LOST SECRETS
OF MASTER MUSICIANS

A Window Into Genius

LOST SECRETS
OF MASTER MUSICIANS

A Window Into Genius

DAVID JACOBSON

SFIM
BOOKS

San Francisco, California

Published by SFIM Books
PO Box 27655
San Francisco, CA 94127
sfimbooks.org

Book design: Jeremy Thornton, Kristofer Herzog
Cover design and interior graphics: Kristofer Herzog, Lorna Stevens
Photographs: Rose Hodges

978-0-9969579-0-8 printed book with color graphics
978-0-9969579-1-5 printed book
978-0-9969579-2-2 – ebook

Publisher's Cataloging-In-Publication Data
(Prepared by The Donohue Group, Inc.)

Names: Jacobson, David (David P.), 1955-.
Title: Lost secrets of master musicians : a window into genius / David Jacobson.
Description: San Francisco : SFIM Books, [2016] | Includes bibliographical references.
Identifiers: ISBN 978-0-9969579-0-8 (printed book with color graphics | ISBN 978-0-9969579-1-5 (printed book)s | ISBN 978-0-9969579-2-2 (ebook)
Subjects: LCSH: Music--Performance. | Musicians. | Music theory. | Music--Instruction and study. | Creative ability.
Classification: LCC ML457 .J33 2016 (print) | LCC ML457 (ebook) | DDC 781.43--dc23

Printed in the United States of America

To Pahtch

To my parents, Joan and Paul

*And to all students in the hope that
they may never be mystified, misdirected,
or become disciples or idolaters
of anyone or anything.*

Acknowledgments

This book has taken many years to write and produce. It is, in fact, akin to a pregnancy and birth, requiring several months of uninterrupted obsession for the creation, and many years of careful attention thereafter to ensure proper growth. Several people have played the role of counsellor and midwife in this process.

I want to thank my friend David Watts, whose encouragement and guidance greatly expanded my concept of what this book could be. My thanks to my friend Kristina Nilsson, Joan Baranow, Leslie Smartt, Paul De Angelis, Julie Murkette and Aaron Brown for their insightful editorial comments, which helped me distill and shape the book.

Michael Nicholas patiently and meticulously helped create the musical examples.

Kristofer Herzog worked closely with me to create beautiful graphics and designs for the musical examples and illustrative figures—essential in bringing the text to life. Rose Hodges was gracious and helpful in creating our photographic illustrations. My thanks to Jeremy Thornton for his subtle and exacting work with me on the design of the book. My friend, Pete Weinberg, was most generous with his time and expertise in many matters associated with the book's production. My very special thanks to Eldon Sellers for his friendship and help.

My students contributed, albeit unknowingly, to the development of this book. My great appreciation, in particular, to my student, Arman Hashemizadeh, for his invaluable conscious assistance.

As always, Audinga Jacobson, whose encouragement, knowledge and belief in this project helped me move forward with confidence, and whose assistance helped free me from many daily tasks, and thereby find the vast amount of time required to complete this book.

DAVID JACOBSON

Contents

Author's Note

This book has been written in a narrative style, intended for a general readership. The musical examples are easily understandable for anyone with an elementary knowledge of musical notation, although to some degree, even without this prerequisite, the essence of the discussion may be gleaned by a careful examination of the graphic illustrations that overlay the musical examples. Illustrations of printed music are labeled "examples." Pictorial illustrations and photos are labeled "figures."

Pages 192–213 of Chapter 18 contain a highly developed analysis of violin technique, which a layman may wish to bypass. Pages 285–307 of Chapter 25 discuss the specific shortcomings of a particular violin method, and may also be sidestepped without ill-effect to the overall argument of the book.

Please note that the names of my school friends at Curtis have been changed. I have altered the names of minor characters in other chapters as well.

Preface

*Here and there individuals stood out far in advance of their colleagues. For example, in the fourteen hundred years separating Galen from Vesalius, the standard of European medical practice was not to be compared with the attainments of either of these men … As a designing engineer Leonardo da Vinci was unequalled until the advent of Vauban and James Watt. In the earlier centuries the **professional** influence as a general sociological fact was mainly a welter of bygone flashes of intelligence relapsing into customary procedures. It represented the continual lapse of intellect into instinct. **But the culmination of science completely inverted the role of custom and intelligence in the older professions.**[1] (emphasis mine)*

– Alfred North Whitehead

The application of intelligence to the unexamined ways of custom can yield profound insight into what is *actually* true or, more scientifically phrased, truer than our accepted paradigms, showing that what is functionally correct often turns out to be the *inversion* of our assumed beliefs. We shall use this approach to look at the field of music and subjects related to its continued flourishing, including an inquiry and exploration into creativity and talent and what suppresses or enhances its development within us. This dialectic is posited via my journey through the world of music and what that sojourn has taught me about both music and life, which are, for me, interwoven. An artistic life is predicated on having the sensitivity to perceive on an intellectual and emotional level what surrounds us. As with all journeys, I started with an idea of what the path would be, but no one can know what is on, or in the road, until you are there. The world of classical music is small. Everyone, no matter where he or she is from, is divided by only three or four degrees of separation. This is to be expected in an art that can be taught well only as an apprenticeship.

In this book I have posited certain ideas—theories—which we will examine. One, among others, is that our *fundamental conceptions* have profound effects on outcome and action, and that shifts in paradigm at this level of consciousness can produce significant change. An example of a shift in fundamental paradigms

---

1 Alfred North Whitehead, *Adventures of Ideas* (New York: The Free Press, 1967), 60.

of historic proportions happened when Darwin's book, *On the Origin of Species,* was first published in 1859. For thousands of years the western world had assumed that life had been designed and created by God, who was an active participant in, and organizer of, world events. Now science seemed to be saying that life had evolved through a process of random mutation, in tandem with impersonal and arbitrary environmental parameters, requiring no outward assistance in the matter. This shock to our general consciousness caused deep societal change. Some of us have still not recovered.

In music we also have sacrosanct beliefs that are rarely challenged. The bolt on the door of inquiry, the greatest inhibitor of advancement in music, is our enchantment with the notion of talent and/or genius. This one question—can talent be understood?—opens a Pandora's Box of further questions. There are performers who all musicians have regarded as possessing godlike qualities. These few people's achievements are acknowledged by most of us as being beyond our understanding. Four were violinists: Jascha Heifetz, Nathan Milstein, David Oistrakh, and Leonid Kogan; two were pianists: Sergei Rachmaninoff and Vladimir Horowitz. Within the history of recorded music almost no one has ever approached their level of mastery. Yet I think it is possible to understand a great deal about their "genius" and in so doing help us all, in particular, and the field of music, as a whole.

I believe that the labels applied to them of talent and genius have stopped us from attempting to understand what they do. Several facts, however, belie their inscrutability: curiously, they all came from the same geographical area, the same era, knew one another, and they approached the act of playing music, at a fundamental level, in nearly identical ways physically.[2] Four of them (Heifetz, Milstein, Rachmaninoff, and Horowitz) used the same principles of phrasing. *This can hardly be a coincidence.*

I have spent many years analyzing these performers' approach to playing, listening to their recordings, slowing down videotapes of their performances, and dissecting whatever they said on the subject of music, or anything else for that matter. *My conclusion is that they play and think about music using concepts that are profoundly different from what is currently taught everywhere; in fact, often the opposite—the inversion—of what is taught.* It is my contention that the precepts used by the performers we will examine are not only fundamentally "true" musically, but require in the expression of these musical ideas a physical approach

---

2   We cannot analyze Rachmaninoff's physical approach, aside from his written descriptions of his playing, because there are no films of him playing the piano. There are, however, many audio recordings, allowing us to examine his musical approach.

that, it so happens, aligns with the body's most efficacious functioning for the physical act of playing. This melding of their particular musical understanding (which we will show is fundamentally true for the nature of music itself, and cannot be dismissed as merely an idiosyncrasy of a small group of acquaintances) and its congruence with the natural coordination and functioning of the body, allowed them to play without mental or physical antagonism.

I call the musical paradigm they employed *bel canto* instrumental technique. I believe the reason these ideas have not been inherited and adopted by later generations is that these performers did not transfer to others what they knew. There are many reasons for this, including societal changes and political upheaval. Additionally, they were too busy performing to develop students from an early age, or if they did teach, their approach seemed to be not unlike a chef who leaves out a few key ingredients in the printed version of his favorite recipes.

This vacuum of knowledge was filled in, *guessed at*, by second-tier musicians and transferred to new generations of musicians as the truth—the way music, technique, and the art is to be understood. Because of the apprenticeship structure of music education, which tends to form self-reinforcing systems not open to external investigation or review, a less insightful, more mundane way of understanding music has gained control and become the way in which we teach and understand music. This bias in the system of education has circumscribed our potentiality, a bias which not only *precludes* the possibility that we can create music and musicians of as high a level as the creators of the art, but has also made our music-making evermore banal. Banality begets spiraling banality. Intellectual malaise is a logical outcome of the way musicians are trained. This book examines why this is to be expected and how this confused training is perpetuated.

None of my discoveries and theories about the methodologies of these great players diminishes their talent and genius. Even with the benefit of knowing more about their process, for most people to come near their level of achievement will be nearly impossible. However, more will come close than presently do. Additionally, I believe this knowledge is *applicable and transferable to all instruments and voice* and will have a dramatic impact on the entire field of music, not only in pedagogy and teaching, but also in performance and composition.

Our analysis of these master players not only shines a much needed and helpful light on how we learn, a subject that affects us all, but allows us to explore the nature of genius itself. Our capabilities and latent talents are often locked within ourselves, a lock, I believe, fashioned out of our inherited and unexamined fundamental beliefs. Our fundamental beliefs are the structure through which we experience the world. We will see throughout this book that what is *actually* true is often the *inversion* of what we were trained to believe.

Our musical inquiry examines many of the knots we unnecessarily tie ourselves into. Both my own experience with learning and my interaction with the students I teach have shown me with magnified clarity that within the same person lies incapability or remarkable facility. The factor causing the difference may be of the most minute kind, yet it exists at a level of consciousness where its effect has far-reaching ramifications. It is one of my postulates that ability and genius are brought forth—unlocked—by having the freedom of mind to allow for fundamental paradigm shifts to occur. In fact, genius *is* a paradigm shift.

Many books have been written about how to play various instruments, but this is the first, as far as I know, to analyze and attempt to explain in simple, understandable terms what great masters are thinking and how they achieve such unsurpassed levels of virtuosity and musical insight. The fact is, one cannot exist without the other. There is no difference or separation between technique and musical expression. Which comes first: musical understanding or technical approach? They work synergistically, but the difference between musicians of the past and today's performers is that the masters of the past's understanding of music was deeper, more moored to an ability to compose tonal, patterned music, had a closer relationship to *bel canto* style singing, and developed in an era, a "micro-culture" of music that valued refinement of spirit and the perception of beauty. The biases and parameters of their "values" *in toto* brought forth the musical potential of people from that era in a particular way, a "tradition of values," that produced musicians who could compose music of profound depth and quality and performers who could express these "values" in their "recreation" of the music. We have inherited this cultural transmission with serious *omissions* in understanding.

I believe that our "system" of music education, which is neither systematic nor thought out, is awash in antiquated and unexamined methodologies. This is creating a paradigm of "accidental" education that is often destructive to students and, therefore, alienating to future participants and supporters of the art.

We will examine how these and other cultural factors are encouraging and unwittingly promoting a state of decadence that is sidelining classical music to irrelevance because our understanding of music is "mechanical." This way of thinking affects the field at its fundamental level—education, performance, and composition. If we do not understand what to transfer as "values" and knowledge, we can only *guess* at what may help students learn to play at the level of creativity of the great artists of the past.

I am proposing that we have been "guessing" wrong. This creates haphazard results in terms of quality, although *predictably* inferior and "shallow" results in general. Mechanical understanding of music begets mechanical performance of music—a belief in "perfection" and a contrived and indirect emotional response to the music that opens the door to "ham-feeling" and commercialism—depriving audiences of a true experience of the music as the composers of the past intended it to be heard. Because the canon of classical music is, at this point, several steps removed from the creators of it, modern composers have lost touch with what *qualities and values* made the great music of the past "great." Their confusion, which is evidenced in their focus on "originality," has misdirected their creative efforts and made their work antagonistic to audiences and performers alike. In pursuit of originality, which I believe does not exist, they have ignored the development of *skill* in the art of composition.

Skill in composing cannot be separated from skill in playing, but because we do not know the "secrets" of tradition and knowledge of the great players of the past we can no longer transfer this skill in playing, which was not based on a mechanical understanding of music, to students. Thus, our lack of knowledge at this *educative* level—learning to play an instrument—is affecting the entire field in a decadent way. Mechanical players are not inclined to compose music, which affects our ability to create new compositions. This means that at the center of the art lies not vitality, but confusion, haphazard results, "perfectionism," commercialism, and a lack of creativity.

Audiences for classical music are disappearing. One of the most important causative factors in this decline is that our dysfunctional educative approach alienates future participants by pervasive bad teaching, produces performers who are mechanical, and, therefore, concerts that are boring, and results in the creation of new music that is antagonistic to everyone but the composer and his friends.

I have used my personal story as a vehicle for showing the confusion and silliness that permeates the classical music world, a situation at the educational level that is often terribly damaging to students, and has the additionally unfortunate effect of preserving, throughout the field, power structures and concepts that are undermining and degrading the art as I believe it was understood by the great musicians who composed the canon of classical music and the performers who were their friends and colleagues.

I use the word art, not business. Music may be made into a business, but that is not what it is. To learn to paint, for example, may allow one to design magazine covers for a living, but to teach painting with the goal of designing magazine covers cheats a student from learning the art, a process that, if done with integrity, requires personal transformation. To learn to play an instrument in order to play in an orchestra or band is not learning music itself and seeing where that takes you. In fact, learning to understand music has no relationship to anything practical at all. Art is a way out of the practicalities that form the structure of our society. It is a doorway to a different world, and the price of admission to this world is the decidedly impractical direct perception of beauty.

The transmission of an art to others is not easy and can never be taught with a cookie-cutter approach. It is my intention to show that, while the learning of the art of music may not be easy, some aspects of it can be made clearer.

To be able to see the true nature of the problems and resultant confusion in music education (which is the foundation of music) it is necessary to slay some dragons. We will examine "blockers" of our creative power: some societal conceptions and programmed belief systems, as well as anachronistic paradigms in the field of music. Many of the societal paradigms that our culture accepts as true are deeply misanthropic and, as such, act as a foot on our throats, stifling our voices. These misconceptions, these inversions of what is true, are a force that prevent creative development. They keep us asleep by forming—in our minds—self-reinforcing systems of thought not open to external investigation or review. The world at its core is creative *every* second, always new. The same cannot be said of our thought processes.

This book suggests some possible remedies. It is my hope that in fixing the foundation, other sillinesses and inanities that are dependent on an idiosyncratic and unscientific approach at the base of the study of music will gradually lose their allure and power, leading to a more democratic, less hierarchical musical "world." These changes, in turn, may lead to an increase in participation and general interest. I use my experiences at the Curtis Institute of Music as examples of the inner workings of the profession of music, but there is nothing unusual about them. My experiences are typical examples of music education as it is conducted throughout the U.S. The system, as it is currently organized, *precludes* any result but haphazard success.

In this book I propose several solutions to these problems, many of which, to my knowledge, have never been attempted. Our current decadent trends and haphazard methodologies may go on despite anything I may suggest that might alter them, but I will take my stab at changing things for the better. Music and society are what our collective minds have created. We all have imperfect knowledge, and are all caught in the same dream. Our social paradigm can only change one person at a time. Yet, once the curtain has been drawn and the situation can be seen with clarity, it is not possible to go back.

DAVID JACOBSON

Introduction

The small, deep processes determine the big. To learn to see anew, one must shift paradigms at a fundamental level.

Why?

Because it seems we are driven by fundamental beliefs and needs that are learned. These may conflict with how our brains function most effectively.

To clear oneself both physically and mentally, it is necessary to eliminate antagonism.

This narrative explicates by implication, and provides a forum for demonstrating that the serious study of music can teach us how to make paradigm shifts that open new possibilities, unlocking latent potentialities. As a consequence of this process we will be able to explore what the concept of talent or genius implies. Is what we do really new or a variation on a theme? Does the road to the mastery of an art lead back to oneself, and in that journey are we untied from the tyranny of outward approval, including the programmed policing of ourselves by our own thoughts?

This book attempts to examine fundamental beliefs that inhibit our ability to be creative. We will include topics not exclusively musical, but in my mind essential to the process of clearing the mind to have the freedom to be creative. I don't pretend to be an expert on these tangential subjects, such as religion or societal structure, but a clear-thinking person will realize that no one is. I comment on these subjects because they fall within the parameter of fundamental beliefs and as such must be included in the dialectic of this book.

Sitting around with friends on occasion, I have told them stories from my past. Everyone does this, and it is somewhat more, or less, interesting depending on how unusual their lives have been, or in direct proportion to how much you like them. Friends have told me that my anecdotes are piquant and that I should write them down. I admit that I have no perspective on the subject. Remembrances from the past can be interesting under alcoholic influence, in the same way that people can seem much more attractive. But just like hooking up when drunk, in the cold light of day all of our huffing and puffing is usually found to be grotesquely self-serving, with only the illusion of any truth.

In recalling one's life it is good to strive to tell the truth, but the problem is that there are as many takes on one's life as there are people who know you. On top of that, my memory seems to change depending on my present mood. So I think we should dispense with the idea that I will tell the truth. The best I can do is to be momentarily honest.

Most people who write about their lives will create a narrative of triumph over hardship, recount numerous accomplishments and successes, and season their memoir with titillating and fascinating anecdotes about the great places they have visited or lived, and the famous people they have known. I will spare the reader all of that. I have had no great successes, have not travelled much, and the famous people I have met have been uniformly unimpressive. My life has not been triumphant. The only thing interesting in my story is the transpersonal.

My purpose in writing this is to show that one can demystify oneself, see through a few layers of inherited programming, go from anger to some understanding, and never or, hopefully, rarely be taken in by authorities, either a single person or society. This occasional clarity allowed me to use my mind more creatively. It removed mental blocks that had kept me stuck, and it showed to me that I was more capable than I seemed to be. I think this is true for everyone.

I attempt no answers for the profundities and mysteries of life, just reflections upon, and insight into the realm of the superficial through the prism of my experiences. Whether or not what I have to say ultimately means anything, I leave to the reader to decide for himself.

Fundamental beliefs begin in the beginning. And that is where I start my story.

ACT I

Genesis

CHAPTER 1

Beginning

I was born in San Francisco in the 1950s and grew up in the suburb of Daly City, a development of identical tract houses in a setting of complete and endless fog. The houses were built by a man named Doelger, whose name I remember because at the gateway to the development an enormous billboard welcoming everyone was signed with his name.

Doelger had been born in the back of his parents' bakery. When he was twelve, his father died, forcing him to quit school in the seventh grade and go to work. According to my father, Doelger was a man in the deepest sense of the word, someone who could create gold from nothing, an alchemist, who had come from a background of poverty and brought to life a real estate empire. He was the stuff of American legend and movie scripts and in direct contradistinction to intellectuals, particularly the intelligentsia of the left, whom my father censoriously denounced as producers of nothing but criticism. Yet this lionizing of the businessman seemed, even to me at the time—I was probably eight or nine when these thoughts occurred to me—to be a tad bit puzzling.

The poets and bards throughout the ages have not chosen the derring-do of the entrepreneur as the subject of their reveries with good cause. The businessman must always have in mind the bottom-line, which circumscribes that he endeavor to achieve his advantage in all situations, making for a certain narrowness of mind that does not usually lead to heroic and unselfish behavior, feats of valor, or hopeless acts of love. The field usually attracts either people who have been disappointed by their abilities (or lacked circumstances that might have allowed them to pursue other more imaginative callings) or those for whom a limited and practical world view is natural. Having the goal of making as much money as possible is bound to temper one's artistic impulses. And in the case of the development of Daly City, as admirable as was Doelger's spirit in overcoming his difficult start, the energy lost by the effort left nothing in his imagination that would have allowed his perhaps latent aesthetic sensibilities to flower.

Doelger built his kingdom of slightly variated assembly-line houses on what had been a cow pasture south of San Francisco. Viewing his creation with today's perspective and cultural values we might wish the visual blight of Daly City to disappear, wistfully hoping the pasture might miraculously return. But in the 1950s the development was a landmark, a monument to the contemporary conception of progress—an efficient use of land, filled with cleverly constructed, inexpensive, but well-made homes. They were new and neat when my parents first moved in at a cost of $16,000 with a down payment of forty percent and easily affordable for my father, who was making $20,000 a year selling cars.

They were also an improvement in living area over what Doelger's company had built in the Sunset area of San Francisco in the 1940s, where each house was crammed so tightly together there was no daylight between them. In Daly City the houses had some space between them—about six feet. The living rooms had exposed wooden beams in the ceiling and a little brick fireplace in which my mother would make coal fires and around which she served us tea every day at four o'clock in keeping with her Irish upbringing. The kitchen had white metal cabinets and a breakfast nook where my mother would help me with my homework and show me how to draw and paint and construct myriad models of fighter planes, passenger planes, and battleships, and teach me how to make three-dimensional maps of the world with paper maché.

My mother had come to the U.S. as an adult. She graduated from Trinity College in Dublin with a degree and gold medal in chemistry, and had decided to see the world. Europe had been ravaged, and the U.S. seemed to be a fresh hope for something new and better. Her father, a lawyer, had been one of the wealthiest men in Ireland. He died when she was four, and a few years later her mother married a well-known patriot and historian who was connected to the insiders of the government and the privileged, smart set of society. His position gave her access to letters of introduction, allowing her to travel in comfort from coast to coast.

She met my father during her six-month adventure in the U.S. and decided to marry him even though he was Jewish, even though her family objected, even though they could not be married in Ireland because no one would marry her to a Jew. She even managed to get a special dispensation from the archbishop of Ireland, approved by the Pope himself, which gave the Church's permission for her marriage with the caveat that she would raise any children that might appear from the union as Catholics. And here she was in Daly City, helping me make models, and serving her children tea in front of a coal fire. My mother is a Romantic, but not the sensitive, poetic type. She is an action figure.

We had a maid named Shirley who took care of us after school. Shirley was a Negro, or as my grandfather would smugly refer to her, a colored, or more gently, a colored person, the term "black" not yet part of the everyday lexicon. She looked as if she'd stepped directly from the pages of *Gone with the Wind* and, through the timelessness of print and a magic spell, had somehow appeared in our kitchen. She always wore an apron and what seemed to be the same pink dress every day, with her hair pulled tightly back in a bun. She was probably thirty pounds overweight—not fat, just plump—with a southern accent and a talent for relaxation.

Shirley ironed clothes and watched television at the same time, usually soap operas, but often game shows. Most of the time the iron stayed up because she would be half-listening, half-talking to me about something, or I would be telling her about school during commercials or in between her participation in the game show. Her husband, Roy, was a mechanic for United Airlines, and because of that Shirley travelled around the country quite a bit because the price of her ticket was only the tax. I might have met Roy, Sr. once. She had a son, Roy, Jr., who I played with a couple of times in our backyard, but not too often. In those days Negroes and Whites did not associate beyond hiring "coloreds" as household help. It wasn't stated, but you knew it. My father always complained that Shirley didn't work, but my mother said that she was nice to us and that was enough.

My mother spent most of her time helping my father with his business. She kept the books. She had worked as a chemist when they were first married, but had given up her job when she became pregnant with me. In our neighborhood women were wives and mothers. The women who had jobs were employed only because their husbands couldn't make enough money. They mainly worked as secretaries. A situation that required your wife to work was considered a shame for the family, as was divorce—an even greater shame—and parents or children involved in such a failure were shunned.

There were no single adults who owned homes. Homeowners were married couples, and if they had no children upon moving into the neighborhood, it was expected that they soon would. Everyone in Daly City was white and all the parents seemed to be the same age. Some were policemen, firemen; even one of the 49ers, Bob St. Clair, a future member of the Pro Football Hall of Fame, lived a few doors down. I remember that he supposedly ate a dozen eggs for breakfast.

My father had gone to the University of California and graduated with a degree in zoology. He applied to graduate school for dentistry and medicine, but was rejected by both schools because in those days, the 1940s, there were quotas on how many Jews could be admitted to a graduate school. So he became a car salesman and, even though selling DeSotos was quite lucrative, he eventually decided that real estate had more of a future, and he got a broker's license. He worked late all the time, even on Sundays. Every night, a few minutes after he arrived home, my mother would serve him a martini or a high ball, and before dinner he would listen to music or play his violin.

My father loved music. He had grown up listening to records of Mischa Elman, Fritz Kreisler, and Jascha Heifetz. In his San Francisco neighborhood this was common in the 1920s and '30s. What was uncommon was that he wanted to play the violin so much that he paid for his own lessons. His teacher was also my first teacher.

My mother told us that my father had a beautiful tenor voice and used to sing ballads and even arias at parties when she first knew him. That part of his persona had long been put to rest by the time my memories begin, but he still played the violin and listened to great singers like Enrico Caruso, Jussi Björling, Jan Pierce, Renata Tebaldi, and Leonard Warren every night. I grew up hearing music—violin and opera records—and watching him play the violin. He practiced two pieces regularly. One was the Bach *A Minor Violin Concerto* with a "Music Minus One" record, which he always had trouble timing with his playing, and the other was the beginning of the Mendelssohn *Violin Concerto*. I don't think he ever played past the first page, but he practiced it every night.

On weekends I would play all day with my friends. Our games would not be considered politically correct nowadays. We ran around trying to shoot each other, either as cowboys and Indians, or soldiers in war games. Our enemies were Japs, Krauts and Redskins. Communists weren't in our minds as enemies of the United States until the fifth grade, when our teachers alerted us to the danger of the domino effect in Vietnam if the North Vietnamese, China and Russia defeated the South, and its potential for a Communist overpowering of the West. Our weaponry consisted of cap guns and a plastic machine gun that had a lever which, when released, would let loose the sound of a round of ammo going off, as well as bows and arrows with suction cup tips, which although seemingly harmless, could still poke out your eye.

There were no play dates. We just played every day after school. Our neighborhood overflowed with kids. There were no drugs except alcohol, and no child molesters, at least none that had been revealed as such. Everyone seemed pretty trustworthy, and it was completely safe to go anywhere, although we weren't allowed off the block.

My childhood was happy. The Sears catalog was my favorite book. When it would arrive in October, my sister and I would spend hours figuring out what we might ask Santa to bring us. I wanted model trains or race car sets, although with a list price of twenty-five dollars I knew I hadn't a chance. The beginning of November until Christmas was a near panic time of excitement and a constant search through the house trying to find where my mother had hidden our presents. They were usually high up in a closet or somewhere behind something in the garage. We would carefully pull and shake the wrapped boxes, hoping and yet at the same time not wanting to see what was inside.

On Christmas Eve we would stay up and try to catch Santa. We left him milk and cookies. We never were able to break in on him—sleep would catch us first—and in the early hours of the morning when we would awake and run out of our rooms to the hearth that served as Santa's gift stand, the milk and cookies would invariably have been consumed.

Both my mother and my father gave me loads of attention. My mother helped me with homework. My father played baseball with me every weekend. And every night, from the time I started the violin at age seven until the time I left home to go to Curtis, my father lay on the couch listening to me practice, usually falling asleep before I finished.

I remember day after day of fog and cold. The sun came out only a few days a year in Daly City. Strangely, five minutes drive away it was always sunny. I knew this from our Sunday trips to visit my grandparents, who lived thirty miles away in what seemed to be eternally sunny Belmont.

To leave Daly City we would often drive in fog so thick you could hardly see ten feet ahead of you. Then, suddenly, a patch of blue in the sky would appear, and within a few seconds the temperature might rise thirty degrees, the world seeming full of promise and adventure. On our return, sadness and dreariness would instantly take its place upon the mere sight of the blanket of fog, and we were cold well before the temperature had dropped.

In the summers we rented a house for a month in Lake Tahoe or the Russian River near Guerneville, swimming and getting sunburnt every day and, whenever I could, I would beg my parents to take us to eat at drive-in restaurants that, in those days, made real milkshakes, and where cheeseburgers were wrapped in orange paper that made them seem even tastier.

As with all things, inevitably summer ran out of time and from the sun to the fog of Daly City we returned from languorous days of swimming to the footles of school.

CHAPTER 2

School

School was perhaps my first great disappointment. Although there have been many that followed: first, second, third, fourth, fifth, and sixth love, career mishaps and dead-ends, and as I passed forty, the growing and never dimming voice in my head that won't stop reminding me that my life will not go on forever and that death has begun a slow march directly at me; yet school, the beginning of that disenchantment (even though I didn't know it at the time) got me in the right frame of mind for all that followed.

As a child, in the years before school, each day seemed fresh. I woke up with eager anticipation and wonderment for what the day might hold in store. My fall from that joy in life began slowly, almost imperceptibly, after kindergarten. The slow darkening of the world was reinforced and guided by television, which I watched passionately and which was designed to preempt questions just as they bubbled up, as they might naturally occur to a developing mind, and to put your curiosity to sleep while at the same time supporting and bolstering the credibility and authority of your elders.

Shows such as *Father Knows Best*, *My Three Sons*, emphasis on "my," *Leave It to Beaver* and on and on inevitably led one to the same conclusion: somehow your parents, your white Christian parents on television, who were always the same age, in particular your father, were always right. You might not trust their analysis, you silly, spirited boy; you might question their methodology, you naively truthful daughter; but they—your parents, that is—knew more than you, and you had better do what they said or nothing good would come of your life. And even if their patiently reiterated and self-assured platitudes did not lead to your complete acquiescence, there was a backup white Christian man in the sky, God, who knew everything and we had to assume that Dad, Mom, and the president were all spliced into this artery of understanding that flowed freely among all white, churchgoing adults.

What was seen on television was a monochromatic world. There were no Jewish parents on television. There were Jewish producers and directors, but television parents and God were Christian, capitalist, white Americans. There were no people of any other race on television in my childhood, except for servants, who could be colored, or Asian if they were gardeners.

Parents were never questioned and in those days men gently guided women through their tribulations. Women and children were thought of in the same way—confused, but harmless as long as they followed what men wanted them to do. So to survive, we all, and certainly I, learned to live up to everyone else's expectations—that is, the written and implicit rules set down by the authorities guiding your life and thoughts, who themselves have been crafted and wrought by the same forces, and so on, as far back as we can go, *ad infinitum*. The system works beautifully to keep everyone in check, with both the enforcers and oppressors being policed by their charges, who in turn have their own underlings to preside over because of the hierarchical nature of the system, or game, as it should more accurately be described.

School is a powerful tool in forging the mental paradigm necessary for the play to continue. The competitive, comparative (good boy, bad boy), and unquestionable nature of the rules of the play shape the mental character of the participants into pleasers desperate for the crowns of laurel given out at the whim and pleasure of the groundskeepers of society, the teachers, who are the first of many checkpoints weeding out the future players from the cannon fodder that is to be left behind and discarded. And for shaping guilt-ridden, self-policing pleasers of power, there is probably no better training ground than a military or religious school. Since my mother was Irish Catholic and allowed to marry my father only if she pledged her children's souls to the Church, and as my family had no affinity for the military, we were all enrolled in the nearest Catholic school.

In Daly City the only Catholic school was Our Lady of Mercy, which was conveniently located only a half-mile down the road from my house. Our neighbor directly across the street, Rosemary Mulready, was the school registrar and drove me to school every day. It was comforting being friendly with an insider, and I'm sure she occasionally smoothed my way.

The school had both a rectory and convent. We were, therefore, taught by the nuns, and occasionally visited by the priests, who seemed very important to us and the sisters, appearing randomly, seemingly by design, in our religion classes, adding a gravity to the subject both by their focused attention on us and by the unpredictability of their visits. Jesus watched over us from the cross in the front of the classroom, and Our Lady watched over us from the corner of the back wall. Her outstretched arms were positioned for an embrace and she wore blue and white robes and a scarf around her hair. She seemed quite pretty.

I should have made the connection that the nuns, who also wore robes and scarves, were also girls. But their arms were always folded across their chest, with their hands hidden up their sleeves; their robes and headdresses were black and covered all their hair, and with names like Sister Henry, or Sister Bernard, I was quite sure they were men, although I think the preface to their names—Sister—may have given me pause. I was confused until the second grade, when I met one who was pretty. That caused me to question my parents and Rosemary, and I was assured by them that even those manly sisters were girls. The pretty nun's name was Sister Roland. I looked forward to school every day that year and was especially well-behaved in her class. Maybe good-looking women create pleasers also.

We studied religion for at least an hour a day in a form called catechism, which provided both the questions and the answers, both of which we had to memorize. What is the Holy Trinity?

The Father, Son, and in those days it was the Holy Ghost, later changed to Holy Spirit. The three faces of God. Three aspects of one God. Everyone, even a seven-year-old, knew it made no sense. But that's where we learned about faith. Faith is a gift, the embodiment of which is to be found in the example of the martyrs, who died rather than betray their faith. We were told that they possessed the highest level of love for God.

We memorized prayers. There were different kinds, like the Our Father, the Hail Mary, and the Confiteor. I enjoyed these assignments. The longer prayers took some work to learn, but we had to perform in front of the class, which I enjoyed. It was such an easy feeling of accomplishment, like cleaning the kitchen floor or scrubbing the toilet is for me now.

There were two different types of sins, carrying very different consequences. One type was venial. Venials were only slightly problematic. If you died, the worst punishment you could receive after death was spending some time in Purgatory. But if people still alive liked you enough to pray for you, you could get out and go to heaven pretty fast. Most people went to Purgatory before Heaven. It was rare that anyone was sent straight to Heaven. You had to have no sins, or be martyred for your faith. There was, however, something that you could do while still alive (assuming you were still going to sin occasionally) that could help once you died. If, while you were alive, you prayed for indiscriminate Purgatorian souls, and you succeeded in getting them out, they would pray for you once you were in. Thus we see in this seemingly innocent arrangement the seed of the Irish or Italian Mafia. I would give good odds on that.

But then, of course, there were mortal sins. And they were very bad. They were really your worst fear because there was no way back. God would shut you out forever. The most troubling scenario when dealing with mortal sin was that you might not even know you had committed one; you could just have had some really bad thoughts. Only God knew for sure.

Some mortal sins, however, were known and clear to anyone. For example, getting divorced was a mortal sin because it was against Church rules, and if you went ahead with it, you would be excommunicated. Basically, that meant burning forever in hell. That was for sure. Your way around the divorce dead-end was being granted permission for an annulment. But I think Rome had to approve it, or as the Catholic authorities phrased it, you needed a papal dispensation. That must have stopped true believers in their tracks. I think going to movies forbidden by the Church counted as a mortal sin. There was a long list of them. I don't know if any books were banned. Murder was certainly a mortal sin. But so was being kicked out of the Church for any reason.

The fear and tension that this training produces makes you hyperaware and diligent, not only for things seen, but for the unknown and unperceived transgressions that you might be incurring by the second. You are living in cosmic proportions from the start and, with every breath, possibly sinking deeper and deeper into unworthiness and potential doom. What you do or happen to think, even for a second, really matters because God sees everything.

I think that Catholicism is the only religion that has private, individual confession. And you confess to an unseen priest who is sworn to secrecy. The reason is not hard to comprehend. As a Catholic you are, in fact, constantly guilty of something, and in danger of being held to account here or in the afterlife. That burden has to be continually sloughed off.

Having the last name of Jacobson in a Catholic school meant that I got special attention, and looks of concern regarding my father, who, aside from being Jewish, also looked like an Arab. His skin was too dark and he bought fancy sports cars and wore tailor-made suits and played tennis. In our Irish Catholic neighborhood he really stood out. By the second grade I knew that my father and I could never be together in heaven. I asked about it several times in class. There was absolutely no doubt on the subject. He was not baptized and, therefore, certainly en route to Limbo. Thinking that that answer was a trifle harsh, perhaps from the scared look on my face, the sisters would add that Limbo was also where all unbaptized babies went.

The real downside of Limbo, aside from the infantile company, is that even though it is somewhere around heaven, hell, and purgatory, it is not close enough to God to be as happy as Catholics will be, or my father could be, if he would convert. The upside of Limbo is that my father would not burn in hell forever. He would be with all the other Jews, who would suffer a similar fate at the end times when we would all be judged.

Neither he, nor any of the rest of my Jewish family, understood the seriousness of their respective position vis-à-vis the Church rules. My father did not take his Limbo limitation with the gravitas with which it was transmitted to me by the nuns in class. I think, or I would like to think, that I was a little skeptical about all this. But I think I believed the sisters and looked at my Jewish family as doomed people, my grandmother and uncles all seemingly happy but not having any idea of the danger they were in. They in turn looked at my mother, the Catholics, the Pope, and the nuns and priests as a bunch of mashuganas.

But I felt pretty bad for my father. Anyway, I wasn't about to question what they said. I really wanted an A.

You see, isn't that where all this sucking-up starts? I wanted that A or the stickers or stars the teachers gave out. We had a chart in the back of the class with everyone's name on it. I used to check it every day. You could see from the front of the classroom that some people had a dazzling display of stars after their names. So everyone knew who had the most, or who had none.

We occasionally got ribbons for first, second, or third place for something or other. There was no honorable mention. Society in those days was not politically correct or sensitive to ordinary people. The term politically correct didn't even exist. There was no ADD, no dyslexia, no family problem or racial issue that was considered applicable to scholastic performance or achievement. Not that all of our present-day sensitivity is meant to change anything in any deep sense. It just means you have a label that explains to everyone why you can't cut it at school, and the diagnosis has the secondary and perhaps even more important effect of increasing the GDP by encouraging drug therapy, special-ed classes, and psychological counseling from people who are often as, or more, confused than their clients.

Doing well was all about obedience to the agenda and goals of your teachers. That sounds reasonable on the face of it. But there is an elephant in the room. The key is that they give you the questions and the answers for everything. What a setup. The school, the authorities, decide what you should question and what the answer to the question is. The wrong questions were ignored with many tactics.

"That's not what we're talking about."

"We don't have time for that."

"Don't be disrespectful."

"This is what God says."

"You must have faith."

"I'm afraid we're out of time."

"You're distracting the class."

"This class doesn't cover that."

Or you were simply ignored, as if the question had been an unfortunate burp or fart that is better left unnoticed in an effort not to embarrass the source. If you asked enough skeptical questions you were branded a troublemaker, a class disrupter, and your parents were notified, or you were forced to stay after school and write some phrase a hundred times, or all of the above at once.

For history class in fourth and fifth grades we had a teacher named Mrs. Stella. She had white hair and wire-rimmed glasses and was quite prim, exactly like what you would expect a school teacher would look like once you know enough to know what they would look like. I assumed that a Mr. Stella also existed somewhere, but it was hard to imagine her anywhere outside a classroom or beside anything or anyone aside from her blackboard.

Mrs. Stella stood at the front of the class and wrote historical facts on her blackboard and we copied them into our notebooks. I really enjoyed that class. She wrote very clearly and I liked the sound of the chalk, which made a thud as she started each new word, and a smooth scraping sound as she wrote because her movements on the chalkboard were so skilled and fluid, probably as a result of having written the same sentences for twenty years. We were judged heavily on penmanship, so I took great care to make sure what I wrote was really beautiful. To get an A we had to memorize what she wrote down. I got all As in elementary school, and loads of stars, even though a couple of times I suppose I went over the top as far as behavior was concerned.

Once we were asked to sign a get-well card for one of the nuns who was sick and in the hospital. The card was passed around and when it came to me, I signed Brigitte Bardot, the sex symbol of the times, and consequently on my mind more than my name. Unfortunately, Sister Bernard checked the signatures, and when she realized that we had an extra, non-registered classmate she forced the class to stay after school until the mystery was solved. After twenty minutes of anguish I raised my hand, the class was dismissed, and I wrote something or other like "I am bad," a hundred times and was eventually released without parental notification. At least I think they weren't told.

Art class got a little problematic once when we were told to draw whatever we wanted and I drew Frankenstein on a surfboard. I really never understood what upset Sister Peter so much about that, except maybe all the chest hair I drew on him. She was absolutely furious, her face turning an exasperated bright red and her voice stuttering out some sort of threat. My parents were called in for that.

One thing I really enjoyed about being a Catholic were all the accessories. We had missals with gold leaf edges and thin parchment-like paper, with a black leather cover that had gold writing on the front. We had rosary beads, which came in different sizes and two colors, black and white. We had small pictures of saints that we could carry in our pockets, as well as statues of patron saints that we could put in our rooms. There was holy water that you could buy, and incense. We had books about the saints, most of whom had been martyred in the most gruesome ways. I know I enjoyed the stories, but I'm not sure it wasn't my grim curiosity about which way they'd be done in that compelled me to read to the end of their lives. For personal adornment we had necklaces with crosses. All the cool kids wore them.

Mass was in Latin, although by around the fifth grade most of the liturgy had shifted to English. I don't remember the songs we sang in Latin masses, but I do remember the switch to folk masses with strumming guitar players feebly singing monotone ballads about Jesus.

Religion class was taken very seriously. After all, it was the law and you had to know the boundaries. This was really the *raison d'être* of the school. We read some of the Bible, not much really. I spent most of the class looking for those passages where someone lay with someone else. Sex was always referred to as laying with someone and I guess that's where we get the term, as in "she was laid." It's biblical. It took me nearly all class to hunt for the sexual passages, but I was never bored in religion class.

Of course, the Bible wasn't taken particularly seriously because Catholics don't need the Bible. We superseded it, after all. We created the Church, God's kingdom on earth where the Pope rules and is, quite fortunately for Catholics, infallible. So for us the Bible is really *passé*. We've carried on the work Jesus began, starting with Peter and Paul, and then the popes and the councils they called together, and we figured out better rules than Jesus did; after all he wasn't around too long and may have missed a few details, which thank God the pope and the cardinals have taken the responsibility to fill in for us. The burden of this is well described in *The Grand Inquisitor.* Of course the tribulations and stress of saving humanity from itself made some of the poor priests child molesters, but I'm sure Jesus would not have understood the burden he left them because, after all, he had to be celibate for only thirty-two or thirty-three years.

So the sisters and the priests at our school were certain, albeit a trifle sad I felt, that everyone in history and not a Catholic will go to hell and burn forever. What about all those people who lived before Jesus? I mean they really had no chance. How about those who lived even before the Bible was written, like the Egyptians? Were they all in hell? I wondered. What about Moses? What about all that killing the Jews did in the Old Testament that God ordered them to do? Were they in hell? Or if God tells you to do it, it means it's alright, like Nixon and Watergate. Religion class really got you thinking. But at least I and most of my immediate family and friends, except for my father, (and with Jews you never knew because Jesus' family was Jewish, too, even though I guess he was Catholic before anyone else, and after being Jewish to begin with) would be saved at the end. This was not an easy class. This was not an easy teaching. But this is what we learned. No wonder Protestants study the Bible so hard. They're looking for loopholes.

But the tough questions kept coming up. Was Jesus a Christian? This question is quite upsetting when asked in a roomful of believers or a classroom of brainwashed children.

Yes, of course. He was the first Christian.

But wasn't he Jewish?

He was a new kind.

But wasn't he supposed to be God?

Yes.

Is God a Christian?

At this point you're labeled a troublemaker and all conversation stops. Or, your doubt is explained by your being under the influence of Satan himself. At any rate, you've ruined everyone's mood.

Still, some things did continually confuse me, such as some people living nine-hundred years, and this Holy Ghost thing, where he appeared as a flame over everyone's head, and sometimes a dove. I asked about these and other incongruities quite a bit in seventh grade, feeling that there was something illogical going on. Sister Benedict would patiently explain that I needed to have faith and that this would come to me by God's grace. But after a couple of days disruption in class, and apparently not enough time for grace to appear, my parents were notified that I would have to stop this annoying behavior or leave the school. And somehow I just figured it wasn't that important after all whether anybody really did live nine-hundred years, or the Holy Ghost was a spirit, a flame, or a bird.

CHAPTER 3

Jake Krachmalnick

I always thought that I understood music. I don't mean this in a boastful way. It's like some people are good decorators because they have a feeling for color and shape. I think that I have a natural musical imagination. From the time I started the violin, I guess even before that, I used to sing a lot. I was always making up tunes. But I was also encouraged in this by my parents, who I think must have thought it was cute. Maybe my constant singing was a way of getting attention. I really can't remember. But when I started the violin I know that I had an emotional response to the music. I remember playing little Christmas carols, or a simplified version of the theme from the Adagio of Dvorak's *New World Symphony*. I loved playing them.

Of course, I hated to practice. To keep me going my father used to write me a practice schedule. Such and such a line repeat ten times, this passage five times. I had to practice one hour each day. For some reason I made very rapid progress and was soon playing Mozart sonatas and Schubert sonatinas, as well as making my way through all the student concertos. I was considered a child prodigy.

I didn't practice much. But I had determination and an untrained musical imagination that made me sound better than I should have if one takes into account that I had almost no conscious idea of what I was doing. I grew up listening to Heifetz, Isaac Stern, and all the great violinists of the time on recordings. My parents took me to the recitals of famous performers and to symphony concerts from the time I was seven or eight. I don't remember very much about them, except that I heard Heifetz, Isaac Stern, Rudolph Serkin, Rostropovich, Oistrakh, Francescatti, Menuhin. Listening to music in the house was a constant activity, and my father, in particular, seemed to me to be obsessed by it. I'm not sure popular music was forbidden, but the first pop music I ever heard was the Beatles live on *The Ed Sullivan Show*. And that was it for years afterwards. My parents loved musicals like *My Fair Lady* and *Carousel* or *Gigi*. Whenever these movies were on television we always watched.

When I was eleven my father decided (I think at the urging of musicians who heard me play and thought I had some talent) that I should change my teacher to someone who was a great player. And that is how I began to study with the concertmaster of the San Francisco Symphony, Jacob Krachmalnick. I think that this transition was very difficult for my first teacher, Willem Wegman. I'm sure that he thought he was doing a fine job. Maybe he was. But Krachmalnick was the concertmaster of the Symphony, and a phenomenal violinist. He had been the assistant concertmaster in the Cleveland Orchestra with George Szell, concertmaster of the Philadelphia Orchestra with Eugene Ormandy, and the concertmaster of the Royal Concertgebouw Orchestra in Amsterdam.

Krachmalnick did not blend in well with any surroundings, either physically or energetically, both aspects attracting one's attention, which is why he had been concertmaster in so many different orchestras. He was a stocky man, about 5 feet 8 inches, and had quite a large stomach. He had a remarkably rough appearance for a violinist, as if he had been in fights as a kid, which he claimed he had, growing up in a poor section of St. Louis. His thick black, curly hair sat on his head like a hat, and what solidified this impression was the fact that his hairline was very low, almost in the middle of his forehead.

His hands were very dry and raw looking, as if he chewed them. But when he spoke and used them to emphasize his speech, his graceful and smooth gestures overrode their gruff, rough look. He was meticulous in his dress, wearing only cashmere sweaters, and slacks and shirts perfectly pressed, and a fragrant cologne that would always stay on my violin for days after he had played it. Even though his appearance, apart from his clothing, was very rough and beaten up, his personal interaction with me was very calming. During lessons he always smoked a pipe, and I loved the aroma. Any difficulty with playing was dealt with carefully, "Let's see, maybe if you do this it will help." It always did. His understanding of phrasing, sound, and color was profound. His only lack was that he couldn't explain anything—he could just show me—and I would copy him as best I could.

The ability to demonstrate is deeply influential if one is talking about interaction with a player who is that accomplished. But imitation without thorough explanation risks missing a fundamentally important point of development that the teacher himself possesses and takes for granted because it has become unconscious in him. Perhaps Krachmalnick could have learned to explain his playing and technique, but he had only two students and had never taught anyone before me. Yet I had a great relationship with him and I think he influenced my character as much as my own father did.

I spent quite a bit of time with him socially. He often took me with him when he visited his friends, some of them musicians, some of them rich people he liked to hobnob with. He'd take me to concerts and, afterwards, to restaurants where he would meet up with them. I was introduced to a world of people I had no access to, people who seemed to me ultra-sophisticated—Europeans speaking German and French and English at the table with no one missing a beat. I don't know if he understood what they were saying. But to them he was the "great musician" and all of these sophisticates were enamored with him.

Krachmalnick, Jake to his friends, was charming. It seemed that he had stories about every famous musician in the world. Photos he had taken of them lined his walls. He knew Stravinsky, Serkin, and Nathan Milstein. He had studied with Heifetz, and played chamber music with him and the great cellist, Gregor Piatigorsky, at Heifetz's house. He was also a friend of Piatigorsky's and once drove me down to Los Angeles to play for him at his house in Bel Air. We spent the afternoon together amidst paintings by Picasso and van Gogh and I listened to them talk about people they knew in common. Jake knew George Szell, Bernstein, and Isaac Stern, of whom, as I recall, he was not terribly fond. Krachmalnick once brought along Josef Krips, the conductor of the San Francisco Symphony, to a recital of mine. Jake knew Jack Benny, and all the famous studio musicians in L.A., many of whom I met through him.

His stories were leisurely, droll, and often way off the social grid. He liked to shock people. He was incredibly generous with his time, giving me three-hour lessons a couple of times a week. With adults he had a reputation for being blunt and crude. When he had a few drinks he often became morose and sardonically bitter. People were, quite naturally, uncomfortable with that. But, in terms of his musical expertise and understanding there was not an ounce of nonsense. I once said to him that I thought he was a great player. He looked shocked and told me that I was absurd. He said he grew up with Milstein, Heifetz, Horowitz. There was no way to compare yourself with that level of genius, he said. That ended the conversation.

Krachmalnick would concertize in Europe in the summer. He always brought something back for me, once even a violin bow he had bought in France. Many years later, when I had developed my theory of how the great players of the past thought about music, I mentioned to him that he also phrased like that. He was unaware of it. He said he just copied what was around him. I made rapid progress in the few years I studied with Krachmalnick, so much so that my life became directed by my musical accomplishments.

CHAPTER 4

Philadelphia

K rachmalnick left San Francisco after I had been taking lessons with him for a couple of years. His bluntness and gruff behavior with his colleagues had gotten him fired from the symphony, traits that followed him everywhere like his own personal weather system, and that as far as his interaction with adults was concerned, rarely saw a sunny day. So Jake moved to Los Angeles, where he became concertmaster of several studio orchestras. He was in his fifties and making stacks of money, but I'm sure this is not where he had hoped to be at this point in his career, the height of his playing, recording the soundtrack for *Loveboat*.

I flew down to Los Angeles every week to continue my lessons with him. My father paid only the air fare, which at the time was about fifty dollars round trip—the same price my lessons had been—because Krachmalnick insisted on teaching me gratis. I left on Friday afternoon, stayed overnight at Jake's house in Bel Air, and came back Saturday evening after my lesson. Jake, Mr. Krachmalnick to me, usually took me out to dinner on Friday, and on Saturday morning to a local Jewish deli, where he introduced me to standards of Kosher cuisine such as lox and bagels, gefilte fish, and kippered herring, the last of which made me appreciate being a Catholic.

When I was fifteen years old Krachmalnick thought it would be a good idea for me to move to Philadelphia and study at his alma-mater, the Curtis Institute of Music. Apparently, he felt I was now too advanced to study with him. By this time I was playing quite a few local concerts, maybe fifteen a year, and had been invited to be the soloist with a local youth orchestra that would be touring Japan. People around me, professional musicians and music aficionados, started supposing aloud that I should go East to study because that's where all the famous music schools were located. The two most acclaimed were Juilliard, in New York, and the Curtis Institute of Music, in Philadelphia. Of the two Curtis was, and still is, the more prestigious because all the students were given full scholarships and the school had only about a hundred students, enrolled from all over the world. Curtis also had a reputation for being more interested in their students' welfare than Juilliard, with its student body of twenty-five hundred, most of whom paid the full tuition. Curtis also accepted high school-age students into their college music program and had tutors for high school studies. This situation, it was thought, would allow me to concentrate on developing into the level of player that it appeared to everyone I was destined to become. I decided to audition for Curtis. I was ambitious and excited to see what I could do.

My mother was the only person who objected. She thought that I was too young to live away from home. But all the men—Krachmalnick, my father, and I—outvoted her, chalking up her reservations to an overactive maternal syndrome of some sort.

I flew with my father to New York to audition for the premier violin teacher in this country and the West (by that I mean outside the Communist bloc): Ivan Galamian.

Galamian, an Armenian, had been born in Persia (Iran) in 1903, but emigrated to Russia in 1916 and studied for three years with Konstantin Mostras at the Moscow Philharmonia School. In 1922 he fled from Moscow to escape the Russian Revolution, moving to Paris to become a student and later, an assistant of Lucien Capet. Supposedly Galamian never pursued a performance career because he suffered from terrible stage fright.[1] He dedicated himself to teaching and had been on the faculty of Juilliard since 1947, and Curtis since 1944. Because he never came to Philadelphia, students travelled to his New York apartment, which served as his studio, for their lessons.

Galamian's apartment was on West 73rd Street in an old building with an elevator that had been there since the early 1900s. It had an accordion metal gate that snapped shut, and space for, at the most, four very thin passengers. His apartment was the size of a house, with rooms going on and on down the narrow hall which seemed to stretch forever. Next to his studio was a waiting area where students could warm-up before playing. Covering the walls were pictures of the famous performers he had taught, luminaries of the violin world such as Michael Rabin, Itzak Perlman, Jaime Laredo, Arnold Steinhart, Pinchas Zuckerman, and many other well-known professionals, signed with words of praise that expressed their heartfelt testimony for the greatness of his teaching. I must admit that to a kid this was impressive. I thought, this is

---

1   Ivan Galamian and Elizabeth Green, *Principles of Violin Playing & Teaching* (New York: Dover Publications, reprint edition, 2013), "Ivan Galamian: A Biographical Sketch," xiii.

where I can learn to play great. I didn't know what that meant, except that it would mean I would be famous like everybody on the wall.

Galamian emerged from the studio. It was nine o'clock in the morning in mid-December. It seemed like nighttime; all the lights were on. Galamian was tall, or so it seemed, compared to my height at the time which was five feet, four inches. His skin was dark and black around his eyes, which were huge and sad. He wore a button-up sweater that drooped around his sloping shoulders. His body was the shape of a bowling pin. He was probably around seventy years old at the time, but looked much older.

Galamian taught students from eight in the morning until seven at night, with a one-hour break for lunch. I don't think he ever left his apartment. He made lots of money, which he never spent. He had no children. He never travelled. He sat in the same chair and taught violin lessons for forty years.

For my audition I played Saint-Saëns' *Rondo Capriccioso* and Mozart's *Violin Concerto No. 4.* I played well and he accepted me as a student immediately. He seemed to think I had great talent, as did his wife, who appeared after the audition from the kitchen and told my father and me that my playing was some of the most beautiful she had ever heard from a student. I reminded her of Michael Rabin, she said. With praise of that measure I would have walked to the moon to study with Galamian. I moved to Philadelphia two weeks later.

Philadelphia, as I discovered, was morosely grim. Not that it's much better now. The streets of downtown, Center City as Philadelphians call it, are narrow, maybe allowing for one or two lanes of traffic. The buildings were tall and stained black, which gave the city a claustrophobic feeling. Fortunately, my parents had arranged for me to live in a suburb of Philly, an upper middle class village called Rydal, with a family who were friends of their friends, the Von Richtensteins.

Mr. Von Richtenstein was a lawyer and Mrs. Von Richtenstein was a homemaker. Both Mr. and Mrs. Von Richtenstein looked the same, like two men—thin, gaunt, and six-feet tall. Their voices were of similar pitch, both hoarse and low, except that he had a German accent. She looked a little stronger than he did. They had two daughters, one my age and the other maybe three years older, which to me, at the time, made her seem like a woman.

When my father left me that first night I think I cried later in bed, finally falling asleep with the thought that I would become a great player as quickly as I could and then return home triumphant. But to truly assuage my depression I let my thoughts wander to a girl I knew. I was always having crushes, intense fantasies about girls I knew and how I would save them from somebody or something, but at the same time somehow see their breasts. I was fascinated by breasts, that being the only sexual part of a girl I could imagine in those days.

One good thing about living with the Von Richtenstein's was that I occupied the entire third floor of the house, a converted attic, one room of which stored a comprehensive collection of Playboy magazines. I had only heard of such things. Now I had fifty of my own.

I took the train into town every day for classes. We were tutored in the usual high school subjects—American history, English, and a language, in my case, French. There were no math or science classes offered. The school was not accredited, a shell educationally, but I had come to Curtis to become a great player, so I devoted myself to practicing.

I practiced at night when I got home from school, maybe four hours. Although I had played nearly every standard etude already, Galamian wanted me to do them again his way. He had his own editions, which we were all required to buy. So I played everything again, his way, with all his fingerings and bowings. If I played a different bowing or fingering from what was marked, he noticed. If I did it again, it was common knowledge that a student would be kicked out of the lesson. As a matter of fact, most of what Galamian noticed was if I played a different bowing or fingering. The lesson was, essentially, one hour of uninterrupted playing.

"Use more bow here." "Save bow here." "Vibrate." "Practice slowly." He spoke very rarely and usually said the same things with a thick accent of some sort, probably Russian, and chain-smoked throughout the lesson. He would occasionally bang out a few notes on the piano with a couple of fingers, or put down his cigarette for a moment and pick up his violin, which lay on the piano next to the chair he sat in, and attempt to demonstrate something.

He would begin by dropping his bow on the string and end by fumbling through a couple of notes. He might do that once per lesson. Galamian never played more than three notes at a time. As far as I could tell he could barely play. I don't think anyone ever heard him play any more than three notes. He never performed. How well could he play? I doubt one person knows.

His etude editions had hundreds of permutations to practice this skill or that, and we were expected to do them all, and he had a scale system with hundreds of permutations and rhythms and we did them all. Lots and lots of playing. Lots and lots of work. No talking. No questions. No thinking. Just hour upon hour of work. After all, if someone else practiced seven hours and I practiced only three, it was obvious that he would be ahead of me. And unfortunately, there were older students who were already ahead. How could I ever catch up? I worked more.

I had music classes in the afternoon—harmony, solfège, music history, and counterpoint. I learned when Bach lived, who influenced him, who taught Beethoven, the dates composers lived and died, the history of musical development, the structure and form of musical compositions. But how this applied to music playing remained a mystery to me. None of it seemed relevant to how to play well. It didn't answer the real question I had: how do the great players do what they do? The connection to playing was never made clear to me, and I'm not sure it's clear to most musicians. They know in theory that they should know music history, but how does it affect the way one plays? They know that harmony does affect expression, but why? Most musicians' knowledge is on an intuitive level only.

This lack of scholarship and investigation is encouraged by our love of the word *talent*. Talent is thought to be ability that comes from nowhere explainable. It is its seeming inexplicability that gives the word romantic power. As we are captives and slaves to Eros, so we are to talent. Talent—the *idea* of talent—puts our minds to sleep.

But it wasn't all bad. Although the teaching style and the work load never changed, the setting did. In the summer we moved from the grime of Philadelphia to the bucolic idyll of upstate New York to continue our practicing at Galamian's summer retreat outside Elizabethtown—Meadowmount.

CHAPTER 5

Meadowmount

The regime at Meadowmount was breakfast at six, practice in your room for four hours until lunch, do whatever you wanted until four, one more hour of practice, dinner, concert, in bed by ten, then repeat it the next day for eight weeks. We lived in rooms six by six with walls so thin you could never get lonely. Boys were separated from girls, and we all lived in prefabricated buildings that housed thirty students.

But it wasn't all work. Upstate New York was beautiful in the summer. While the humidity wreaked havoc on instruments, it released other sensations in the mind and body that also wreaked havoc, but of a much more intensely pleasant and sensual nature. It was nearly jungle weather and the aroma of the grass, trees, and earth was distilled by the heat into an aphrodisiac for the mind and body. In Curtis all the girls were older than I was, but here I was surrounded by a hundred girls from Juilliard prep who were my age. It was hot, both during the day and night, and in the languor of the summer air my mind became entranced. This is where I first fell in love. Her name was Lisa. She was a cellist.

I was sixteen and she was thirteen and kind of tomboyish, a tall lanky girl, very pretty, actually a beautiful girl. She was always alone. We just started hanging out. It was very innocent. At night we would walk and look at the stars. The dark country roads were empty, most of them only dirt roads. We walked along, heading nowhere in particular, just away. The air was hot and saturated with moisture mixed with the aroma of the nearby corn fields and pine trees that surrounded us. The sound of cars in the distance made the world seem as if it had disappeared and only we remained, apart, away forever, like the town Brigadoon, and we looked up and could see the night sky ablaze with stars.

Fireflies seemed to light our way and the chirping of crickets screened us from what lay beyond the road. I breathed in her perfume, a sort of oil, as if every pore in my skin could feel her without touch. Her voice in the darkness seemed so close, as if she were talking directly in my ear. We were alone in the world, the dark, and she was mine, and I didn't feel scared or lonely for the first time I could remember. I held her hand and kissed her. I couldn't stop thinking about her, and I suppose I was really in love.

That first summer at Meadowmount, my first time away from home for an entire summer, was a beautiful dream, a reverie I both dreamt of at night and lived in during the day. My perfect world with her and my dreams was abruptly destroyed when my parents unexpectedly arrived a week early to visit. They took me out to dinner, and I invited Lisa to come along. I think they liked her.

The next day my parents informed me that they were taking me with them, and that I would be leaving that day to travel with the family throughout the East Coast. They had arranged my early departure with Galamian. There was nothing I could do.

I could barely talk for days. All I could do was think of her. I was in pain, literally.

My mother grew alarmed by my strange behavior and confronted me.

"What's wrong?" she pleaded, "Are you sick?"

I shook my head.

"Is it drugs? Have you been taking drugs?"

I shook my head.

"What is wrong?" she asked desperately.

She looked at me. I could see she knew.

"Is it a girl? Is it Lisa?"

I nodded yes.

She smiled.

But I still felt wretched. Sick even, I missed her so much.

CHAPTER 6

Curtis

Eventually I moved into the city from the suburbs. The commute took too much time, and nearly everyone else in the school lived near Curtis. So my grandparents travelled back East to help me find an apartment with another student who was also sixteen. We found a place on the corner of 16th and Locust Street, only three blocks away from the school, a one bedroom apartment, part of a much larger unit that had been divided and fallen into disrepair. My friend took the living room/kitchen area as his room and I had the bedroom. This is where we practiced.

My roommate was from Korea, and introduced me to the combination of spam, white rice, and butter. It is delicious. We lived on that, supplemented by Hamburger Helper and Shake 'n Bake. Vegetables were not allowed into the apartment. Our kitchen habits on several occasions proved problematic for our next-door neighbor, an elderly woman, who complained to the manager that hamburger was coming up through her bathtub drain.

My Korean friend was the most advanced violinist in the school. At that age he could play everything—all the Paganini caprices, every major concerto, all the Bach unaccompanied sonatas. We were agog. He was a chill guy. He never showed off or bragged. He practiced at tempo, concert speed. I don't think I ever heard him work anything out. On any given morning he might play through three major concertos, only occasionally having to stop to fix anything. How good was he really? I don't know. I only know that several years later he won some major competitions and was living in a little apartment in Paris. I never heard of him after our school days together. I think he's famous in Korea.

I had another friend, a pianist, named Portnoy. He was thirteen at the time. He could also play anything. He never practiced for more than an hour unless he was pushed by circumstance and even then, never more than an hour and a half. He studied with Rudolph Serkin and Mieczyslaw Horszowski. Portnoy was constantly reading. The subject did not seem to play any part in his choice. If it was in a book, he was interested. Even at that age he seemed to have encyclopedic information, a human search engine. He was also completely modest about his ability.

Each week he was expected to bring in a new piece for Serkin or Horszowski. For some compositions he would receive two or three lessons, but everything had to be memorized after the first week. He could learn and memorize a Mozart concerto in a few days. He listened to music constantly, introducing me to myriad performances and composers. Portnoy went to every concert he could, and dragged me away from practicing to go to many of them. It was difficult for him to convince me to stop practicing, but he was extremely skilled at it. But from Portnoy I probably learned more about music than from any teacher or class at Curtis.

Unlike most of the students, Portnoy lived with his family and commuted to school from Levittown, a suburb of Philadelphia. On weekends I often went to stay with them. All the houses in Levittown were exactly the same for mile upon mile. The walls were like paper, the doors to the rooms hollow, and the windows aluminum-framed. You could hear everything that was spoken or breathed no matter which room you were in. Portnoy had one brother and two sisters, all younger than he was. His mother worked for the U.S. Postal Service, and his father worked harder doing something that I was never quite clear about. He was always having bad luck.

They seemed to struggle with money, at least it seemed so to me, but were very generous, and became like a second family to me. Bernie Portnoy, Mr. Portnoy to me, was a short, stocky, bald-headed man, with strong, huge arms like Popeye. I think he had only a high school education. He was around fifty years old, but had already had two heart attacks by the time I first met him. To Mr. Portnoy, his son was a genius, nothing less, and, apart from his continual business problems, young Portnoy was the focus of his attention. The family dinner became an occasion for a recitation of his son's accomplishments and mental prowess, to which he would always add, "He's not like you or me. He's a genius." And what could we all do but agree, which didn't seem to set too well with Portnoy's sisters and brother who were also at the table listening to their father's nightly paean. But it meant so much to Mr. Portnoy that he be allowed to think this way about his first-born, that no one ever offered a bit of dissenting opinion, including young Portnoy himself.

This scenario occurred every time I visited, for years, and always ruined the dinner, but not the food, which, despite the stifled conversation, was kosher and delicious. Mr. Portnoy was very religious, and quick to point out to me that I wasn't really Jewish, reminding me nearly every time he saw me, either because he never remembered that he had told me before, or because he was concerned that I didn't remember. Not that that meant anything to me, but I suppose he felt better knowing that I would now realize my true position before God.

As the Curtis years went by all the little Portnoys grew up into regular white-collar folks, getting married soon after college and all making a lot more money than their older brother, who after graduating from Curtis was only able to find work in a cigar store in downtown Philadelphia. He languished there for a year, until a former dean of Curtis heard about his predicament and invited him to enroll at the New England Conservatory in their Artist Diploma program.

When I entered Curtis I was a sophomore in high school and had been a straight-A student. I had received a scholarship for high school in a new experimental school in San Francisco, the Urban School. Classes had four or five students and the teachers were PhDs. The faculty was ultra-liberal, which did not align well with my parents' political views. Afraid that I would become a Communist, they transferred me to the top public school in the city, Lowell.

I liked Lowell, with its rather scholarly air. Nearly every member of the student body was Asian or Jewish. I was there only a couple of months when it was decided by me, my father, and Krachmalnick, that I should enroll in Curtis. As I mentioned previously, I was accepted immediately and joined the school during the middle of the year, which seemed like a promising start.

Galamian had told my father that I would receive one lesson per week from him. At the time, everyone except for a couple of students, alternated lessons with his assistant. However, when I arrived at Curtis I was informed that I too would be temporarily studying half of the time with his assistant, but that this situation would soon change. It didn't. Not that weekly lessons with Galamian would have been different, as I soon discovered. As I said, Galamian rarely spoke in lessons. His main admonitions were practice slowly, play in tune, keep your bow parallel to the bridge, and do his fingerings. He did not demonstrate in any way that could be understood by the word. He also rarely answered questions. His usual response to any query was "Practice slowly."

I liked his assistant Paul Makanowitzky. He was a short, pugnacious man with a military haircut and nervous edge, who, had a casting search for the protagonist in the movie *Taxi Driver* been ongoing, would have surely eclipsed Robert De Niro for the role. He was considered to be quite eccentric, not only using a viola bow to play the violin, but also letting everyone know that he carried a gun with him wherever he went. He didn't say much, either. If I had questions, he referred me to Galamian, who had been his teacher. I soon learned to not bother asking.

Makanowitzsky left after my first year and was replaced by Jaime Laredo, who until recently still taught at Curtis. Laredo was a concertizing violinist at the time and often absent from lessons because of it. He also never answered questions, referring me to Galamian instead, who had also been his teacher. I asked other students if their lessons deviated from this format. No. It seemed that everyone was having the same experience. When I asked other teachers at Curtis, violinists, how to do something I was struggling with, they told me that they didn't want to interfere with Galamian's teaching. After all, they said, he is the greatest teacher in the world.

Galamian's monosyllabic style was quite at odds with the verbal fluency of the book he wrote on violin playing. It wasn't until many years later that I realized he didn't write it. An appreciative student had authored it with Galamian's imprimatur.

Leopold Auer, the teacher of Heifetz, Milstein, and many other great violinists wrote about the dynamics of a teacher's educative interaction with a student:

> My very fortunate experience as a pupil of Joachim's convinced me that the violin teacher should never confine his teaching to word of mouth. In spite of all verbal eloquence a teacher can call to his service, he will never be able to inculcate properly, to compel the pupil to grasp all the delicacies of execution, if he is unable to illustrate, by means of the violin itself, whatever he asks the pupil to do. Purely verbal teaching, teaching which only explains by means of the spoken word, is dumb teaching.[1]

How would one describe teaching that never demonstrates *or* answers questions. Is that double dumb? Can you be dumber than dumb? Is dumb similar to unique, not measurable by degrees? What if no one in the school demonstrates or answers questions? Can you have a perfect storm of dumbness? A cascade of ineptitude?

I did what I was told, but I still had those nagging questions. I wanted to know how Heifetz or Kogan played. No one around me sounded like them. The main aesthetic of string playing in Juilliard and Curtis in those days, was (and still is) can you play fast and loud, and slide, which means executing glissandi. The aesthetic was a kind of *faux* Fritz Kreisler, or "mock" Heifetz, who both added ample glissandi to their interpretations. But none of the students or teachers sounded like those great old guys. They seemed like comical imitations. In fact,

---

1   Leopold Auer, *Violin Playing as I Teach It,* Dover Publications, (New York, 1980), 7.

many thought the music was funny, even though they would be serious in a concert. The students were often clowning around with the way they played great music. I was never able to relate to it. I believe it shows a lack of feeling, an innate superficiality. I saw the same thing recently on a visit to Curtis. I don't know why those people are musicians.

The milieu of the school did not help build aesthetic sensibilities, although the building itself, an amalgam of two mansions was quite beautiful. But it was an oasis in the battlefield of downtown Philadelphia.

CHAPTER 7

Center City

Center City Philadelphia, where Curtis is located, comprised a very small area, only a few blocks. Its boundaries were Market Street to the east, Broad Street to the south, Walnut Street to the north, and Spruce Street to the west. Outside of this perimeter lay a black ghetto, and within it, office buildings, houses from the eighteenth and nineteenth centuries, a one-block park called Rittenhouse Square, restaurants, and a homosexual ghetto.

Coming from San Francisco an active and visible homosexual presence should not have shocked me, but in Philadelphia, the city of brotherly love, it was more uninhibited than I was accustomed to. Men openly kissed and fondled each other in restaurants and groped one another while walking down the street. This, along with the tall, blackened buildings and claustrophobic narrowness of the streets, which together blocked the sun, contributed to a general seediness.

The police were conspicuously visible at all hours. I had never seen such an active police presence in a city, and would not again until traveling to Jerusalem many years later, where soldiers carried machine guns on their shoulders as they rode busses and dined in restaurants. In Philadelphia, the police, intimidatingly huge, fat men, patrolled the streets and alleyways in jeeps. One might suppose that their vigilance contributed to a sense of well-being in the city, but their aggression and ubiquitous presence gave me the impression that an occupying army had taken charge.

The mayor, who looked like a Mafia don, was Frank Rizzo. Charges of police corruption and brutality appeared regularly in the paper and local news. Although often proved, nothing seemed to change the violent tenor of the city. It was an odd mixture of influences, as if the educated class had emigrated to New York, or somewhere with more opportunity, and those who remained were blue-collar white people unable to leave or too uneducated to want to, blacks with angry ghetto malice, and exhibitionistic homosexuals who seemed like perverts. At night rats ran amok over the streets and gutters and, often, in the subway, one or two could be seen perched on the platform as if they were passengers waiting for the train.

There was a theater in Center City on Walnut Street called the Aard Cinema that showed porno movies all day and night. No one under twenty-one was supposed to be admitted. I was sixteen and five-feet-four, but Portnoy and I dressed up in sports jackets to look older and they'd let us in. This is where I first learned about sex. In those days porno movies were called stag films. Everything about the theater, the film, the area, and the employees seemed illegal. The theater smelled like a combination of pee, cum, and disinfectant. There were only men in the seats and no one looked at each other, except for perverts who would try to catch my eye and motion for me to sit near them. Perverts stood in the back of the theater playing with their crotch and waiting. For what, I never dared to look.

The performers in the movies wore masks that shielded their faces. There was no plot, often just two or more scrofulous people, underfed and old, having sex on a bed. Some of the women were pregnant or having their periods and would bleed all over their partner. The first time I saw one of those films and discovered what sex was like, I let out a gasp. Yet curiosity bade our return and some of the films were not as disgusting.

Every two weeks I took the train to New York for lessons. The school gave us fifteen dollars for the round-trip fare. I looked forward to the trip, often traveling with other Galamian students. I sat in the dining car, which in those days still had tablecloths and waiters, enjoying a full-course meal, watching the New Jersey landscape of electrical grids, power lines, and warehouses go by, which although not Switzerland, was a respite from Philadelphia.

Our destination was Penn Station in New York, a dark and filthy place filled with bums and perverts hanging around the bathrooms and people lying passed out on the floor of the terminal. Usually we took the Broadway Express up to 72nd Street. After the lesson, on the way back to Penn Station we would walk down Broadway, passing by Juilliard and Lincoln Center, and meet a couple of friends for a meal in Chinatown. Sometimes we walked down 8th Avenue and bantered with the thirty or more hookers lining the street, or we would explore Times Square, where in those days you couldn't move ten feet without being offered girls or every drug imaginable, or both.

I often capped off my New York excursion with a visit to one of my favorite eating establishments, Tad's Steak House, where, if I remember correctly, you could get a steak for $1.99. I would then take the train home to Philadelphia and start to practice as much as I could before my next lesson.

ACT II

The Play, Eden,
and The Fall

CHAPTER 8

The Play

VALUES CREATE "CULTURES" AND "MICRO-CULTURES"

Thus far our story has dealt with situations in which our protagonist has been thrown about from here to there. He has had very little, actually no, overview of the ways of society and the world. At this point I think it is time to look more deeply into who's pulling the strings of the play. To do this I will attempt to answer a question that was recently put to me. I met a very wealthy man at a party, whose daughter, he told me, had graduated from Oxford with a degree in English literature, yet speaks like a "valley girl." He asked me why she did this. Here is the answer I would have given him had there been the time.

It seems to me that from the moment of our birth we are all groomed to be actors. Our first roles are bit parts in Family Theater. This theater has existed for thousands of years; we have birth orders, traditions; we are son, daughter, student, a member of a generation. Even our name can assign us a role if we are David, Jr., Edwin III, Matilda, or Sunscape. Our role, or roles, make one's course of action clear. If you are a son, then such and such will follow regarding your relationship to your mother; if a daughter a different plot coalesces. A play of a different sort is required with your father, who has a script with your mother (his wife), and yet another with his own father. If you are a male your role, by necessity, differs from a female's. This is partly genetic, due to inherent differences between male and female, but these differences are reinforced and exaggerated by social custom, such as the fact, for example, that in some cultures only the sons inherit the family wealth, which, in itself, creates dramatic tension.

We are all prodigies in the realm of the theater. Because we are trained actors at a young age we become adroit manipulators of others, yet are, in turn, easily manipulated ourselves. The older we grow, the more masterful and unconscious our role-playing becomes. So when the mass media suggests novel roles for us to perform, in addition to what is already in our repertoire, we are skilled enough to play along. The media produce theatrical events to beguile us to watch the ads (which are themselves mini-theatrical events) of the businesses that pay the media to create the shows. These productions have stock characters—roles—whose *interaction* create the story. Or, often, stock characters are put into a situation, and the different roles react to the *event*, creating a story. The media creates roles with which we can identify, designed to garner our interest. Foreign films from countries such as China, France, or Japan are difficult for American audiences to identify with because the customs and roles seem unrelated to us. So we don't watch them as much.

Roles serve another function as well. Formalism and rigidity in adherence to the roles societally prescribed for us create and preserve hierarchical relationships. If one refers to their boss or teacher by a first name, the tenor of the interaction is altered. Mr. This or That, or Dr. So and So, or Ms. Girl acts as a modifier between both parties and circumscribes a relationship of power. Perhaps it is necessary. Sometimes it is just desired. Dad and Mom are dad and mom even when their children need walkers themselves.

The way we speak is a role in itself, as Bernard Shaw so cleverly elucidated in *Pygmalion*. Eliza Doolittle, a lower-class London flower girl, is taught the speech affectations and accent of an aristocrat, trained in the manners of the upper-class and is instantly accepted into the swell's world, whereas, before her reeducation, they would have had nothing to do with her. Therefore, we could say that *every role contains implicit values, creating a "micro-culture" of its own within our broader values and culture.* A boss must behave and dress in conformity to our customary expectations of a boss. At home his wife may tie him up and whip him for his sexual gratification, but at the office no one would suspect his predilection. The priest is disposed to appear holier than he may be once he dons the surplice. The vestments have their own values, often in conflict with his own, as has been demonstrated by recent events in the Catholic Church. What is essential to the maintenance of the role motivates action. In other words, *the role creates action implicit within it, yet the values implicit in the role are often in conflict with the desires of the person playing the role.* This conflict creates tension, which is also influenced by the paradigm of the setting. The college professor who lusts after his student would not have the same dilemma if she was not in school, or in his class, or forty years younger than he is.

Let's return to the Oxford/wealthy/daughter/valley girl. The valley girl identity that she assumes casts her, by definition, as "a spoiled, materialistic, pretty girl who shops excessively and is promiscuous." She wants to be included in the cliché, which coincidentally helps support the media's business interests. Is this role "created" by the media? In fact, the cliché is middling true because droves of girls want to identify with it (that's how it became a cliché) and try to conform to the expectations the role demands. When they identify with it they are expressing their values, which embed them in the "micro-culture" of those values. Those values, or belief in the importance of being a "spoiled, materialistic, promiscuous, hoping to be seen as a pretty girl" *will bring forth* a certain set of circumstances into their lives. *The role is, therefore, the puppeteer.* Is our Oxford girl choosing this consciously, or is she in an environment that saturates her with these ideas so effectively, in the hope she will buy a lot of "stuff," that she adopts them with as little consciousness as the tan she acquires walking from boutique to boutique?

One of the hallmarks of great drama or comedy is the ability of the author to illuminate the confusion that continually occurs in our minds about who we are from one moment to the next in juxtaposition to the roles we play. Take, for example, Othello. He is a renowned and valiant general, but he is also gullible and insecure. He loves his wife, Desdemona, yet can be tricked, by a "friend," into murdering her for an adulterous deed that never occurred. Nothing here is as it seems. Iago is not his friend; Othello is not a great man. He "loves" Desdemona, but murders her.

Or Hamlet. Hamlet is a prince and son, which prescribes he take action to avenge the murder of his father, who was the King. But he is given this task by a ghost and is, therefore, filled with doubt about the validity and course of his action. Was his father murdered? Why did his mother so quickly marry his uncle? Why does she seem happy? One causative factor of his doubt is that he believes that if he is intrinsically, deeply, a prince he should be inherently more decisive and courageous than he seems inclined to be. His agonized choices end up killing everyone who is important to him, including himself. How can a prince act in such a confused manner?

Because he is just an ordinary, confused man, playing a part that he believes in, but the part, or parts, that make up his identity are really an artificial cultural happenstance. One may believe that by birth he has an inherent divine right to be a Prince or King, and because of this divine dispensation is intrinsically different from and better than other men and, therefore, entitled to rule them. By law this may be so. But is any man so different from another that he should be considered royal and another's ruler? If Hamlet had rejected the notion, the role of princedom, he would have had no need to act, or at least not in the ways he chose, and therefore, an entirely different story would have unfolded.

The drama is his inner conflict between who he thinks he should be and who he is. He loved Ophelia, but as a prince could not be with her. His confused, conflicted behavior drove her mad and set into motion events that killed her. Hamlet's role is in conflict with his underlying inclinations.

No one is born Jewish or Muslim, or Catholic or American. We, meaning adults, *assign* children these identities, *which contain implicit values, creating a "micro-culture" that unfolds from the assigned identity.* The role is conjured by us, but believed and acted upon by our progeny, with the interesting twist that they, and we, forget that it is all concocted by us to begin with. *Roles are psychological paradigms that have no concrete reality*, unlike, for example, the sun. Whatever you name the sun or believe about it, it is still itself. When we are born, and before we are born, the sun exists. No one creates it by teaching it to us.

Mass media does not have the inclination to show how ambiguous and conflicted our roles are since they help create them. It is likely that most people don't want to confront the obvious implications of our unstable identity because if we are not the sum of our roles, who are we? I think we are nothing. But not nothing in the sense that we commonly understand. *We are not definable.* We cannot be *fully* known or described, and scientifically speaking, neither can anything else.

Because there is no foundation to the suggested reality "bought" by our minds, we are *conditioned* to be easily swayed, or "sold" by other suggested "micro-cultures," roles, or packaged truths. There are many to choose from in our cultural paradigms. They will all set forth circumstances implicit within the context of the role.

One of them is the myth of the common man, the regular Joe. Joe has his regular girl. We'll call her Jane. Joe didn't go to college because it's for sissy liberals and eggheads. Joe hangs out with the guys at least once a week. He plays poker and bowls, and is obsessed with sports. He is fifty-two years old, but wears a baseball cap back to front in the style of a fifteen-year-old on his weekend trips to the mall. He has a flat screen TV that he bought on Black Friday, the biggest size you can find, which dominates the living room like a window into darkness. Joe and Jane look at it with the same admiration some reserve for the Pietà.

Joe may be a plumber, or a car mechanic, but he is an independent guy. He hates unions. He wants to be rich, so he invests his money in the lottery every week. He has been married to Jane a long time. They eat at fast food restaurants and have three kids who want to be rock stars. Well, maybe not. They want to join the military or be fashion designers.

Nowadays Joe goes to church. He is a born-again Christian because Jesus saved him from the previous Joe model that was a hard-drinking man. In those days he routinely beat up his wife and kids (this is the Joe model that was a union man) but now he and his wife go to therapy on television. Finally he sees and accepts that unions are ruining profits.

He flies the American flag from the porch of his tract house and only buys American-made merchandise, unless he is at Costco or Walmart and there is a great deal on a new accessory for his TV or stereo. Jane shops with her credit card. Well, she used to. Now it's food stamps. She has never travelled outside the U.S.; it's too foreign. She has a job to help ends meet, and wants to have more kids, even though they can really only afford two less than they have. And now even less because Joe can't find any work. But they are noble citizens. Their kids will join the military to see the world and be able to afford college. The possibility of dying or having your leg shot off is part of the chance one must take for opportunity.

Jane talks to her mother every day, several times. She still defends her decision to marry Joe, who her mother always knew was a loser, albeit charming. If she had married Robert, says her mother, who loved her and now has his own computer company, she could have been rich. The stories about him being gay are just vicious rumors. Not every man gets married. He needs to find the right person. He would have married Jane, says Mother several times per week. Mother made the same mistake herself by marrying Jane's father, a drunk and a womanizer. Or, in another version, maybe she loved him, but he died on the job in the coal mines, or out at sea in the National Guard when a wave swept him overboard. The role has dictated the script, which was originally written by the media. Individuals put them on.

Because the "Joe" role has no *intrinsic* reality, being absorbed unthinkingly from television, the "player" of "Joe" can easily slip into another suggested role. Perhaps the cowboy role will work for a while. There are many models to choose from. Clint Eastwood, for example, was a magnificent cowboy, although he probably never rode a horse until he made a movie. The same is most likely true for John Wayne. I doubt if we would find either of them sleeping with a bunch of cows under the stars. John Wayne was as much a cowboy as George Bush, a supposed "cowboy" who went to Yale. The cowboy myth is the lone dude who is free. He has no interest in money. He has his horse, and other dudes, maybe a squaw somewhere that he visits after a long cattle drive. He spits wherever he wants. If someone pisses him off, he shoots him because the law is for sissies. Cowboys never work for anyone for long—they pull themselves up by their own bootstraps, whatever those are, and ride away. They're outwardly mean, but inside they care—if someone beats up a woman too much they will intervene.

Paul Newman in *Cool Hand Luke* is a modern cowboy. The movie shows what happens to cowboys in the real world. He's thrown in jail for defacing parking meters while drunk, and because he won't submit to the rules of the prison, he is eventually killed. Jack Nicholson, in *One Flew Over the Cuckoo's Nest,* plays a modern cowboy type who won't conform to rules and is eventually lobotomized. Now we have gay cowboys, to show the soft, interior underbelly of the Eastwood/Wayne model. I always thought John Wayne walked funny. Why would anyone want to be a cowboy? In the real world the cowboy model will land you in jail or A.A., or the morgue. Apart from that, there are very few roundups left to participate in.

If being a cowboy doesn't work for a guy he can pick again. We have the conquerer role. He takes what he wants and is fought by other guys who want what he takes. He, in turn, is pursued by women who want what he has. But he takes the one who doesn't care. Or maybe she played him all along? This is the smart, gutsy, power myth—the myth that makes investment bankers sexy. I hate to tell you guys, your fear is correct. The chicks are after you for your money.

For women there is the sincere, unnoticed and overlooked average girl, who because she has a good heart is eventually recognized by a rich man for the wonderful, real person she is, and gets to marry him. She could be a hooker, as in *Pretty Woman,* or just an insecure charmer as in *Brigdet Jones's Diary.* Her reward is always to marry above her station, which creates its own problems, causing her to be cast as the gold digger, or the "it's a shame how low the family will be brought down by marrying the servant" heroine.

If she marries at her level she has to struggle (the regular Joe model) but get through it because of God. Her husband will lose his job, or she will get cancer, or one of their kids will get cancer. Or she will invent something and become rich, which will upset everything. But in the end they will understand that money doesn't change love. Or maybe it does. There is the "family is the greatest thing" myth, there is the "friends are the greatest thing" myth, there is the "I am unappreciated and unnoticed but if I keep being unappreciated and unnoticed for years, *60 Minutes* will finally find me" myth.

Lately our current proselytized social paradigm seems to be the desire to be average, not elitist, not a snob, just to be one of the regular "folks," one of the masses. Yet, ironically, everyone also wants to be special and one of the privileged, but in a certain prescribed way, *a way that coincidentally, and interestingly, is congruent with the preservation of the values of the mass media itself.* Their achievement, or what makes them special, never places them in opposition to power structures. For example, they don't want to be famous for ending world hunger, nor do they want to be special and elite because of any erudition or intellectual achievement. They want to be famous. Their achievement can be for eating the most cheeseburgers in one sitting, having sex with someone famous, exposing humiliating events in their daily lives on reality TV, or being rich—the reason and means an unimportant footnote.

I suspect "folks" trained by the media would view people such as Jefferson, Hamilton, Marie Curie, Einstein, Liszt, Brahms or Rachmoninoff as aesthetes and snobs. Perhaps the pursuit of knowledge for its own sake has been given up nowadays or can be excused only as a means to an end. These remarkably intelligent people represent values of their *own* making, arrived at by clear perception, a "micro-culture" that led to discoveries in science, political thinking, and the creation of great music. Yet the "culture," the society at large must be capable, must have the *latent and implicit possibility* that such people can emerge or be formed. The development of individual potential is not separate from the values of society because *what we value is the culture that we create.* This resultant culture *generates* an environment of potentialities, which as a system, *precludes* possibilities, development, and discoveries not latent within the roles (and their implicit values) assigned us by the cultural system.

Unfortunately, if we look carefully, we will see that the truth is the *inversion* of what we are led to believe—for most of us, our values are not our own. Is our culture? It is our *unnecessary identification* with our *mechanically* adopted roles that circumscribes our potential. Our *roles* are pulling the strings. They, therefore, color and filter the *insight*—the *feedback*—that we receive from our interaction with the world.

The *generative* power of underlying values and beliefs within a "culture" or "micro-culture," *unfold* potentialities. We can make an interesting parallel with the generative power of the underlying rules in language acquisition, which creates dead-ends (parameters) in facility (concepts such as "head-first" or "head-last"). These parameters result in a defining, or limiting, of the physical facility necessary to utilize that particular language, as in a Japanese speaker's inability to pronounce an English version of "r," or many such examples in all language speakers. Language parameters circumscribe—*form*—a language. It may even be that the facial expressions common to speakers of the same language, which without uttering a word can make it obvious that one is not "native" to American English (as in the case of the smile of a native of France), can be explained by the limitations, or underlying grammatical rules, of each language. These rules form the muscular configurations necessary for the pronunciation of words unique to that language, and therefore, the muscular bias of the facial muscles, which, ultimately, form facial expressions.

In the same way, it is possible that role parameters may be just as drastic psychologically. Because values determine bias (which allows only certain intuitions to appear to the mind), intellectual development—intelligence and creativity—is very likely dependent upon psychological settings, which may either bring forth intelligence or entrap one in confusion. If the bias and limitations within the unconsciously accepted belief system inherent in a role or roles does not lead one to a deeper understanding of what may be true, factual, then the normal brain process of "creatively" constructing a reality (which seems to be a built-in paradigm for everyone) will be led astray into a cul-de-sac of limited or blocked intelligence and perception. On the other hand, if the "bias" of "values" happens to be such that they would unharness the mind by seeing *through imposed* ways of perceiving reality, creativity from another source could be brought forth—the wellspring of intuition, or some may say God.

The built-in limitation, or parameter in this case, would be the "value" of searching for what is true, even though that may never be completely realized. This is, in a sense, the "value/culture" of scientific inquiry. Yet scientific approaches are often distracted from the search for what is true to the search for what may be "practical," which can end in very destructive results for us all. "Values" create "culture," which creates potentiality circumscribed by the parameters or limitations of the underlying beliefs, which may include having no certain, "set," beliefs at all—which would be truly scientific. Therefore, it is highly probable that one's values, *regardless of whether one is conscious of them or not*, are an active determinant of potentiality. We shall see that this is undoubtedly true for the development of musical ability. *Foundational* biases allow for ability to be *brought forth*, or *preclude* such a possibility, often directing efforts to dead-ends, because the interaction, the *quality* of the feedback—through visualization and insight—is inseparable from the *quality* of the structural settings.

CHAPTER 9

Eden

...it is the culture and environment, not the language, that lead to differences in how readily one or another mental ability is put to use.[1]

– Stephen Pinker

Leopold Auer helped produce two of the greatest violinists of whose playing we have direct knowledge—Jascha Heifetz and Nathan Milstein—along with a slew of other marvelous violinists. These players, born in the late nineteenth century and early twentieth century, living until nearly the end of the twentieth century, sound very different from us. Many musicians today, including myself, think that they sound better. Understanding how the great playing of the past differs from the present is not easy to grasp. It is a matter of *values*—values create culture. What previous generations valued musically is different from what we aspire to. We may hear the difference, but don't understand or value it. We don't know why we should.

In describing this difference people will say that performers of past eras favored more glissandi (sliding between notes), more rhythmic freedom. Perhaps they will notice a similarity between the sound of the instruments and singers. People often say that the great players of the past were not as brilliant technically and that they sound "old-fashioned."

There is one problem.

These performers studied, socialized, and were often close friends with many of the composers whose *oeuvre* has become the *canon* of classical music. In many cases, as composers, they were the source of the music themselves. If performers, they played in the way their composer friends, who were often their teachers and mentors, imagined music should be played. They were all cultivated people. And they sound entirely different from us. Our way of understanding music is different from that of the people who composed it, who created it. *We do not understand their values. Therefore, we cannot understand their music.*

---

1 Stephen Pinker, *The Stuff of Thought* (New York: Viking, 2007), 148.

THE SOIL THEY GREW IN — A "MICRO-CULTURE" OF ART MUSIC THAT EXISTED FOR HUNDREDS OF YEARS

I recently attended a luncheon at a winery whose vineyard and small garden is not irrigated, dependent entirely upon rainfall. The gardener in charge explained that everything concerning the process of cultivating the garden and the vineyard is interconnected with the mineral content of the soil, the amount of rain, when the rain appears, how closely the vines and plants are spaced. The plants and animals on the property absorb the taste and characteristics of what is in the soil. It is one indivisible system.

For example, they raise chickens on the property. If the chickens are fed salmon scraps, the next day the yolks will taste of salmon; everything is inseparable from what it grows in, eats or breathes. Most of us are not as sensitive to this symbiosis as is this gardener, whose farming system is dependent upon a thorough understanding of the relationships between the garden, the sun, the rain, and his manipulation and support of those connections.

This type of structural interdependence was a key factor in the development of classical music in Europe for hundreds of years. In fact, the interrelatedness of composer, player, and student reads like the *Book of the Generations of Adam* from the fifth chapter of *Genesis*. Let's begin with the lineage and influence, the "soil" of Leopold Auer. We will leave out the word "begat."

Auer was born in 1845 and studied the violin with Jakob Dont, who in the middle of the nineteenth century wrote a book of twenty-four caprices that are part of the canon of violin pedagogy and technical development. Dont's teacher was Pierre Rode, who also composed famous caprices for the violin that are a standard part of the pedagogical tradition. Rode's teacher was Giovanni Battista Viotti, another great violinist and composer. We are now back to the 1700s.

Auer also studied with Joseph Joachim, who was a great violinist and composer, and a close friend of Brahms. Joachim's mentor was Felix Mendelssohn, and one of Joachim's teachers was Ferdinand David, a great violinist and prolific composer to whom Mendelssohn dedicated his violin concerto. Mendelssohn knew Robert Schumann and Hector Berlioz, who knew Frederic Chopin and Franz Liszt. Auer socialized with these people. He writes that at gatherings in Joachim's home:

> I met Ferdinand David and Johannes Brahms...I also made the acquaintance there of Clara Schumann, Robert Schumann's widow; Ferdinand Hiller, director of the Cologne Conservatory,...as well as a composer of distinction;

Niels Gade, Denmark's greatest composer, and many others, a veritable host
of artists who were passing through Hanover…[2]

He played chamber music with Joachim, often works newly written by
Brahms with the composer in attendance. He performed Beethoven's *Kreutzer
Sonata,* with Brahms at the piano, in a concert. He was friends with Pablo de
Sarasate, Henryk Wieniawski—famous violinist/composers—and the composer
Carl Goldmark.

Auer studied composition and wrote a few pieces, although not on the level
of his acquaintances. He was, however, admired enough by Pyotr Tchaikovsky
to be chosen as the dedicatee of his violin concerto. Auer also knew the
great composer/pianist Alexander Glazunov, who was the director of the St.
Petersburg Conservatory when he was a professor there.

The violin department of the St. Petersberg Conservatory, where Auer taught,
had been founded by the great Belgian violinist/composer Henri Vieuxtemps in
1861. His successor was the previously mentioned violinist/composer Henryk
Wieniawski, who had been a student in Paris of Joseph Massart, who also
taught the renowned violinist/composer Fritz Kriesler. Vieuxtemps knew
Paganini, as did Heinrich Ernst, another great violinist and composer. Ernst
knew Joachim, who, as we mentioned, was one of Auer's teachers. This is an
intricate web of relationships, acquired knowledge, and skill (see figure 9-a).
Let's take a closer look at the interrelationships.

Arcangelo Corelli (1653–1713), violinist/composer, taught Francesco
Geminiani (1687–1762), violinist/composer and music theorist, the violin.
Antonio Vivaldi (1678–1741), violinist/composer, learned the violin from his
father, Giovanni Battista Vivaldi (1655–1729?).[3] Gaetano Pugnani (1731–1798),
violinist/composer, was a pupil of both Corelli's and Guiseppe Tartini's (1692–
1770), another violinist/composer. Pugnani's most famous pupil was Giovanni
Battista Viotti (1755–1824).

Viotti's students included Pierre Rode (1774–1830), *who taught Auer's teacher,
Jakob Dont,* Charles de Bériot (1802–1870) and Rudolphe Kreutzer (1766–1831),
all of whom became famous teachers and composers themselves. Kreutzer is
considered the founding father of the nineteenth century French school of
violin playing. He taught August Duranowski, whose technical discoveries
inspired Paganini. Kreutzer also taught Antonio Bazzini (1818–1897), who knew
Paganini, and became a celebrated composer of violin music and opera, teaching
composition to the great opera composers, Pietro Mascagni (1863–1945) and

2 Leopold Auer, *Violin Playing as I Teach It* (New York: Dover Publications, 1980), 8.

3 All records of him are lost after 1729.

Fig. 9-a

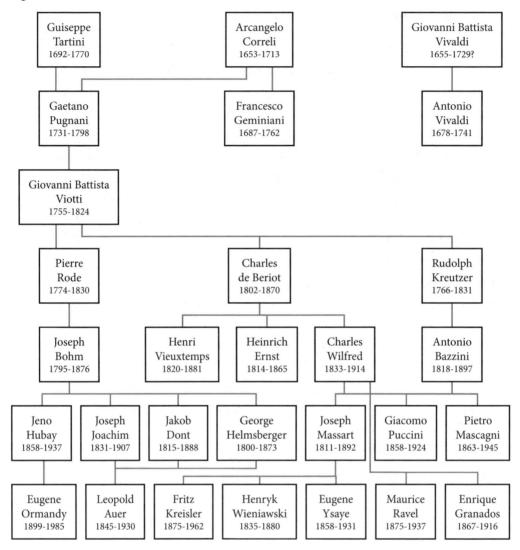

Giacomo Puccini (1858–1924). Bazzini also taught Joseph Massart (1811–1892), who was the teacher of Kreisler (1875–1962), Henryk Wieniawski (1835–1880), and Eugene Ysaÿe (1858–1931), all three famous composers and performers of violin music. Massart was a friend and musical collaborator with Liszt for many years.

    Paris was the center of intellectual life in Europe in the nineteenth century. One could find Berlioz (1803–1869), Liszt, Chopin (1810–1849), Eugène Delacroix (1798–1863), and Victor Hugo (1802–1885) gathered in a single drawing room if he was fortunate enough to be invited to one of George Sand's soirées. Camille Saint-Saëns (1835–1921), a great pianist/composer, was a friend of Liszt's and Berlioz'. Even Richard Wagner lived in Paris for a few years, from 1839 to 1842.

De Bériot, as noted previously, was a student of Viotti's. He taught Henri Vieuxtemps (1820–1881) and Heinrich Ernst (1814–1865), both wonderful composers of violin music. De Bériot's son, Charles Wilfrid, was a pianist who taught the composers Enrique Granados (1867–1916) and Maurice Ravel (1875–1937). Pierre Rode was the teacher of Joseph Böhm (1795–1876), who taught Jenő Hubay (1858–1937), Joachim (1831–1903), Jakob Dont (1815–1888), and George Hellmesberger (1800–1873), all violinist/composers. Auer studied with Dont, Hellmesberger, and Joachim.

Hubay taught the conductor, Eugene Ormandy, the violin. Ferdinand David (1810–1873), who, as we mentioned, was a frequent guest at Joachim's house when Auer was a student, was a pupil of Louis Spohr's (1784–1859), a friend of Mendelssohn's (1809–1847), and a prolific composer as well as a violinist. Mendelssohn had heard Chopin in one of his rare performances.[4]

The web of influences could not be tighter unless they intermarried, which some did. Liszt's daughter, Cosima (1837–1930), married Richard Wagner (1813–1883). Robert Schumann (1810–1856) married Clara Wieck (1819–1896), the daughter of his piano teacher, Johann Gottlob Friedrich Wieck (1785–1873). Clara Wieck Schumann, who was also a composer and considered a great pianist, became a close friend of Brahms. Johann Wieck also taught Hans von Bülow (1830–1894), who was also a student of Liszt's, (and a composer as well) and whose daughter, Cosima, von Bülow married, before she left him to marry Wagner, with whom she had had an affair for several years.

There were the Russian composers, "The Five" whose mentor and teacher, Mily Balakirev (1837–1910), had been influenced by Mikhail Glinka (1804–1857) into creating a Russian nationalist music. The group included César Cui (1835–1918), Modest Mussorgsky (1839–1881), Alexander Borodin (1833–1887), and Nikolai Rimsky-Korsakov (1844–1908). Rimsky-Korsakov taught Igor Stravinsky (1882–1971) composition.

Sergei Rachmaninoff (1873–1943) taught the great singer Feodor Chaliapin (1873–1938) the title role of Boris Godunov, in Mussorgsky's opera, which became the singer's most famous role. Rachmaninoff was taught piano by his cousin Alexander Siloti, a pianist/composer (1863–1945), who was a pupil of Liszt's, who had been a pupil of Carl Czerny's, who was a student of Ludwig van Beethoven's, who was a student of Joseph Haydn's. Rachmaninoff was also taught piano by Nikolai Zverev (1832–1893), who taught the pianist/composer Alexander Scriabin (1872–1915) as well. Zverev's students lived at his house.

---

4   Chopin performed in public perhaps twenty times.

He regularly hosted social gatherings which included well-known artists and intellectuals from Moscow and St. Petersburg.

Rachmaninoff's harmony teacher was Anton Arensky, a pianist/composer. His counterpoint professor was Sergei Taneyev, who had studied composition with Tchaikovsky and piano with Nicolai Rubenstein. Tchaikovsky was a mentor to Rachmaninoff. Taneyev also taught Reinhold Glière, Scriabin, Nicolai Medtner, and Jules Conus, whose son married Rachmaninoff's daughter. Vladimir Horowitz's mother had studied piano with a student of Theodor Leschetizky's, who was a student of Czerny's. Horowitz's friend and mentor was Rachmaninoff.

Richard Strauss (1864–1949) was taught composition by his father. The cousin of composer Max Reger (who taught the conductor George Szell composition) was Hans von Koessler (1853–1926), who taught composition to Zoltán Kodály, Béla Bartók, and Ernst von Dohnányi. The violinist Jascha Heifetz's first violin teacher was his father, the concertmaster of Vilnius's orchestra, and his next teacher was a student of Leopold Auer's. After that start he travelled to St. Petersburg and studied with Auer. Nathan Milstein's first teacher was Pyotr Stolyarsky, who also taught David Oistrakh. Stolyarsky was a student of Auer's.

This is a garden of biblical proportions. It almost seems with soil that rich anyone begotten from it would grow into an expert musician. These musicians socialized with the aristocrats and nobility of Europe as well as with artists from other disciplines. This interaction and communication influenced them profoundly. Rachmaninoff said, when asked how he composed, that he put all his life into his musical compositions. To write music on his level you can't be living in aboriginal Australia or, unfortunately, most areas of the United States.

THEY ARE TRAINED

We place a high value on thoughtlessness. The ability to perform a task without practice or understanding is regarded as a sign of talent. The highest level of musical talent is commonly thought to be uncultivated. The world of music is rife with expressions such as "he was just born playing like that."

"He has a golden throat."

"He didn't learn from anyone."

More commonly, "I didn't learn from anyone," if the artist refers to himself.

We want to believe that someone is born an artist, hatched fully formed from a musical egg. Why do we need to believe this?

Why do we value the idea that someone did not have to work hard or learn from someone else? An investigation into the background of great talents reveals that they were not accidental and never hatched fully formed. As great as Horowitz was, even he had to be *taught* to play. As Milstein comments:

> Horowitz's development, as that of any genius, was natural to a great degree. The seeds were tossed into the ground back in Kiev; his mother [who had studied with a student of Leschetizky] began teaching him music, and then Sergei Tarnovsky took over and did a lot for him. Then Volodya's work with Felix Blumenfeld played a major role in his development. Blumenfeld was the uncle of Heinrich Neuhaus, who taught Sviatoslav Richter and Emil Gilels...Later Rachmaninoff became an incredible authority for Horowitz... *The influence of a major musician like Blumenfeld* [a great pianist who was taught composition by Rimsky-Korsakov] *is crucial in one's youth. Later, the seeds can grow on their own; the genius's gift blossoms getting nourishment from its environment. That's what happened with Volodya.*[5] (italics mine)

Here is Milstein describing his own development:

> In Petersburg we lived in an enormous house on Gorokhovaya Street. We got up early, at seven. We had breakfast: bread and butter, and tea. Following the example of the rich Abelsons we also had cheese. Then Mama sent me to the store for groceries. After that, I would go to my music stand and practice the violin...I was practicing maybe four or five hours. At last Mama would say, "Go eat."[6]

Milstein's mother left her husband and other children to live with him in St. Petersberg.

Paganini, in his mid-thirties, spoke about his father's involvement with his studies to his friend Schottky:

> He soon recognized my natural talents, and I owe to him the first fundamental principles of my art...one can hardly imagine a stricter father: if I did not seem industrious enough, he would compel me to redouble my efforts by hunger. I suffered very much physically, and my health began to give way, and yet there was no need for such severity. I exhibited great enthusiasm for the instrument, and studied it increasingly in order to discover new, and hitherto unsuspected effects.[7]

---

5 Nathan Milstein and Solomon Volkov, *From Russia to the West* (New York: Henry Holt and Co., 1990), 192.

6 *Ibid.,* 18.

7 Dr. Herbert Axelrod, *Paganini* (New Jersey: Paganiniana, 1979), 16.

He didn't "pick up" playing, or composing, for that matter. He studied composition with Francesco Gnecco and Ferdinando Paer, both famous opera composers, having already received from his teacher, Giacomo Costa, a full musical training in harmony, counterpoint, and composition as a boy.

Van Cliburn's mother was his first teacher. She had studied with a student of Liszt's. Yo-Yo Ma's father was a music professor and his mother a professional singer. Sarah Chang's father was a professional violinist. Evgeny Kissin's piano teacher *lived* with his family. Maxim Vengerov's parents were both musicians.

THEIR VALUES CREATE THEIR CULTURE, WHICH CREATES THE MUSIC

I think we should let them speak for themselves. No one else can do them justice or adequately paraphrase the emotion and intensity of their thought.

Shostakovich:

> Music in which the composer expresses his thoughts truthfully, and does it in such a way that the greatest possible number of decent citizens... will recognize and accept that music, thereby understanding his country and people. That is the meaning of composing music, as I see it.

> Can music attack evil? Can it make man stop and think? Can it cry out and thereby draw man's attention to various vile acts to which he has grown accustomed? To the things he passes without any interest?[8]

Borodin, about whom, Shostakovich told the following story:

> Rimsky-Korsakov would visit Borodin and ask, "Have you written anything? I have." Borodin replied. And it would turn out to be another letter in defense of women's rights.[9]

Chopin:

> "Nothing is more detestable than music without hidden meaning."[10]

Rachmaninoff:

> My constant desire to compose is actually the urge within me to give tonal expression to my feelings... Study the masterpieces of every great composer, and you will find every aspect of the composer's personality and background

---

8   Josiah Fisk, *Composers on Music* (Boston: Northeastern University Press, 1997), 355.

9   *Ibid.,* 355.

10 *Ibid.,* 257.

in his music. Time may change the technique of music, but it can never alter its mission.[11]

Referring to Liszt and Anton Rubenstein he said, "Their greatness was not the hollow shell of acquired technique. THEY KNEW."[12]

"What?" we may well ask.

Richard Strauss:

> The melodic idea, coming straight out of the ether, which suddenly overtakes me, which appears without any material stimulus or psychic emotion emerges from the imagination, immediate, unconscious, without benefit of the intelligence. It is the greatest of divine gifts, not to be compared with any other. Poetic inspiration can still have a connection with the intelligence... melodic inspiration is the absolute revelation of final mysteries.[13]

Wilhelm Furtwängler's insightful comments about creation:

> Consider the situation of the creator, the composer. He starts from nothing, from chaos, so to say. He ends with a completed work. His movement towards this goal, the task of bringing form to chaos, is via the path of improvisation. *Improvisation is the basic form of all true music...* In conformity with the laws of organic life every "spiritual event" represented by a work of music carries within it the urge towards completion, fulfillment... We might define a piece of music as an improvisation seeking a fulfillment—a fulfillment expressive of its in-dwelling musical form yet remaining, at every moment and from beginning to end, improvisation...
>
> How does it appear to its interpreter, the performer?... When one turns one's attention to the way the piece has grown, the way one passage has evolved into another in logical sequence, and when one thus comes to see more and more of the composer's creative vision of his work *in toto,* then, and only then, will all the separate parts be seen in their true function, arranged in their proper order, with their own character and flavor. If the work is the chronicle of a "spiritual experience," each individual moment can only receive its meaning from its position within the context of this chronicle and in accordance with the psychological laws that govern it.

---

11 *Ibid.,* 235.

12 James Francis Cooke, *Great Pianists on Piano Playing* (New York: Dover Publications, 1999), 215.

13 *Ibid.* 8, 211.

It follows from this that for every musical work...there is only one approach, one manner of interpretation, that consistently proves to make the deepest impression, precisely because it is the "correct" interpretation.[14]

Tchaikovsky writes about composing:

It is absolutely necessary for a composer to shake off all the cares of daily existence, at least for a time, and give himself up entirely to his art-life... Everything else is forgotten, the soul throbs with an incomprehensible excitement, so that, almost before we can follow this swift flight of inspiration, time passes literally unreckoned and unobserved...Unfortunately...external hinderances are inevitable. A duty has to be performed, dinner is announced, a letter arrives, and so on. This is the reason why there exist so few compositions that are of equal quality throughout. Hence the *joints, patches, inequalities, and discrepancies.*[15]

I doubt if any of these people would be watching football with the gang while chugging down a few brewskies on their Sunday afternoons.

THE SUBTLETY OF RHYTHMIC NUANCE

Carl Maria von Weber on rhythm:

The most difficult problem of all is to unite voice and instruments so they blend in the rhythmic motion of a piece and the instruments support and enhance the voice in its emotional expression, for voices and instruments are in their very nature opposed to each other. Because of breathing and articulation singing calls for a certain fluctuation in the measure that may be compared to the uniform beating of waves against the shore. Instruments (particularly strings) divide the time into sharp segments comparable to the swinging of a pendulum. Truth of expression demands the blending of these contrasting characteristics. The beat should not be a tyrannical restriction or the driving of a mill hammer. On the contrary, it should be to music what the pulse beat is to the life of man. There is no slow tempo in which passages that demand a faster movement do not occur and thereby prevent the feeling of dragging. Conversely, there is no presto that does not call for slower execution of certain passages, so that the expression will not be marred by overzealousness...These interpretive insights are to be found in the sensitive human breast alone, and

14 Wilhelm Furtwängler, *On Music: Essays and Addresses,* translated and edited by Ronald Taylor, "Principles of Interpretation" (USA: Scolar Press, 1991), 11–12.
15 *Ibid.* 8, 157–158.

if they are lacking there, then neither the metronome, which can only prevent gross blunders, nor our highly inadequate markings will help.[16]

Debussy:

You know my opinion of metronome markings: they are right for a single measure, like "roses, which exist but for a morning;" there are "those" who don't hear music and who, because of this, use the markings to hear it even less![17]

Josef Hoffman, the great pianist:

"You should not play with the metronome for any length of time, for it lames the musical pulse and kills the vital expression in your playing."[18]

This family of relationships through which the art of music evolved in Europe was a near Garden of Eden for the development of musical ability. Yet, as in the biblical story, there were forces present and accumulating that were gradually coalescing—as a result of the values and culture at large—that would subsume this musical village, this micro-culture, tearing it apart and expelling what was left scattered throughout a comparatively infertile world.

---

16 *Ibid.*, 63–64.

17 *Ibid.*, 198.

18 Josef Hoffman, *Piano Playing*, "Piano Questions Answered" (Toronto: Dover Publications, 1976), 59.

CHAPTER 10

The Fall

Style is traditions, and the secrets of those traditions could be [surmised] by the young novice only among great singers, the perfect models consecrated by fame. [Traditions] elude scholastic instruction. Only the performing model, taken from life, can inculcate and transmit them. So that if those who possess the great, true traditions disappear without leaving disciples on their level, their art vanishes, dies.

– An observation by Rossini to a friend.[1]

VALUES/CULTURE AND TRADITIONS OF THE MICRO-CULTURE, "EDEN," ARE LOST

Rossini was speaking about transmitting the "secrets of the tradition" of the great *bel canto* singers, but his illustration about how these "secrets" can be lost is applicable to all facets of musical tradition.

As we have described, the "classical" music that we have inherited evolved through hundreds of years of development that grew as a result of the interaction of a close-knit community of artists centered in Europe. This organic expansion of skill and complexity included the evolution of the instruments, the concert halls, the teaching, the virtuosic insights and abilities of performers and composers, the composers that melded all these aspects and facets into their work. The assertion of individuality in composition, performance, and instrumental technique came through this concentrated matrix of training and association aided by proximity and a nearly interbred community of values, *particular* musical values. These values circumscribed potentiality, creating within their explicit and implicit parameters one of the greatest accomplishments of civilization—what we label "classical music."

As we shall discuss, the system of transferring esoteric musical knowledge broke down on many levels. We have inherited a chaotic assemblage, a confused

---

1   Richard Taruskin, *Music in the Nineteenth Century* (Oxford University Press, 2010), 40.

and incomplete memory of what that tradition was because the centers of its continual rebirth were destroyed by a variety of factors. We shall examine how this happened—one breakdown at a time.

COMPOSERS LOST INTEREST IN PAST FORMS

…it has never been the performers, today or in the past, who defined the style of reproduction, but the creators. This they did indirectly, through the new challenges and new visions in their works, which also changed our perspective on the past, or *directly as performers themselves.* It was the creators, the composers, who provided the performer with the *raison d'être* of his activity: their very existence gave him a sense of direction and acted at the same time as a constant, if unconscious controlling influence which protected him from the most blatant of misconceptions.

All this was only possible, however, as long as composers felt themselves to be the natural heirs and consummators of the past, to which they had a living relationship. But since the "New Music," that is to say, since contemporary composers began to see themselves as being in opposition to the "Old Music" and thus to their own past, they inevitably lost all relationship to this past. They were no longer willing or able to create a style of performance for a past that no longer interested them, leaving it instead to the professional interpreter.

This was the moment when the question of interpretation raised its head and when the public grasped, unconsciously, what an alarming degree of importance the interpreter had suddenly acquired. He found himself holding in his hands a treasure of incalculable value—the whole of the past—with no higher authority to which to appeal for help. This moment marked the beginning of the *ludicrous* overestimation of the interpreter, the performer— an overestimation to which he himself had tended from the outset…as a result of perpetually confronting the public. But it also marked the onset of a move to escape from his power, to restrict his influence, to lay down the path he should follow. On the one hand there emerged the view that there was no such thing as an objectively correct performance but that everything was a matter of taste, and that each individual and each age had the right to refashion the past according to its own requirements…On the other hand we had the crabbed, soul destroying demand for literal interpretations. Those propounding this view would dearly love to pronounce a sentence of death on anyone who departs one iota from the composer's written text, restricting performance to exactly what is recorded and thereby reducing any subjective freedom to the smallest degree imaginable.

We can now begin to understand why it is no accident that these two apparently contrary trends in performance should make their appearance in one and the same age. There even seems to be a causal connection between them, as though they had a common origin, were like the two sides of a coin, or two streams flowing from a single spring.

This common origin is in fact simply the sense of uncertainty that has taken hold of all aspects of our contemporary musical life....[2] (italics mine)

Composers had been the vanguard of the musical traditions of this European micro-culture, of its *musical values*. Even when expanding upon traditional methods their approach was based on a deep understanding of the *values* that created the culture of the past. They were, generally, expert player/performers and often, as in the case of Bach, Beethoven, Liszt, Chopin, Wieniawski, and Vieuxtemps (we could go on and on), not only teaching composition but instructing students in the art of playing. All of Leopold Auer's violin teachers were also composers, as we have noted.

Gradually, as Furtwängler mentioned, composers lost interest in past forms and began believing that having deep knowledge of the past was not essential to what they wanted to compose in the present. Composition became specialized, gradually separating itself from the *techniques of playing* that had been developed and integrated into their compositions by virtuoso/ composers. These technical/musical advances had been the foundation of the great performer/player's compositions, but were gradually not utilized or valued by composers who now sought a new means of expression. *Composers began to separate themselves from performing and playing.* This began to shift the parameters, the "culture," of musical "values."

Musicians, becoming evermore commonly not trained in the art of composition, began to misinterpret the printed score, believing that the *abstraction* of the printed music was music. They became confused about what the abstraction on the page represented. As we shall explain, this shift began to "mechanize" interpretation, and performers, gradually, could no longer "re-create" a printed page of music with the improvisatory spirit and understanding, the "values," with which it had been composed.

Although composers gradually stopped performing the pieces they wrote, they were still, even until the 1950s, expert players. Yet, as we mentioned, most expert players did not compose, perhaps because the emerging compositional styles being taught were often antagonistic to the technique of virtuoso playing.

2 Wilhelm Furtwängler, *On Music: Essays and Addresses,* translated and edited by Ronald Taylor, "Principles of Interpretation" (USA: Scolar Press, 1991), 8.

This began to sever the connection of the *development and application* of virtuoso instrumental technique to, and with, compositional approach. This rift, this disconnection, between composing and performing continued to grow until we now often have composers who cannot play *any* instrument, and musician/players who cannot compose or improvise. Additionally, nowadays players are no longer taught, as was Auer (who could compose), *by teachers who can compose,* a fact which encourages mechanistic music-making, a divorce of the creative process from the realization of the printed page.

Yet we have slid still further into decay, a shift in "values," a shift as to what constitutes "quality" itself. *It is now seriously claimed by the administrations of major music schools that a teacher need not be able to play an instrument at an expert level at all.* Hence, we have the height of decadence, a method of teaching developed by Shinichi Suzuki, an amateur violinist, whose approach is based on his attempt to teach *himself* to play the violin. His deeply flawed "method" has been eagerly adopted by well-known music schools, while being proclaimed and marketed throughout the musical world by his followers as an enlightened approach to not only music education, but education *en masse.*

THE GREAT PLAYERS STOPPED TEACHING

The industrial revolution of the late nineteenth century created an expanded middle class who had the extra income and desire to attend concerts. The business potentialities within the field of music continued to grow because of technological breakthroughs throughout the twentieth century. Travel became increasingly more comfortable, allowing artists to play the same programs in diverse places. The development of the phonograph enabled instrumentalists and singers to perform, in a sense, a few thousand concerts per night. As Marshall McLuhan wrote, "the media is the message"—the medium, in this case technology, carries within it its own message, affecting our behavior beyond the information it transmits. Thus, through the sale of records and improved methods of travel and communication (advertising), a few performers were able to make a great deal of money, and had no time, necessity, or interest in teaching and passing on what they knew. What they "knew" was their edge, their advantage.

It is here that we see another breakdown in the transference of esoteric knowledge. Auer, who could compose, was taught by great violinist/composers, and bequeathed what he knew to Heifetz, Milstein, and anyone else he taught. His pupils did not, or were not able, to do the same. *A few of Auer's pupils, in particular, developed the musical art of playing the violin to an incredible level of expertise. It is this tradition—its musical values/culture that has been lost.* This has contributed to our *pervasive* confusion about musical "values." (We shall see in later chapters that this knowledge was not simply a result of unthinking "talent," but is a sophisticated system of musical thought and technique far superior to what is currently known.)

I believe that within the musical enclaves of Europe and Russia a select group of performers understood deep truths about music as *a system of thought*—a language—and through the application of *bel canto* principles of phrasing to instrumental technique developed an approach to technique and musical thought that works *in congruence.* Because of the innate "structure" of music and the technique needed to play it, this approach, which happens to be fundamentally correct on many levels, gave them a considerable musical and technical advantage. One's musical understanding and one's technique is a "structure" in that, congruent or not, the two form a system of relationships. This means that if a few "key" underlying factors in one's assumptions about either music or technique are correct, or *incorrect*, the end-result is greatly affected. Consequently, the end-result lies in the beginning, the fundamental level—*success is dependent upon how one understands or misunderstands the* **structure** *latent within music and the technique necessary to play it at a high level.*

"VALUES" CREATE THE MUSICAL CULTURE OF SOUND, WORKMANSHIP, RHYTHM, VIBRATO

A *bel canto* way of playing music was ubiquitous in performances of the past, although it would not have been defined as such. We can hear this in classical music recordings until the 1940s; we can hear it in early recordings of popular music, jazz, and "big bands." Gradually this tradition began to disappear. Their concept of tone, of vibrato, of rhythm and phrasing is entirely different from, and superior to, today's players. This way of playing was "in the air," yet not deeply understood except by a few people (who knew each other). Players of the time learned this way of playing by imitating others, not really knowing what they were doing in an organized way, as my violin teacher, Jake Krachmalnick (who was a great player), admitted to me. This was a "culture" of sound and musical aesthetics that was apprehended *intuitively.*

However, I believe that a few people developed this way of playing music into an aesthetic system. This *bel canto* amalgam with technique ended with Heifetz, Milstein, and Horowitz, the last performers who *knowingly* used this musical/technical approach that, as we shall see in later chapters, happens to be intrinsically and objectively true. This style, its values, gradually faded away.

To put the matter simply, the great musicians of the past played more vocally, more smoothly, and had a more beautiful, refined sound than what is presently heard. They developed their technique from an "understanding" of the music they were playing, which emerged from inherited values and a cultural milieu that was "in the air" for most musicians, but not deeply understood. They lived alongside the composers, and in many cases were fine composers themselves. They were highly educated musicians. They taught others what they knew, their values, and the "culture" of music. Wieniawski taught. Joachim taught. Liszt taught.

The great pianist Artur Schnabel's analysis:

> *In the past almost every musician was composer, teacher, performer.* Then the enormous expansion of musical activities led to an unfortunate separation of these activities. The teachers who, naturally, were not all on the same level had to face new tasks. Rules, conventions, and standards, intelligible for persons without a helpful background had to be established. *The growing emphasis on the mechanical, on methods, formulas and standardization, is symptomatic of this development*... Notions, ideas, knowledge have to be simplified, reduced to formulas, further and further removed from the goal. Truth is lost or forgotten.[3] (italics mine)

REMOVED FROM A COMPOSITIONAL FOUNDATION, MUSICAL TRAINING AND PERFORMANCE BECAME MORE SUPERFICIAL

This is to be expected. The composer creates from an inner necessity, a compulsion. He creates to express feelings that cannot be articulated in any other way. The energy and knowledge required to bring forth his vision is enormously complex and not easily distilled. He cares about his creation as one might for a child. A performer will never have this bond with the composer's creation. He may have strong feeling for the piece, but his labor on it will be of a different sort, involved, but not of the same order. The performer does not need the same depth of musical knowledge to play the music adequately. However, to "re-create" the music, ideally, a performer should be well instructed in the art of composition.

When Horowitz plays a piece of music written by his mentor and friend, Rachmaninoff, who learned his art from Tchaikovsky, there is a seriousness brought to bear in the effort that cannot be separated from his proximity to the composer. The friendships and social interaction between composers and virtuosos, most of whom studied composition, was an essential component of

---

3   Artur Schnabel, *My Life and Music* (New York: St. Martin's Press), 129.

their unusually deep knowledge. Once that milieu was broken up by war and revolution this cross-fertilization diminished, eventually fading into mere self-promotion. *The knowledge was all they had left, yet this gave them an advantage over other performers.* When they died, the knowledge died with them.

MASS DESTRUCTION IN EUROPE

The transmission of esoteric musical knowledge was dealt a catastrophic blow by the wars of the twentieth century. Europe committed suicide/murder in an unprecedented orgy of blood that continued in Eastern Europe for many years after the ending of World War II. For the purposes of our discussion we will list only a few of those countries where classical music had been developed to the highest level. The death toll for World War I in these countries was:

- France 1,677,800
- Germany 2,476,897
- Italy 1,240,000
- Russia 3,311,000
  plus 9,000,000 deaths from the Russian Revolution (1917–1922).
- Austria Hungary 1,567,000

World War II:
- France 567,000
- Germany 6,633,000–8,393,000
- Russia 23,954,000[4]
- Lithuania 353,000
- Poland 6,000,000
- Italy 454,000
- Latvia 227,000

These numbers are simply staggering—insane. This apocalyptic era created an artistic diaspora, ending the musical "village" that had nurtured the art's development for hundreds of years. We can only guess at the emotional turmoil suffered by those displaced to the U.S. Additionally, there was no similarly well-developed, musically cultured soil for European musical traditions to take root in. Here are the conductor Otto Klemperer's comments upon first arriving in the U.S. after the Second World War:

> I've explained to you that since I haven't been able, up to now, to relate
> spiritually with any American being, this means that it will never happen to

---

4   It is estimated that Stalin killed another fifty million people from 1927 to 1953.

me. I came to this country at too mature an age, and it is now quite impossible for me to link myself with the environment and with the people. Most of all, the absence of romanticism or warmth, makes me feel far more alone than if I chose to be alone in a warm environment.[5]

In another letter he writes:

They're intoxicated with comfort and nothing else. The ambition of every one of my musicians is to buy a car.[6]

COMPETITIVE PERFORMERS

Nothing is more terrifying than a teacher who knows no more than the students are to know. Whoever wants to teach others *may conceal the best of his knowledge*, but must never be a dabbler.[7] – Goethe (italics mine)

Great artists in the West stopped teaching, but they were not idle. Displaced European star performers were busy protecting their turf, which is the concert arena, seemingly uninterested in passing on the art. Horowitz eventually received fees of several hundred thousand dollars per concert, lived in a townhouse on the upper East Side of New York with servants and paintings by Picasso. Why would he teach anyone to play the piano like he did (although he was taught his style by his teacher Felix Blumenfeld, who was a great pianist)?

The students being developed in the conservatories around them posed no threat because no one understood the old style. The inheritors of this knowledge did not teach in a serious way. Horowitz lay down on a couch and yelled out suggestions to the few students he would listen to. Heifetz also "played" at teaching, which is apparent from viewing the videotapes of his master classes at USC. Rachmaninoff did not teach nor did the violinist Nathan Milstein. Students are potential competitors. If your wealth depends on your knowledge, it is unlikely that others will be made privy to your secrets. Unfortunately, because of this situation, we have a gap in knowledge that could not be filled even if our current "stars" would teach.

The aforementioned players received training that was the equivalent of learning mathematics from Niels Bohr or Einstein, not, as is common now, from someone who graduated high school and learned algebra. At this point we are several steps removed from the geniuses who created the canon of

---

5   Joseph Horowitz, *Classical Music in America* (New York: W. Norton & Co., 2005), 324.

6   *Ibid.*, 324.

7   Heinrich Schenker, *Counterpoint,* Book I, translated by John Rothgeb and Jurgen Thym, edited by John Rothgeb (Ann Arbor: Musicalia Press, 2001), 19.

Western classical music. *Therefore, for many years, and currently, the type of playing that is promoted and taught by professional musicians at conservatories and universities in this country is the product of second-tier players who have become well-known teachers because there was no one who knew any better.* Lacking the *tradition*, the *values* that the older players possessed, but would not, or for some reason could not explain or pass on, modern teachers did the best they could. Without deep knowledge they could create only mechanical musicians—hard workers, but musicians who could never be as good as the more deeply trained players of the past.

THE U.S. BECOMES THE CENTER OF MUSIC

Here is Arnold Schoenberg's analysis written in 1948:

> Today's manner of performing classical music of the so-called romantic type, suppressing all emotional qualities and all unnotated changes of tempo and expression, derives from the style of playing primitive dance music. This style came to Europe by way of America, where no old culture regulated presentation, but where a certain frigidity of feeling *reduced all musical expression.* Thus almost everywhere in Europe music is played in a stiff, inflexible meter, not in a tempo, i.e. according to a yardstick of freely measured quantities. Astonishingly enough, almost all European conductors and instrumentalists bowed to this dictate without resistance. All were suddenly afraid to be called romantic, ashamed of being called sentimental. No one recognized the origin of this tendency; all tried rapidly to satisfy the market, which had become American.[8] (italics mine)

Classical music had been transplanted to American soil. After World War II the American market dominated Europe. How did music fare?

THE U.S. IS A CULTURAL DESERT

It is a bit superficial to assert that the U.S. is a cultural desert. It is certainly not fair to the 16 million Indians who were eliminated by the influx of Europeans. But what else can a "land of opportunity" mean? Although Europeans brought some "traditions" with them, often the main reason for their emigration was to escape from somewhere horrible to somewhere safe, or they came here to exploit an opportunity. A few settlers with an opportunistic mindset would not create commercialism as a cultural paradigm, but multiplied by

---

8   Arnold Schoenberg, *Style and Idea,* edited by Leonard Stein, translated by Leo Black, "Today's Manner Of Performing Classical Music" (US: University of California Press, 1984). 320.

millions, this outlook can take on a religious zeal. Hence this country's focus on commercialism, which views life not with an appreciation of intrinsic worth, but with an eye for what "opportunity" can be created from the exploitation of a situation for monetary benefit. The art of classical music did not land in a true desert, but in the land of commercialism, where its value was understood as its potential profitability.

THE ART IS LOST

In his book, *50 Secrets of Magic Craftsmanship*,[9] Salvadore Dalí wrote that like Vincent van Gogh, who cut off one ear for love, he would gladly cut off *both* ears to know how Vermeer had mixed his paints. The secret, the recipe, was never written down. Dalí thinks the reason is that it was common knowledge among the close-knit world of artists in those days, a method so ubiquitous that no one bothered to preserve it. The musical world was also a small, insular group. Charles Rosen describes in his book, *Piano Notes*, how relatively few works comprise the canon of music for the piano:

> It would take only eight hours to read through all the Schubert piano sonatas, less if you skip the repeats, and about another five to become acquainted with everything else he wrote for solo piano…In about six months of sight reading for three hours a day, one could go through most of the keyboard music of Bach, Handel, Mozart, Chopin, Schumann, Mendelssohn, and Brahms. Another few months and one could add Haydn, Debussy, and Ravel. Another hour and a quarter would suffice for all of Schoenberg's piano music…and an hour and a half will get you through Stravinsky…and ten minutes each for the piano works of Anton von Webern and Alban Berg.[10]

There was no need to preserve understanding when musical activity emanated from only a few cultural centers in Europe. The insularity of artistic communities acted as a form of quality control. Everyone knew each other and who the masters were. When these centers were destroyed by two World Wars and the Russian Revolution, leaving the culturally barren but hospitable setting of the U.S. as the repository of European musical culture, the traditions became dissipated and lost.

---

9   Salvador Dalí, *50 Secrets Of Magic Craftsmanship* (New York: Dover Publications, 1992). Chapter 1, 13.

10 Charles Rosen, *Piano Notes* (New York: The Free Press, 2002), 97.

SECOND-TIER PLAYERS BECOME FIRST-TIER TEACHERS IN THE U.S.

Second-tier players became professional teachers and controlled music educational standards and practices, "values," through association with major educational institutions, thereby, gaining influence and power. The centers of music gradually shifted from a few European capitals to a few cities in the U.S. after World War II, but the U.S. was not fertile ground for this transplantation. We, for reasons that are beyond the scope of this book, or possibly any book, have never developed as a national music, music that requires many years of education and sophistication to compose and play. Our music has arisen from the poor or working classes—jazz and pop, folk, country, rock, etc. Self-taught instrumentalists are sufficiently skilled to perform these genres.

European classical music is centuries old. The music is heavily intertwined with their religion, philosophy, poetry, painting, sculpture, and literature, and even with the architectural knowledge that built the concert halls where the music is performed. The social movements, the struggles of the people of Europe, are in the music. It is a profound reflection of their lives and of human existence that is understandable only if one is willing to put in an effort equal to the depth of the medium. The instruments themselves took hundreds of years to evolve. Stringed instruments are considered works of art and many are worth hundreds of thousands of dollars, some, even millions. Learning to compose the music and playing an instrument masterfully takes years of apprenticeship and is a lifetime endeavor. The only skill that is taken this seriously in our society is athleticism—sports. This country has no indigenous art that requires this level of skill. When classical music is transposed to our society we understand its purpose to be playing in a band or orchestra and we equate its complexity and sophistication to jazz. This is at best naive, at worst a perversion.

A six-year-old can play the roles in kabuki theater. But what is the point? There is no understanding. If all we see as an audience is shallowness, or learn music through a superficial educative process as students, eventually, as a society, we forget what the point of it all was and what its expressive possibilities are. It becomes entertainment, not art. This is the danger of a performance, market-based approach. Everyone wants to learn fast. They want results, achievement, fame. Understanding the "values" that create the "culture" of the art is seen as an unnecessary waste of time, and the "source," the inspiration from which the art was created, is eventually forgotten. A famous teacher in Russia used to boast that he could teach a monkey to play the violin. But he added, "What is the point?" Without deep understanding you have nonsense—no sense. We have tried to fill in this lack of background with "music appreciation" classes. What result would "science appreciation" classes have on the public's knowledge of science? The very attempt to teach it in a shorthand version trivializes and mocks the subject. When Europeans fled here to escape the danger in Europe we did not have the background to carry on their tradition of music. We still don't. But at least they were able to survive.

THE U.S. AFTER WORLD WAR II

Ivan Galamian taught at Julliard and Curtis for thirty-five years. Galamian was a bureaucratic teacher, and as such was and is the common level of the music professor of today. He was a product of the teaching of Konstantin Mostras, (who composed very interesting etudes for the violin) and Lucien Capet, *but he was not privy to the "secrets of the tradition" transferred to* Auer from Joachim, Dont, Hellmesberger, Wieniawski, Sarasate, Brahms, Clara Schumann, and on and on, which Auer transferred to his students. Auer produced far superior results to those of Mostras, Capet, or Galamian.

As we have seen, Auer's premier students did not teach, or if they did, were unable or unwilling to pass on these traditions in a coherent way. What Galamian did do was attempt, as had Carl Flesch, to methodize the study of the violin. But in this simplification of approach, which Schnabel had spoken of above, the *aesthetics* of music have been submerged, and "technique" has been *imposed* upon the music. This is an inversion of the relationship of technique to music, which must be that *technique arises and is formed, as a necessity, from an understanding of the aesthetics and "truths" of music,* which, as we shall discuss later, *creates an entirely different, and far superior, type of technique.*

Because of his position in Juilliard and Curtis he attracted ambitious and talented people who worked hard, but the spirit and method—the milieu—was regimented, unquestioning, and unquestionable. The legacy of his teaching is the pervasiveness of players who have "technique" but shallow musical insight, which affects their technique. If technique is not used to express sophisticated musical ideas, it is merely used to demonstrate mechanics—good worker playing.

Galamian's method is essentially based on rote learning, the repetition of contrived pattern endlessly repeated, hoping that this training will prepare one for any contingency. Therein lies the problem—*his contingencies are not essential to the contingencies met in musical expression.* They are abstractly and unnecessarily complex and based on a *misunderstanding* of the "culture and values" of classical music as it was understood by the creators of it—a misunderstanding, in fact, *of the nature of music itself.* We shall devote several chapters to the nature of this misunderstanding and confusion. Yet, at this point, it is only necessary to note that a *mechanical* approach to an art dependent upon subtle expression, intuition and spontaneity *inevitably, and logically, leads to authoritarianism and its byproduct, commercialism—selling.* Let's take a moment to explore this theory.

The act of creation must be nourished from a wellspring of intuition. Some call this inspiration, others God. It need not matter by what name the source is labeled. What is important to apprehend is that the source itself is not definable, or understandable—*it is a mystery*—and those dependent upon this source for their work realize it does not come from themselves. This realization counteracts and contradicts authoritarianism. When playing an instrument is divorced from composition or improvisation what can be left but the over-evaluation of the printed text, which is a compromise, an abstraction, of the original idea because the word, the sign, is never the thing itself. Therefore, when an art is separated from the act of creation and is *mechanically* reproduced, it is liable to enter the land of perfectionism because mechanism is thought to be *perfectible.* Yet whatever is *alive,* creative, is in a process of ceaseless movement and change. But what is "perfect" cannot change because alteration changes its "perfect" state; perfection cannot be an aspect of something alive, vital. Perfection is, therefore, an illusion, a product of intellectualism and is, in essence, neither alive or dead. *It is not real; it is a phantom.*

Without an understanding of the *spirit* of the music, *the values, the culture,* the *"recreation"* of the printed page cannot be possible. What *is* possible is the mechanistic reproduction of the symbols—a computer can do this quite well. A human being can be made to do this, but only by turning himself into a robot. Hence, a mechanistic approach is in its very nature rote learning, which is devoid of creativity. This creates a fundamental problem—music is supposed to be played with feeling, but what feeling can a mechanic have? *A mechanic can only pretend to feel.* This is the genesis of ham-acting, and ham-playing, by necessity engaged in by those who have no understanding of what they reproduce, yet desperate to "feel" something. Unfortunately, it is *"understanding," merging, a "oneness"* with the material that creates "feeling." It can come from no other source. To "understand" in this way is not easy. *How one might be able to do this is the subject of this book.*

This disconnection from "true" feeling allows commercialism to enter into the arena of art. Devoid of inner-feeling the performer/artist "sells" his performance to the public by layered-on "expression" and physically overt demonstrations of involvement, essentially "hamming it up." Yet the art of classical music was never intended by the composers as a commercial vehicle, as we have seen in the previous chapter in remarks made by the composers themselves. When this music is commercialized, the effort to sell it, to make the "product" "approachable," attempts to change its nature into "pop" music, which is not what classical music is, but what it may yet become. One must elevate oneself to art, not pretend the art is perceivable without effort from the perceiver.

With a mechanical approach as his method (which is inherently unthoughtful) a player/student—because of his lack of mental rigor or development of critical, creative thinking—becomes susceptible to domination. Having learned to play mechanically under the tutelage of an authoritarian teacher and milieu, he has been "prepared" to be dominated in his professional life by claims of authority in all sorts of guises, one of the most popular and destructive being the cult of the conductor. This edifice of confusion and decay *is the result of a system of education that is fundamentally unreflective, mechanistic, and uncreative.*

If a system of teaching an instrument is based on fundamental assumptions about music *and* the functioning of the body that are incorrect, the result will be flawed and limited, leading to a block of one's potential for creativity and intelligence. Unfortunately, Galamian's system of playing and understanding music has formed hundreds of violinists who carry on his unreflective and flawed approach, many of whom are currently in positions of influence. *They, therefore, affect not only the educative world of violin training, but all other aspects of the field of music itself*—the pedagogy of other instruments, compositional training, and performance values. Galamian's legacy was amplified through Dorothy Delay, herself a Galamian student, who began her teaching career as his assistant. She continued his superficial approach. In this system, students, if they play well at all, do so in spite of what they are taught, and never as well as they could had they been given a more correct set of fundamental premises. This shallow, mechanical approach continues unchecked because, in the field of music, professional teachers *instruct students isolated from critical review or oversight.* The main reason for this lack of institutional oversight and research is that the possession, or lack, of "talent" is viewed as a *primary* causative factor in the success or failure of a student. This is also believed by the teachers themselves as a primary explanation, which becomes an apology, in a defensive sense, for their own deficiencies. As we shall begin to see in this book, the *actual* situation is much more complex.

THE SOVIETS

The pre-Revolution Russians who were artists and musicians had been part of an upper middle class intelligentsia. They were fluent in several languages, educated in art, literature, poetry and philosophy. Their approach to music cannot be divorced from the "values" of this refinement of mind. When the Russian Revolution began, many artists and musicians fled the country. Those who remained were forced to choose sides in the civil war—Red or White. The Reds were Bolsheviks, mainly workers and conscripted peasants. The Whites were the intelligentsia, members of the middle class, pro-democratic reformers, pro-monarchists, landowners, liberals, non-Bolshevik socialists, and others who were against a *coup* by the peasantry.

The Whites lost the war. The middle class and intelligentsia were murdered, sent to prison, or intimidated into silence. It is estimated that nine million Russians were killed between 1917 and 1922. H.G. Wells visited St. Petersburg in 1920:

> It was the first time a modern city had collapsed in this fashion. Nothing had been repaired for four years. There were great holes in the streets where the surface had fallen onto the broken drains; lamp-posts lay as they had fallen; not a shop was open, and most were boarded up over their broken windows. The scanty drift of people in the streets wore shabby and incongruous clothing, for there were no new clothes in Russia, no new boots...The death rate was enormous, and the population of this doomed city was falling by the hundred thousand every year.[11]

Some of the Russian culture remained, but the power structure—the heads of institutions, conservatories, schools—was controlled by Bolsheviks, the peasants. The intellectual pursuits of the previous era were not allowed. Cultural institutions and music were tightly circumscribed by a brutal totalitarian state. In 1932 Stalin, at his whim, starved seven million people to death in Ukraine. In Stalin's time even a performer of David Oistrakh's caliber was in constant danger. In his own apartment building there were arrests by the NKVD, neighbors taken in the middle of the night and never heard from again. Thousands of people were rounded up every night and shot in NKVD prisons. Stalin and his allies murdered over fifty million people in the Soviet Union between 1927 and 1953. To put it mildly, these factors caused a shift of "values" and "culture" in the micro-culture of music.

---

11 H.G. Wells, *The Outline Of History,* Volume II, "Twenty Years of Indecision and Its Outcome," Part 5 (New York: Garden City Books, 1949), 1131.

Yet musical knowledge remained somewhat intact in Eastern Europe until the Soviet breakup in the 1990s, but under very different and horribly difficult circumstances. Intellectual freedom was gone. Great players had to teach. Therefore, the training was still at a high level, but artistic freedom was under a watchful eye, one that always threatened imprisonment or murder for anyone a committee decided to be suspicious of. David Oistrakh and Mstislav Rostropovich and many other musicians still worked closely with composers as in the earlier days of Russia. They were friends with great composers such as Shostakovich, Prokofiev, and Khachaturian, who all wrote masterpieces for them to play.

There is a difference in the playing style of the Soviets from the *bel canto* approach of Horowitz, Rachmaninoff, Milstein and Heifetz, as we might imagine. The Soviets—Gilels, Richter, Oistrakh, and Kogan (who was a colonel in the KGB), to name a few—were great artists. But the entire value and cultural system of Russia had been destroyed. Knowledge of how to play remained, but developed in a brutish society. They did not inherit the *bel canto* melding of instrumental technique and musical expression that the older Russians had perfected, although recordings of Prokofiev playing the piano and conducting suggest that this way of thinking was "in the air" or that he may have been *conscious* of it himself. The Soviets were, and are, more athletically minded in their interpretations and less creative than the older Russian, pre-Revolution, generation.[12] Additionally, as in the West, gradually players were not trained to compose, *which created the same disconnection in interpreting the musical text* that has made *all* performers continually more mechanical in their approach.

In spite of this, one will find that Soviet and Eastern European trained string players and pianists are *far superior* to what the West has produced. Their success is not genetic or in the soil. *It is a result of a well-designed system of training*, which although inferior to the old Russians, is still far superior to what the U.S. and Europe have organized. Teaching was considered a serious responsibility and a source of prestige, rewarded by a better life and better living circumstances if one could produce star students. The training of students was begun from an early age and the teaching of teachers and maintenance of their standards was tightly, even severely, controlled. Several outstanding players were created, but we have not heard, or heard of, many of these great players because they were trapped in communist countries. Many

---

12 Although the Soviet school of playing possesses a well-developed understanding of how to use the body when playing, and an elevated concept of beauty of sound, how could they not be affected by living in such a brutal environment?

extensive treatises were written on playing the violin, the piano, and a variety of musical subjects, including one by Pyotr Stolyarsky, the teacher of Milstein and Oistrakh, that remain in Russia or exist untranslated in the West. (A few have been translated into German.)

This discrepancy between Western musicians' lack of technique and the Eastern Europeans' greater skill was often explained when I was a student, and continues to be explained, by the old saw that the Eastern Europeans possessed "technique" but were not musical, and Westerners were musical but did not have flashy technique. Thus, it was proclaimed that someone can be a great musician yet not have great technique. This is never true. As we shall see, music is a system of thought, and as such has inherent truths and rules that allow for its most efficacious functioning. To express the music one's body/mind must be in congruity with the system of music itself. Technique, in its true sense, is the ability to channel the music's emotive power through the system of the body and instrument without antagonism, or incoherence, to any part of the system. *If there is a lack of technique or facility, there must be a lack of expression.* Inspiration may appear and be given its full flight only when technical mastery is achieved.

In summary, Eastern Europe and the Soviets retained knowledge of the old traditions, but the threat of murder, imprisonment, the intimidation of dissidents by the totalitarian police state that controlled all their cultural institutions, made those traditions more regimented, less refined generally, because they were produced in a brutal society. The U.S. possessed only *remnants* of the old European knowledge—individual artists, performers and composers, most of whom did not pass on to students what they knew in any organized way because there was, and is, no structure here do so. In the past, esoteric knowledge had been transferred to new generations by the proximity of composer, teacher, and performer to one another. Once that world was destroyed everyone else was left to figure everything out as best they could.

The result of all this confusion and dilution has been a gradual decay of the art. Soviet artists are a step removed from the Russians of the past. In the U.S. a violinist such as Isaac Stern, a product of this country, is a step down in understanding from the Russians like Milstein, and probably a step removed from his teacher Naum Blinder, a student of Auer, who Milstein thought was a fine violinist. Then came the Israelis, *who were trained by musicians who had escaped Eastern Europe and the Soviet Union.* They were brought here by Isaac Stern, who exerted enormous political power in the musical circles of the U.S. The way he chose to wield it was to promote performance as salesmanship, not a renaissance of the training that would revive European culture. (The fact that Europe had persecuted Jews for centuries may have contributed to his lack of interest.) Next to appear on the classical music scene were Asian players, some well-trained. *Yet one will always find a Russian teacher* lurking in the background, either directly or as the teacher of the teacher.

The music scene as we currently know it was shaped by concert managers influenced by Isaac Stern and, through him, Dorothy Delay. Performers promoted by them were taught and encouraged to draw attention to themselves in a way that can only be compared to ham-acting. Little attempt was made to link performance with insight, understanding and real feeling for music because, at this point, the knowledge of the musical community was devolving. This lack leads to a desperate effort to show off, because, in the absence of real knowledge, to fill the void and create a feeling of confidence, the performer feels he needs to add on extraneous effort to "sell" his performance.

Expression without understanding requires obedience to an authority—mimicry. It is always overblown, drawing attention to itself because the performer is designing the performance for the effect of being noticed. This type of performer is the "smiling as they play" type or uses the "eyes floating up to heaven" approach. A true artist is not self-conscious of his feeling or response to his medium. His response is unfiltered and immediate, natural and uninhibited. It is, therefore, not overdone and need not draw attention to itself to be effective. The best advice ever given for music performance is delivered by Shakespeare via Hamlet's instructions to actors:

> …do not saw the air too much with your hand, thus, by use all gently, for in the very torrent, tempest, and (as I may say) whirlwind of your passion, you must acquire and beget a temperance that may give it smoothness. O, it offends me to the soul to hear a robustious periwig-pated fellow tear a passion to tatters, to very rags, to split the ears of the groundlings, who for the most part are capable of nothing but inexplicable dumb shows and noise. I would have such a fellow whipped for o'erdoing Termagant. It out-herods Herod. Pray you avoid it.
>
> Be not too tame neither, but let your own discretion be your tutor. Suit the action to the word, the word to the action, with this special observance, that you o'erstep not the modesty of nature. For anything so overdone is from the purpose of playing, whose end, both at the first and now, was and is, to hold, as 'twere, the mirror up to nature, to show virtue her own feature, scorn her own image, and the very age and body of the time his form and pressure. Now this overdone, or come tardy off, though it make the unskillful laugh, cannot

but make the judicious grieve, the censure of the which one must in your allowance o'erweigh a whole theatre of others. O, there be players that I have seen play, and heard others praise, and that highly (not to speak profanely), that neither having th' accent of Christians, nor the gait of Christian, pagan, nor man, have so strutted and bellowed that I have thought some of Nature's journeymen had made men, and not made them well, they imitated humanity so abominably. Reform it altogether!

And let those that play your clowns speak no more than is set down for them, for there be of them that will themselves laugh, to set on some quantity of barren spectators to laugh too, though in the mean time some necessary question of the play be then to be considered. That's villainous and shows a most pitiful ambition in the fool that uses it.

Serious musical compositions are akin to a dramatic play. Would an actor smile his way through Macbeth, pleased with how well he spoke the lines? Would an actress draw attention to herself and thereby disturb an audience's experience that the play is "real" and that an auditor is somehow looking through a key hole, trespassing on events they should not be witnessing?

These stage antics, which include winks to an audience, dancing on podiums, ecstatic looks to the heavens, are well-known to concert goers. The supposed artistic aims of many of today's performers are greatly compromised by their stage personas, putting them into the category of entertainer, not artist, which would be acceptable if that had been the intention of the composer who slaved away to express emotions too subtle to be spoken or telegraphed. They have an *inverted relationship* concerning their relative importance to the music and are in the wrong arena of performance—a rock band would be a better fit. If the actors who Hamlet addressed had used today's standard approach for a musical performance he would have had to abandon his plot to expose his uncle's murderous act to the court by presenting the foul deed in a play. The King's court would have been laughing so hard they would have missed the whole point.

The educative divorce of playing an instrument from compositional and improvisational skill (I do not mean jazz) creates at the base of the art, by necessity, a mechanical approach to playing because without deep understanding what else can one do? Mechanism at the center of learning has been obfuscated by authoritarianism, and in performance is masked by ham-feeling. Because the performance of music is essentially perfectionistic, dead, and emotionally contrived to sell the product, which is the performer, the auditor's experience is fundamentally compromised. The audience is not hearing what the music was intended to be. They are the victims of a bait and switch akin to thinking their partner married for love, but actually it was all a pretense—your partner wanted your money. The relationship is essentially insincere. Eventually the hollowness of it becomes apparent and the initial emotional thrall dissipates until all that is left is a remembrance of what had been hoped for.

As an audience we are cheated by this unfortunate situation, as is the music. Audiences sense that the relationship between participants is insincere, fake. Some continue to participate by habit, as in a marriage long empty of love continuing with a wistful memory that once there had been passion. Boredom, at heart disappointment, becomes one's emotional ally. Younger people are brought by to visit, but leave at their first chance because what to you seems normal to them is lifeless, and youth is not yet resigned to an end. This is the house of classical music.

From this overview we now return to the story of a particular life.

ACT III

Educatio

CHAPTER 11

Confusion

I think Krachmalnick must have instilled in me some feel for the old way, the way of Auer and all the great Russians, unfortunately without any conscious understanding of what that was. It was transmitted to me more as a sense of sound, of some sort of connectedness between notes. The taste of something true, if even for an instant and not understood, is never forgotten, putting me in a position that made it impossible for me to believe in what I was being taught. Immersed in another system of values, although equally unreflective, I became lost. The Juilliard, Curtis, American way of playing wasn't for me and was as difficult to accept as it would be for a straight man to live in a homosexual world. I had no internal model, approach, understanding, or sympathy with what surrounded me that would have allowed me to put a step forward with confidence. It seemed to me that no one knew what they were doing. I became continually more depressed. I practiced hard, maybe five hours a day, but my playing got worse. I didn't believe in what I was being taught by Galamian or anyone else. No one he taught sounded like those old masters. I failed a harmony class because I almost never attended. That was the first F I had ever received in my life.

Before I had entered Curtis, I was performing public concerts probably fifteen to twenty times a year. During my six years at Curtis I performed only three times. Galamian had no studio classes, so none of us performed anywhere all year except in lessons. We played orchestra concerts, and perhaps one chamber music concert. But we mainly practiced. At Meadowmount one might perform, but I did only twice in four years. And there was a reason for this. I was getting worse.

I had been an unconscious player as a kid, and as I got older Galamian was turning me into an unconscious player who could no longer remember what had worked and was being given an approach that was making me worse. His method was tying me up into physical and mental knots, and I was not alone in this. Nearly all of our contemporary players have technical problems and musical confusion. They just would never admit it publicly.

The conundrum was that he was supposed to be the best teacher in the world. He was also the leading teacher at Juilliard and Curtis. Where can you go if this is the best? I got more depressed. After three years at Curtis I could hardly think. I had used to be able to do math problems in my head. Not any longer. I could hardly hear myself when I played, as if I had cotton in my ears. I went to school and walked around town in bedroom slippers. No one noticed anything—if they did, they kept it to themselves. But I kept practicing.

I completed all my music classes by the fifth year, but decided to stay on; Curtis lets you do that. Some students who enroll at thirteen stayed eight or nine years. Anyway, where was I supposed to go now that I played worse than when I started? How did I know that? Galamian told me that I used to play better.

By this time I lived alone in my Center City apartment. I had stopped paying the phone bill. I could barely get out of bed. I apparently missed three orchestra rehearsals. The school secretary tried to call, but since my phone didn't work she couldn't reach me. Three weeks before I was to graduate, I was told I had been expelled from school.

There were only a few things that could get you expelled from Curtis. One was failing a class twice. Another was studying with a teacher who was not on the Curtis faculty, for which the great violinist Joseph Silverstein, who was a student of Zimbalist (who was a student of Auer) and who later became the concertmaster of the Boston Symphony, was expelled. The third was three unexcused absences from orchestra rehearsal.

I was stunned. The secretary told me that when she discovered that I had missed three rehearsals, she called up Galamian. She asked him what to do. He said if I had broken the rules, I should be kicked out. And that was that. I appealed to Jaime Laredo, who intervened with Rudolph Serkin. I had never met Serkin in my entire time there, a school of ninety students, but I guess even Serkin thought that this punishment was too much. I was allowed to graduate from the year before, since I had completed my studies, but my transcript would show that I had been expelled. I could not graduate with my class.

I couldn't tell anyone—I was too humiliated. I was worried that I could never get into graduate school because of my transcript. So I moved to New York and tried to freelance. I kept taking lessons with Galamian. That didn't last long. Soon I couldn't bear to look at him.

It was many years later that Krachmalnick told me what a difficult time he had at Curtis.

He started at Curtis when he was only thirteen years old; his family had moved with him from St. Louis to Philadelphia. His first teacher was the concertmaster of the Philadelphia Orchestra. Krachmalnick also studied with Efrem Zimbalist, a famous violinist and a pupil of Leopold Auer, but it was with this first teacher that he had serious problems. Apparently this teacher hated Krachmalnick so much that he sabotaged his progress as a student.

A student orchestra conducted by Koussevitsky was assembled for a concert tour of South America one summer. Krachmalnick auditioned—he was probably seventeen—and won the concertmaster position. When his teacher heard about it, he called up Koussevitsky and said that there had been a mistake and that Krachmalnick could not leave the country because of a prior commitment he had not told them about. This, Krachmalnick told me, was a lie. His teacher suggested that another student of his take Krachmalnick's place. Krachmalnick was dropped.

He found out soon enough about the betrayal, but didn't understand why this man hated him so much until many years later when Krachmalnick became the concertmaster of the Philadelphia Orchestra himself. He told me that at one of his first concerts as concertmaster he noticed that his old teacher was sitting in one of the first rows scowling at him. The teacher came backstage afterwards and approached Krachmalnick, saying, "You used to come and watch me years ago, and I knew you were waiting for me to screw up. Now you know how it feels."

Krachmalnick told me he grabbed him by his necktie and said, "Don't ever come back here again."

He said he was taught nothing at Curtis that he could remember, but did recall that Zimbalist often started out the lesson by saying, "Impress me." He said he learned by watching great players and picking up what he could. It might have helped me to know that Krachmalnick had not had such a great time at Curtis. But who knows? At any rate, I was in quite a situation.

CHAPTER 12

Opportunity

I wasn't trained adequately for anything. To officially graduate high school I passed a high school equivalency test in Philadelphia because the high school tutoring classes at Curtis were not accredited by the state. Also, a Curtis diploma was not an accredited college degree, although it was worth something because the school was so famous. I don't think I had learned a thing academically since I was a freshman in high school. On top of this, I could no longer play that great. I was tied up in knots. So I did what I could. I played shows on Broadway, subbed in the City Ballet and Opera, and even played a little strolling violin at the Plaza Hotel.

I can't say I was pleased with all this, although I did enjoy watching the Broadway shows. But New York must be the loneliest place in the world if you are single; more accurately, single, broke, and having the emotional development of a teenager. It was as if I had grown up on an island of children, like the story, *Lord of the Flies*. I had had no adult guidance in my life. My parents knew nothing about the music business. They trusted that Curtis would prepare me for something. I didn't need to be controlled, but there was no one around me for years who took any interest in me whatsoever. None of my teachers had ever asked me how I was doing. No one had noticed that I was a walking dead child-person. I had been taught nothing except shame. I had no idea how to interact socially, how to relate to adults, how the world worked, and I was angry, confused, and disillusioned. I had lost any trust in people, yet trusted them to an absurd degree because I was looking for someone to save me from all this. There was no one. What I needed was wisdom. But that cannot be given to you and is not easily uncovered.

Emanuel Feuermann wrote about this phenomenon in his unfinished treatise on cello playing, *Notes on Interpretation:*[1]

---

1 Seymour W. Itzkoff, *Emanuel Feuermann, Virtuoso*, Emanuel Feuermann, "Notes On Interpretation," (Alabama: University of Alabama, 1979).

> The prodigy is completely unprepared for the future as an independent,
> thinking human being; he is completely defenseless. This development—which
> is considered normal—is similar for most musicians.

The teachers and administrators in the major conservatories are products of this system and its values. This is the "culture" created within the field.

No music school tells you the truth about the opportunities for employment as a musician. Why would they? If they did, most conservatories would have to close their doors. In writing this book, I wanted to learn the true statistics for finding employment in symphony orchestras. I obtained much of this information from a study entitled *Musical Chairs: A 28-Year Study of the Supply and Demand of Orchestra Musicians in America* by Brandon Van Waeyenberghe, conducted with support from the College-Conservatory of Music at the University of Cincinnati, The Corbett Foundation, and the Otto M. Budig Family Foundation. This is, as far as I know, the only serious study undertaken on this subject. It becomes obvious why after seeing the abysmal facts.

There are, give or take, sixty-one professional orchestras in the U.S. Of these, ten pay over $100,000 per year. Perhaps twenty pay over $60,000. Most pay in the $20,000–$30,000 range and are financially unstable. They pay "per-service." There are about eighty-five members of an orchestra.

There are between fifty to eighty positions available each year that pay over $60,000 per year that are advertised in the *International Musician*, which is the main source of professional job listings. These positions *are open to anyone in the world*.

Between 3,500 to 4,000 students graduate each year from U.S. colleges with performance degrees. If we assume an average of sixty-five positions available each year paying over $60,000 and divide this by an average number of qualified graduates—3,750—looking for those positions, there is a 1.73% chance of being hired. If we then add to this pool foreign applicants, perhaps one hundred, and assume that students will attempt for more than one year to acquire a job they have trained for their whole life, we arrive at a different probability. Would they try for eight years? We now have, perhaps, a pool of 30,100 candidates vying for sixty-five jobs, which is a .2% chance of acquiring a job. The study cites an example of an opening for trumpet in the New York Philharmonic in 2005:

> If every trumpet player currently playing in one of the top 61 orchestras
> auditions for the position, it would result in 182 applicants. Add to that the
> number of brass graduates in 2006 with an emphasis in trumpet (800 graduates

with an estimated third of them studying trumpet) equals 267 potential job seekers just entering the workforce from all education levels. Conservatively add another dozen as dark horse and international candidates and potentially 461 trumpeters could audition to become the next Principal Trumpet of the New York Philharmonic.

This is a very conservative estimate—a .2% chance of getting the job. It assumes that the only people who try for a job are those who have just graduated or those who already have one. It is more probable that the pool of qualified applicants is also composed of people who have not been able to acquire a position for a few years. The actual number is more likely at least six to eight times higher, which means the potential job seekers are conservatively 267 × 7 (1,869) plus 182, plus players from other countries, which is a .04% chance of landing the job.

From 2002 to 2010 the average number of students who graduated per year with performance degrees for string instruments was about 1,100. About one-half of these, 550, are violinists. Advertised openings for orchestra positions paying above $60,000 per year average about forty openings for strings. About one half—twenty—are for violinists. If we assume that someone would try to obtain a job for eight years, this means that 4,400 potential applicants could try for those spots. If we add in another one hundred foreign players to the mix we get 4,500 people who are qualified for the job, which is a .4% chance of being hired.

The number of advertised jobs has dropped by 50% in the last twenty-eight years, and continues a steady decline. Yet, the number of students graduating with degrees in music performance continues to go up. Many orchestras are in desperate financial circumstances. A few, five or six, are financially healthy, but have dwindling attendance. What does this suggest? There is no growth in the field. Orchestras in major cities are being propped up financially by major donors, not increased ticket sales. How long can that last?

Unlike a degree in English literature or sociology, a degree in music is not transferable to other more employable disciplines. Music performance degrees are obtained by practicing an instrument, not by furthering one's general knowledge. While some may say this success rate is similar to ice skating, no one gets a degree in ice skating, thereby wasting their college years pursuing a degree in something with almost no hope of employment, and, additionally, no furtherance of their academic background. There is also not a vast industry depending on the ice skater pursuing ice skating for a living. No one pays thousands of dollars for a formal education and a degree in ice skating.

There are no colleges or universities that have teachers who make a living from teaching undergraduates and graduate students ice skating. There are no professional groups who demand support of millions of dollars to keep their ice skating enterprise in the black. Yet, in classical music, a vast economic structure *depends on students believing that they can be musicians* and that there is something of interest for them to do once they graduate. At least ice skaters know the truth.

I would bet that trying to join the NBA has better odds. But even if it didn't, the potential payoff is different. Basketball players can make millions of dollars, as can actors, as can baseball or football players. Some orchestra musicians can make well over $100,000. Maybe a few—twenty—can make over a million. Of course, the students who are practicing hour upon hour are unaware of these odds, or perhaps they think that they will get lucky.

Let's say they do. They obtain a position in a major orchestra. They're making well over $100,000. Yet, their entire musical experience consists of doing what a conductor tells them to do. That is all. If they are a section player, such as cellists or violinists, their job is to blend in with everyone else in the section. They may be in that seat for forty years because of tenure. The same small group of conductors direct all the major orchestras for thirty or forty years, and the orchestras play with the same small group of soloists. Perhaps they will find that stimulating.

Orchestra musicians, however, are among the most bitter, unhappy people in any field of employment. Harvard psychology professor Richard Hackman ranks orchestral musicians below federal prison guards in job satisfaction in a paper, "Life and Work in Symphony Orchestras."[2] This is understandable. Players quickly become much worse, and lose whatever musical integrity they had, because they are forced to be automatons. The main criterion for passing through an audition is the ability to play with a metronome, even to the point where fast passages are practiced with a click on each note to see, literally, if you can play like a machine.

The great violin pedagogue, Carl Flesch, wrote about the fate of the orchestra player in his book, *The Art of Violin Playing,* observing that a position in an orchestra:

> demands the entire renunciation of his personality, of his artistic convictions, of his individual trends of taste; complete subordination to the will of the conductor, who forces him to accept his own human and artistic qualities— hence the denial of his own ego, the compulsory acceptance of an alien

2 Published in *The Musical Quarterly*, Vol. 80, No. 2 (Orchestra Issue, Summer, 1996).

individuality… Even the highest wage can never compensate for the inner distress which clings to the whole profession.[3]

If one hopes to play chamber music for a living, in a quartet for example, the reality is that you are married to three other people for your continued success. One change in the group transforms it totally. There are, perhaps, seven or eight groups in the world that play most of the concerts. When you play a concert, the fee is split four ways. You pay your own travel expenses. Quartets need a base position at a university to make enough money to survive, and those situations are already taken by tenured groups.

Most people who graduate with a degree in music start to do what are called gigs. A gig is a one-shot affair. Or there are what are called "freeway" symphonies that require a commute of often two hours to play in a small regional orchestra and a musician is paid perhaps $70 for the night's rehearsal. Perhaps a musician will be able to "sub" in a high-paying orchestra for awhile. But the orchestras have a lengthy list of people to call and there is nothing steady in that. In the summer work often dries up. Musicians can play weddings. Interestingly, even in Juilliard, wedding "gigs" are promoted on their website as employment opportunities for students. (A different caliber opportunity from the summer experience a law student at Harvard would expect of an internship at the Supreme Court.) So ex-students can hang on for a while, keep practicing, and hope that they can get a job that most people eventually end up hating.

There are other opportunities. You can be a soloist, a star. This is possible for violinists, cellists, pianists, singers of all types, and one violist. There may be ten people in the world who are violin soloists and can make a living this way, maybe ten pianists, one violist, and a few singers. The same people play every major concert venue year after year for a generation or more.

You could be a conductor. The famous conductors, maybe ten of them, attempt to conduct all the big orchestras, sometimes having multiple appointments. You may hope to find a job conducting a university orchestra, but those conductors get tenure. You can conduct Broadway shows, or play in them, but Broadway is using less and less live music, and the music written for the shows is at best Andrew Lloyd Weber level, which is usually a simple tune with a rock beat. If you play a wind or brass instrument, there may be two or three orchestral positions that you can hope for within an orchestra. There are only six or seven orchestras that pay a base salary above $130,000 in the country. These positions are protected by tenure, so you often have a case, as in the New York

---

3 Carl Flesch, translated by Frederick H. Martens, *The Art of Violin Playing*, Book Two (New York: Carl Fischer, 1936), 79.

Philharmonic, where a principal player, such as Stanley Drucker, held his position for forty-nine years.

Maybe you can teach? Public schools attempt only the most superficial music education and even then it is being cut. Maybe you can teach in a university? You run into the problem of positions protected by tenure, and if you do obtain a job your pay will be around $30–$70 an hour if you are not a professor. If you are a professor you may make much more, maybe $150–$250 an hour. Those jobs are limited. Maybe a couple of handfuls in the country. Additionally, at a college level, what are you in good conscience preparing your students for? You could teach at a conservatory. They will charge students $90 an hour and pay you $45-$60 an hour at the pre-college level, more at the college level, but again, you are usually preparing your students for nothing. There are no jobs.

If you are a pianist, you can accompany instrumentalists, usually bad ones, as most are, and obey them for a living. But if you can become an elite accompanist you can make good money. There are very few of those because there are very few soloists who can make a living. Here is how the pianist Artur Schnabel describes this relationship:

> A star (singer or instrumentalist) receives hundreds of pounds for a part, his or her pianist perhaps only ten or twenty or so. He may be more musical than the "star" but probably feels too depressed and degraded to try his best. Where he should lead, he has to obey. Almost all violin and cello virtuosos compel pianists to subordinate the requirements of the music to their employers vainglory or limitations. Nearly every fiddler tells his pianist that under all circumstances he is too loud—he does not mean he is too loud for the music, but too loud for his fiddle.[4]

This is the reality.

There was, however, one good thing about moving to New York. At least I was out of Philadelphia.

---

4   Artur Schnabel, *My Life and Music*, St. Martin's Press, 138-139.

CHAPTER 13

New York

When I arrived in New York in the late 1970s it was a very different place from what it has become. The city was nearly bankrupt and quite dangerous. People were leaving the city, not moving in. Socially, I found things very difficult. Nearly everyone seemed to be a couple, and women who weren't already in a relationship were terrified of strangers. So I stayed to myself. I had one friend from Juilliard I hung around with, but whenever I spent time with him I always ended up feeling worse. I only gradually realized that he was always putting me down, which is common among guys and something that probably wouldn't have been that bad, except that I was too down already to fight back mentally and just shrug it off. I took everything to heart. He was always with this girl or that, constantly finding new ones. I felt totally inept and unable to connect with women, so I had no girlfriend. I stayed in New York for five years, still practicing four hours a day. I don't know what I was playing, but I kept at it.

I tried a few lessons with David Nadien, who had been the concertmaster of the New York Philharmonic, also a student of Galamian's (really, it's like a hall of mirrors). He always wanted to be paid in cash, which I found a bit off-putting, since he was very wealthy for a musician. At least he would demonstrate, something that I had not come across for years. But again, I had the same problem—he was trying to teach me the way he played. Not that he wasn't an excellent player. But I wanted more than that.

The explanation "this is how I do it" is not a sign of thorough investigation. It seemed to me that it should have been possible for a teacher to describe how anyone played—good, bad, or indifferent—and explain what was better or worse in diverse artists' technique or musical approach in a way that could convincingly prove the point of view of the teacher, or maybe not. That way a student is not forced into the position of having "to take it or leave it" and learn by unreflective imitation or imposed authoritarianism.

Anyway, by this time my friend Portnoy had graduated from the New England Conservatory and was teaching piano at Boston University for a miserly sum of money, considering his skill. He had become friends with a famous concertmaster, Raphael Druian, who had retired from his position with the Cleveland Orchestra and was teaching at the university. At Portnoy's suggestion, I played for Druian. I suppose he liked me; he offered to teach me for free and helped me obtain a full scholarship to Boston University. So I moved to Boston.

By the time I arrived in Boston I had become so nervous internally that I couldn't eat in front of people without my hands shaking so much that the food would fall off my fork. But in Boston I began to calm down. Boston was like some sort of heaven on earth to me. I found a mother-in-law apartment in a wealthy tree-lined section of town near BU called Brookline. I had lived in downtown Philadelphia (a black, gay ghetto), which was horribly depressing, and then the West Side of Manhattan in a studio apartment infested with roaches.

Unlike Brookline, there are no trees in New York, unless you are in Central Park, and the only life I saw there apart from thousands of people on the streets were insects running around the sidewalks, and even sometimes crawling up the walls of restaurants. A girl I had taken out sucked up a baby roach through the straw of her gin fizz, and later the same evening a bum exposed himself to us as we sat chatting in the glass-enclosed terrace of a restaurant. Occasionally I would see a dog being walked. So finally living somewhere clean and upscale, closer to what I had grown up with when I lived with my parents, was a great relief.

A university has a completely different atmosphere than a conservatory. There are normal people there. They haven't practiced their whole lives. They went to a prom. They worked in national parks in the summer. They relax on weekends. The girls were pretty. And they were all friendly. I was amazed. All these pretty girls, and all friendly. The women in conservatories are usually obsessed with themselves, as are the men, and spend their entire lives practicing. They are super-ambitious, super-driven, practicing all the time. Many of the male teachers are predatory and chase after the good-looking females. It's a tough situation for a regular guy. Yet there is some sexual advantage in music schools because most of the men are gay. But the driven nature of the women ruins it anyway. Everyone is a nervous wreck, probably because they gradually start to realize that not only are they taught nothing real and paying a lot for it, but on top of it all there is no work for them once they graduate. I think that's why everyone, including the teachers, is so nervous.

The savvy, or skeptical, reader could easily say at this point, why go on? Cut your losses and go back to school and get a degree in something you like. And that is reasonable. My mind did not see that. I knew that I hadn't learned anything since I was fifteen. I figured I could change that. I remembered that I used to be able to play well and I thought that that ability must still be in me. I didn't want to just give up. Aside from that, I had crippling shame about my situation because of my expulsion from school. Shame does not make for clear thinking. I did not even appear on the Curtis alumni list until I worked up the courage to call them many years later and asked them to put me on the list.

I kept things secret. I felt trapped. There are always options A to Z, and even more. At the time my mind was seeing options A to B, or narrower. Because I didn't know anything except the limited reality of the music world, I didn't know what else might be interesting. What I didn't realize was that the information I was seeking didn't exist and could never exist in the system of education as it was structured, because the system is not self-reflective or scientific. I would have to find it out myself. The answers that I needed had no blueprint, no certain path. There was no easy way and no one, except for me, who could untangle my mind. So I figured that I better get started.

CHAPTER 14

Paradigm Shifts

U pon settling into Boston I decided to educate myself. Maybe I could get some new presuppositions, since the ones I had didn't seem to be getting me anywhere. I began by reading Shakespeare—all the major plays. I studied philosophy, most of which I couldn't abide, although I did enjoy Plato's dialogues, especially the detailed, methodical reasoning with which Socrates guided his coterie of disputants through randomly suggested polemics. Even when it seemed certain that there could be no successful defense of an argument or Socrates' query had decisively and satisfyingly been sated, he inevitably had a new twist that sent the whole dialectic further down the rabbit hole. I read the Bible—the Old and New Testaments because of its fusion with our cultural foundations of law, government, politics, and literature. I studied psychology—Freud, Karen Horney, Alice Miller, R.D. Laing. I discovered Douglas Hofstader and Gregory Bateson. Their ideas about systems theory, in particular, were illuminating. This influx of knowledge began to shift my assumptions about the world.

Raphael Druian, my violin professor at Boston University, had done his best to help me. But I still had the same problem. I didn't like how he played, not that he wasn't excellent. He simply had his faults like everyone else, his main one being that as he practiced and worked out a piece his performance became more and more controlled emotionally, and more and more small sonically and, therefore, evermore dull to a listener.

I became aware of one deep-rooted belief in particular that had kept me stuck—if one were truly talented, whatever was attempted could and should be accomplished without effort or thought. I had been trying that approach with little success. So I decided to see if I could *think* my way out of the ditch I was in. I began to study great players.

THE BEGINNING OF CHANGE

"The mechanics of playing are easy for everyone," proclaimed Nathan Milstein to an incredulous Pinchas Zuckerman in a filmed interview.[1] Apparently they are for some people. Milstein went on to say:

> Think how to achieve quality. Practicing does not achieve quality. You achieve quality only when you can do it [playing] *without opposition, without difficulty. Because difficulty opposes your possibility of doing better.* (italics mine)

I had studied with some of the most famous violin teachers in the world, all of whom had their particular approaches. Very good players had been created, but none on the level of whom I, and nearly everyone else in the business, regarded as the greatest violinists: Jascha Heifetz, Nathan Milstein, David Oistrakh and Leonid Kogan. These four eclipsed all others. Interestingly, they all came from the same era and area: Russia. Two of them, Milstein and Heifetz, were students of Auer's, and Oistrakh and Milstein[2] were students of a student of Auer's, Pyotr Stolyarsky. Milstein was friends with Horowitz and Rachmaninoff, two of the greatest pianists. And they were all at a level far beyond what anyone has since achieved. Maybe there was something in the Russian soil that could account for this. Or maybe they just knew things about playing that no one else did.

Leonid Kogan,[3] who came from the same lineage (his teacher, Abram Yampolsky had been a student of a student of Auer's), training, and geographical area, but was born twenty years after Milstein, visited Curtis when I was a student there and listened to us play. He was quite blunt and characteristically sardonic. According to him, we were not being trained correctly, which he made unquestionably clear by his condescending smiles and "stage whispered" comments in Russian that required no knowledge of the language to understand. What was the difference between what we were learning and his approach to playing?

I could not answer that question for many years. Everyone I asked could only tell me how he played himself. I suppose I could have tried to study with one of those greats—they were all still alive. But Heifetz did not teach in a serious way and Milstein did not teach at all except for master classes. The

---

1   *Nathan Milstein—In Portrait*, DVD, (Christopher Nupen, 2007).

2   Milstein's first teacher was Stolyarsky, who recommended him to Auer when Milstein was twelve years old.

3   Kogan was a "Soviet" style violinist, who although a great player, was less imaginative than Heifetz, Milstein, Horowitz and Rachmaninoff, who as we shall see, all approached playing and music in nearly identical ways.

only knowledge I had of them was through their recordings or watching them in a concert, which was rare and not helpful. When one watches a master player perform it is very difficult to understand what he does differently from other players that might explain his superiority. He may sound better. But how, or why, is not obvious. It takes time to absorb, and in real time what is being observed goes by too quickly. Additionally, you have to be an expert to understand subtle differences, and you have to be close enough to observe detail. No one sold seats a foot away from Heifetz. Oistrakh and Kogan taught in Soviet Russia—behind the Iron Curtain. Milstein taught master classes occasionally, I even played in one. But his pedagogical *metier* was playing passages at full speed, without any explanation. "Play like this," he'd say. It's amazing, but useless pedagogically.

I was able to gain insight only when videotapes and DVDs of these great players became available. Because of this technology, I could watch Heifetz every day for hours, and with a proximity impossible in real life circumstances. Another miracle was that *I could view their playing in slow motion.* There is no sound, but, if you know the piece, the notes they are playing are understandable. In this unique way, I was able to take hour upon hour of lessons from them all for over ten years.

I tried to change my playing to align with what I observed. It wasn't easy. I had to guess a lot. If I noticed something unusual or interesting, I would test it by incorporating this new idea into my playing and see if I would achieve a different and better result. I would then postulate that if this were true it would suggest that Milstein, or whoever I was watching, must have had such and such a thought process that would have led him to do such a thing. *I was, essentially, trying to understand how they thought.* I learned viscerally that one change affects everything else because the body and mind form a system. A seemingly minor adjustment in one hand would affect the other, or even my neck or back. Sometimes even the most innocuous changes would injure me. It seemed sensible to me that if I continued logically, step-by-step, answers would come. They might, but it could have taken five lifetimes. Fortunately, other forces stepped in and reached out a helping hand. This is the part of the story where love intervened.

I am strangely honest, in the sense that I would never do something that I felt was not true. I had been in relationships with many wonderful women, but somehow I could never get myself to marry them. Not that I didn't ask. I asked quite a few times, but not until I had left them and was dissatisfied with someone else. Then, gradually, I would be filled with regret and remorse that I had so cavalierly thrown away such a wonderful person. So I always came abegging back, although not for long because the relationship inevitably carried on from where it had left off, albeit after a brief period of bliss. As I understood this pattern of return more clearly, through several iterations with other girlfriends, the moment of joy became progressively shorter, and the dissatisfaction more predictable, until I no longer tried to go back and took to drinking a bottle of wine instead.

When I first saw Audinga I thought she was beautiful. I am very shallow about beautiful women and easily enchanted by them. But she seemed very Russian, very difficult, so I avoided her. I found out later that she avoided me for different reasons. She thought I was arrogant. I had noticed her for about a year before I finally talked to her. We went on a date and were married three months later.

My dates with her were very tiring. We talked a lot. I thought that she was very interesting but was exhausted after discussions with her because, I reasoned, her Lithuanian, somewhat Russian accent made it very difficult for me to understand what she was saying. I have learned after many years with her that the difficulty is not language. The difficulty is that nothing gets by her. Her diligence does not come from a sense of superiority. It is because she cares passionately about what is real—true—because she really cares about people. I think that is our bond. We disagree on nearly everything else. Yet, to me, one's response to life is the only indication of character that can be trusted. You know people by how they treat life.

Audinga is a great violinist. She would never say so because it means nothing to her. She had studied in Lithuania with two violinists who were outstanding players. Her first teacher, Alexander Livontas, was a student of David Oistrakh's, and of Milstein's first teacher, Pyotr Stolyarsky, (who, as I mentioned, was a student of Auer). Livontas was a renowned soloist in Eastern Europe, a great violinist. He died at the age of fifty-three when she was ten. She then studied with Victor Radovicius, who also studied with Stolyarsky and Oistrakh and who was also a great violinist. Because of this stellar training she was able to fill in some of the blanks in my inquiry, such as which muscle in the right arm controls the motion of the bow, which would have taken me five hundred years to understand. She was trained in the Soviet style, a schooling whose inadequacies are more of a creative, nuanced nature rather than a lack of technical skill. When we were first married, she worked with me for hours helping me make the changes I had been seeking. I still fought some of what she said because I am not a trusting sort of person, at least not anymore. But she had one approach with me that was very powerful. She believed in me, and I could trust, because of her character, that it was not because of some nonsensical reason.

All through this learning process I became increasingly aware that physical changes beget mental shifts. And vice-versa. *Mental shifts will change physical motion and ease.* These shifts allow, or bring forth, new concepts to the mind because one becomes, to some extent, a different entity if the change is basic enough. I learned that I was more malleable than I would have guessed, but that change needs to be at a fundamental level to bring the mind/body system into another paradigm.

I remember having discussions with a friend when we were students at Curtis about how Horowitz played. My friend thought that one "secret" might be Horowitz's posture at the piano—his low arms—or that his fingers were flatter on the keys than most pianists. He would copy these mannerisms. It made no difference. He still sounded the same.

I realized years later that these mannerisms are outward manifestations of deeper thought processes. *They are the result of ideas that are not obvious.* Copying the outward will not lead you to understanding. To understand what they do—the great players—you have to see into their underlying concepts. Their fundamental assumptions determine the quality of the complex end-result we see. That is why, to improve in a real sense, it is important to go deeply into one's fundamental presuppositions.

In discussing how to develop great levels of skill, there are two important components. One must break down the activity into its essential elements, but in such a way that the discrete bit is the essence of the whole; and, one's mind must be flexible enough to allow paradigm shifts to occur. Conscious, repetitive practice of the bits (the amount you can control) will form the correct neural connections and the process of assimilating this new approach will inevitably speed up.

Part of the learning process is that with the new sensation, mental pictures (visualizations) and linkages will appear where before they had been unseen. What seemed unrelated will gradually, or sometimes suddenly, appear as a simple idea repeated over and over with slight variation that ties everything together into a simple whole. One's mind must be allowed to roam into these new areas *unimpeded by fear.* Confusion will last in this process until a new mental picture appears. Of course, the process is endless, but what leads to success is the ever-deepening understanding, both in physical feeling and in mental pictures, that is always being strengthened, and oddly, at the same time, shifted.

Real, profound change—paradigm shifts—can occur only when fundamental presuppositions are shifted. An interesting example of a paradigm shift would occur if, after talking to a stranger for a few minutes at a party, I discovered that he was related to me, not just distantly, but that my father had had an affair thirty years ago and that this stranger was my half-brother. That would shift our relationship fundamentally. But not only my relationship with him.

This would affect my ideas about my father, my mother, my family story. Now I might understand why I was suddenly sent away to boarding school, or why my mother was in the hospital for those few weeks many years ago. As an adolescent I had been confused and hurt because my father seemed distant and morose. His indifference had been a factor in my decision to volunteer for the army. After being wounded in Iraq, losing my right arm below the elbow, I had never been able to have a close relationship with anyone. I now felt deceived and betrayed. Yet further investigation reveals that my father's affair had happened before I was born, and that my mother, even though they were married, had disappeared without explanation for six years, leaving him alone and confused.

Nothing is now the same, and events that had previously been inexplicable and interconnections that had not been noticed, beckon you through a portal that unexpectedly appears.

CHAPTER 15

The "Secrets" of the Masters

It seems clear that the creative development of science depends quite generally on the perception of the irrelevance of an already known set of fundamental differences and similarities. Psychologically speaking, this is the hardest step of all.[1]

– David Bohm

THE OPPOSITE, THE INVERSION, OF WHAT WE ARE TAUGHT

I mentioned previously that one deep-rooted belief suppressing my development was that I believed if I was truly talented I ought to be able to do difficult things without thinking. That idea had put me into a classic double-bind because if I had to think to be able to do something, even if I ended up able to do it, the result (even if the result was what I wanted and met my expectations) would still be inferior (in my own mind) because I did not have the "talent" to do it without thinking.

Once I understood the colossal stupidity of this shibboleth, my energy was let loose. Unfortunately, this didn't occur to me until I was about thirty-five years old. Anyway, getting back to our inquiry, what I discovered while watching my tapes in slow motion is that these great players, the violinists I was trying to understand, have—at a fundamental level—identical physical approaches. In real time they look different from one another, but slowing down the tapes and carefully scrutinizing their movements revealed that in slow motion they look the same. The great cellist Emanuel Feuermann makes a similar observation in an unfinished treatise he wrote on playing:

> *It is surprising how few rules and principles there are* and still more surprising how completely they change the entire style of playing. Believe it or not, my dear friend, the really outstanding string players, whether Kreisler, Casals, or Heifetz, are similar to each other in the way they use their muscular systems

---

1   David Bohm, *On Creativity,* Routledge, (New York, 2010), p.16.

and handle their instruments and bows. The main differences lie in their different personalities, talents, and ideas, and only to a very small extent in their techniques, for which, again, physical differences are accountable.[2] (italics mine)

I began to wonder; Why do they all play in the same way? And, if I tried to change my playing to match what I was seeing, would I improve? I had been trained differently from what I was observing and I wondered if there was something deeper going on than a difference in physical approach. What did they know that I didn't? None of them left any description of their methods. In fact, I am not aware of any detailed description of playing written by a great player. Emanuel Feuermann attempted to write a treatise on cello playing, but died before finishing. Chopin also tried to write one for the piano, but died before he could complete it. Maybe it's bad luck to attempt it.

Some will say that geniuses (whatever that means) don't understand what they do. I will use a quote from Nathan Milstein as a refutation of that argument:

> Great artists create their own style, their own technique. You hear people talk about the "spirit of Picasso." That "spirit" is the direct result of Picasso's technique. And the revelations of Van Gogh stem from his technique, too! The creator's individuality is made manifest through the new technique he develops. That holds for painters, and composers, and performers. It's why you can recognize the playing by Horowitz or Heifetz immediately, in the first few bars, and not only by their merits but by their mannerisms.[3]

It is clear that Milstein knew what he was doing. But it is also clear that he believes his knowledge is his edge. As we investigate and, I believe, ultimately understand much of what he and these other players do, it will become clear that they are not in much danger of being equaled. It is, in fact, so difficult to do what these masters do, even if you "know," only those who deserve to understand, who have the talent to do it, who can clean their minds enough, will ever come near it.

Chris Sharma, considered to be the world's greatest rock climber, has traversed routes across bare rock throughout the world that seemed impossible. He is a pioneer in the sport and has an interesting insight into what is possible:

---

2   Seymour W. Itzkoff, *Emanuel Feuermann, Virtuoso*, Emanuel Feuermann, "Notes On Interpretation," (Alabama: University of Alabama, 1979).

3   Nathan Milstein and Solomon Volkov, *From Russia to the West* (New York: Henry Holt and Co., 1990), 191.

Climbing is an evolution, where the standards today are the combination of the efforts of all of us who are climbing right now and all the people before us…standing on each other's shoulders…The hardest thing is to do something the first time. Someone has to have that vision, [to say] "Oh, that's possible." And once that's done, then other people can see," Oh yeah, it is possible." And it becomes way easier for other people to do it, too.[4]

I believe master players are conscious of what they are doing. One crucial piece of evidence in support of this is that they can reproduce what they do consistently. They are able to learn new pieces at the same level of excellence. They, also, always sound like their own playing. The common belief that someone can do something without knowing what he is doing, from raw talent, and reliably reproduce it, even under pressure, makes no sense. Apart from that, these players all took lessons to *learn* their craft. All of this implies that they had a system, and a system has parameters.

Could they have explained it? Perhaps not in words. Yet if there is true desire, there is always a way. A great player could say, "I can't explain what I do in words, but I invite you to watch how I learn a new piece." This never happens. Glenn Gould said that he could state the principles of piano playing in fifteen minutes. Did he ever do it? He wouldn't even admit that he had had a teacher (who, by the way, was a great pianist).

The fact is, they knew that there are fundamentals from which they operated and that their playing was a result of this basic mental conception combined with the training of muscle memory to reproduce those basic skills at will, with a little intuition thrown in.

We all know that the purpose of technique is to have the skill, physically and mentally, to allow a player to perform without impediment. It is using only the muscles that are necessary and not more. Technique is also knowing how to learn. It is knowing how to make a piece expressive. It is the ability to control nerves in performance. Technique is the beauty of the sound. It is using the body effectively and naturally to master demanding physical and mental complexities with ease. Technique and musical expression are intertwined, inseparable. The end-result seems like a magic trick. But how do you get it?

4   http://www.northcountrypublicradio.org/news/npr/15825820/rock-climber-chris-sharma- chases-next-king-line.

Let's start with a few ideas from the philosopher Gurdjieff:

> A man must first of all understand certain things. He has a thousand false
> ideas and false conceptions, chiefly about himself, and he must get rid of some
> of them before beginning to acquire anything new.
>
> False ideas are produced by the forms of our perception.
>
> One must learn from him who knows.[5]

Our ideas create our consciousness, our perception, our potentialities. Or, as
Milstein puts it, an artist is his technique, his understanding. And to kick off
our inquiry, here is more insight from Milstein: "Invent. If somebody doesn't
know what invention means he should stop violin playing." So let's take his
advice and explore, invent, and maybe discover a few things that will allow
us to make a fundamental shift in perception.

THE INQUIRY

I started small. I asked myself two questions:

"What is the smallest unit of music?" and...

"Can I play at least that like Milstein or Heifetz?"

One note is not music. It could be noise. Even Chopin agreed with me on this.
Is a pair of notes the smallest unit of music? Pairs are everywhere in nature.

It seems natural to think that way, and I remembered reading in a book by
Douglass Hofstadder, *Godel, Escher, Bach,* that computers think in on-off bits.
Therefore, I started with that idea. But then I realized that some music is written
in three. Was my inquiry already doomed? Fortunately, I remembered reading
that the French music theorists of the seventeenth century regarded three as
a variation of duple meter created by the extension in time of the second beat.
So I left that issue aside for the time being. I wondered, can I play two notes
like Milstein? Or Heifetz? Or Kreisler? Because if I can play two notes, I can
link them to two more. Then maybe I can play a piece and sound like them.
But which two? The downbeat to an offbeat, or the offbeat to the downbeat?

So I listened to the great players and tried to copy them. I chose slow pieces
because I posited that people think in paradigms, regardless of whether they
are conscious of them. We are creatures of pattern. If you want to understand
how someone thinks musically, you just have to listen to their slow playing.
Fast passages are really sped up melodies. They usually play fast the way they
think slow.

---

5   P. D. Ouspensky, *In Search of the Miraculous: Fragments of an Unknown Teaching* (New York:
    Harcourt, Brace), 20, 40.

Here is a key for the symbols that will be used in our musical analysis:

○ ∞   pairs of offbeat to downbeat or up- to down-bow cycles

V   up bow

⊓   down bow

⌐⌐   bracket for groups of notes (phrases, neighbor note reductions, etc.)

⟶   sign for the direction of motion or depicting downbeats

I tried to make just four consecutive notes—two pairs—sound like Milstein. I chose the first movement of Handel's *Violin Sonata No.4 in D Major*. This is the opening of the piece.

15-1a

After some experimenting, I found that if I rebarred the piece and played square, that is, playing the "new" downbeat to the offbeat, ex. 15-1b, I sounded very similar to Milstein. Here is the piece rebarred.

15-1b

But this was confusing. Could he really be thinking something that different from what was written?

I then realized that he played his offbeat so much, and the downbeat so little, that if you played it rebarred and recorded it, it sounded like him. I then assumed that he thought in pairs of notes, swinging his offbeat into an unaccented downbeat *(ex. 15-1c).*

15-1c

The easiest way to show this is on a simple etude *(ex. 15-2a).* The ratio of offbeat "fullness" to the downbeat is about 2:1; the downbeat receiving approximately one-half the fullness of the offbeat.

15-2a

If I chose any sixteenth note passage and rebarred it, the recording would sound very similar to Milstein. Here is the etude shown on the previous page rebarred, but this experiment works with any passage of music *(ex. 15-2b)*.

I then began to check my results with other great performers' recordings. I guessed that since Milstein and Horowitz were friends there was a good chance that they thought alike. So I looked for a Horowitz recording of something slow. Scarlatti's *Sonata K. 466*, ex. 15-3, seemed easy to understand. Horowitz phrased the same way as Milstein.

The pairs are grouped in this way, but completely linked to each other. He is playing in very long phrases comprised of pairs of offbeats to downbeats. These link to form larger groups, but the larger groups are themselves linked until the piece ends. I checked Fritz Kreisler. The same. Heifetz, ditto.

Most instrumentalists try to imitate singers and I knew from my reading that Chopin had studied *bel canto* singers:

> The best way to attain naturalness in performance, in Chopin's view, was to listen frequently to Italian singers, among whom there were some very remarkable artists in Paris at the time. He always held up to pianists their broad and simple style, the ease with which they used their voices and the remarkable sustaining powers which this ease gave them.[6]

---

6   Jean-Jacques Eigaldinger, *Chopin: Pianist and Teacher* (Cambridge: Cambridge University Press, 1986), 44, original source was Karasowski, II, 93.

Even more interesting is the following:

> His [Chopin's] playing was always noble and beautiful, his tones always sang,
> whether in full *forte* or in the softest *piano*. He took infinite pains to teach
> his students this legato, *cantabile* way of playing. "Il (ou elle) ne sait pas lier
> deux notes" [He (or she) doesn't know how to join two notes together] was
> his severest censure.[7]

Horowitz, also, studied *bel canto* singers:

> Horowitz began to study the art of the Italian baritone Mattia Battistini…whom
> Horowitz considered a "forgotten genius." He memorized details of Battistini's
> performances, fascinated by his plasticity of phrasing, breath control, tonal
> shading, and lyric expressiveness…It did not bother him that Battistini had
> habitually taken what some might consider shocking liberties with an aria.
> "Even if we don't agree with such exaggerated freedom, there is much we can
> learn," he said. "It is better to control an abundance of spontaneous feeling
> that to hide that not enough is there."[8]

So I checked great singers. I listened to Jussi Björling sing the "Flower Song"
from Bizet's opera, *Carmen*. He phrased in the same way as Milstein, Heifetz,
Kreisler, and Horowitz. Again, I must repeat that the small groups are all tied
into each other. My circles are simply a convenient way to show what I believe to
be the thinking behind the singing. Here is an excerpt from the aria *(ex. 15-4a)*.

---

7 *Ibid.*, 46. The original source was Streicher/Niecks, II, 34.

8 Glenn Plaskin, *Horowitz, A Biography of Vladimir Horowitz* (New York, William Morrow and
   Co. 1983), 282. Horowitz studied Guissepe Anselmi, Alessandro Bonci, as well as the Russian
   tenor, Leonid Sobinov.

Many great singers sing like this. Here is an analysis of an excerpt from Mozart's, "Voi Che Sapete Che Cosa è Amor," as sung by Frederica von Stade (*ex. 15-4b*).

A close examination will show us some of what is going on. There are no accents on the downbeats. In fact, there are no accents at all. The music flows seamlessly from one note to the next with a constant forward rolling. This is a hallmark of *bel canto* singing,

Bel canto style is difficult to define, and if you asked contemporary vocalists what it is, they would probably say they can't explain it, find anyone who can teach it nowadays, or find anyone who sings this way anymore. They will say that Maria Callas was one of the best examples of this art.[9] But what is it? To begin with, it is essentially smooth connection between notes—what we call *legato*. That is how it was taught. One note to one note. Vowel sounds are the basic core sound. Consonants (which are accents) impede flow and have to be carefully overlaid on a smooth, connected foundation. If this is your goal, other steps must follow.

One must have physical ease. Without ease there will always be a forced quality to the connection, to what happens in-between the notes. There can be no extraneous muscle use. Smooth connection leads to smooth sound. Smooth sound is not pushed. That would make an accent. Smooth sound has to be released. Released sound has a different quality. I would say that it has *quality*. Implicit in quality is refinement. Smooth, released sound has the space, the capacity, for nuance. We could call this the "culture" of sound. If smoothly connected unforced sound is an important *value*, a "culture" of "understanding," other ideas must, by necessity, follow.

If you think about it, the downbeat has a natural sense of arrival. It has intrinsic weight. Why add to its heaviness by focusing on it? I think this is what the great *bel canto* singers understood, at least instinctively. In fact, smoothness and physical ease allow for *concentration of power*. Nothing is lost in extraneous muscle usage. *This is the essence of great athletic skill.*

---

9   I don't agree. Her phrasing is often heavy on the downbeat, unlike Caruso, Björling, or Horowitz's favorite singer—Mattia Battistini.

Bruce Lee, the master of martial arts, wrote about this subject:

> The outstanding characteristic of the expert athlete is his ease of movement,
> even during maximal effort. The novice is characterized by his tenseness,
> wasted motion and excess effort. That rare person, the "natural athlete" seems
> to be endowed with the ability to undertake any sport activity, whether he
> is experienced in it or not, with ease. The ease is his ability to perform with
> *minimal antagonistic tension*. It is more present in some athletes than others,
> but can be improved by all.[10]

So it would appear that *bel canto* singing is aesthetically and athletically
correct. Has this approach been used by instrumentalists? I think a few have
figured it out.

They're all dead.

All the instrumentalists whose playing I have selected to deconstruct play
their instruments in *bel canto* style. *Bel canto* singing, this tradition of musical
expression, is what they valued. It so happens that the composers who wrote
the music did, too.

NORMAL, AVERAGE PLAYING

Here, below, is an example of normal musical thinking for an instrumentalist.
This is how everyone is taught to understand music. This is how all orchestral
music is played, and how most (I would say all, but I can't know everyone) of
our recent soloists and conductors think musically. I will use an example of
how everyone, with small variation, is taught to phrase the second movement
of the Tchaikovsky *Violin Concerto (ex. 15-5a).*

15-5a

10 Bruce Lee, *Tao of Jeet Kune Do* (Ohara Publications), 43.

The phrasing and thought process line up precisely to the note grouping as printed on the page. Each main beat is given a small emphasis, which has the effect of chopping up the musical line into a bar at a time, thereby destroying any melodic sweep. The three beats per bar are divided (1, 2, 3), whereas even with this approach, one could still swing the third beat into 1 and 2, giving a division of (3, 1, 2), thereby alleviating some of the monotony of playing a bar at a time. But even that is never heard.

Here is an example of a faster piece of music from Handel's *Violin Sonata No.6 in E (ex. 15-5b).*

Typically, downbeats, which are usually played with down-bows, are emphasized, making this, as in example 15-5a, very "beaty." An "early music" player devotee is even heavier on the beat than most musicians and for some reason believes that their approach is historically sanctioned. Unfortunately, what is usually bequeathed by the historical, unrecorded record is the memory of the last bad performance, as Gustav Mahler was wont to say.

This thinking revolves around and orients itself to the downbeats. Since this is a *fundamental* concept, by which I mean this is the basis of one's musical thinking, the result of this orientation has dramatic and unfortunate consequences regarding technique and musical performance (which are in essence the same thing) for anyone caught in this matrix.

For one thing, the inner beats are lost. The offbeat becomes a *reflection* of the downbeat and does not link naturally to the next pair. There is a space between the groups because of the double accent—the *emphasis* on the downbeat, which has a natural feeling of arrival, as we mentioned. The offbeat never recovers from the power of the downbeat. Successive repetitions of this pairing will inevitably amplify the downbeat's percussive nature. As the drama, or tension, increases—in a crescendo, for example—you will notice, if you listen for it, that the first note of the successive pairs (the downbeat) inevitably, because of this fundamental thinking, becomes progressively heavier and more percussive. Therefore, the offbeat gets lost even further.

The music seems to stay in place, like a ball bounced in one spot, or a picture changed on a static easel, or as if you were marching in place. Marching is numbing, mentally. Music that marches in place encourages sentimentality because it lacks the vital, creative energy natural to the imbalance of forward motion. In other words, because there is no *flow* to the music—which is against music's nature, as stilted speech is to conversation—the static music-making created by this square, heavy downbeat playing encourages artificial mannerisms, which leads to contorted, unnatural understanding, and ultimately to exaggerated expression.

As the tempo increases, the offbeat is lost even more. This creates the need to actively pump out the notes that are being "swallowed." We call this "digging in." Projecting. In reality, it is straining. There is will in this dynamic, force. It is aggressive and overdone. It is hard work. Unfortunately, this square, heavy downbeat way of thinking about music *is how most musicians are trained to play.*

Liszt, who valued a *bel canto* style of playing, was aware of the problem and comments on this banal approach:

> Often the vulgar maintenance of the beat and of each bass note of the measure (1, 2, 3, 4) (1, 2, 3, 4) clashes with both sense and expression. There, as elsewhere, *the letter kills the spirit* and to this I could never subscribe, however plausible might be the hypocritically impartial attacks to which I am exposed.[11]

When he conducted:

> Rather than confining himself to the bar line and conducting with regular accents, as so many conductors did and still do, Liszt looked for metrical pliancy, drama, and color. His highly unorthodox beat outlined the rise and fall of a phrase rather than coming down heavily on the first beat of the bar... [He was] more interested in phrase than accent.[12]

A quote from a previous chapter bears repetition in this context. Carl Maria von Weber was aware of the discrepancy between a vocal and an instrumental approach. As he wrote:

> The most difficult problem of all is to unite voice and instruments so they blend in the rhythmic motion of a piece and the instruments support and

---

11 Josiah Fisk, editor, *Composers on Music* (Boston: Northeastern University Press, 1997), 109.
12 Harold C. Schonberg, *The Lives Of The Great Composers,* Chapter 13, Virtuoso, Charlatan—and Prophet, Franz Liszt (New York, W. W. Norton & Co. 1981), 208.

enhance the voice in its emotional expression, for voices and instruments are in their very nature opposed to each other. [Only if taught in our commonly accepted way.] Because of breathing and articulation, singing calls for a certain fluctuation in the measure that may be compared to the uniform beating of waves against the shore. *Instruments (particularly strings) divide the time into sharp segments comparable to the swinging of a pendulum.* Truth of expression demands the blending of these contrasting characteristics.[13] (italics mine)

I will henceforth call this approach "square" phrasing because of its tendency to form short accented units of notes, partitioned as the music has been written, but in essence, ironically, destroying the line and flow of the music. Square playing has no forward motion, creating heaviness and, as a result of these two traits gives birth to loud, heavy sound. The innate stasis of the music literally digs a hole for itself, whereby the emotion of the music becomes translated into accents, pushed sound and slower tempos, with little detail between beats because the offbeat is overshadowed, creating no space for nuance. *Square playing is a symptom of a misunderstanding of the nature of music.*

Loud playing is an outgrowth of heaviness. This is different from *power* in sound, which still has quality. By quality we mean that even within increased volume lies room for nuance. Loud playing lacks this quality and is currently pervasive in orchestral performance, solo performance, and singing. As defined by *Webster's International Dictionary* the word "loud" has a definitely pejorative flavor:

Loud
1. marked by intensity or volume of sound
2. clamorous, noisy

Loudness does not allow for subtlety; nuance need not apply. All of this reminds me of an inadvertent haiku a friend blurted out:

> Everywhere the Jay goes, he screams.
>
> Why?

Or, as the great pianist Moriz Rosenthal once observed: "Platitudes are best delivered with a thundering voice."[14] But I suspect a more insidious aspect to his statement: *Loudness turns everything into platitudes.*

This square conception of music has other consequences as well. Because of its reliance on main beats, or rather the undervaluation of inner beats, musical time is felt to be what occurs *at* the beat. This creates a dependence on

---

13 *Ibid.* 11, 63-64.

14 Mark Mitchell & Allen Evans, *Moriz Rosenthal in Word and Music* (Bloomington: Indiana University Press, 2006), 125.

metronomic rhythm and the metronome, the killer of all musical expression. As Rachmaninoff wrote: "The most mechanical playing imaginable can proceed from those who make themselves slaves to this little musical clock, which was never intended to stand like a ruler over every minute of the student's practice time."[15] Yet it is this musical clock that is the heartbeat of every orchestra in the world. One's ability to play in lockstep with its click is the key to admittance to the ensemble. It for this reason that conductors, most of whom function as human metronomes, are deemed necessary to hold a large ensemble together.

Here is Arnold Schoenberg on the subject:

> Using mechanical devices immediately eliminates every problem. At the age of forty I still wanted to be a conductor—especially when, as often happened, I heard a poor performance. But after studying the work in question thoroughly and trying to formulate my feelings in conformity with those of the composer, I found myself facing so many problems that I cried out, "How fortunate that I do not have to perform this work now!" When subsequently I heard a performance of this work, it seemed as if the conductor had taken a wet sponge, easing all traces of problems by playing the whole movement in one stiff, inflexible tempo.[16]

In music based on this paradigm everything is stable. The problem is that music should feel improvised, fresh, and off-balance. Square playing is psychologically dull music-making. Players get bored. So do audiences. Therefore, a performer must create superfluous, contrived excitements: throw his body around, grimace, toss her hair, look towards the ceiling with wonder as if a vision from heaven has appeared. You have to become strangely, unsimply, even in some cases grotesquely creative to make the music captivating. This is what we see in many of our current performers.

Another problem with this approach is that it is intrinsically unathletic. It is hard on the body to play with a down motion that is repetitive. The action of "downness" breaks physical flow and does not allow a player to get into a physical groove. The more expressively you try to play, the more the down emphasis ties your body into knots, often resulting in playing-related injuries. This square concept will never achieve the same physical ease as the *bel canto* approach. Thus, it is impossible to attain the same level of virtuosity and mastery that has been reached by musicians who play by *bel canto* rules derived from *musical values which are innate and implicit in the nature of music.*

---

15 James Francis Cooke, *Great Pianists on Piano Playing* (New York: Dover Publications, 1999), 213.

16 Arnold Schoenberg, *Style and Idea,* "Today's Manner Of Performing Classical Music" (U.S.: University of California Press, 1984), 322.

THE BEL CANTO APPROACH
(THE OPPOSITE OF WHAT WE ARE TAUGHT)

Let's now examine a *bel canto* instrumental approach. Let's take a look at how Milstein phrases our previous Tchaikovsky excerpt *(ex. 15-6a)*. I must emphasize that the pairs are all linked in one seamless outpouring of music.

This is also how Heifetz phrases this movement, and I am sure Kreisler, although we have no recordings of him playing this piece, but their musical thinking is essentially the same. Their thinking, phrasing, is oriented to the offbeats and the offbeat's interaction and relationship to the downbeats, or main beats.

Here is Heifetz's phrasing of the previously examined second movement of Handel's *Violin Sonata No.6 in E Major (ex. 15-6b)*. There is a constant flow and smoothness with this conception. The downbeats are not reemphasized. They have an implicit importance anyway because they are points of arrival.

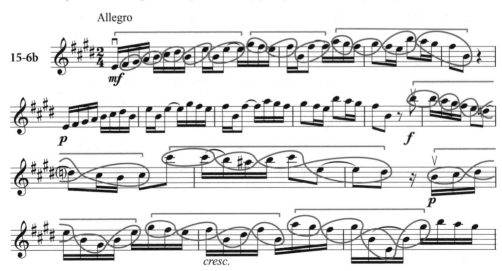

Glenn Gould phrases in exactly the same way *(ex. 15-7)*. This is an excerpt from *Variation 1* of Bach's *Goldberg Variations*, but he uses the same thinking for everything he plays—from Beethoven's *Emperor Concerto,* to Webern's *Five Pieces for Piano.* There is much more involved in this approach than I am presently showing, but I don't want to get ahead of myself.

15-7

Thinking of music in this way demands an entirely different technical approach—one that eliminates downbeat emphasis. This also has dramatic physical and technical consequences, which we will explore in a moment.

Everything we have said thus far leads us to an obvious question: Why is it that this discrepancy exists between how music is printed and how our models of excellence play or sing it? It is, in fact, reasonable to assume from looking at the printed organization of music that the performance translation should be grouped in the form in which the music is printed. Here is a well-known but historically aurally transmitted tune,"Happy Birthday" (originally known as "Good Morning to All"), as it would appear in print *(ex. 15-8a)*.

15-8a

If sung with adherence to the bar-line segmentation the words would be grouped as follows: (Good), (morning to), (you, good), (morning to), (you, good), (morning dear), (children, good), (morning to), (all). The first word of each parenthesized group would receive an accent because it is the first beat of each bar. To speak in this way would sound mechanical and segmented. Yet this is how musicians are trained to understand the printed page of music, which as a result sounds equally mechanical and segmented.

If sung or played by ear the phrasing would inevitably be as follows *(ex. 15-8b)*.

How is this difference explainable?

Music has existed for thousands of years. A flute made from the bone of a bear was discovered in Europe and has been carbon dated to 40,000 BC. Music could not be written down with any reliability until the eleventh century when a monk named Guido of Arezzo invented a system of notation. Our modern notation dates from perhaps the sixteenth century. This shows how difficult it was for humans to capture music in an abstract form.

For thousands of years music had been understood as what it is in itself—sound, pitch, rhythm. This has changed. We now believe with great certainty that what is *literally* written is music. Yet written music, as with written language, cannot convey every nuance and shading possible for the evocation of the imagined scenario of the author. What is written are symbols, after all, and the symbol is not the thing itself—it is an *abstraction*. It is reasonable to assume that an abstraction cannot contain every element of the source—that the source is beyond this containment. Furthermore, in a work of art we should hope that the symbol is pregnant with meaning and layers of comprehension. If it is only to be taken at face value, and the symbol is all that there is, then it is simply trite.

In *The Gutenberg Galaxy*[17] Marshall McLuhan points out that the medium of print glorifies the word. It stratifies the senses in troubling ways, raising the level of the *directed* gaze, which is necessary to be able to read, to *a way of viewing the world*. Yet in its deepest sense, the reality of the world is beyond the classification (and the mandatory simplification of its properties) inherent in the language used to describe it. We are trained to observe the world through words and concepts that have become concretized by the medium of print as if these abstractions were, in themselves, the "ground" of reality. *Print segments perception.*

Music suffers the same fate. The printed version of compositions is worshiped. Our segmentation of performance from creativity (composing) obscures the possibility of a more subtle interaction between composition, performance, and creativity. This schism promotes the exaggerated tenet we currently have of the

---

17 Marshall McLuhan, *The Gutenberg Galaxy* (USA: University of Toronto Press, 1963).

written score as the final truth, which becomes perfectionism. Specialization (performers separated from the act of composing) perverts the art. Notation has limits in what it can literally convey, as I am sure any composer is aware. In fact, if you listen to Rachmaninoff play his own compositions, or Prokofieff conduct his own Fifth Symphony, you will hear that they phrase in this offbeat to downbeat way, and not in the way that is literally depicted in the score. In fact, they perform countless nuances not written in the score. The idea of following the score with computer-like accuracy is sophomoric. You can't tell performers everything.

Here is Carl Maria von Weber on the subject:

> There is so much to be said on the subject of markings that I might be tempted to develop it further were I not warned by frustrating experience. I consider them superfluous, useless, and I fear, easily misconstrued. Let them remain, but to be used only with caution.[18]

David Bohm:

> The main function of a language symbol is not to stand for or represent an object to which it corresponds,... it initiates a total movement of memory, imagery, ideas, feelings, and reflexes which serves *to order attention to and direct action in a new mode that is not possible without the use of such symbols.*[19]

I believe that our confusion about what written music attempts to convey is, in part, a direct result of our divorce of composition from playing, a marriage that ended in the early 1900s. But let's continue our inquiry. What we have thus far uncovered has further implications.

---

18 *Ibid.* 11, 64.
19 *Ibid.* 1, 82.

CHAPTER 16

"Laws" of Music, Visualization, and Other Discoveries

Einstein... gave his main attention to broad and deep questions relating to general concepts that had previously been largely implicit and taken for granted in a rather habitual way.[1]

– David Bohm

No one has ever described the process of re-creation, reconstruction, more strikingly and more profoundly than Wagner in the legend of how Siegfried's sword was reforged. There was no way in which even the most skillful craftsman could weld the broken pieces together. Only by grinding the fragments to dust, thus returning to the primordial state—the state of chaos which preceded the act of creation—can one reconstruct, recreate, the work in its original form.[2]

– Wilhelm Furtwängler

To understand music, to "re-create" the written page, must we "grind the fragments to dust," or are there *deeper principles* at work in music applicable to both creation and re-creation that go beyond our preconceptions, beyond the printed text, which may help us contact the essence, the primordial state, itself?

"Laws" of Music

We are investigating. We are on a search to understand. There are implications to what we have discovered. Music is a system of thought (all thought is a system) and as such has inherent parameters that circumscribe the system. So I will now posit a theory that is, I believe, a basic truth, not a "value," about music—a "law" if you will.

THE THEORY OF PAIRS

- *The smallest unit of music is a pair of notes — the offbeat to the downbeat.*

This fundamental paradigm shift is a Pandora's Box of possibilities and implications. Ralph Kirkpatrick has expressed some interesting thoughts on this subject, and while not stating explicitly that music is pairs of notes at its

---

1 David Bohm, *On Creativity,* (New York: Routledge, 2010), 59.
2 Wilhelm Furtwängler, *On Music: Essays and Addresses,* translated and edited by Ronald Taylor (USA: Scolar Press, 1991), 13.

fundamental level, he is aware of the negative aspects of a heavy downbeat and the controlling function of the inner beats:

> *The notion that the downbeat is accented has done enormous damage. One can hear it daily. I prefer to lay emphasis on the preparation to downbeats,* rather than on their accentuation. Preparation can be so convincing that a hearer may not notice whether or not that which was prepared has been omitted…
>
> *The inner portions of measures and the subdivisions of beats are always their most active parts.* It is in these that every experienced ensemble player makes contact with other players and responds to them. These, rather than the downbeats, are the things of which the skillful conductor makes use in establishing characterizations, instead of mechanically plowing forward like a metronome. These subdivisions of measures and beats make it possible constantly to regenerate a tempo, to recapture it if it has slipped in one direction or another….[3] (italics mine)

Schoenberg voices a similar opinion:

> Change of speed in pulse beats corresponds exactly with changes in tempo. When a composer has "warmed up" he may feel the need of harmonic and rhythmic changes. A change of character, a strong contrast, will often require a modification of tempo. But the most important changes are necessary for the distribution of the phrases of which a segment is composed. *Over accentuation of strong beats shows poor musicianship*…To people who have never heard the great artists of the past who could venture far-reaching changes of every kind without ever being wrong, without ever losing balance, without ever violating good taste—to such people this may seem romantic.[4] (italics mine)

Furtwängler's insight into the problems of creating musical flow while cueing the beats is also apropos to our discussion:

> *The power to affect a note, and this cannot be emphasized too often, lies in the preparation of the beat, not in the beat itself.* We are talking about that brief, often minute instant when the beat falls, before the actual orchestral sound itself…Would it not be possible to envision a manner of conducting which dispensed as far as possible with these terminations, these brief fixed moments, and have recourse only to the beat and its preparation?[5] (italics mine)

---

3 Ralph Kirkpatrick, *Interpreting Bach's Well-Tempered Clavier,* Chapter Four, The Rhythmic Approach (New Haven: Yale University Press, 1984), 68.

4 Arnold Schoenberg, *Style and Idea,* Today's Manner Of Performing Classical Music (US: University of California Press, 1984), 321.

5 *Ibid.* 2, "The Tools of the Conductor's Trade," 21.

Our theory is useful in a number of ways and has far-reaching implications. In a lighthearted way it could be compared to a musical "E = mc²." This one idea shifts the whole game. For one thing, this concept is helpful in analysis. With this as a template, we have effectually created a microscope with which to observe anyone's playing; to examine, to understand, in fact, *their basic musical thinking.* It is easy to explain what people do, both expertly and clumsily, with this theory as a constant. We can use it to see what does not conform, which makes it possible to diagnose problems in individual players *or* teaching methodologies. This is because the pair of "offbeat to downbeat" controls the music *between* the beats, the glue and flow of music. Playing in this pairing of notes not only allows a performer great control over details, but using this paradigm as examiners (analysts), allows us to see clearly how well one note *connects* to another, *a lack of which is often the source of technical problems.*

There are further implications. Implicit in the very nature of the pair is forward motion. The offbeat is *pulled* to the down. This fact brings us to another theorem, a "law."

- *Music rolls forward in time.*

I believe this is a fundamental truth—a "law," not a "value." The intrinsic tension of the offbeat releases to the downbeat, like a cadence. Because of the pull towards resolution, this pair of notes has *inherent* drama. As a musical statement *a pair is complete in itself.* It is also, by nature, off-balance, thereby creating movement that rolls the music forward; one pair flows into the next in an endless loop of action and resolution, like a row of dominoes falling endlessly forward.

Music unfolds, flows, through *time.* That is its essential and primary nature, just as when we walk or speak. The physical motion of walking and the rhythm of speaking fall forward. There is direction to our words. Similarly, when we walk forward we are constantly off-balance. Moving forward is an adventure.

Music works similarly. Since there is an innate flow and intrinsic drama when the offbeat leads to the downbeat, it is possible, by phrasing in this way, to be simple and direct in our "re-creation," yet be very expressive. The music is meant to work this way. The innate, inherent drama of the movement of the pairs *creates* energy. One doesn't need to add it on. It takes you—carries you—quite naturally. In addition, forward motion, a *rolling* quality to music, is physically easier on the body because it creates *uninterrupted* flow in the motion of playing.

The best advice ever given for music performance is delivered by Shakespeare through Hamlet:

> Speak the speech, I pray you, as I pronounced it to you, trippingly on the tongue [let the music roll forward as does natural speech]. But if you mouth it, as many of our players do, I had as lief the town crier spoke my lines [square, metronomic playing].

Unfortunately, as I mentioned previously, all orchestras play in a square, metronomic way. It is unavoidable, given the way musicians are currently taught to understand *printed* music, and exacerbated by the presence of a conductor beating time.

This shift in musical understanding that we are discussing—a more forward rolling way of playing—has practical applications for both dance and opera companies. An orchestra that played music in this way (which currently does not exist) would have a dramatic influence on a dancer's performance. Music that has forward motion is more natural to move with, and one can envision that another level of virtuosity and expression might suddenly appear, perhaps even different choreography. The same would be true for the onstage movements of singers in opera productions. Forward rolling music would encourage more fluidity, more action.

Rhythm is not found on the beat any more than a metronome is required to speak in time. The inner beats of words are the syllables, which unfold quite logically, naturally, and understandably without a mechanical time-beater. The "syllables" in music are the offbeats, the inner beats, which is where the true pulse of the music lies.

If it is true that the smallest unit of music is a pair of notes, then we can make a further assumption, a "law," that, as will be seen, opens a new world of possibilities.

- *There are limited ways to play two notes.*

This is a fact, not an opinion. My route to this realization came by way of my astonishment at how perfect the posture of both Milstein and Heifetz is when playing. They used no shoulder rest, which for most people is a necessary addition to violin playing. The shoulder rest is used to hold the violin in place, freeing up the arms to move with ease. If one does not use a shoulder rest the violin must be held (cradled is a better word) in the left hand, and *rest* on the shoulder or collar bone while the left hand/arm shifts around the fingerboard continuing to vibrate the notes with the left arm and hand. This is incredibly difficult to do and not hold the violin tightly. Astonishingly, Milstein could even raise his head off the instrument while vibrating or playing difficult passages. I could not understand how.

As I studied Milstein on videos year after year I began to have a theory. His bow motions are unusually free; his left fingers appear to scarcely touch the strings. Everything is fluid, easy, and light. He seemed to only *lift* his fingers.[6] I began to wonder—is it possible to play with no conscious downward motion of the left hand, or the right, and is this why Milstein can stand with perfect posture and play with such ease? If he can be that relaxed in his head and neck area, and simply rest the violin on his collar bone, *there must be no physical action from playing that pushes down.*

I posited to myself the theory that Milstein was aware of only the *up motion* of his fingers. I went about seeing if this was possible to do. I knew, or assumed, that he thought in pairs of notes, offbeats to downbeats. So I tried to see if I could train myself to feel as if my fingers were already down, and then lifted, as a way to circumvent any conscious down-motion. I went back to basics, a book of etudes by Kreutzer, and found one that might work. Here is *Etude No. 9* from Kreutzer's canonic book of studies *(ex. 16-1)*.

I played the first note, F, then stopped the bow, leaving it (the bow) on the string. I put my fingers down on A and G. I then slurred (played in one bow) A and G. If I lifted A, G was "revealed." I felt as if I "peeled" away A to reveal G. I realized this is one way to play a pair of notes, ex. 16-2a, and yet be aware of only *one* motion. Very economical.

If I stopped my bow long enough in between setting up pairs of notes, I found that I could no longer "remember" that I had put my fingers down. Once I had "forgotten" about the "down" motion, I "peeled" A/G again. I found that I could shorten the gap in between setting up the pair, eventually not stopping the bow at all. Yet I would be aware only of the feeling of A being *already down* (as if putting down my finger had never occurred) and lifting the "already down" finger to reveal G. I realized that I could put my fingers down, but in such a way that they seemed to have *already been down (ex. 16-2b).*

This left-hand smoothness helps to connect the notes, and with a very simple physical motion. In addition, this smoothness allows the bow to connect—or

---

6   Watch Milstein play Paganini's *Caprice No. 5*, in *Nathan Milstein, Mozart, Paganini, Falla, Novacek, etc.*, DVD (EMI Classics, 2008).

grip—the string better because there is no percussive action from the left hand that disrupts the string's vibration. I now had two ways of playing pairs of notes with *one* motion: "setting" one note and peeling it away to expose the other, and "setting" one note and putting the next finger down in a way that seemed as if it was already down.

I tried to think of other ways to play pairs of notes. The simplest is two notes on separate strings. In this case, I could play two notes with *no* left-hand motion *(ex. 16-2c-e)*. I now had three ways to play a pair of notes.

I had noticed in my video investigations that Milstein's shifts (changes of position on the violin) from note to note were extremely smooth. Most players have a jerky look when they shift. Was there a way to simplify that motion? An idea occurred to me: the *shift, itself, is the note.* In other words, starting from a "set" note (we are still talking about pairs of notes), the action of the shift—the motion itself—is the note. There is no movement and then arrival. *The journey to the note is the note (ex. 16-2f and g).*

I now realized that there are only four ways of playing pairs of notes with one conscious motion. *These four movements explain all left-hand motion no matter how seemingly complex the music.* (If one does not think in this way, there are literally thousands upon thousands of ways to play notes.) Moreover, these ways of playing pairs of notes allow for greatly streamlined motion, in fact, only one motion per pair. This helps to create and explain Milstein and Heifetz's physical ease. Here are the four ways to play a pair of notes *(ex. 16-2).*

Example [a] is "set-peel," [b] is "set-drop" (except that the "drop" should feel as if the finger was already down), [c–e] are "two for nothing," [f] and [g] are "set-shift."

VISUALIZATION

The figure-eight

As I practiced this new method, another idea popped into my head. A pair of notes is a cycle. Pairs connect to each other. It occurred to me that maybe a good visualization of this would be a figure-eight. I thought of the base of the eight as the offbeat, and the top of the eight as the downbeat. This helped me time the movement of the fingers of the left hand. The figure-eight is conceptual only. *It is not a description of motion.* I should mention that there is not one "correct" picture. Whatever comes into one's head that assists in a smooth connection between notes is what is natural for them. *The pictures, the visualizations, will change as the understanding deepens.*

Visualization in playing scales

I remembered reading that Heifetz had said that if he had only thirty minutes to practice, perhaps two-thirds of the time would be devoted to playing scales. It is a truism that all master players stress the importance of scales. Feuermann, probably the most technically developed and perfected cellist, wrote that playing a perfectly smooth scale was perhaps the most difficult thing to achieve. I decided to apply my new method of thought to scale playing and see what I would find out.

This three-octave C major scale is divided into pairs of notes.[7] Here is a breakdown of the scale conceived in this way *(ex. 16-3a).*

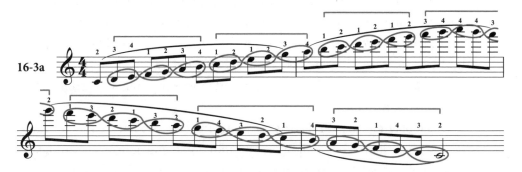

The figure-eights are one endless loop, a groove like a racetrack. For clarity, I have broken the figure-eights apart, three pairs per group.

Figure 16-a, on the next page, is an in-depth look at ex. 16-3a. The *motion* of the left hand pairs has been broken into figure-eights. The following numbers represent the types of left-hand pairs utilized:

    1 is "set-peel"
    2 is "set-drop"
    3 is "two for nothing"
    4 is "set-shift"

The colors are red for offbeats, and black for downbeats. The scale reads from right to left for reasons that I will soon explain.

---

7 The numbers above the notes are fingerings.

Fig.16-a

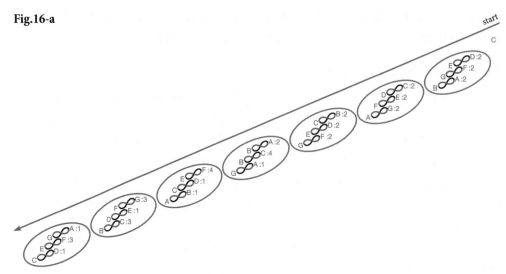

Three pairs are linked to form a chunk, or phrase. The scale is seven "chunks," groups, of three pairs. This illustration, Fig. 16-a, demonstrates that one is able to play *six notes (three pairs) with three conscious motions.* We could say, therefore, that the brain is working half as hard, or at half the speed. Interestingly, *the mind joins the pairs on its own*; that is an easy matter once the individual *groupings of pairs* are solidly in the mind.

When playing, and this is true for music in general, a pair of the offbeat to the downbeat should be thought of as an indissoluble structure, not unlike the double helix of DNA. One might say the that two notes form a double-stop, even though they are not played simultaneously. Yet the structure is permeable, in that other pairs can connect, attach, to it *(ex. 16-3b).*

16-3b

Interestingly, the act of *visualization,* which we are demonstrating here, affects physical motion and is an important factor in explaining great technique. This is an interesting discovery: *thought—visualization—affects the body's response to the thought through deep processes that cannot be consciously accessed.*[8]

---

8 I advise the reader to experiment with this himself. This is *pictorial* visualization. But there can be aural "visualizations," concepts, as well. It is well-known that if a player sings a phrase and then tries to match what he sang with what he plays, the outcome will be affected. Yet how he sings is subject to influence and suggestion—flowing, accented, smooth, etc. Internal conceptions, even as unconscious assumptions, affect outcome.

For example, if we now imagined the C major scale shown in ex. 16-3a visualized as shown in Fig. 16-b, the *sound produced*, the *bowing*, and the physical *feeling* of the left hand will be affected.

Fig. 16-b

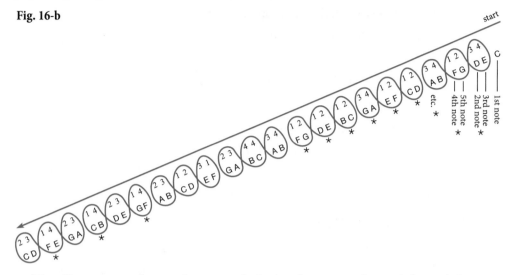

The illustration, the circles as a whole, read—move—from right to left, following the arrow. But the notes (the letters in the individual circles) and the numbers for the fingers (the fingerings), read from left to right *within each individual circle marked by an asterisk* because that is how the left-hand fingers line up when the fingers of the left hand are biased to the outside, as we shall explain in detail in Chapter 18. Additionally, all such figures—16a through 16f—use the same angle of motion.

This visualization is not to be taken too literally. We are attempting to present a picture of what *might* come to a player's mind intuitively if he were to set the parameters of his approach to the biases we have been discussing. The pairs of notes in the figure come from right to left because this is how they appear in my mind, not as they are printed in the music, which is left to right. I suspect this right to left mental shift is a natural visualization when offbeats are used as the instigators of the flow of sound. This picture cannot be an exact one-to-one correlative relationship to what may appear in the mind, only an approximation.

As depicted, the example will, hopefully, convey a sense of sound and motion that is biased to an up-bow feeling for the left hand and bow, which affects the sound (which we will also explain presently), and will also show—if one can use this picture when playing the scale—that how one thinks influences and organizes the mind/body in ways that are not accessible to conscious understanding.

People may have different visual intuitions from one another when grouping offbeats to downbeats. As I mentioned, these pictures may shift as one goes deeper into this process, this sort of alignment. Yet *it is a fact* that visualization has a *guiding* effect on physical motion and the coordination of the body and is a key factor in the acquisition of musical/technical mastery.

Pairing applies to all double-stop scales. For example, these pairs of thirds, ex. 16-4, are all played as "set-shift."

A scale represents, in simple form, the physical motion and mental paradigms that comprise an actual composition of music, i.e. chunks, groups, of pairs of notes played by the left hand *in only four ways*.[9] I realized that I now had a simple method for the coordination of the left hand that I could use to play any piece.

THESE INSIGHTS REDUCE COMPLEXITY

Fast passages or slow melodic lines break into these *limited* patterns of pairing. Paradoxically, this seemingly complex method greatly *reduces* left-hand complexity. It has the added benefit of concurrently phrasing the piece *at the most basic level*. For example, here is Gluck's "Melody" arranged for violin and piano from his opera *Orpheus and Eurydice* (ex. 16-5).

The third-finger, F, releases to the E/F pair, the F "drops," the next pair, G/F, is "set-peel," the second-finger, E, is a "peel" of the preceding F, the E "peels" to D, which is a "set-shift" pair. The second-finger, D, releases, "peels," to C♯. This gets us through the first two measures.

The second-finger, A of measure 3, is already down and vibrating before the bow moves. The shift to B♭ *is* the note (B♭), which is released to "reveal" A, which swings, musically speaking, into the B♭ of bar 4 as a "set-drop." The next A is a "peel" of the B♭. At the end of bar 4 the C♯/D pair is a "set-drop," the next pair, E/D, which takes us to bar 5, is a "set-peel." The dotted-quarter, D, "peels" to C♯ of the pair C♯/D, the D moves to G♯ (which is the shift), which brings us to A of our last pair, G♯/A, which is a "set-drop."

Following the path of the pairs of the left hand is the *phrasing structure and rhythm of the piece*. This shows, interestingly and importantly, that *the inner*

---

9   This method of thinking applies to all string instruments—viola, cello and bass—which are, after all, simply different sizes of the same design.

rhythm is inseparable from the phrasing. In other words, *rhythm is phrased*, and cannot, therefore, be merely metronomic. The "movements" of the left hand, conceived in pairs, is the musical bedrock, the mental organization of the music itself. It is also a physical "feeling," a feeling that is, *in itself,* sensually expressive. This is an *inseperable* part of what constitutes "musical expression."

DELVING DEEPER

This made me remember something that Heifetz had said in an interview: "It [the process of practice] has to be coordinated. First the fingers. Then your left hand with your right hand. That has to be synchronized."[10] This is not much to go on, but I added other statements he made such as: "Practicing for me is a combination of putting two things together. First, I study the piece. I call this mental work. Then, I start to practice the piece. I call this physical work. I have to combine the two before I reach any goal." Another time he said:

> It appears that the mastery of the technique of the violin is not so much of a mechanical accomplishment as it is of a mental nature...If an artist happens to excel in some particular skill, he is at once suspected of knowing some "secret" means of doing so. However, that may not be the case. He does it just because it is in him, and as a rule, *he accomplishes this through his mental faculties more than through his mechanical abilities.*[11] (italics mine)

Heifetz puts it plainly—his advantage is the way he *thinks.* Putting all this together, and it isn't much to go on, I decided to see what an inquiry into bowing would reveal.

The bow is a cycle

I have watched videotapes in slow motion for many years—twelve and counting. As I said earlier, I gradually realized that Milstein, Heifetz, Kogan, and Oistrakh all play very similarly when the motion is slowed down. At real-life speed they seem different because their hands and body types are different. One thing struck me as unusual. They use a tremendous amount of up-bow compared to most violinists.

Violin teaching in the West thinks of bowing as an *active down-bow* and an up-bow that somehow returns, a rebound from the down motion. This is commonly taught and easily observed in performers from the U.S. and Europe.[12] This is logical given that an active down-bow aligns with the common understanding

---

10 *Heifetz in Performance*, DVD (RCA, 2004).

11 Dr. Herbert Axelrod, *Heifetz* (New Jersey: Paganiniana, 1976), 131-132.

12 This is true of Galamian's method of teaching as we shall examine thoroughly in Chapter 26.

of music—what is literally depicted by the written notation—which, as we know, segments the notes into groups of so-called "strong" and "weak" beats. Therefore, we find that players commonly employ an *active* down-bow on the downbeat and an up-bow aligned with the offbeats or weak beats.

Our investigation has made it clear that Heifetz and Milstein thought about music in an opposite way—the *inversion*, in fact. Their bowing technique reflects this in a predictable way since, as we have seen, their understanding of phrasing is the *opposite* of what is commonly understood. Therefore, their *up-bow* is very *active* and their down-bow seems to float, or fall, down. With Heifetz in particular, if you watch in slow motion,[13] all his longer-length down-bows go completely to the tip of the bow. And you can see that he is watching this. It seemed to me, especially from watching Heifetz, that perhaps he, and they, thought of bowing as an up-bow to down-bow *cycle*. So I experimented. I assumed that they "set" this cycle from the up-bow, and that the "up" was active and the "down" passive. This would coincide with offbeat to downbeat phrasing.

Putting both hands together—the layering of thought

Since the bow also operates on a cycle of up to down, I wondered whether if, conceptually, I laid this on top of the left-hand figure-eight, I might have found an easy way of integrating the motion of *both* hands. With string instruments up-bows usually play offbeats, and down-bows, downbeats. Therefore, to play this example detaché—separate bows, ex. 16-6,

the conceptual "figure-eight" picture in my head looks like this *(Fig. 16-c).*

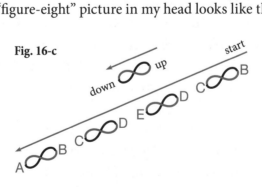

Fig. 16-c

13 Watch Heifetz play Gluck's *Melody* or *Sweet Remembrance* by Mendelssohn in the DVD *Heifetz & Piatigorsky—Historic Performance Film Footage,* Kultur Video (2005), in slow motion, noticing how attentively he watches his bow returning to the tip at the end of the up to down cycle.

The bow, also, falls into figure-eight patterns. *This does not describe the physical motion of the bow. This is a mental picture of a system only.* Actual bow motion is straight across the strings of the instrument, decidedly not a figure-eight. In the previous example, the color red begins at the start of the up to down cycle. The down-bow "falls" and the process resets and starts over. (The up-bows are colored red—they are the offbeats.) The up-bow requires twice the energy of the down-bow "fall," but with *no accent.* Therefore, the down-bow seems to be *half* the speed of the up-bow. *Conceptually the figure-eights fall in the same track; the same up to down motion is repeated with different notes and left-hand motions as a base.*

The motion of bowing, the "actual" movement of the arm

The bowing cycle, the movement of the right arm, is *initiated by the plug-in to the triceps muscle*, a point just above the bone of the elbow. This small spot controls all bowing motion, a fact known in elite Russian and Soviet pedagogy, not in the West.[14] Other muscles may be involved, but even the *thought* of other muscles being involved will subtly engage them and result in inefficient muscular coordination and antagonistic muscle use.

Heifetz and Milstein have fundamentally identical bowing technique and phrasing. Heifetz said in an interview in 1918:

> *The true art of bowing* is one of the greatest things in Professor Auer's teachings… bowing as Professor Auer teaches it is a very special thing…The movements of the bow become easier, much more graceful and less stiff.[15] (italics mine)

When watching Heifetz and Milstein, the right arm bowing motion seems to move from the outside, in. The bow moves across the string at a 90° angle, *but close observation shows that the right arm travels at another angle.*

---

14 Both Carl Flesch's and Ivan Galamian's books on violin playing mention the that right arm moves, or opens, from the elbow. The elbow is not a muscle. There is no mention of the muscle used in bowing by any treatise on violin playing that I have read. Chapter 18 has a picture of the plug-in to the triceps (*Figs. 18a and b*).

15 Dr. Herbert Axelrod, *Heifetz,* (New Jersey: Paganiniana, 1976), 129.

It is the motion and *direction of the right arm* to which one must pay attention to facilitate fluid bow movements *(Fig. 16-d)*. This awareness is a subtlety that confers great benefit. With this perspective, the right *hand* becomes the true "tip" of the bow.[16]

Fig. 16-d

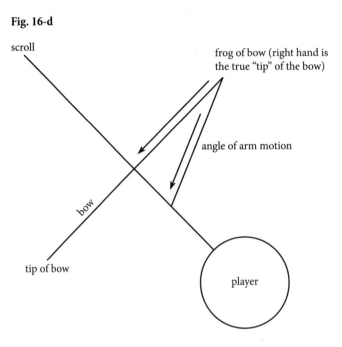

The left hand paradigm matches the right

The timing between the finger motion and the directional changes of the bow is that the finger of the left hand is placed on the string just before the bow changes direction.[17] In other words, the left finger is always "set" before the bow moves. Is this why Heifetz learns the left hand first? Perhaps, but I think that Heifetz is hinting at more than that. I believe he follows *the organization of the left-hand movements as his blueprint for playing*. The left hand is legato; it is the substructure of his thinking and is based on smooth connection. It does not articulate. What I realized from this was that Heifetz is saying the left hand leads the right in a fundamental way. *The right follows the thinking of the left.*

Therefore, the right arm, in terms of *different bowing possibilities and varied articulations*, is a *less fundamental* aspect of the process than the left. That is why he said, "First the fingers. Then your left hand with your right. That has to be synchronized."

---

16 Chapter 18 explains this in detail.

17 The Appendix has an explication of this, example, A-6.

The bow movements are also, fundamentally, legato. From legato as a base, the right hand and arm articulate and color the *fundamental structure of the left* by moving the bow with more, or less, weight (controlled by arm relaxation and, occasionally, index finger articulation) and speed. This gives variety to the basic connected, legato structure.

A NEW FIELD OF ANALYSIS

My guess is that this is the sort of analysis these great players do. This not only includes phrasing, inner rhythm, bow groupings, and left-hand movement, but flow in physical movement and music as a whole indivisible act of expression. Their approach is from the inside, out—*the underlying values and structures of music create their technique.* Most musicians *apply* fingerings and bowing strokes moored to a conception of music that is metronomic, guided by an erroneous understanding of what the *written notation* of music represents— which is understanding music from an abstraction (as if one could understand swimming in water from a picture of a lake). Unable to see through the symbols, they dutifully reproduce an abstraction. All the dots and dashes are observed, the tempo accurate to the metronome, the sound clean with all the notes in place. The page of symbols has been followed accurately, *yet the music itself has not been touched.* A mechanical approach *imposes* itself on the music through *will power* and an erroneous understanding of the written page.

The great performers we are studying are the opposite of mechanical—their playing is an organic, alive, *inward to outward process*, beginning with an insight into what the music *actually* is, beyond the way it is literally depicted. An organic process derives energy from what is implicit, what is natural in the music, and allows musical expression to flow *from the essence of the music, the proper functioning of the body through flow in response to musical "values," the "feeling" of the music, and the correct engagement of the instrument as an acoustical system.* This is what the great players understood and studied. Of course, when Heifetz or Milstein says that he studies a piece of music, I am sure he also means the form, the harmony, the piano or orchestra parts. But everyone does that. When Milstein says, "Practicing does not achieve quality," and talks about his "special" technique, which in his own words is what "creates" him, I think he is referring to *this* (what we are discovering) kind of analysis.

These players have made several *not easily* intuited paradigm shifts. First, they do not see the music as what is literally written. Next, they base their technique on this deeper understanding of music, beyond the abstraction of print, finding the essence itself—the flow of music—which is beyond the markings on the page. They have also made paradigm shifts in understanding motion, seeing the true, or *actual* movement of the arms' and hands' motion *vis-à-vis* the instrument, not distracted by the arms' and hands' *apparent* movement on the instrument. I am suggesting that paradigm shifts of this sort, and many others we will discuss, are part of what we mean by genius. However, this is not a sufficient explication in itself.

These shifts allow a different sort of feedback, or intuition, to present itself to their consciousness. This cannot be analyzed or understood. Yet one shift allows for others and it is this continual accumulation of *insight* that creates mastery, which never reaches a final level. The insight of the masters we are studying is as far from normal professional level playing as the Sun from the Earth. We have two biases, two realities: one filled with problems of mechanics, coordination and interpretation; the other, where these problems *do not exist*.

COMBINING WHAT WE HAVE LEARNED THUS FAR

Using the methods of analysis we have thus far described, I have given an example of the coordination of the hands for a small segment of the last movement of the Tchaikovsky *Violin Concerto (ex. 16-7)*. The numbers below are fingerings. The numbers on the top represent the type of left-hand pair.

Here is a mental picture in figure eights *(Fig. 16-e)*. The numbers are the left-hand pairings. This is how, on a base level, one must think through the piece.

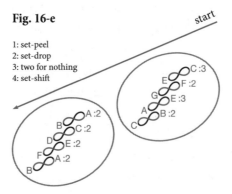

We could also use, for ex. 16-7, the visualization for the left hand, and basic "up-bow released sound" that we described with Fig. 16-b, which would give us Fig. 16-f, shown below. The numbers are the fingerings for the left hand. The illustration, the circles as a whole, as in Fig. 16-b, read—move—from right to left, following the arrow (which represents an up-bow bias to the sound). But the notes (the letters in the individual circles) and the numbers for the fingers (the fingerings), read right to left *within the individual circles marked by an asterisk* because that is how the left-hand fingers line up with an outward bias of the left hand *(Fig. 16-f)*.

Fig. 16-f

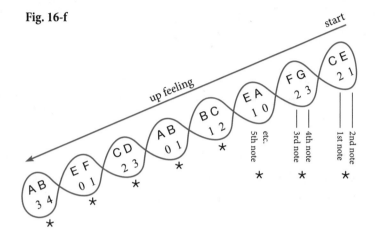

There are "over-layers" of thought to this level, such as the grouping of pairs, and the coloring—nuance—and phrasing of notes. A passage such as this excerpt is really a fast melodic line (as are all so-called "passages"). This group of notes is *phrased* and each note manipulated—one note longer, another brought out by emphasis even at a fast speed—as if it were a slow melody. In other words, it is intentionally *not* even, or *even*, depending on the melodic contour as envisioned by the artist/performer. At any rate, a passage like this is never played mechanically, metronomically even, by the masters we are analyzing.

The left-hand pairs do not always match the right

The basic overlay is not always that simple—it often does not coincide with the left-hand pairs. Yet *all* bowings can be broken into up-to-down cycles. For example, a common grouping of the bow is found in this passage from Mozart's *Violin Concerto No.5 in A Major (ex. 16-8a)*. The passage, starting in measure 3, is bowed as three pairs of up-to-down. This makes playing it much easier because, grouped as three pairs of two, the action of the bow is always essentially the same—up-to-down.

The left hand follows pairs of offbeats and downbeats, ex. 16-8b, making the passage sound fuller, which in this case makes the overlay of the bowing pattern *different* from the substructure of the left-hand pairs.[18] (This is also true for ex. 16-5, Gluck's "Melody").

COORDINATION

The next insight I had was that *physical movement is the musical expression.* What do I mean by that? To the connoisseur every extraneous and not properly worked-out movement can be *heard.* The more perfected and directed you want your expression to be—clean, rich sound, perfect legato, no physical or mental conflict, one total mind/body coordinated system—the less room there is for anything that has not been worked out completely. (Yet there still must be the space to make the performance seem improvised in the moment, fresh, which we will discuss in the next chapter.) Our model allows for *complete awareness and control of the coordination of both hands,* using the basic phrasing as the foundation. It reminds me of something that Bruce Lee said about coordination:

18 The appoggiaturas do not affect the left hand pairing. The notes must still unfold in time.

Coordination is by all means one of the most important considerations in any study of proficiency in sports or athletics. *Coordination is the quality which enables the individual to integrate all the powers and capacities of his whole organism into an effective doing of an act...*

Muscles have no power to guide themselves, but the manner in which they act, and consequently the effectiveness of our performance, depends absolutely on how the nervous system guides them. Thus, a badly executed move is the result of impulses sent to the wrong muscles by the nervous system, or sent a fraction of a second too soon or too late, or sent in improper sequence or in poorly apportioned intensity...

Well-executed movement means the nervous system has been trained to the point where it sends impulses to certain muscles, causing them to contract at exactly the proper fraction of a second. At the same time, impulses to the antagonistic muscles are shut off, allowing those muscles to relax. Properly coordinated impulses surge with just the exact intensity required and they stop at the exact fraction of a second when they are no longer needed.

Therefore, learning muscle coordination is a matter of training the nervous system and not a question of training muscles... Training for skill is purely a matter of forming proper connections in the nervous system through precision practice. Thus, we can attain skill only by actually doing the thing we are trying to learn.[19]

This last statement is brilliantly true: "We can attain skill only by actually doing the thing we are trying to learn." This shows the shallowness of the often repeated platitude that developing talent is mainly achieved by practicing for hour upon hour, or our current popularly specified 10,000 hours. One must practice what one wants to do *correctly* or the brain will *not* develop the coordinated capacity to master the skill, no matter how many lifetimes of practice one devotes to acquiring mastery. Therefore, to develop skill at the highest level is an extremely *narrow* path that must be set to *specific parameters*—which, as we have noted with any system, circumscribe potentiality—*plus* practice.

---

19 Bruce Lee, *Tao of Jeet Kune Do* (Ohara Publications), 43-44.

The Application of These Ideas to the Piano and Other Instruments

Because all musicians play *music*, musical *truths* apply equally to all instruments and voice. This leads to the inevitable conclusion that *the technique and musical thinking for all instruments is fundamentally the same.* Different instruments simply have, physically, different ways of playing pairs that will facilitate one conscious motion per pair and the elimination of accentuated "down" motion. Therefore, Milstein could learn from the great pianist Rachmaninoff:

> Rachmaninoff taught me to listen closely to music, to find various connections and influences in it. The most amazing discoveries await a musician on that path.[20]

Fine pianists are taught to play with a prescribed array of hand gestures and arm movements that are meant to elicit the desired sound and expression of the music.[21] This works up to a point, but the vocabulary of gestures, in which each may have a nearly infinite variety of touch, will not necessarily convey the drama of the offbeat to the downbeat unless one is *conscious* of this paradigm. As with violinists, and all other instrumentalists, pianists are ubiquitously taught to play music with an active downbeat, the phrases segmented as the music is printed. Their musical/technical approach would be more effective for expression and facility if *overlaid* on a foundation of pairs of notes. This is, in fact, what one hears in the playing of Rachmaninoff, Horowitz, Glenn Gould, and, although not a subject of our inquiry, Prokofiev (a rare recording of him playing his *Toccata*, for example). The deep underlying movement of the notes in pairs is of a higher logical type, more fundamental, than the hand gestures required to play the piano effectively.

Therefore, I am suggesting that the piano, also, has only four ways to play pairs of notes. Interestingly, they are very similar to the left-hand organization of the violin and certain strokes in bowing. One might say that a pianist's hands and arms "bow" and the fingers select the individual notes. Underlying this, however, must be the foundation of pairs, which is the *movement of the music through time, unfolded through the constant interaction of the offbeat to the downbeat.*

Because Horowitz and Milstein were friends, I decided to assume that they influenced each other, and that what worked for Milstein (no conscious

---

20 Nathan Milstein and Solomon Volkov, *From Russia to the West* (New York: Henry Holt and Co., 1990), 120.

21 One commonly hears pianists who have been taught to "type" as the motion of their fingers on the keys. This is simply bad technique.

down motion, phrasing in pairs, releasing sound, and many other violin "techniques") might have worked for Horowitz and vice-versa. This sort of cross-fertilization—violinists influencing pianists, pianists influencing violinists, singers influencing instrumentalists and vice-versa—is not as unusual as it may seem. Chopin's piano teacher was a violinist.

We have a verbal clue from Rachmaninoff, who was a mentor of both Horowitz and Milstein, that the basic technical and musical approaches of different instruments might be similar. He said that when he played he felt as if his fingers "grew out of the keys." This would imply that he was connected to them, which would mean his body weight was sinking—down. Since he used the word "grew" I take that to mean that he felt attached to the keys by "roots." A plant grows upwards and is connected to a base, but the attachment does not come from being *pushed* down. Likewise, the weight of the arms and body "rests" and is, therefore, attached to the keys. If Rachmaninoff's essential setting was "down" that would mean that to play he had to "release" the down setting, which is similar to Milstein and Heifetz's violin technique.

We have almost no verbal clues from Horowitz about how to play aside from a fascinating interview he gave to *Etude Magazine* in March of 1932 entitled "Technique: An Outgrowth of Musical Thought," where he states exactly this, that his technique is an outgrowth of his musical thought.[22] He also mentions, interestingly, that he emphasizes what he calls the *intermediate notes* as a good violinist does (we can only guess that he meant Milstein):

> He (a good violinist) does not *lose* the *intermediate tones*; they are all there. But the listener does not hear them obtrusively. Each falls into place, and the emphasis is on the last tone to which the others lead. So if I play all the notes steadily along, without graduation, or without relating one to another, and without climactic or guiding emphasis, I have said nothing, even though I may have played the notes correctly and in correct time. *But* if I play in such a way that every finger *feels* its tone, as it has learned to do from the sensation of the fifth finger, then I have my effect.[23] [The balance of the hand to the fifth finger is also used in violin technique.]

This is the musical illustration in the article, ex. 16-9a, but the example is unmarked, which is extremely odd. Had it been marked I feel certain that it would have shown the pairing of notes.

---

22 This is the last time that Horowitz spoke so candidly about piano technique.
23 This will be discussed in detail in Chapter 18.

The following from Chopin's "Ecossaise" in D flat, op. posthumous 72/5, (1826):

He [a good violinist] plays thus, ex. 16-9b:

Ex 16-9b is unmarked—an obvious error—therefore, we have no way of knowing what Horowitz means by *intermediate* tones. He goes on to say:

> In my own technique, the fifth fingers (both right and left) are the basis for playing runs, chords and octaves… The fifth finger I might call the "guide" through passages of scales or arpeggios ("runs"), chords and octaves. It is almost as if the fifth finger, with its acute sensitiveness, strength and control, taught the other fingers how to play. In scales and other passages I play as the violinist does. A *good violinist does not play all the tones with equal strength.*

THE MISDIRECTION OF ATTENTION

If one were to experiment with letting the fifth finger of both hands be the "guide" to the hands, I suspect one would begin to notice that attention directed thusly affects the movement of the *arms* when playing.

As in the playing of the violin, most players give their attention to the movement of the hands *on* the instrument, not the movement of the arms themselves. We have discussed that in violin playing the movement of the bow across the strings is at a different angle from the *movement of the right arm when bowing.* Directing one's focus to the movement of the bow hinders the freedom of movement that *naturally* occurs when one is aware of the movement of the right arm itself.

Additionally, most violinists give their attention to the movement of the left hand aligned to the *strings* of the violin. When combined with the *usual* focus of violinists on the movement of the bow, the left hand when shifting, and the action of bowing, will seem to be *perpendicular* to one another. This way of thinking about playing obfuscates the fact that *when the left-hand fingers are properly balanced by an outward bias of the base of the fingers to the fifth finger, the "pinky,"* which we will discuss in Chapter 18, an *abstract* congruence (visualization affects motion, as we have noted) of the finger motions of the left hand, and the left arm's motion when shifting, is formed with the *right arm's* movement. If aligned in this way, the movements of the left arm when shifting, the left fingers' movement, and the right arm when bowing, will be seen to be *parallel* to one another. *This confers an extraordinary advantage in technical ease.*[24]

A comment by Heifetz seems to support the idea of focusing one's attention to the *movement* of both arms:

> When changing strokes at the frog, you should have the feeling that the bow is a continuation of your arm, and part of the wrist. Just as the violin, on the other hand, is a continuation of the [left arm]. It should be the same as a gun or a rod—it should become part of the arm. *When the arm and the bow oppose each other, it then is an awkward pull and you find yourself struggling.*[25] (italics mine)

This *misdirection* of attention by players seems to be common in piano technique as well. The hands seem to move *parallel* to the fall-board of the piano, but if one's attention is directed to the fifth finger's "lead," it will be obvious that both arms *actually* move at an *angle to—and into—*the fall-board. Awareness of the true movement of the arms[26] when traversing the piano keys makes one's movements considerably more relaxed and, therefore, as in violin playing, creates a great technical advantage. With this insight in mind it becomes quite obvious when watching Horowitz play that this is, in fact, how he moves his arms when playing scales, arpeggios, chords and octaves.

Observing most pianists, the movement of the hands across the keys appears to be controlled from the spreading of the elbows and is a far less natural movement than the arms seeming to move *into* the fall-board. This *movement* of the arms into the piano's fall-board is so similar to violin bowing (when

---

24 This left hand outward balance, bias, is very obvious when watching Milstein, Heifetz, Kogan or Oistrakh play. Watch Heifetz play octaves in Paganini's *24th Caprice* from the DVD mentioned in footnote 13. Watch Milstein play Novacek's *Perpetuum Mobile.*or any other piece in *Classic Archive: Nathan Milstein—Mozart, Paganini, Falla, Novacek, Brahms, Beethoven, Bach*, DVD (EMI Classics, 2008).

25 Samuel Applebaum, *The Way They Play*, Book 1 (New Jersey: Paganiniana, 1972), 78. Artists' comments about playing are typically enigmatic and impossible to understand unless one already knows what they mean, which would mean, of course, that the question need not have been asked.

26 The arms "hang," relaxed, from the wrist. The same is true for the right arm, the bowing arm, in violin technique.

attention is directed to the angle of movement for the right arm) that I would
almost suspect that Horowitz must have discussed this with Milstein.[27]

MORE PARALLELS BETWEEN THE VIOLIN AND
PIANO TECHNIQUE

In Milstein's book, *From Russia to the West*, Milstein claims that he uncovered
the secret to Horowitz's sound:

> Horowitz invented his own special position for his hands when he played.
> [He was taught this from his teacher Felix Blumenfeld.] Take a look at his flat
> fingers! Observing him play, I learned how to imitate his sound on the piano.
> Of course I can only do a few notes à la Horowitz, separately with [the] left,
> separately with the right hand. His secret was this: after hitting the key hard
> (like the hammers in the piano itself) he immediately released it. That gave the
> "Horowitz resonance." If you continue to hold on to the key, it stifles the sound.[28]

There is no *banging* of the note. What Milstein says must be tempered by
close observation. The fingers move up, although remaining close to the key,
(or staying on the key). The flat position of his fingers places more fat of the
finger on the keys, which gives a more resonant sound than a typing position.
To play chords, Horowitz does the same motion—up. So does the great pianist
Emil Gilels, as slow motion analysis of the opening chords in his DVD of the

---

27 I would also wager that the movement of Horowitz's arms is initiated by the plug-in to the triceps
muscle, as is the bow arm of a violinist. The awareness of this motion (that the arms move at an
angle to, and into, the fall-board, and the basic motion itself) is a subtle matter, not easily gleaned,
because the movement of the hands and arms on the keyboard is often only a very short distance.
Yet even in small movements, this bias in motion is a great benefit technically because this motion
is simply the extension of the arm. Balancing to the fifth finger would also imply, *would suggest*,
(perhaps) that the fingers of the left hand subtly rotate clockwise at the base of the fingers, and
the fingers of the right hand subtly rotate counterclockwise at the base from a player's viewpoint
when playing. This does give both hands an open feeling. All reaching for notes maintains this
subtle internal balance for the hand, including pivots, effectually balancing the hands to the fifth
finger and making this bias the"guide" for all finger and arm motion. This advantageous bias may,
perhaps, explain Horowitz's unusual curling of the fifth finger of the right hand when playing
scales. Curling the finger in this way turns the base of the fingers outward from the players' point
of view. My suspicion, (I base this on the fact that so many other aspects of piano technique are
similar to high level violin technique) is that Horowitz found that with this outward bias of both
hands he could play off this "angle into the fall board" (described above); the fingers, hands, and
both arms moving along with, and playing into, the same abstract line formed by this angle.
Therefore, at a subtle level both arms could feel as if they always moved in *parallel* motion. This
would be identical to high level violin technique, and, likewise, confer an enormous technical
advantage, aiding in the emergence of synchronicity, discussed in Chapter 18, page 216.
28 *Ibid.* 20, 191.

Tchaikovsky *Piano Concerto No. 1* will show. Otherwise, the chords, if played with a strike downwards, sound more like a slap in the face than a resonant, musical expression of energy. Whenever I hear a pianist or an orchestra play the ending chords of a piece in this "struck" way, I can't help but think I'm watching the last few knockout blows of a heavyweight prize fight or one of the frequent scenes of face-slapping with Moe, Larry and Curly in episodes of the *Three Stooges*. To play chords that ring, violinists must use the same motion that Horowitz or Gilels would employ—the motion of the bow on the strings must be across and off, which is up.

Let's return to Horowitz. It appeared to his friend, Milstein, that he released his fingers to achieve a resonant sound. It also appears this way to me when watching him in slow motion. This implies an up-motion. Could he have been trying to avoid conscious down motion, too?

From a book written by his piano technician, Franz Mohr,[29] we know that Horowitz had his piano action set up in such a way that the keys went down very easily, but back up fast. In observing him play, it is clear that the weight of his arms and body is relaxed and down, sinking into the keys, but not pushed. A fast uptake, but easy down motion of the keys, suggests to me that he wanted to feel only "up" motion so that the sound "released," and that his movement on the keys was horizontal, and up. This is similar to how Glenn Gould set up his piano and how he plays physically. Interestingly, Rachmaninoff, Horowitz, and Gould all phrase in essentially the same way—they swing their offbeats into the down, and if you overlay this theory of "pairing" notes while listening to them, it is easy to hear this.

One has to work hard to meld the clues left from great players into a coherent framework or system of approach. The opportunities are often right in front of us, yet we don't see them. For example, I have a friend who owns a piano shop and is also a fine pianist and composer. I asked him if he knew how Horowitz had set up his piano.

"Oh, yeah," he said nonchalantly, "His piano goes on tour. When it came here I weighed the keys. I have the numbers."

"Have you ever set up a piano like that?" I asked.

'No," he shrugged.

"But wouldn't you learn a lot from understanding why he might have liked it that way?"

"That's just the way he liked it."

And that is as far as he went with it.

---

29 Franz Mohr, *My Life with the Great Pianists* (Grand Rapids: Ravens Ridge Books, 1992).

Glenn Gould apparently wrote to Steinway & Sons many times asking that they adjust the action of one of their pianos so that it would play like his favorite Chickering, which had easy down motion and fast uptake. The interoffice letters show that they thought his request was absurd. Gould may have been crazy, but not about piano technique. He had a reason to like easy down-action and fast uptake. Obviously, he required that to play in his style. It would be interesting to seriously examine that Chickering.

VIOLIN TECHNIQUE APPLIED TO THE PIANO AND OTHER INSTRUMENTS

The easiest application of violin, or string technique, to the piano is the idea of "set-shift." Set-shift makes playing octave passages on the violin and piano much easier and, in part, explains the easy fluid motion you see when Horowitz, Milstein or Heifetz plays them. Here is an example of the pairing for an octave scale on the violin *(ex. 16-10a)*. Each pair is "set-shift." To play a group, a phrase, of eight notes requires only four conscious motions.

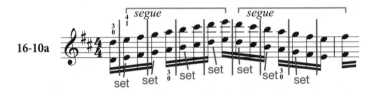

16-10a

Here are some examples from pieces. In this passage, ex. 16-10b, from the third movement of Dvorak's *Violin Concerto in A Minor*, the grouping is three pairs per chunk. Therefore, six octaves are played with three conscious motions.

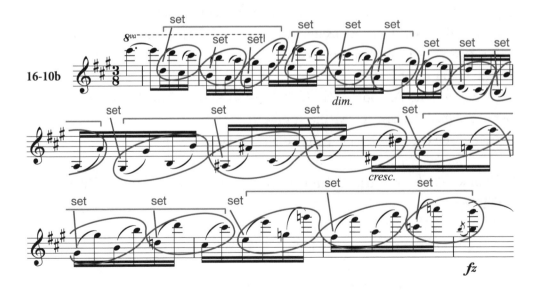

16-10b

There is almost no difference between playing "set-shifts" on the piano and the method used for the violin. Here are some examples from the piano repertoire. This is Liszt's *Sonata in B minor* as it appears on the page *(ex. 16-11a).*

This example, 16-11b, is the substructure of pairs of "set-shift."[30]

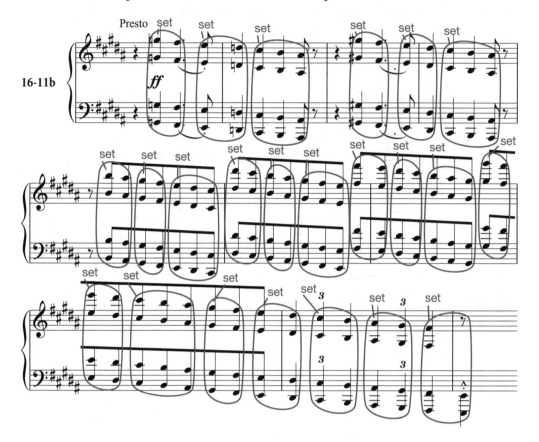

16-11b

Ex. 16-11c is the chunking, grouping, of the pairs into phrases. The entire passage is a repetition of the initial pattern.

---

30 "Set" means that the fingers are *on* the "set" note before playing. The "set" note of the pairs is the offbeat. The note that is "set" should feel as if the hand has always been there from long before. This applies to the "set" part of *all* the types of pairs that we have discussed and shall discuss. The space, the time, to "set" the pairs, or "set" the first note of the pair, will gradually lessen to the point where all one will feel is that the "set" note is somehow immediately "set," meaning it is "set" in the *rhythm* of the note, as part of the rhythmic flow.

If one depresses the "set" key from the air it is very possible that a double-motion will occur to play the note. Careful observation will show that the finger will first touch the key, and then in an *extra* motion proceed to depress the key. Or, often, the finger may be on the note but the player will lift it before depressing the key. *All* double motions are a waste of energy, and to the subtle ear will sound, as musicians say, "not clean," meaning there is a slight extraneous noise, lack of connection, or "schmutz," around the notes.

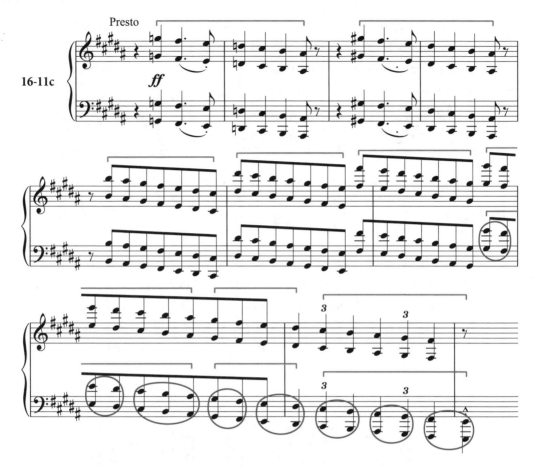

Set-shift pairing also works for the cello. In ex. 16-12a, from Tchaikovsky's *Variations on a Rococo Theme* for cello, measure 376 through the first half of measure 378 are repeated groups of octaves, two pairs at a time, forming four-note descending scales. In the *second half* of 378 the pairing is the same, but the *movement* is different. Our first group of A/D, A/G♯, after beat two, is easier to play if, after the shift to D, D is a "set" that moves to A, from which one plays the following G♯ as a shift. (Usually it is easier to shift from a high note to a low note.) The next two groups follow the same approach, "setting" from the high note of the group.

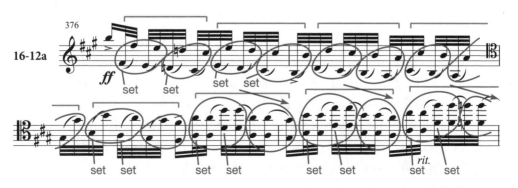

The passage is much easier if the foundational level, which is really octave double-stops, is mastered before overlaying the bowing *(ex. 16-12b)*. In other words, one must learn the left hand first.

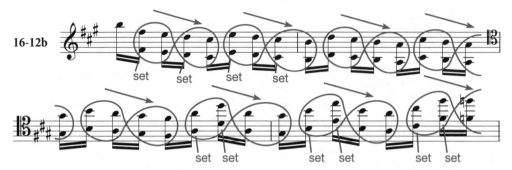

16-12b

You have to be creative with your groupings. Some passages require a variation of pairing—"pairing" pairs—such as this octave passage, ex. 16-13a, from the aforementioned Liszt's *Sonata in B Minor* for piano. In this case it is easier to group pairs with other pairs, which still creates an offbeat to downbeat pairing—the pair C♯/B is the *offbeat* to the pair E/D♯, the pair F♯/E♯ is the *offbeat* to the pair G♯F♯, etc.

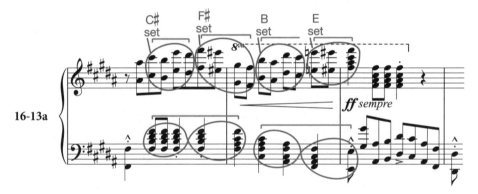

16-13a

This next passage, ex. 16-13b, from Paganini's *Caprice No. 4* for violin, is played in the same way. The scale in tenths is easier to play grouped as shown in measure 2. When played in pairs one will notice that the first shifts are the same for each two pairs when going up the scale. In measure 2, when playing the pair of tenths, G/B♭ to A♭/C, the first finger moves a half-step, the fourth finger a whole-step. In the next pair, B♭/D to C/E♭, the first finger moves a whole-step and the fourth finger a half-step. The shifts, *in pairs*, are the same for the *first finger* in the next two pairs going up. In the descending part of the scale the first finger moves, when thought of as pairs, as whole-steps, F/E♭ to D/C, then B♭/A♭ to what would be G/F if the scale continued. All the passages in tenths found in this caprice are made considerably easier by this sort of analysis, as are all passages in tenths, in general.

Measure 4 is easier to play when grouped as "paired" pairs (just like the previous example for the piano, ex. 16-13a), and linked as offbeat to downbeat pairs. If done correctly, four notes (all shifts), feel as if you were only playing two shifts.

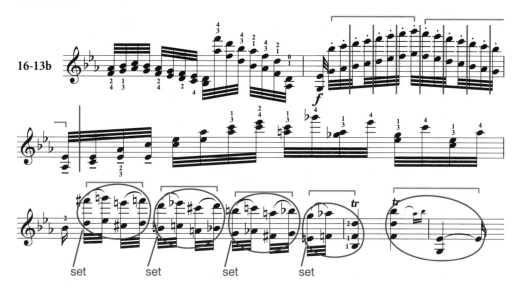

Here is an example of "set-shift" pairs from a virtuoso violin piece by Wieniawski, *Scherzo-Tarantelle (ex. 16-14a)*. The first pair (in this case the triplets are basically a major sixth with an open D string) is a "set-shift" of a minor third in a *down* direction; the second pair is a "set-shift" up a minor second. The next two pairs move in a mirror image of this—the first pair moves up a minor third, and the second pair, down a minor second. This realization makes the passage easier.

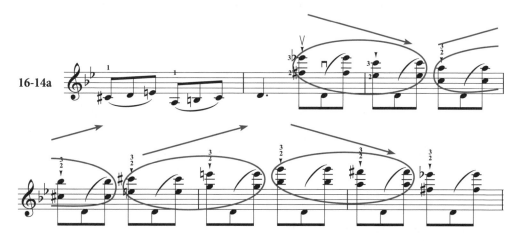

Understanding *pattern as movement* is very useful. This octave passage in Mendelssohn's *Violin Concerto in E Minor* can be difficult *(ex. 16-14b).*

16-14b

The movements, however, form easy patterns. The first pair of octaves, G/A♯ (B♭ is easier mentally than A♯), stays in place. The second and third pairs, C♯/E and G/A♯ (B♭), move in parallel motion, both shifting down the *distance* of a major third; the last two pairs, C♯/E and G/B, shift up a third. Therefore, the thinking when playing this passage is "stay, shift down twice, shift up twice." The next passage, starting in bar 5, is a bowing variation of the same octave pattern. Therefore, the left-hand motions are identical.

SINGING IN PAIRS

"Pairing" can be used to analyze vocal technique. If one thinks about it, *there is only one way to sing a pair of notes—"set-shift."* I believe that this is not a far-fetched connection—it is a *"pattern that connects"*[31] string instrument technique with singing. A violin, or any string instrument, can get some sense of singing by playing an aria on one string with only one finger. You will find that unless you group motion as "set-shifts," every note is a shift. In fact, every note *is* a shift, but pairing the notes gives you *one motion* per pair and is much easier. (I must remind the reader that the shift *is* the note, not "movement," and then a note is "arrived at." That is a double motion, a waste of energy, and will make an accent.) Therefore, I am postulating that it is possible that the concept of "set-shift" might be transferable and useful to singers. For example, here is the famous aria from Bellini's opera *Norma,* "Casta diva," *(ex. 16-15a).*

---

31 A precept of Gregory Bateson's from his book, *Mind & Nature—A Necessary Unity,* describing the oneness of nature.

The grouping of the pairs is meant to connect with each other. If I am correct, and the physical technique of singing is similar to the problem of playing octaves on a string instrument in that each note is created by a shift, then we can be bold enough to assume certain things. The first note of the pair is what I call "set." (This is an attempt to describe the physical "feeling" and mental paradigm.) The first note should feel as if it is a starting point. The second note is created by a single movement to the note; the journey to the note *is* the note itself. Once the pairs are mastered, the "feeling" of singing in pairs is joined to each pair (the pairs will connect themselves), eventually binding the pairs into phrases. Yet the phrases flow from one to another because, once the music starts, it is a single flow of energy.

In reality, music is in constant falling forward motion until a piece is over. Even a "rest" is not a stop in the *flow* once the music has begun. This is also true of fermatas, which are dramatic pauses in music, not dead zones. Action is merely suspended, itself action because of unresolved tension, which is the audience waiting for the music to begin again. I should more accurately say that we are waiting for the "sound to begin again" because *the silence of a fermata is the music.*

A closer examination of ex. 16-15a shows that the piano part is phrased in the same way as the voice, creating clear ensemble congruence and curing Weber's conundrum of matching instruments with vocal inflection *(ex. 16-15b).*

16-15b

With this way of thinking *there is no difference between the phrasing of the piano and the phrasing of the singer.* Additionally, it can be easily noticed that *little notes always join, or lead, to big notes,* as is evident throughout the aria. This facilitates flow, and is another musical "truth," a "law," which seems to have no exception, applicable with success to all instruments.

Here is another example of musical analysis that may apply to pyrotechnics in singing *(ex. 16-16)*. In the "mad scene" from Donizetti's *Lucia di Lammermoor* we find operatic difficulties such as this passage. Here may be an easier way to think about it. We can see that these groups of fast notes are really just embellishments,[32] or very simply put, ornamented scales. In measure 3 an embellished A♭ moves to B♭ (a pair), then a similarly embellished C to D, another pair, and so forth. This is probably much easier than singing in the groupings "literally" printed in the music. For cleanness one may still have to break the ornaments into pairs of "set-shift" as a base.[33]

16-16

---

32 We shall examine this way of thinking more thoroughly in Chapter 17.

33 We again notice that the phrasing of the piano part is clearly synchronous with the voice.

MORE WAYS TO PLAY PAIRS IN PIANO PLAYING

There are only three other ways to play two notes in piano playing in addition to "set-shift." The second way is "set-lift." The first note of the pair (which is the offbeat) is lifted at the same time the next note (the downbeat) is put down. You can train your mind to feel only the release of the offbeat, thereby playing two notes with only one motion. Here is a good example from the opening of Rachmaninoff's, *Prelude in G♯ Minor,* Op. 32, No. 12 *(ex. 16-17)*. In this example, the musical group begins on the *fourth* note of the opening, D♯, but could also begin on the *second* note, D♯, depending on which grouping is easier and/or sounds better. Our first "chunk" is three pairs, all "set-lift." In this passage it is always the D♯ that is lifting, and this is where one's awareness needs to be directed. The downbeats should have no accent. The weight of the arm is down, and it is the weight of the arm, heavier or lighter, that controls the crescendo.

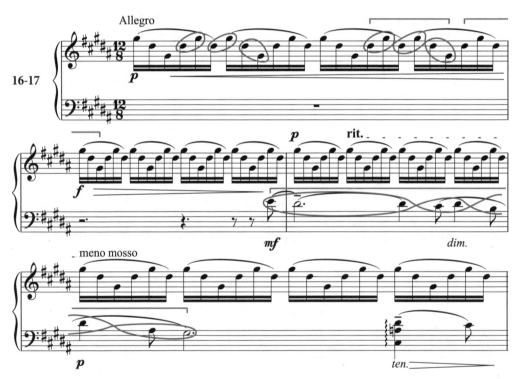

16-17

Two hands alternating is also "set-lift." The hand that plays the offbeat lifts as the other hand descends, simply a different version of the above-described motion of alternating fingers. A good example of this is the excerpt from the last movement of Tchaikovsky's *Piano Concerto No.1 in B♭ Minor,* ex. 17-6c, found in our next chapter in the section describing octave transpositions on the piano. Interestingly, basic "set-lift" (finger motion) can be practiced effectively by using ex. 16-1, Kreutzer's *Etude No. 9,* which works as well for piano technique as it does for the violin.[34] It cannot be practiced the same way, but if one's attention is directed to the releasing of the offbeat (not to the playing of the downbeat, which will occur by the lift of the offbeat) the learning effect will be the same as for violin technique.

The third way of playing pairs is "set-peel," or "set-slip," whichever term one prefers. This occurs between chromatic notes, a black key to a white key. Horowitz often uses this in melodic passages. It can be used to create "gluey" connections between chords, using the voice leading to make smooth chord connections. (It is more accurate to think of chords as "individual" voices that connect melodically and happen to create chords as they flow forward.) Chopin used this sort of "slipping" of one finger between keys to achieve a more legato, *cantabile*, connection:

> He often used the same finger to play two adjoining notes consecutively (and this not only when sliding from a black key to a white key), without the slightest noticeable break in the continuity of line.[35]

The fourth way of pairing is "set-release," which is used in passages of repeated notes, such as in this example from Schubert's, *Impromptu in A♭ Major (ex. 16-18)*. The second note of each pair is a "release," an "up" motion, that does not leave the key. The passage should have no feeling of downward motion. Note that syncopation, when paired this way, *leads* to the beat (another "law"), and is much easier to play.

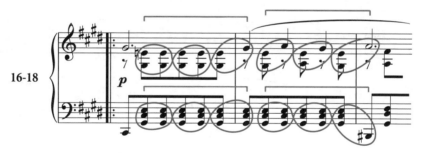

16-18

This technique, or way of thinking, ("set-release") is a possible answer for playing the octaves in Liszt's arrangement of Schubert's *Erlkönig*, which according to Charles Rosen, contains perhaps the most difficult octave passages written for the piano.

---

34 All of Hanon's etudes for the piano are perfect for practicing this as well.

35 Jean-Jacques Eigaldinger, *Chopin: Pianist and Teacher* (Cambridge: Cambridge University Press, 1986), 46, original source was Mikuli, 4.

WIND AND BRASS INSTRUMENTS PLAYING PAIRS

Wind and brass instruments also use finger motion to play notes, but may have even more limited ways to play pairs with one motion than do string instruments or the piano. Certainly the phrasing is identical. For example, here is an excerpt from Mozart's *Concerto for E♭ Horn*, K.495 *(ex. 16-19a)*.[36]

The pairs are a more *fundamental* level than the phrasing slurs—musical connection does not stop at the end of a slur. This is a good example of the difficulties with notation. If a player makes a break at the end of the slurs, the melodic line will be broken into several bits instead of being heard as one long line.

In this next example from the last movement of the same concerto, ex. 16-19b, I have divided triplets into *three pairs of two* instead of groupings of three. In playing groups of three the last note of the three is often lost, not heard well. Grouping in pairs helps bring out every note, which makes the passage sound fuller. Moreover, if one were to experiment with this idea, it will become obvious that pairs of notes are easier to play than groups of three. The brackets are a suggested grouping, phrasing, for the pairs.

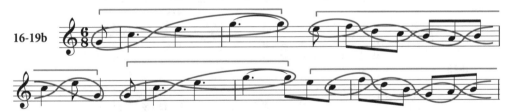

Here is an example from Strauss's *Concerto in D Major for Oboe and Small Orchestra*. In this excerpt, ex. 16-20, we see pairs of notes that are endlessly linked. The brackets attempt to show larger groupings, but in this case the piece is really one long phrase, an unbroken line falling endlessly forward. As in singing, the two notes that make up each pair have to be smoothly connected. That is step one. Two notes should feel as if they are being played with only one motion. Once this is accomplished, the pairs are linked to each other, which they do on their own, and then combined into larger groups. But, as in our example with singing, this linkage does not stop until the piece is finished.

---

36 The first note, D, is played as F natural above middle C. The notes are played a major sixth below what is written.

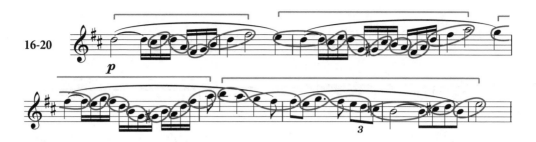

16-20

PAIRING TIME SIGNATURES

The theory of pairs has implications for time signatures. We have noted that *rhythm is phrased.*[37] Metrical pulse is also phrased. This alters commonly held beliefs and could be considered another musical "law"—*pulse (beats) and rhythm are phrased.*

Musical pulse cannot be mechanical because the *measurement* of time is psychologically based. One may measure time mechanically with a watch, but that is still a psychological decision. One's ordinary experience with time is that it flows in a varied stream, depending on one's mood. Because playing music comes through one's body, it must be played in *human* time. It cannot be mechanical because the body is not a mechanism. Therefore, musical time must be subtly shaped.

In ex. 16-21a we see that 3/4 can be grouped as (2, 3) (1, 2) (3, 1), *which joins two bars* and eliminates the squareness of (1, 2, 3) (1, 2, 3) or (2,3,1) (2,3,1).

16-21a

Pairing works well in waltzes, mazurkas, etc., creating long lines to the music. Examples 16-21b through 16-21e show groupings of six beats to a bar, either in 6/8 or 6/4. These divisions are helpful in many works of Chopin and Liszt. This is especially useful in pieces by Chopin, where the bass provides the pulse around which the upper lines "nuance."

16-21b

16-21c

---

37 Percussion instruments are also subject to the musical "laws" we have been discussing—released sound, phrased rhythm connecting the offbeat to the downbeat, grouping notes into phrases, and, artistically, fitting into the fabric of an ensemble. The term percussive is, indeed, an unfortunate descriptor. Percussion instruments are "struck" to *release* a sound of *quality*. The purpose is not the "striking."

Additionally, this grouping helps clarify the pulse when rests are added to (or notes subtracted from) the beats of the bass line, as often happens in compositions by Chopin and Liszt, as shown in ex. 16-22e1, from Chopin's *Minute Waltz.*

Ex. 16-21f shows that in 2/4 beat two leads to beat one, which creates movement, not the usual heavy downbeat and lighter upbeat, which creates a feeling of marching in place, or, more accurately, stomping in place.

The next example, 16-21g, shows the movement of pairs in 4/4.

MORE ON THE UNAPPRECIATED AND NEGLECTED OFFBEAT AND ITS USE IN ENSEMBLE PLAYING

The implicit power of pairing the offbeat to the downbeat brings us to another truth, a "law:" *The offbeat controls rhythmic nuance.* Rhythmic nuance *is* rubato. Therefore, the control of the offbeat to the downbeat controls the musical drama. Thinking by the beat causes one to miss the details *in between* the notes, which is the connective tissue.

Control of the inner beats is the *"control"* in ensemble playing. This means that training musicians to play in this way will allow them to play in large ensembles without needing someone to beat, or depict, the time. In other words, a conductor is not necessary to hold ensembles together because *if music is properly understood it has its own intrinsic cohesion.*

Most orchestral music is a *seemingly* complex interaction between the various instruments of the orchestra. In fact, it is written very skillfully so that all the musical lines played by the performers are actually interwoven, just like a play. For example, every instrument has "hand-offs" to other players, like passing the baton in a relay race to the next runner. This is found without exception (there may be one, but I don't know of it) in all ensemble music, including all orchestral music, and including the interaction of instruments and voices in opera. *These interlaced relationships are easily controlled by an understanding of the connective power of the offbeat.* Here is a very simple example from Mozart's opera *The Marriage of Figaro (ex. 16-22a).* The score makes the intertwined and interdependent nature of music easy to see.

16-22a

Ex. 16-22b highlights the unity of rhythmic and melodic flow among the different instruments. The "many" are really one—an interwoven tapestry of melodic lines joined by the glue of the offbeat moving to the downbeat.

16-22b

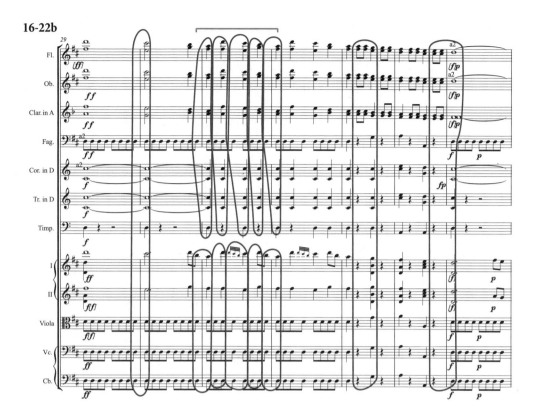

This way of thinking has important ramifications for the technique of piano playing, which will be discussed in our next chapter. Looking at a score with this approach also affects the role of the conductor and his relationship to the coordination of an ensemble—a topic to which we will devote an entire chapter.

CHAPTER 17

Skeletal, or Compositional, Thinking

I happened upon up another clue about playing from a filmed interview that Milstein had with Pinchas Zuckerman. In the film,[1] Zuckerman plays the opening of Mendelssohn's *Violin Concerto in E Minor*, and Milstein sings the same phrase. This is the printed version of the piece *(ex. 17-1a)*.

Milstein says, "I 'see' the music like this," and he sings *(ex. 17-1b)*.

This is clearly a *skeletal version*. Zuckerman then plays the opening to Mozart's *Violin Concerto No. 3 in G Major* and Milstein again says he "sees" it like this and sings a skeletal version of the piece. Here is the printed music *(ex. 17-2a)*.

And the version Milstein sings *(ex. 17-2b)*.

Unfortunately, and astonishingly, neither Zuckerman nor anyone else present asked Milstein why he "sees" the music like that or what good it does

---

1 *Nathan Milstein—In Portrait*, DVD (Christopher Nupen, 2007).

him, but we can make some guesses. Milstein does three things in his version of the Mendelssohn. First, he "sees" a note that repeats itself as just one note; second, he "sees" G/F as F, and third, he "sees" C/E as C. In the Mozart, he eliminates the neighbor note. These examples can be interpreted in various ways. I choose to see it as skeletalizing a piece. I think that he tries to "see" a group of notes in its most threadbare form. This creates a skeleton of basic ideas from which he *hangs* extra notes.

Is this advantageous? If you try it, you will see that it reduces complexity and is easier on the brain. It is also more akin to the way a composer develops a piece—from a simple generative idea to complexity. Additionally, "hanging" notes onto a skeletalized form *has an improvisatory feel and gives the music being played a more spontaneous sound.* This *freshness* is no small matter in the "recreation" of music. Milstein is not playing from the printed page. He is going deeper. He "sees" what the page represents beyond its abstract form. He sees the *music* hidden behind the print. As we continue in our inquiry, we will also.

VARIATION

The variation of pattern is not only an essential aspect of music, but also a deep principle in life. If we look carefully it becomes apparent how similar everything is. Take, for example, our faces: two eyes, two ears, two nostrils, the mouth is divided in half; or our bodies: two arms, elbows correspond to knees, arms to legs, ankles to wrists; or, our link to other animals: hands to paws, claws to fingernails. Or the crossover to other natural forms: veins to rivers, breath to fog. Veins look like trees, grass could be hair.

The variation of simple elements through DNA is a key process of life and creates the diversity of all living creatures. As I mentioned previously, it is a logical conclusion from the observation of our shared characteristics that we are all one system, and that living forms are related at fundamental levels with nonliving forms.

The variation of simple ideas also creates language. This is described by Noam Chomsky and Morris Halle in their book, *The Sound Pattern of English:*

> The class of possible phonetic representations is of course infinite. Similarly, the class of phonetic representations designated as well-formed sentences in each human language is infinite. No human language has a limit on the number of sentences that are properly formed and that receive a semantic interpretation in accordance with the rules of this language. However, *the grammar of each language must obviously be a finite object,* realized physically in a finite human brain. Therefore, *one component of the grammar must have a*

recursive property; it must contain certain rules that can be applied indefinitely often, in new arrangements and combinations, in the generation (specification) of structural descriptions of sentences. Every language, in particular, contains processes that allow a sentence to be embedded within another sentence, as the English sentence *John left* is embedded in the sentence *I was surprised that John left.* These processes can apply indefinitely often to form sentences of arbitrary complexity. For example, the sentence *I was surprised that John left* can itself be embedded in the context *Bill expected_ _ _ _ _,* giving, finally, *Bill expected me to be surprised that John left,* after various obligatory modifications have taken place. There is no limit to the number of applications of such processes; with each further application, we derive a well-formed sentence with a definite phonetic and semantic interpretation.[2]

We shall see that recursive patterns and variation are also fundamental to the art of composition and to the acquisition of virtuoso technique. Variation creates music.

THE MOTIVE—THE RECURSIVE PROPERTIES OF MUSIC

One of the helpful aspects of the way Western classical music is written, as far as virtuoso playing is concerned, is that compositions are based on the repetition of only a few fundamental ideas. The theorist Heinrich Schenker explains this in profound depth. Here is a condensed version:

Pattern is implicit in a note's structure. Each note is pregnant with the overtone series and, in fact, our tonal system is derived from the overtone series in each note. The foundation of the harmonic system is the perfect fifth and the major triad, which are derived from the most audible tones of the overtone series. Through the repetition of a couple of chords, a main key area can be established for an idea, the motive, to live in.

The motive itself is created through repetition and its journey, through variation and tonality shifts, creates—generates—the drama of the piece. These modulations, or tonal shifts, are in relation to, and variations of, one center. Each key could be a center itself, depending on the surrounding support of chords. The chordal shifts in a single phrase are a subset of the tonal shifts of the work itself. The entire piece folds "out" of itself, unfolds (as does a book from an initial idea). Western classical music is essentially variation of tonality and motive, which create a character or characters for a musical drama. Through variation these motives are transformed and their origin obfuscated. The

---

2   Noam Chomsky and Morris Halle, *The Sound Pattern of English* (MIT Press, 1991), 6.

motive is a seed from which the piece grows, as if hatched from an egg. *This method gives a composition organic unity.*

It is my opinion that this "hatched from an egg," or "grown from a seed factor," is a huge help to the performer, or "re-creator," because through seeing the piece in a simple way, where complexity is hung on a skeleton of simple ideas, it is possible to take the work as a whole and reduce it to *a few simple physical movements that are repeated. These physical movements are recursive.* Here is an excerpt from Debussy's, *Doctor Gradus ad Parnassum (ex. 17-3a).*

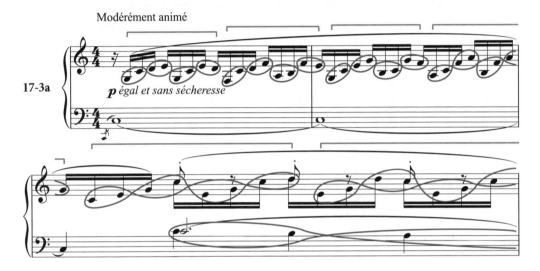

17-3a

As you can see, the first note of the pair is an offbeat. This lifts at the same time the finger that plays the downbeat goes down. With practice, as with playing the violin, (where I learned to play with no conscious down motion), a pianist can train his mind to feel only the offbeat "up" motion. He plays, in this case, eight notes with only four conscious motions while, coincidently, phrasing the piece correctly at the same time, assuming there are no downbeat accents. (The quarter notes in the bass in bar 3 are "set-lifts," just as in the right hand, but at one-quarter the speed.) The entire piece works this way physically ("set-lift") because this basic musical idea (which must be expressed physically) is repeated throughout the composition. Here is another similar example from Bach's, *The Well-Tempered Clavier Book I, Prelude No. 2* in C minor *(ex. 17-3b).*

17-3b

If the group of notes from the previous example by Debussy, ex. 17-3a, was slowed down and became a slow melody they would be played physically in the same way. In fact, later in the piece they are *(ex. 17-3c)*.

Therefore, melodies also can be played this way, and seem to be done so by Horowitz. An easy application of this approach can be seen in the following example, Mozart's *Piano Sonata No. 16 in C Major*, K.545 *(ex. 17-4)*.

The first pair, C/E, is "set-lift," which brings us to G/B, in which the G lifts as the B is put down. The next pair, D/C, is a "set-lift" also. The left hand of bar 1 follows the same pattern. The pair, G/E, is a "set lift," as is G/C. The only motion one should feel is the lifting of G. In the right hand of bar 3, G is the lifting of A, and the next pair, C/G, is the lifting of C, followed by F/E, which is the lifting of F as E is put down. If you think in pairs that connect, you should feel no conscious down motion for this entire segment and, of course, throughout the piece.

MUSICAL TAPESTRY AND COORDINATION

If we examine ex. 17-3b from another perspective it becomes obvious that, in pairs, the first three pairs of the first phrase move in parallel motion between the bass and treble, the last pair in contrary motion *(ex. 17-5a)*.

This *pattern of movement* between the hands appears throughout the prelude with only slight variation. In piano playing, pairs of notes between the hands can move in parallel (by that we mean the same direction) and contrary motion between the fingers of both hands or movements of the arms. Both hands can stay, one can move and one stay, etc. Sometimes one note moves to two notes or four, or various combinations.

Therefore, when thinking in pairs of notes the possibilities of movement in *direction* between the hands and fingers is *limited*. Additionally, one will always find *simple patterns of movement in pairs of notes* throughout a piece because compositions are motivic, which means that *only a few basic patterns* will reappear—in varied form. This applies to even the most complex pieces of music.

If we examine ex. 17-4 from this perspective we can see that music written for the piano is, in itself, an ensemble of separate voices[3]—the many—interacting as a single interwoven musical tapestry of sound *(ex. 17-5b)*.

This approach—linking *separate voices* through the interaction of offbeats to downbeats—works for any *ensemble of instruments,* as demonstrated in

---

3   Studying the piano is, in a very real sense, the study of ensemble playing.

Chapter 16, ex. 16-22b. In reality *there are no separate voices*. This is a common confusion and a subtle, but important point. No voice or "part" in a piece of music can exist without the whole. The notion of separation is an illusion. All voices contain the others—they are created by each other. This idea—there are no separate voices—influences the coordination of the individual player or the different instruments of an ensemble. Henceforth, it should be assumed that any example of piano music, or any combination of instruments could, and should, be thought of in this way.

In ex. 17-5b, if one aligns the juxtaposition of the moving eighth notes in the bass (for example, with the melodic quarter notes or the entrance of the melody after a rest) *with* the beat, a player must *"time"* the coordination between the hands. This will tend to reinforce beats, breaking flow. But if one is aligned to the inner beats, no "timing" for an entrance—or counting—is necessary because the inner beat *leads* to the melodic half-note entrance in measure 3 and *naturally* coordinates with other voices (melodic lines). This is a subtle point, but one which touches on ensemble playing in general. *Alignment to beats requires timing; alignment to inner beats is a natural flow.*[4] In ensembles, timing—musical coordination between players—implies cuing, which in the case of large ensembles, requires a conductor. Playing from the inner beats, however, creates a *self-binding* tapestry of interdependent musical lines, *each one containing the other.* This interplay *leads itself*, thereby eliminating the need for cues and for a "cuing leader."[5]

Here is another example, the *Prelude in A minor* from Bach's *Well-Tempered Clavier Book II*, ex. 17-5c, which shows the intertwined nature of so-called separate voices. Played in this way the player becomes aware of the "glue" of the pairs, the fullness of the sound, and the physical flow and ease that naturally occurs when the implicit connectedness of the notes is brought to light.

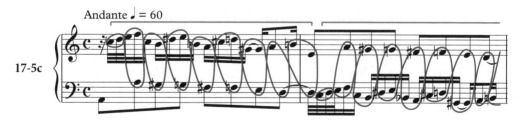

17-5c

Andante ♩ = 60

---

4 Individual practicing or group rehearsing must be slow enough to integrate the off-beat's coordinating role.

5 If properly rehearsed and trained orchestras would have no need of a conductor to coordinate performances. We will discuss this in detail in Chapter 22.

Articulation may be *added* to smooth connection, but as we have seen, *flow* is more fundamental than articulation. Without a base of connectedness, performance will be compromised.

In ex. 17-5d, Chopin's *Minute Waltz,* Opus 64, No.1, we see an analysis of the motion of the pairs. The accompaniment forms a pattern that continues the same physical movement for the left hand, even though this repetitive pattern is obscured by rests. This is a good example of the fact that rests are not silence. They are a continuance of the pulse, motion, and phrasing of the piece.

Ex. 17-5e views the piece as a self-binding tapestry of musical lines. The coordination of the hands is a repetitive pattern because of the *motivic* construction of the piece.

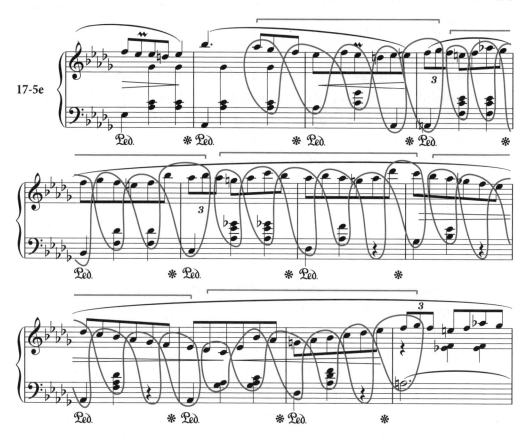

17-5e

In this next example from the first movement of Chopin's *Piano Sonata No. 2 in B♭ Minor*, ex. 17-5f, we can see the effectiveness of this type of analysis for ensuring the coordination between the hands, which, because of this detailed picture, not only becomes very straightforward, but shows us, in the smaller brackets, an inner melody (which Horowitz clearly brings out in his performance of the piece) that is used in the second theme of the movement.

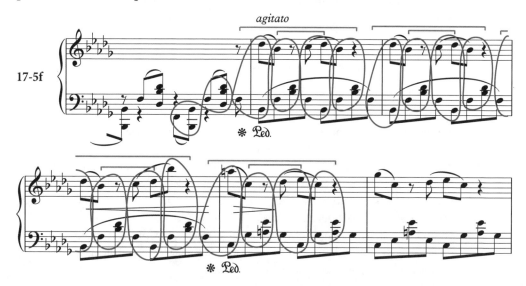

17-5f

One of the difficulties of playing with an orientation to the offbeat is that coordinating the hands is more complex—*unless this method of analysis is used.* Most players simply line up with beats, which seems to be much easier. But to any auditor willing to make a comparison it becomes obvious that orienting to the beat inevitably sounds mechanical.[6] In comparison, the understanding and playing of the deep structure sounds richer, fuller. Because there is more "glue" between the notes, the possibility for nuance and subtle control over phrasing, color, tone, rhythm, and physical realization is greatly enhanced.

The detailed understanding of the coordination of the hands is *inseparable* from the fundamental phrasing. This approach *makes learning much faster, deeper, and easier for any pianist* because *he is practicing what the music actually is—the deep-level coordination and phrasing.* It is the *lack* of the incorporation of this substructure that inhibits the potentiality of a player, presenting itself as musical and technical deficiencies, which are really symptoms of a deeper problem.[7]

Once the substructure is deeply understood—by using this sort of analysis— one may begin to develop the ability to play pairs of notes with only *one* conscious motion. The next step would be to join the pairs into a phrase through an *overall* physical motion, which may become a simple gesture of the wrist and arm, for example. Analysis of this type finds subtle patterns that are normally easy to overlook. My guess is that it is this sort of substructural understanding (coupled with the insight and intuition that will present itself to a mind with this bias) that helps make technical/musical wizardry possible. This is truly technique that is an *outgrowth of musical thought.*

The self-binding musical tapestry created by the relationship of the offbeat to the downbeat and the fact that seemingly separate voices contain all the other voices is a result of musical laws *more fundamental* than phrase markings, articulation, tempo, and bar lines. We have already mentioned these laws, but we will remind the reader that:

- The smallest unit of music is a pair of notes—the offbeat to the downbeat.
- Music flows forward in time.

---

6 This brings to mind Schoenberg's complaint about metronomic conductors, who by their mechanical approach "solve" all the expressive complexities in a piece of music by overlooking them. Similarly, pianists deceive themselves by believing that an accurate reproduction of an abstraction, which is what the printed music is, is desirable or even possible. This simplistic, unnuanced approach gives many performers the illusory comfort that they are being thorough, when in reality they rarely touch the essence of the music itself.

7 The lack of understanding of the deep coordinative structure is what forces pianists to resort to the ubiquitously employed pedagogical cure-all for overcoming technical deficiencies—practicing in varied rhythms. The problem lies at a deeper level.

- There are limited ways to play pairs of notes.
- Rhythm, musical pulse (beats), must be shaped, phrased.
- Little notes join, or lead, to big notes.
- The offbeat controls rhythmic nuance.
- Syncopation *leads* to the beat.

To these we will add another law:

- *There are no separate voices.*

OCTAVE TRANSPOSITION

An advantage pianists have, in terms of simplification, is the fact that on the piano identical passages occurring in different octaves—a frequent compositional device—are played with the same fingerings. This means that a pianist may seem to play lots of notes, but actually plays no new material. The opening of Beethoven's *Emperor Concerto* is an example. The same figure happens in three different octaves *(ex. 17-6a)*.

Octave variation to elongate passages is ubiquitous in all classical music, but only in the piano is the fingering and physical setup of the instrument identical in every octave. Therefore, a passage such as this one from Lizst's *Gnomenreigen* is really not as complicated as it may seem at first glance *(ex. 17-6b)*.

Or this example from the last movement of Tchaikovsky's *Piano Concerto No.1*, ex. 17-6c, which is a one-octave chromatic scale played between both hands repeated three times. This an example of "set-lift" between two hands—as one hand comes up, the other hand descends. If your mind is trained, you can play this pair with only *one* conscious "up" motion.

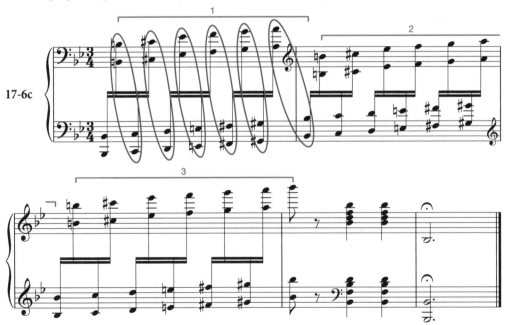

BEETHOVEN, PATTERN AND SKELETIZATION

Seeing through the obfuscation—or camouflage—of variation makes Beethoven's music much easier to play because his approach is deeply embedded in pattern. For example, here is an excerpt from his *Sonata No.9 for Violin and Piano*, the "Kreutzer." The initial motive of a pair of adjacent notes is repeated over and over throughout all three movements of the piece, ex. 17-7a-g. A look through the entire piece shows that this basic idea *is* the piece. (I am leaving out harmonic analysis.) In measure 82 the two-note pattern is repeated as filled-in octaves, E/D♯. In measure 75 it is trilled half-notes, and on and on.

Ex. 17-7b is another variation of the two notes.

Or here, ex. 17-7c, where the G♯ of the pair, A/G♯, is ornamented, and the passage is repeated three times.

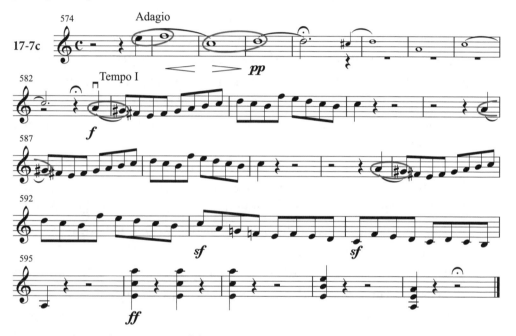

He continues this variation of the two notes into the second movement, ex. 17-7d,

which is morphed into the theme for the third movement, ex. 17-7e,

which becomes ex. 17-7f,

and ex. 17-7g.

In truth you could go on and on. He does.

This is analysis, but very different from the analysis of the classroom because this helps the actual playing of the piece. *This is an untouched field of analysis that would be very useful to performers.* Why? *Because the repetition of the motive is also the repetition of the physical movement needed to play it.* Just as a piece can be understood as the variation of motives, it is also a variation of a few physical movements and mental paradigms. It is this way of looking at music that makes it "simple" and allows the performer to enter into the realm of virtuoso playing and mastery.

This is certainly not to say that analysis of form and harmony is not useful. But it has to be tied to performance and compositional technique, which is unfortunately rarely taught to students with any depth unless they are composers. In other words, it has to be applied *practically* to have any impact on the education of musicians.

Here is another example of apparent complexity being resolved through compositional understanding. This excerpt, ex. 17-8a, is from the third movement of Vieuxtemps' *Violin Concerto No. 4,* which Heifetz flies through in a way I could never understand until I realized it is a pattern of two stepwise notes obfuscated by an upper neighbor. The piece suddenly became almost "easy."

As we can see, when simplified the melody is just stepwise motion *(ex. 17-8b).*

This idea is then reworked into a faster version *(ex. 17-8c).*

The skeletal understanding makes the passage much easier to play *(ex. 17-8d)*.

In this passage from the second movement of Prokofiev's *Violin Concerto No.1*, ex. 17-9a, G/A♭/G is really just G. I have indicated the other simplifications based on this idea.

Starting in the sixth measure after "35" of the same movement, an extremely difficult passage begins *(ex. 17-9b)*. It is really just an ornamented chromatic scale, as shown in ex. 17-9c. With this understanding as a "base" the passage is much easier to play.

However, to match the eighth-note accompaniment in the orchestra, which should be phrased over the bar line, there must be layering of thought when playing the passage—the sixteenth notes are grouped as offbeat to downbeat eighth notes, congruent with the proper phrasing of the accompanying instruments, but divided into three pairs of notes per group (*ex. 17-9d*).

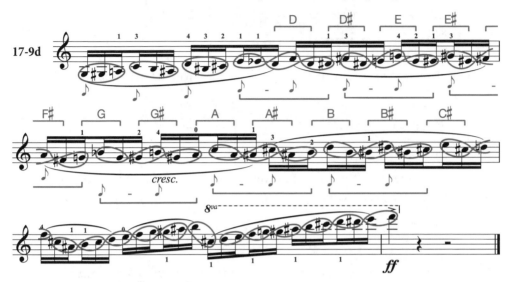

There must be congruence between the thinking—the musical approach—of the solo part and the accompanying parts.[8] Without this, interactive flow among players is impossible. A soloist must incorporate the phrasing that he wishes for the accompaniment into the *fabric* of his solo part and vice-versa—the accompanying players must integrate the nuances of the solo line into their own part. In reality, as we mentioned, there are no separate lines—each contains the others.

In example 17-10a, from the same movement, the physical motion and thinking for both hands is varied slightly in ex. 17-10b. The left and right-hand movements are identical to ex. 17-10a, except for a slight shift in the timing of the bow changes.

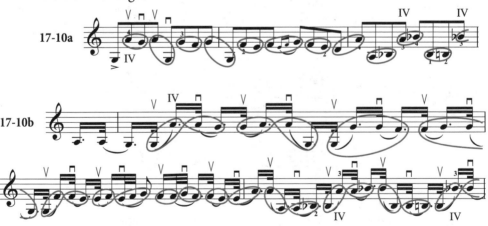

---

8   As we shall see, this does not require a conductor. An ensemble's congruence requires musical sophistication from the performers.

Something else that Milstein plays better than almost anyone else are scales, both chromatic and diatonic. I think he groups them in a simple way. In a chromatic scale, every four pairs covers a perfect fifth; every three pairs cover a perfect fourth in triplets. For example, in Paganini's *Caprice No. 5*, I think Milstein groups his notes in this way *(ex. 17-11a)*.

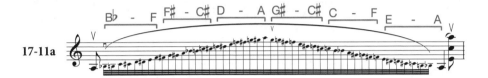

This way of thinking can be applied to the Strauss *Oboe Concerto*, also making sure that the penultimate note of the scale links over the bar line *(ex. 17-11b)*.

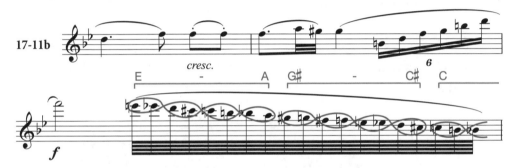

This also works in combination with "set-shifts" for glissandos, such as in this passage from Tchaikovsky's *Violin Concerto*, ex. 17-11c,

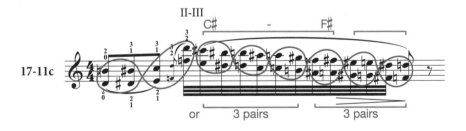

or for chromatic octaves on the piano as in another excerpt from Liszt's *Sonata in B Minor (ex. 17-11d)*.

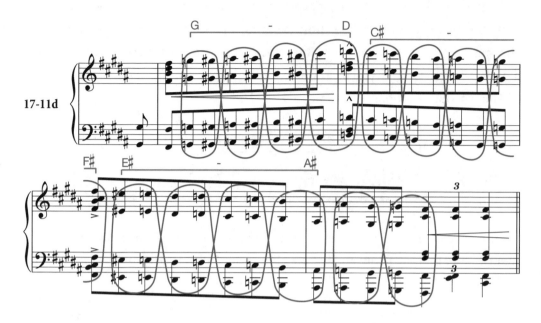

17-11d

or this famous passage from the Dvorak *Cello Concerto in B Minor (ex. 17-11e).* This is a combination of "set-shift" and grouping a chromatic scale in perfect fifths.

17-11e

For diatonic scales, every four pairs covers an octave. Here is an example from Bruch's *Concerto for Violin in G Minor,* ex. 17-12, but this would obviously work for any instrument. This a very useful way of thinking for playing long scales that span several octaves. It is easier to control the passage, to not get ahead of yourself mentally, using this grouping—octave to octave.

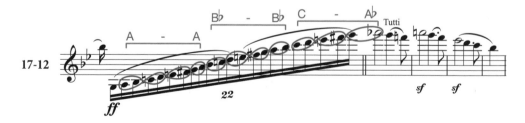

17-12

Paganini's *Caprice No. 17* is a combination of diatonic and chromatic scales *(ex. 17-13)*.

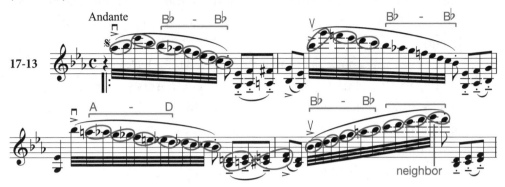

Skeletalizing neighbor notes and repeated notes can bring a freshness to performance, a way of interpreting the written page that we suggested Milstein often employed. For example, in another excerpt from Bruch's *Concerto for Violin in G Minor* the simplification suggested makes the solo part sound subtly improvised, more free *(ex. 17-14)*. These ways of thinking are not separate from technique. If the first note of the violin's entrance is a completion of the orchestral part, then in a sense the solo part starts with the ascending scale of the woodwinds, which is more interactive. The bracketed notes of measure 3 of the solo part is another helpful grouping. Thinking that the double notes of D, C, B are really just a scale in thirds is easier for the mind than grouping them the way they are written.

INTERPRETING THE MUSIC

This brings us to an interesting point. How accurate is the score, and am I not guilty of "interpreting" the music in a way that interferes with the composer's intentions?

For one thing, music of all eras was expected to be looked at creatively until the twentieth century. With the ability of composers to control suggested tempos through the metronome, some pedantic types began to believe in the "completeness" of the score, and to undervalue and misunderstand the need for an interpretation of the written music.

There is no doubt that a performer has a responsibility to accurately portray what a composer has arduously, patiently and carefully written. He is, as Stravinsky noted, the intermediary between the composer's crafted work, which is *not* an improvisation, and the judgement of the public regarding the work's merit. In this sense, the composer is at the mercy of a performer's technical skill and musical values.

Yet the page does not make a single sound on its own. The first act of "interpretation" is the *sound* of the instrument, which is a direct product of the training and mind of the performer. It is his skill that creates the timbre. Timbre *is* nuance, which in itself is too subtle to be notated. In addition, rhythm is never metronomic. An experiment with a computer reproduction of a score is enough to tell any listener that machine accuracy does not sound very good, unless you enjoy the ticking of a clock. In fact, we have demonstrated that *rhythm is phrased*. Pitch has variables and room for discretion—leading tones are an obvious example—but there is also play in intervals such as thirds, sixths, tenths, seconds, sevenths, etc. Composers and performers are in a symbiotic relationship. Here is Milstein's view:

> Stravinsky tried to create a myth of the composer who knows—exactly and definitely—how his music should be performed… Stravinsky, in my experience, didn't understand at all how his music should be played. Few composers do! Even Beethoven didn't understand how his music should be presented. Composers don't know how to make their own music sound good. That's why they need cooperation, not confrontation, with performers.[9]

What Milstein may mean is that there are fundamental truths about the nature of music itself, and the qualities *inherent* in the instruments, that are more elemental than the way the composer organizes sound on the printed

---

9   Nathan Milstein and Solomon Volkov, *From Russia to the West* (New York: Henry Holt and Co., 1990), 130.

page. These fundamental truths are not particular to one piece of music. They are a substructure, deeper than a composer's phrasing marks, perhaps implying something in the *essence* of the composed music that lies beyond a *composer's* conception of the piece's ideal interpretation.

If composers are upset with the level of players' "recreative" skill, they had better go about making certain that students are well-trained. On the other hand, nowadays, as we shall discuss in a later chapter, perhaps composers should learn how to play an instrument expertly and develop the skill, the craft, to compose music that is *coherent* to performers and audiences.

In our next chapter we shall assemble what we have learned thus far into a system of music/technique.

CHAPTER 18

Technique: A Three-Part System

Playing an instrument is a system. There are three interacting components—each a complex subsystem of its own—that must function harmoniously:

1. One's body, which must include one's mind.
2. The instrument—the violin—which forms a system with the bow.
3. The music played.

Each component has its own internal rules and relationships. To play well one must maintain the integrity of each subsystem, integrating them with one another without compromising the integrity of any component part. "Technique" is the integrated mega-system. That which does not contribute to the harmonious functioning of all three systems, or is not congruent with the ideal functioning of any individual system, cannot be considered valid technique.

THE MIND/BODY SYSTEM

Playing an instrument is a physical activity. It is physical action that must bring forth sound, and if there is physical action there must be more, or less, effective ways of performing such movement. For the body to move with coordination, the muscles must work without internal antagonism—with flow. The skill of a player is dependent on the fluidity of his physical actions. From fluidity comes power. This is especially applicable to any physical activity that requires repetitive action and precision. Precision, what musicians call "solid" technique, is only possible when the muscles of the body work in congruence with one another. Unreliability and injury are the constant byproducts of a physically incorrect approach to muscularly repetitive tasks.

The body is put into action by thought—the mind. Therefore, of primary importance to the mind/body system is the *intention* to create physical flow—the smooth connection from one movement to the next. *The way one thinks of, or about, movement affects movement itself.* Other important factors in the mind/body system include the physical strength and psychological make-up of the student/performer. The type of strength necessary for playing the violin is suppleness supported by core muscle strength—power from the inside out. Psychologically, the mind must be able to focus, have the inner freedom to trust intuition, and the insight to perceive deep pattern.

THE INSTRUMENT/BOW SYSTEM

Until it is played, an instrument is neither asleep nor awake. It may have function—as an object of art to a collector or, in the case of a piano, a decorative accent to a salon, but it does not function as an acoustical system. In the same way that the ideal functioning of one's body as a system of movement demands adherence to inviolable laws of its own structure, the violin/bow as an acoustical system also has needs—requirements—for its most efficacious functioning. These needs are satisfied, more, or less effectively, through the physical *touch* of the player.

An instrument's purpose is to create sound. The sound must be *brought forth*, a subtle and elemental truth. To bring forth sound one must draw it from within the instrument. One can do this violently, coaxingly, or many degrees in between. The spirit and touch administered circumscribes the potential. In this sense a violin functions as a live entity—it gives back what it receives. Heaviness and percussive action on the system, by either the bow or the left hand, are dampening to the flow of the vibrations in and through the violin. Therefore, one must *release* the potential for sound from the instrument, which requires, fundamentally, that the *touch* of the player spin forth the sound.

Additionally, the *quality* of an instrument and bow is an essential component to the playing system. The setup of the violin must be ideal—the string height neither too low nor high, the instrument itself capable of creating focused sound. The bow must be well-balanced and supple. It is through interaction with the violin/bow system that a student experiences the physical feeling of playing. If the system is not functioning properly, the student cannot establish a correct physical relationship to the violin, nor can he gain an understanding of the tonal possibilities of the instrument.

THE MUSIC SYSTEM

Music is a system of emotional communication that employs pitch—notes—as its medium of message. Individual notes have no commonly agreed upon meaning within a culture, unlike words, which although in essence abstract, gain specificity by general assent. For example, the word "dog" is no more an actual dog than the word "koko" could be. We just agree that it represents some entity that looks and behaves a certain way.

Musical notes have *no* meaning until the composer arranges them in such a way that their meaning becomes somewhat understandable. Music can never be specifically, digitally, understandable, and that is one of its most useful properties for an artist. It can, therefore, be structured through artifice to express that which can never be understood specifically—the nuanced emotions and feelings of our experience of living. A composer creates meaning in a musical composition primarily through the construction of pattern and by exploiting the recursive and generative properties inherent in the patterns themselves. These patterns are expressed in time—they unfold. Therefore, *two primal elements of music are pattern and pattern's unfoldment, or flow, through time.* Ergo, music flows forward in time through pattern, as does language, which Shakespeare advises us should be spoken "trippingly on the tongue."

How do these three systems—the mind/body, the instrument/bow, and the music—form a well-functioning, interactive system? This is the problem facing anyone learning to play the violin. Is there a factor that underlies and integrates all three systems?

There is—flow.

Of primary importance in the mind/body system is *physical flow, the smooth connection from one movement to the next.*

Of primary importance in the instrument/bow system is the release of sound from the instrument, which requires that *the touch of the player spin forth, release the sound through the flow of vibration within the instrument.*

Of primary importance are two elements in the music system—pattern, and pattern's unfoldment, or flow through time. *Music flows forward in time through pattern.*

To summarize: the mind/body system, through flowing physical action, interacts with a man-made acoustical system—the violin and bow, which is designed to react through flowing touch—to spin forth pitches organized by a composer's mind into recursive and generative patterns that unfold and flow forward in time to create contrived meaning. The underlying structure that binds all three systems is flow. Whatever impedes flow destroys the interaction of all three systems as a mega-system.

Therefore, it so happens that the fundamental elements necessary for the ideal functioning of each of the three systems are congruent—to produce ideal sound requires ideal bodily flow, which happens to be the same flow that moves music forward. All three systems are recursive in structure (which shall be explained in the following sections), like the Russian nesting dolls—a doll within a doll within a doll within a doll—meaning that complexity in the system is born from *simple principles* pregnant with developmental possibilities.

COMBINING THE SYSTEMS

Foundational violin technique must be a triple helix "seed" in which all three systems needed to play (the mind/body, the instrument/bow, the music) are wrapped around each other developing a single interactive structure that remains coherent for each separate element. As with the development of life, this seed—template—will form a system of interaction with itself and the environment (in this case with the student, the instrument, the music, and the teacher) that will *bring forth* the correct intuitions about how to learn, assuming the basic setting of the system is *fundamentally* correct. In other words, expertise arises from the *system* interacting correctly—a correct physical/mental foundation, a correct instrument/bow foundation, and a correct mental approach to the music. The interaction of the systems which leads to expertise awakens intuitive responses—too subtle for explanation in words—that *lead* to mastery. *Mastery cannot be taught.* However, none of these factors are entirely genetic. They are environmentally educed.

Foundational technique could be understood in another way. We can use a computer as an example. Hardware is meta-information, which is information about information. It is the template, the instructions, that allow the computer to understand *how* to understand information—content. Hardware is a higher logical type than content. The foundational violin technique that must be learned from the start is akin to hardware. It is the instructions, the muscle memory in the body and the information given the mind—an indivisible unit—that is the template on which all content (musical compositions) must be laid. If one's muscle memory, which is meta-information, is incorrect, all future development is limited because the technique required to play the violin and the music written for it are an intricately *interwoven* system.

THE MIND/BODY/INSTRUMENT/MUSICAL SYSTEM

A system is more than the sum of its parts. The information created by the interface of the subsystems cannot help but communicate something. It is not indifferent. There is interaction between this information and the student—feedback. Through the experience of feedback, a student *teaches himself*. In the mega-system of playing the violin, the teacher and the skills being taught (the comments the teacher makes, the physical demonstrations, the technical advice, the values/culture tradition that the teacher transmits) open up possibilities; these possibilities are, in turn, circumscribed by the doors of possibility the "experience" of the teaching presents to the student (what the teacher does or does not know, how thorough the developmental approach is, the psychological relationship between the student and the teacher, etc.). If the student has the correct feeling in his body when playing (guided by the knowledge of the teacher), this "experience" will teach the student about the *interconnection* between the quality of one's movement and the sound produced.

If the quality of touch is correct, the violin plays—responds—differently, in step with the changed approach of the student. This feedback from the instrument may give a student further insight about the technique of playing or even the expressive possibilities of the music, which may be seen (or never seen) *only* when the student is ready to bring them forth. This affects the mind of the student yet again, altering his understanding of music, which alters his understanding of what he is being taught by the teacher—what seemed to the student an unnecessary detail may now open his eyes to its greater significance. This interactive process can be an endless loop of learning, as long as what is being taught creates no built-in limitations. The most dangerous limitation is incorrect foundational muscle memory. Muscle memory is almost impossible to alter.

All music is based on the variation, or recursive properties of pattern, at least in the music we label classical, as is the technique required to play it. When understood in this way, technique and musical expression are seen to be an inseparable whole. This process of becoming aware of pattern within pattern in technique and in the music goes on *ad infinitum* if the channels of one's mind and body are clear. The music and the technique to play the music are born from the same seed—the variation of simple elements that are pregnant with the potential for the development of complexity through *connecting pattern*.

The repetition and modification of pattern is how a composer creates artfully contrived meaning in the equally contrived harmonic language of music. Without pattern, the sounds—the notes—would have no coherence to the mind and could easily be perceived as noise. To create meaning in music the musical material must be manipulated and expressed through the form—structure—of a composition. A piece of music is based on musical ideas called motives, which through rhythmic, tonal and dynamic variation create a unified "whole" grown from a single seed developed into a seemingly diverse structure.

This process is recursive. Within a simple basic idea, a motive, lies all the generative possibilities of the composition. A composition is, in its simplest form, tension moving to resolution. It is driven forward, unfolded by thousands of mini tension-resolutions (harmonically, rhythmically, dynamically) all giving birth to the myriad offspring of the initial idea. The instrumental technique for playing this music has the same recursive properties. *Within its fundamental structure is embedded all advanced technique. The recursive properties of the music and the technique to play it interact.* They are eventually seen to be the same. Music and the technique required to play it at a high level are an inseparable whole. Therefore, knowledge of compositional technique is an essential element of instrumental technique.

To play the violin seems very simple. One hand moves the bow across a string, the other hand stops the string with a finger, altering the string length, which changes the pitch. That is the essence. How this is done is the art. What is learned is stored as muscle memory—correct or not—and in most cases cannot be unlearned, at least not without enormous effort. Therefore, usually, the end lies in the beginning, a true case of predestination.

The technique of the violin is transmitted by the example of a teacher's playing and by the "hands-on" transfer of the physical feeling and touch involved. It, therefore, follows that a teacher must be a master player. How else can he know the subtleties of touch that constitute a correct foundation? The training is really an apprenticeship in the "secrets of the tradition," which must be within the teacher or he transfers an inferior foundational bias.

THE ESSENTIALS OF VIOLIN TECHNIQUE;
THAT WHICH MAINTAINS THE INTEGRITY OF THE THREE COMPONENT SYSTEMS—THE MIND/BODY, THE VIOLIN/BOW, AND THE MUSIC—AND MELDS THEM INTO A LARGER SYSTEM.[1]

FUNDAMENTAL BOWING TECHNIQUE

1. There are four planes of movement for the bow, one for each string.

Each string is a variation of the other (recursion) or, one could say, within the correct playing of one lies the correct playing of the others. The two middle strings, the A and D strings, are the core settings. The G and E are played in relationship to them—when playing the G string, the bow is biased to the D

---

1   The following description works equally well for playing the viola, which is simply a larger violin with different strings—A, D, G and C. Most of what follows could be applied to cello technique as well. We know that Feuermann was influenced by watching Heifetz play.

string; when playing the E string the bow is biased to the A string. This reduces the overall arc from the G string to the E string.

At an expert level of technique the bowing plane feels as if it is one plane—as if one played on a single string. The logic of this is fairly apparent—if it is a reduction of angle that makes a smooth connection from the A to the D string, for example, it is a similar negation of angle to play from the A to the E, or from the E to the G. Ultimately, if one is expert at the negation of angles between strings, it becomes apparent that there is but one plane. This perception, made real through training, is physically efficient, satisfying the need for smooth physical connection. It is also mentally efficient—conceptually it is easier to play one plane for the bow than four.

Changing strings is executed by the arm moving as a unit to change the plane of bow motion, controlled by the deltoid muscle and the base of the triceps muscle working in congruence. The basic skill for changing strings is the same for any tempo. A faster tempo requires more precision, but to the expert player all string changes require the same precision, like a surgeon with a knife—clean and precise. The violin requires, fundamentally, the same touch of the bow for all four strings, even though they require subtle differences. These differences arise out of a systemic unity—all four strings are variations of the other. *The flow of the physical allows the flow of the musical.*

2. *The right arm bends at the elbow, controlled by the muscle at the base of the triceps, the plug-in of the triceps (the soft spot just above the bone of the elbow, Figures 18-a and b).*

Fig. 18-a

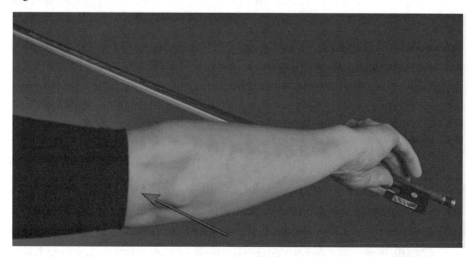

All bowing, fast or slow, is controlled by this muscle. How complicated it would be if, muscularly, every bow stroke emanated from a different starting point.

Fig. 18-b

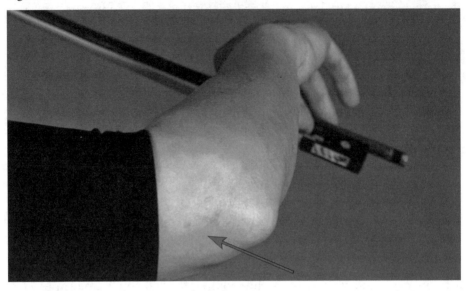

As with the instrument itself, which has four strings—each a variation of the other—so also must the movement required to play the violin be recursive in nature. As in science, ideally a theory should have a simple beauty to be considered a fundamental truth. Of course, this presumes an elemental coherence in the system of life itself. Whether true or not on a fundamental level for life, for a musical system to function properly it must have coherence.

The bow moves across the string, the forearm closing and opening, activating (spinning) the string. This is true for any tempo and for all bow combinations and strokes. Long, smooth, connected bows are the source, the seed, for all more complex bowing patterns and strokes. (All bowings, excluding staccato—which is controlled by the focused squeezing of the plug-in to the triceps—are varied combinations of up to down motion.) All fast, detaché passages are sped-up legato bows.

3. The bow moves parallel to the bridge.

A right angle, 90°, formed between the bow and the string is the angle that most effectively sets the string in motion. This is true for all four strings and allows for congruence in physical motion and congruence with the instrument's design, which places the bridge in the same relationship to all four strings, meaning the bow must do the same. The wood of the bow tilts away from the bridge at about a 45° angle.

4. Fast bowing is perfect slow bowing speeded up.

Fast passages are sped-up melodies; within correct slow playing, fast playing is born. This is an example of an inherent truth in music (connection between notes) coinciding with the most effective use of the body—the need for the body to base athletic movement on smoothly connected motion born from perfect slow motion. One need not look far to prove the truth of this assertion. Tai Chi is a martial art practiced in slow motion. Speed up the movements, and gestures that had seemed innocuous can inflict severe damage to an opponent.

When I was a student at Curtis there was a listening room in the library that had a phonograph that could play records at 16 rpm. We used to listen to 32 rpm records at 16 rpm. When played at half-speed the recordings of an artist of Jascha Heifetz's skill showed that every note he played was perfectly connected, almost glued, to the next. He sounded even more perfect when slowed down, which means that he must have learned from slow to fast—an example of perfect slow playing being "sped up." The stickiness between notes manifested in his slowed-down playing is a good demonstration of an elemental truth of the musical system: a composition is a single outpouring, an exhalation without break until the end of the piece.

5. The up-bow is active, the down-bow is passive.

The movement of the bow is a cycle from up to down. Up requires effort, down happens of its own accord and need not be accentuated. Eventually this approach creates a groove of action, but the "up" remains subtly active, the "down" a floor from which the "up" rises. An active up-bow satisfies the instrument's sound system because the "up" bias creates more flow, more spin to the string. Therefore, *the up-bow "sets" the sound*, which the down-bow maintains. The opposite, a "down" bias, *deadens* the sound because the down is already heavy—aided by gravity—and need not be doubly blessed by any conscious help.

Up-bow to down-bow cycles are in congruence with the requirements of the musical system because up-bows usually occur on offbeats. The movement of the offbeat towards the downbeat inherently propels the music forward, creating a natural *liaison* between the offbeat and the downbeat. This way of thinking about bowing, so correct physically, coincidentally, and very conveniently, phrases the music correctly as a byproduct.

6. The right arm moves at a different angle than the bow.

The tip of the *bow* is not the true tip. The true tip is the *right hand* when extended. This is difficult to perceive because, physically, the frog (the lower part of the bow), when playing at the tip of the bow, seems to be the furthest away from the body. But conceptually one should envision the extended right hand as the tip—the "outside."

When playing up to down pairs, *the right arm*, at the plug-in to the triceps, feels as if it moves from the outside, in. One will notice more readily that the *right hand* moves, from the outside, in. To simplify this, we could say that the right wrist is *pulled* into the body on an up-bow, the motion initiated by the plug-in to the triceps muscle. The down-bow returns with one-half the energy of the up-bow.

When bowing, the player should focus primarily on the *movement of the arm*, not the bow. *If focused on the right arm movement*, one will notice that when one is at the tip of the bow, the right hand/arm is extended. The right hand is the "true" tip when one is focused on the *movement of the arm* because the arm moves from the outside—where the arm is extended—to the inside, where the right hand is now close to the body *(Fig. 18-c)*.[2]

Fig. 18-c

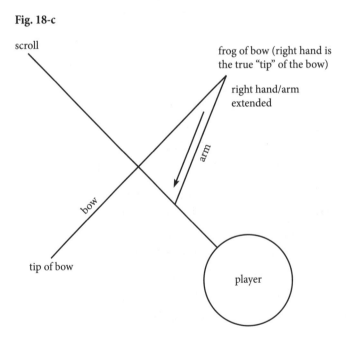

---

2 This feels, for the up-bow to down-bow pair, as if the right arm moves "inside-out," which it does. The arm moves from the *outside* of the body *into* the body for the up-bow; it moves *from* the body, *out,* on the down-bow, which is an "inside-out" movement for the pair.

The *actual* movement of the arm is not apparent because the angle at which the right hand holds the bow causes the bow to move across the strings at a 90° angle, while the arm moves towards the body on an up-bow at about a 22° angle.

With awareness of the motion of the right arm as one's primary focus, it becomes obvious that the *width* of the path of the bow is considerably different from what it appears to be if focusing on the bow itself. The path of the right arm is considerably *narrower*, and therefore the bow path is more easily controlled. This narrower path, or groove of action, makes it much easier to negate angles when crossing strings *(Fig. 18-d).*

Fig. 18-d

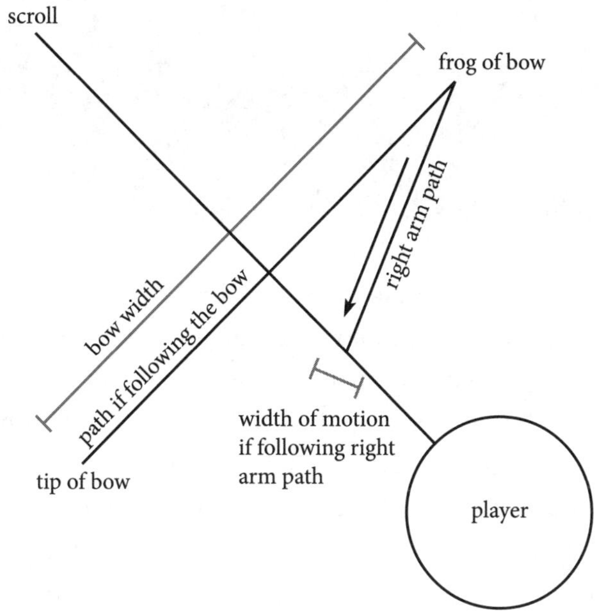

scroll

frog of bow

right arm path

bow width

path if following the bow

width of motion
if following right
arm path

tip of bow

player

7. *The right arm is held up by the deltoid muscle, with the arm hanging from the right wrist.*

Figure 18-e is our duplication of Heifetz's right arm alignment on the G string.[3]

Fig. 18-e

elbow is lower
than the wrist

The elbow must be lower than the wrist. This "dip" at the elbow makes the right arm feel very relaxed. (*All* bowing planes have this relationship of the elbow to the wrist.) Bowing forms planes of action—*the plane* of the *motion* of the right arm when performing the bowing cycle from up-bow to down-bow. This motion is very subtle, yet extremely important, because all bowing derives from the mastery of this basic flowing motion. This movement is generally described as up and down, but can also be described as the right hand being pulled *into* the body and returning *out* without any effort at all, with the weight of the arm relaxed down, the arm suspended, hanging, from the deltoid muscle and the right wrist.[4] Figure 18-f shows the correct wrist/elbow relationship at the frog.

---

3 The same angle can be viewed in *Heifetz in Performance*, DVD (RCA, 2004), at the end of his performance of Rachmaninoff's *Daisies*.

4 I would describe, or visualize this motion, as opening a drawer on the up-bow, the plug-in of the triceps initiating the wrist moving into the body, and the drawer closing "by itself," or being drawn by a magnet, on the down-bow. One could also say that the arm contracts on the up-bow and extends for the down-bow.

Fig. 18-f

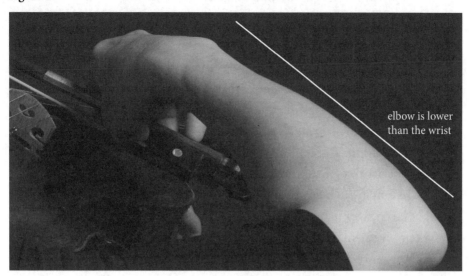

elbow is lower
than the wrist

8. *There are three ways the bow moves in up to down pairs—on the same
   string, clockwise string changes, and counterclockwise string changes.*

Counterclockwise string changes (the arc of the right hand in space) are
the most difficult—moving from a lower to a higher string on an up-bow to
down-bow cycle. Clockwise string changes (the arc of the hand in space) are
easier—moving from a higher to a lower string on an up-bow to down-bow
cycle. Counterclockwise motion occurs when moving from the G string (on
an up-bow) to a higher string, for example, the D string (on a down-bow). It is
much easier, for example, to move from the E string (on an up-bow) to the A
string (on a down-bow), which is clockwise motion for the arc of the right hand.

Skill in executing smooth string changes must be learned at slow speed and
experienced in many different situations, only gradually being attempted at
fast tempos. The *negation* of angles between strings is of crucial importance.
Eventually, at the highest level of skill, as mentioned above, the bow seems to
move in a single plane, and has these three variances within the overall back
and forth motion.[5] One must be trained to be aware of these string changing
distinctions to circumvent the difficulties often encountered in a musical
composition. Changes of bowing (whether notes begin on an up or a down-
bow, thereby eliminating counterclockwise motion, for example) and fingering
choices can alleviate inherently awkward passages in a composition.

---

5 The arc of the right hand in space, whether clockwise or counterclockwise, is what is seen by an
  observer. The player *should not consciously* move his hand in clockwise or counterclockwise motion.
  To the player, the bow must seem to move on a *single plane* from up-bow to down-bow. It is the
  attention to the *movement of the arm* when bowing that makes this achievable. The *start of the up-
  bow*, which is understood as the right arm as a whole, "sets" the angle for the bowing pair.

9. *All bow strokes are slight modifications of legato bowing.*

Seemingly different bow strokes are actually embedded, implicit possibilities within perfect legato, offspring brought to life by a slight change of the weight of the arm, a slight pressure from the index finger, more arm weight for chords, etc. As in any athletic endeavor, flow is an essential foundation to all movement. All articulation is derived from smooth underlying connection. *This must be true if music is a single exhalation.* Articulation is an ornament, icing on the cake, of connection. To play any spiccato stroke (off the string) is a matter of lessening the arm weight and adjusting the tilt of the bow by raising the wrist slightly. To employ firmer articulation one must focus the arm weight, often through the engagement of the index finger, as is the case for a martelé stroke. The basic movement of the bow remains the same. It could more correctly be said that there are no bow strokes, just subtle shadings of legato, using more or less bow, more or less weight.

10. *The index finger of the right hand must move "with the hand" on the down-bow.*

If the index finger moves in an opposite direction from the down motion of the bow and hand, an antagonistic relationship will develop between the flow of the down-bow and the "stuckness" of the index finger. This is often a source of constriction in the flow of the down-bow and should be carefully watched. The finger should move *with* the bow, which also creates a desired *passive* "pull" on the down-bow. The right wrist must be *very slightly* pronated by *subtly* turning the hand and wrist to allow adequate weight and contact of the index finger with the bow.

11. *The bow must be placed between the fingerboard and the bridge at a point on the string that creates a core sound.*

Core sound is a quality of sound that is full, round and focused. It is created most easily on up-bows (in tandem with a correct cushion on the tip of the left fingers when contacting the string, which we will presently describe), at a point between the fingerboard and bridge. This point is found quite naturally when the up-bow is used as the "set" of the sound. The production of core sound is the basis of the correct physical feeling for playing and a good example of the interrelatedness of all aspects of technique. The act of producing a core sound sets the string to a certain tension, that, as a consequence, develops the muscles of the left hand and right hand properly, and even evolves the sound of the violin itself. An instrument will improve its playing qualities if played correctly. An unskilled player will diminish the instrument's tonal quality, and not just when he is playing it, but for all who follow.[6]

Core sound heightens the response of the instrument, focuses it. As the instrument's response increases in subtlety, the physical effort required to bring the instrument to its potential brings the player's muscular efficiency to a heightened level. In this state there is the possibility of physical, instrumental, and musical nuance—artistry.

These meta-techniques must be learned at slow speed, gradually, without antagonistic muscle use. They must be continually practiced slowly and consciously in application to the content of different pieces of music. A student learns these techniques and this way of thinking in the simplest possible forms, only gradually adding complexity while maintaining the intrinsic technical and mental approach. It is for this purpose that etudes were written, as well as pieces specifically written for students.

FUNDAMENTAL LEFT-HAND TECHNIQUE

1. *The "set" of the fingers and hand is based on the two middle strings, the D and A (as is the "set" of the bow).*

The angle of the finger on the string is essentially the same for each string, the G and the E being set in relationship to the D and the A strings. There is almost no movement of the left arm when the fingers move from string to string within the same position.

When fingers are placed on the string, the tension of the string changes. This affects the bowing, again showing the systemic nature of technique. The coordinating complexities are enormous and the process of joining fingers with the bowing and producing good sound cannot be hurried or complicated by introducing too many different factors simultaneously.

For this reason a beginner must first become adept at playing open strings. This may take a couple of months. A teacher such as Leopold Auer devotes an entire method book to various etudes and simple accompanied pieces designed to develop enough bowing skill so that the use of the fingers of the left hand will not disrupt the functioning of the right. It may take a few months before a student uses all four fingers in the first position because each finger must be somewhat "set" before another can be introduced.

---

6 The hysteresis of resonance patterns suggested by Chladni figures.

2. *The placement of the fingers on the string is an essential component in producing core sound.*

There must be a cushion on the tip of the fingers so that the flesh envelops the string. This not only affects the hand's agility, but greatly affects tone and intonation. In conjunction with proper bow technique, this placement of the fingers produces a round sound. This cushion is created by a subtle pulling back of the fingertip when it is placed on the string. The finger must rest firmly, yet not forcefully on the string. Development of this skill must also be carefully watched and trained *(Fig. 18-g)*.

Fig. 18-g

Everyone must play the instrument with their fingers and a bow; human hands are essentially the same. Yet the way the instrument is touched will reveal a master's hand or an amateur's, and these differences can be discerned by playing a single note. It is the quality of the *touch* upon it to which the violin responds. It is the touch that creates the tone, which is the foundational expression of the music.

Fig. 18-h

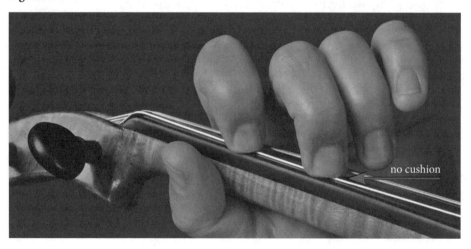

3. The action of the fingers must be, like the bow, smooth and connected—
legato.

As with the bow, so with the fingers. Smooth connection is a physical and musical necessity for both musical and physical flow. Any percussive action of the left hand on the strings is not only potentially damaging to the hand, but will also disrupt the bow from its track of movement, its groove so to speak. Percussive action also breaks musical flow. *Expert left-hand technique eliminates conscious down motion of the fingers.* The fingers feel as if they have always been down and are released or peeled off the string, lifted up. In the same way the bow motion of passive down-bows is the "floor" from which the up-bows rise: the fingerboard is the "floor" from which the fingers rise. When all four fingers have been introduced it becomes possible to move on to an essential element of left hand technique—the hand forms a frame.

4. The left hand forms the frame of a perfect fourth between the first and
fourth fingers.

The hand is balanced from the fourth finger. The hand can be divided into three parts. The second, third and fourth fingers form a unit, as does the first finger and, separately, the thumb. In other words, the hand is balanced from the outside to the inside. This is true *regardless of the finger pattern being played in the music* and is also similar to the bow motion, which also moves from the outside, in.

The proper setting and forming of the left-hand structure necessary for playing takes a long time to develop, evolving for the first few years of playing. This development must be carefully watched and guided. The proper balance of the hand is not only necessary for the efficient movement of the fingers, but adds strength to the fingers, which on their own have little and can only be brought to effective use in proper relationship to the hand and arm as a whole.

The fingers of the left hand must be able to move in a few different ways. They must move up and down (on and off the string), they must be able to slide up and down the string, and they must be able to move laterally across the strings. These movements must be done while maintaining the correct frame and balance—a counterclockwise rotation at the base of the fingers[7]—which makes it possible to play on several strings at once, while keeping the intrinsic relationship of the fingers to each other. Why is this crucial? Because the violin has no marks for individual notes, they can be found only in relationship to each other, like crossing a stream one rock at a time.

---

7 The fingers feel turned "out."

The correct development of the left hand is crucial to all advancement. A proper frame is an egg of latent possibilities. This setting is transfered throughout the violin, shifted up and down the fingerboard into areas called positions, all of which could be looked upon as variations of the first position. In other words, first position contains all the others. It is the seed for every position, an example of recursion. The principles of sound production are not different in higher positions, nor does the intrinsic problem of finding the notes change. As one goes into higher positions, one could say that the violin seems to shrink, meaning it "plays" the same, only feels smaller.

5. The fingers of the left hand are played in groups, rarely one at a time.

This not only strengthens the individual fingers, but preserves the frame of the hand. In general (there are exceptions), the number of the finger used requires the same number to be used. Thus, the first finger is supported through the frame of the hand; the second is supported by the first finger, placed on the same string on a note of the key being played; the third is supported by the first and second; the fourth by the first, second, and third.

Placing several fingers down simultaneously has another beneficial effect— it aids the violin/bow system by eliminating percussive finger action on the string. If a finger is already down when it is sounded, the connection from one note to another is smoother, more legato. Playing fingers in groups is also efficient from a muscular perspective—it satisfies the athletic requirement that all unnecessary motion be eliminated.

Embedded within this basic technique (another example of recursion and a crucially important aspect of technique) is the possibility of using the same basic hand-set to move fingers to other strings simultaneously. This creates double-stops. On a single string, an interval of a second becomes, on two adjacent strings, a sixth or a fourth. An interval of a third on one string is a third or a seventh on adjacent strings, or an interval of a fourth on one string can become an octave or a second. A single finger on two strings produces a fifth. Without a solid frame—a properly developed left hand—the playing of double-stops is impossibly difficult. It is only double-stop practice that can develop the frame to a virtuoso level, another example of the systemic inviolability of technique.

At an advanced level, the frame of the hand is set by two double-stop perfect intervals—an octave between the first and fourth fingers and a perfect fourth between the first and second fingers, the second and third fingers, and the third and fourth. These two intervals balance the hand in two directions.

One direction is the fourth finger on a higher string than the first, the other the fourth finger on a lower string than the first. In the hand position biased to the fourth finger on a higher string, the double-stop intervals are octaves, and sixths within the frame; when the hand is biased to the fourth finger on a lower string than the first, the double-stop intervals are thirds and fourths. When the hand is set to play both an octave *and* perfect fourths between the third and fourth fingers, the second and third fingers, and the first and second fingers, the bias creates a hand "set" that can play all double-stop intervals with the greatest accuracy and ease. This subtle "set" is very helpful because there are "hidden" perfect fourths in sixths—when moving from sixths with the first and second fingers to sixths with the third and fourth; there are "hidden" perfect fourths in all thirds. Likewise, there are "hidden" perfect fourths in all single-note scales and arpeggios across adjacent strings.

6. *The base of the fingers (where the fingers join the hand) of the left hand must be turned subtly to the right (a counterclockwise rotation at the base of the fingers) from the player's point of view (Fig. 18-i).*

Fig. 18-i

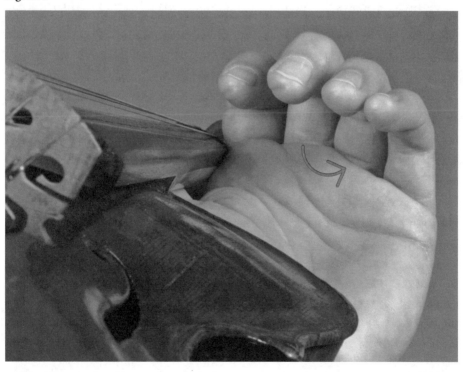

In other words, the left hand must feel open. This allows the fingers to move more freely. Visually, because of the unusual position of the left hand, which must be turned to the left from the player's point of view, the fingers of the left hand will seem to cross the player's hand. The reality is that the *base* of the fingers should turn so that they *open* the hand. This is, again, a subtle matter, a feeling achieved physically through *visualization* and *subtle* motion of the hand and fingers.

This is what is meant by balancing the hand to the fourth finger (the fifth finger in Horowitz's description). In this position the first, second and third fingers will feel or seem (*a visualization*) as if they are to the left and in front of, the fourth from the player's point of view. It is a mental and physical construct of a subtle nature, but creates powerful results in terms of left-hand ease. The fourth finger will be relaxed and not stretched.

Fig. 18-j

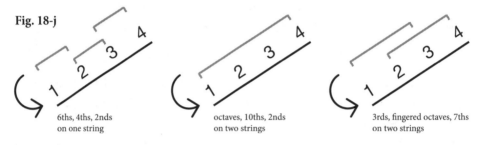

6ths, 4ths, 2nds   octaves, 10ths, 2nds   3rds, fingered octaves, 7ths
on one string   on two strings   on two strings

Figure 18-j shows the mental abstraction, or visualization of the left hand balanced to the fourth finger, or open feeling, when playing double-stops—sixths, octaves and tenths, thirds and fingered octaves. This balance, or perception, is true for *all* left-hand configurations. *The hand will not look this way,* but must feel this way for several other useful congruences to come into play. In other words, the fingers, *no matter what configuration when playing a group of notes,* should feel as if they align to this abstraction. Thus, it is again evident that *mental paradigms influence physical motion* in extremely subtle, yet important, ways.[8]

Therefore, when the left hand plays this chord, ex. 18-1a, which can be played throughout the violin, the fourth finger will *feel* as if it is behind and to right of the third finger—from the player's point of view; the third finger will *seem* to be behind and to the right of the second finger; the second will *seem* to be

---

8   These are visualizations, abstractions, which means there is "play" in the description. We are describing mental and physical processes that cannot be described in every detail with precision, and never could be. For example, one may tell someone to be aware of their breathing. But how aware can one ever be? We can notice that we breathe and to some extent understand subtleties of this process, but we will never be able to access how the cells are affected, what is happening in the lungs with precision, etc. It is for this reason that visualizations are important in accessing processes that will to some extent remain hidden from our conscious awareness. Yet, visualization, (how we think) can directly affect those deep structures.

behind and to the right of the first. This will be true *even if all the fingers play on the same string.*

18-1a

When playing this chord, ex. 18-1b, throughout the fingerboard the left hand should align in the same way.[9] This means that the manner in which the fingers of the left hand set themselves, or "reach," when playing fourths, thirds and seconds as double-stops must keep the fingers turned out (counterclockwise rotation at the base of the fingers) by *not* turning the hand and fingers "in" (which would be a clockwise rotation at the base of the fingers) to reach these double-stops.

18-1b

When this is done the mind will "see" the fingers align *in the same way* for ex. 18-1a as for the chord in ex. 18-1b—the fourth finger will *seem* to be *behind* and to *the right* of the third—from the player's view, etc.[10]

Figures 18-k and 18-l show the conventional understanding of finger alignment, which will create the feeling of the fingers crossing the hand. This will make the hand feel closed, as if it turns inward, and is the effect created when balancing the hand to the first finger. (The first, second and third fingers will feel as if they are behind the fourth.) In this position the fingers feel as if they stretch. *This must be avoided.* Additionally, in this muscular bias, the movement of the left arm will be turned ever so slightly more to the left from the player's point of view. This puts a slight strain on the arm and gives a different sense of the motion of shifting—more strained, less ease.

---

9   This is a sort of violin koan. If ex. 18-1b can seem to feel the same as ex. 18-1a, that is the essence of the matter. The feeling of the "balanced outward" hand position would also be the balance of the hand for playing every musical example for the violin that is used in this book.

10 The proximal phalanges of the fingers are turned at the base.

Fig. 18-k

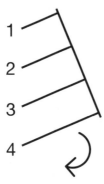

Fig. 18-l

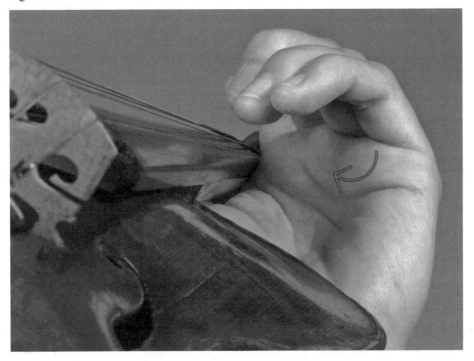

7. *When balanced to the fourth finger, which opens the hand, the fingers of the left hand form an imaginary line with the line of the right arm when bowing.*

If the fingers can play off this line—which is *an abstraction*—the action of the left hand's fingers and the motion of the left arm when shifting, which moves along this line, act in congruence with the motion of the right arm. This alignment affects shifting and makes it apparent that the motion of the left arm, when shifting throughout the violin, is *parallel* to the motion of the right arm when bowing (*Fig. 18-m*).

Fig. 18-m

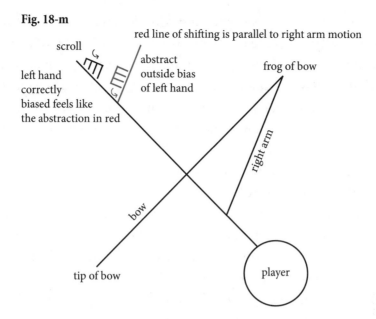

Normally players place their attention to the *left hand* moving up and down the fingerboard *parallel* with the strings, and their attention to the *movement of the bow across* the strings. This means that the motion of the left arm/hand and the bow motion across the strings are perceived to move *perpendicular* to one another. This creates *tension*, Fig. 18-n, and reminds us of something Heifetz said that we quoted in Chapter 16.

> When the arm and the bow oppose each other, it then is an awkward pull and you find yourself struggling.[11]

Fig. 18-n

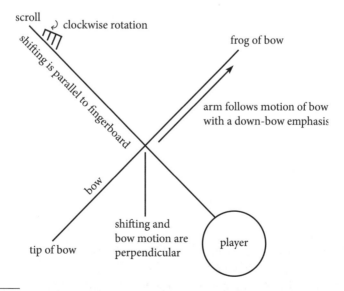

---

11 Samuel Applebaum, *The Way They Play*, Book 1 (New Jersey: Paganiniana, 1972), 78.

When one is focused on the *movement* of the left and right *arms,* a different physical reality presents itself to the player. If the left hand is aligned to the open hand position we have described, the movement of both arms will be seen to be *parallel* with one another. This is a *subtle* matter, as we mentioned. At first glance, the left hand may seem to move parallel to the strings, which creates a 90° angle to the bow motion, but the left *arm actually* moves at the same angle across the strings as the right arm when bowing, even though the left hand moves up and down the fingerboard.

The width of the path of the bow, or line of action for the right arm movement *is very narrow,* as we have shown in Fig. 18-d, making the elimination of bowing angles when crossing strings quite simple, which makes bowing much easier. This helps make the right arm path become one plane, which then *aligns with the line* for left-finger action and shifting. The awareness of this congruence between the arms makes playing *much* easier physically for both arms,[12] creating great facility in shifting throughout the fingerboard and ease in bowing, and is essential in achieving virtuoso technique of the highest order. At this level of awareness, there is no up and down shifting.[13] One moves from one point on the abstract line, formed by the bias of the left hand, to another point on this line.[14] The line is the *actual* motion of the arm when shifting in alignment to this bias. A sort of technical wizardry may then become possible *(Figures 18-o and 18-p).*

---

12 My guess is that this congruence of left and right arm motion, as well as the balancing of the hand, is applicable to cello technique as well.

13 The feeling of up and down shifting is a result of the left hand/arm's movements when shifting being aligned to the direction of the strings.

14 The distances when shifting seem much smaller because the shifting motion of the left arm is more streamlined.

Fig. 18-o

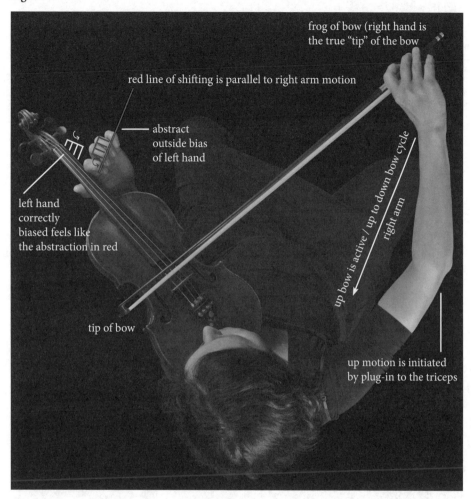

Fig. 18-p

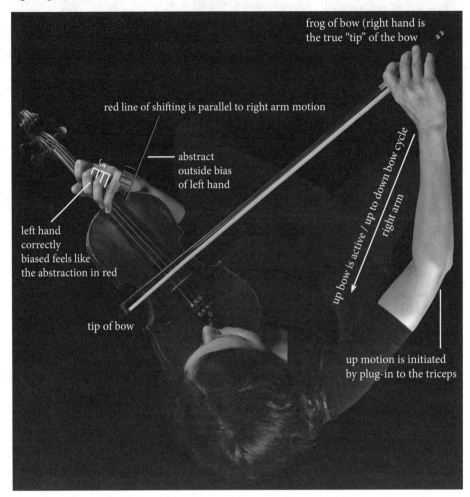

frog of bow (right hand is the true "tip" of the bow

red line of shifting is parallel to right arm motion

abstract outside bias of left hand

up bow is active / up to down bow cycle

right arm

left hand correctly biased feels like the abstraction in red

tip of bow

up motion is initiated by plug-in to the triceps

8. *When changing strings with the bow, if a finger is to be played, it must be set on the new string before the bow is moved.*

This forms a double-stop. This is true for both melodic and virtuoso passages.

9. *Vibrato is an ornament to a core sound.*

Vibrato is not the basis of sound, it is an enhancement of core sound. If the basic sound is well-rounded and focused, it takes very little motion to make a note "vibrate." Vibrato is an oscillation of pitch, from under the pitch *to* the pitch. The motion is actively up, passively down, as with the bow. Vibrato motion is *set* to up-bows *because up-bows "set" the sound*. This "up" vibrato motion must stay "up" on down-bows, which has the effect of concentrating the sound and, helpfully, acting as a brake on the down bow (which should be passive), another example of the congruence of correct physical motion with inherent properties of the violin. Because it is physically easier to vibrate on up-bows, *"up-bow with vibrato" sets the sound.*[15] This also, naturally, places the contact point of the bow nearer to the bridge without effort, an important factor in producing an unforced core sound. (Another example of the ideal for the violin/bow system being congruent with the ideal for the mind/body system.) When vibrating, the hand and fingers must remain balanced to the open hand position.

10. The fingerboard is divided into three areas.

It is easier to imagine the fingerboard divided into three areas—lower, middle and higher. The middle is neutral. The first position is set in relationship to the fifth position, which is the center of the fingerboard. The player plays from fifth position down to first position and from fifth position up to higher positions.

11. When playing in offbeat to downbeat pairs, there are only four ways to play a pair of notes with one motion.

As we have discussed, instead of thousands of possibilities for playing notes, playing in pairs means that no matter how complex the piece, all left-hand motion can be explained by four movements—set-drop, set-lift, two-for-nothing and set-shift.

Ultimately, expert violin technique is a matter of the mind/body finding the correct physical *angles* to allow the system to function efficiently. The player's neck must be in a certain relationship to the shoulders, the shoulders to the arms, the violin to the floor, the fingers to the string, the bow to the violin. The room for variance is very slight, which is why the posture of great masters such as Jascha Heifetz, Nathan Milstein and David Oistrakh is so perfect. *Without aligning in this way, the system would not work.*

DEVELOPING SKILL

One gains skill by perfecting technical "hardware" and applying it to new situations. A student, therefore, learns how to learn. Feedback from the application of the basic hardware to new situations refines and perfects the basic template. This allows the student to concentrate on finer and finer points of execution. The recursive nature of an individual composition—the variation of the same motive, its development and unfolding—means that the physical

15 The vibrato can be visualized as moving "up" to the abstract line (mentioned in section 7, above) that the left hand and arm move with, the line that is parallel to the right arm's movement. This allows the player to focus the vibrato. But the subtlety of vibrato is complex. The appendix discusses Heifetz's method of vibrating in detail.

motion to play the motive is repeated in varied form, although this is not immediately apparent unless one is aware of technique on the subtlest level. Without thorough training in foundational technique, these elemental physical patterns—which are embedded in the music itself and are a key factor in the acquisition of virtuoso technique—remain unnoticed, hidden from the player.

To develop the meta-techniques we have discussed, students must practice scales, double-stop scales and arpeggios. Scale practice trains a student how to move from note to note sequentially with smoothness, reinforces where the notes are in relationship to one another, and forms and develops the correctly balanced left-hand structure (playing to the abstract left-hand line) necessary for playing pieces. As part of this system of training, the great violin virtuosi of Europe wrote etudes to develop and incrementally reinforce basic skills—meta-technique—and to concentrate on one aspect of technique for several pages at a time in varied form. Pieces demand the use of several variations of meta-technique at once and, perhaps, for only a measure or two. If pieces are learned without the support of scales and etudes, a student cannot develop the "hardware" to play the compositions properly. For 250 years, etudes and scales have been used successfully to train expert violinists in Europe and Russia.

As is obvious from what has been described, the recursive nature of the technique means that expertise is the offspring of very few seeds. For the technique of the left hand, the "seed" is the *frame* of the hand, which includes the balance of the hand. For the bow, the "seed" is *pairs* of legato bows. The more perfect the seed, the more perfect its derivatives.

How does this work as a system in practical application? As a result of training and compositional knowledge, a student learns to see *essential, fundamental* musical patterns in a particular composition. These musical patterns must be made manifest through physical motion. Since the musical composition is based on pattern, the bodily movements to play the piece are based on pattern. Additionally, there happen to be patterns fundamental to playing the instrument that are congruent with the patterns of music itself, beyond any unique composition.

Bowing is physically efficient when thought of as up to down pairs. Up to down is a cycle. This physical efficiency does not change at faster speeds or with more complex combinations—mixed bow strokes. The body works best when "up" is active and "down" is passive.

It so happens that the instrument reacts best to this understanding of bow motion. The sound is meant to be released. Any pushing or percussive action on the string by the bow or fingers of the left hand will reduce the spin, the flow, of the vibration of the string. Therefore, *the most efficient physical method of bowing and of left-hand motion happens to be the most correct, given the nature of the instrument/bow system.*

This way of bowing makes it easier to produce core sound, which brings the instrument to its full sonic potential. Core sound also brings the body to its maximum physical effectiveness. In this state, both the instrument and the body are finely tuned for maximum power and subtlety of expression, which are dependent upon *subtlety* of physical motion.

The sound of the violin is most easily released when initiated by the up-bow with the down-bow acting as a momentary break in an up-bow feeling. Correct vibrato motion focuses the sound and, helpfully, acts as a brake on the downward motion of the bow. The release of sound from the instrument at slower speeds is the same when playing faster—the bow motion is still up to down pairs. But it also so happens that an active up-bow leads the music forward to the downbeat, in congruence with the need of the music system to unfold forward in time.

This has a further musical effect. The active up-bow to passive down-bow affects the phrasing. Down-bows usually occur on downbeats. To emphasize a point of arrival with a heavy down-bow would be a double accent, breaking phrases into bar lines and destroying the musical line, which by nature must unfold forward over the bar-line.

This forward horizontal motion is also congruent with the requirements for flow in physical motion because the horizontal unfolding of the physical action of the music is functionally easier for the body than downward emphasis, which leads to antagonistic muscle use and bad posture. A "down" emphasis on downbeats leads to a break in the flow of the body's motion, which is most efficient if the motion is not broken by downward emphasis that, coincidentally, preserves the musical line.

When a player has "worked out" a piece, we can simplify everything to:

1. The bow moves on a single plane of grooved up to down cycles (if the angles are negated), moving with different speeds, weight and distance, depending on the context.

2. The left hand plays in pairs of notes (there are only four), maintaining an outward turning of the fingers at the base, creating a particular balance of the left hand that maintains this feeling *no matter what finger combination is being played.* The fingers play off the abstract line formed by the left-hand bias; the left arm shifts with this line, which is parallel to the *actual*

movement of the right arm when bowing (creating a "gluey" left hand/ finger relationship to the string and bow, which helps form the groove, the one-plane possibilities for the right arm). The vibrato moves up to this abstract line.

3. Playing is *constrained* by musical values.

What *emerges* from this system of technique is *synchronicity*—deeply coordinated potentiality for doing. The offbeat to downbeat nature of music, which is really a *wave* of movement, is in sync with the *physical* realization of the music. The natural pairing of the notes is in sync with the four ways for the left hand to play the pairs. This is in sync with the pairing of the up-bow to down-bow, which is the cycle for all bowing. The fact that both arms actually move in parallel motion and in cycles of "up to down" means that the entire system *synchronizes* mentally and physically to the *wave* of offbeat to downbeat, the baseline movement of music in time that, very likely, aligns to the way our brains function, which is in waves.

It is the limitations, the inherent bias, of these "values" of sound and the *constraints* of "culture" in the performance of this music that creates *depth* of approach and *detail* of execution. These are melded with inherent truths of the nature of music. If it were not for the *limitations and constrictions* of what constitutes "quality," combined with an accurate understanding of the truths within each subsystem of "technique," one could never arrive at the genius level of playing evidenced by the subjects of our study. The "limitations," guidelines, upon "quality," force one to go deeper into what is possible. The incorporation of these "limitations" with the *objective* truth for the effective functioning of the subsystems, allows the mind to go to ever deeper layers *unimpeded*.

It is our "forgetting" of the "values" of this European cultural creation that has opened a wide door of "valid" participation, wide enough that performers cannot go deep inside the music itself and have lost their way by having too much freedom *from* musical "values." If playing in metronomic rhythm, somewhat in tune with a wide vibrato that approximates intonation, unrefined sound, and solving musical problems with "literally" obeying a score is good enough, we will see that good enough always gets a little easier.

CHAPTER 19

Religion

To understand how great players thought about playing I had to learn about thinking itself. For the moment we will take a side journey in our story and venture into my revisitation with religion. Religion is a natural corollary to philosophy and psychology. Years ago I discarded any interest in organized religion, which seemed to me robotic and cowardly, although to gain insight into the workings of my mind I studied religious, philosophical and psychological topics for hour upon hour. Russian literature, in particular, often combined all three subjects and I read stories by Tolstoy, Dostoevsky and Chekhov with enthusiasm. Yet I continually bogged down in *The Brothers Karamazov*—the insanity of the characters could never hold my interest. I made several tries at it, four or five, never getting much beyond Father Zossima's teachings. But I read the chapter on the Grand Inquisitor many more times than that and it was the ironic flavor of Ivan's tale, with which I was naturally in accordance, about the "necessity" of the Catholic Church's reorganization of the teachings of Jesus that attracted my interest.

My research eventually expanded beyond the boundaries of my living room. In Cambridge there was a monastery where, aside from the singing of Gregorian chants by the monks during mass every morning and every afternoon at five o'clock, continual silence was observed. The monastery was built of stone and surrounded by a high, ivy-covered wall that enclosed a garden of sycamore and elm trees with pebbled pathways leading to a chapel. Sitting on the aged wooden benches hidden beneath the drooping elms, or walking in the garden and throughout the seemingly ancient buildings, I could easily imagine I had been transported to sixteenth century Florence. The public was invited to visit overnight, and I often spent silent weekends with the monks in the middle of Cambridge, yet centuries displaced.

There is a romance to religion, particularly in association with incense, Gregorian chant and buildings from the sixteenth century that has great appeal to me. I always thought that it would be an easy escape from everything if I could only believe or experience anything mystical. Alone in the chapel of the monastery in the middle of the night, sitting on the cold stone floor with the scent of incense lingering in the air, I would try to be still enough to, perchance, have a vision of something extraordinary. I had grown up with stories of miracles from my days in Catholic school. We read books about saints, and in class watched religious movies filled with healings and visions, so in some way I still carried the hope that I might have missed something. My favorite religious movie was the *Song of Bernadette*, a story about a peasant girl who had frequently "beheld" the Virgin Mary at a spring in Lourdes. My favorite relatives were my Irish grandmother's brother, who was a priest, and her first cousin, Edward, who was also a priest and had been a missionary in Africa. So when events brought me back for a second look at religion I was not entirely disinterested and decided to revisit my childhood teachings to see if there might be any truth to the whole business.

There comes a time in everyone's life when you would like to be able to believe that God cared about you, or would give a hint that He even existed. That time came for me after a disappointing love affair when I was thirty-five. I loved her and she could never make up her mind between her past boyfriend, who unfortunately never seemed to be past, and me. She was always going from one of us to the other in confusion and guilt, until I suppose she couldn't stand it anymore and left us both, and town, for what seemed to be an endless tour of the country with a Broadway show. She was gone for three years.

My passion for her had been intensified by the competitive instincts her lack of preference for me had spawned. To my mind I was clearly superior to her ex-boyfriend, who was some pathetic doormat who refused to let her go. Constantly missing her, not being able to live without her, he was lonely and depressed and his moanings and groanings were so frequent and loud that even I felt sorry for him. My addiction to her was expressed with a different set of arguments, rhetoric and behavior. I was possessive and jealous and mad as hell. It never occurred to my simple, naive mind that she was expressing her preference, which was for neither one of us. This outcome was a devastating disappointment for my movie-filled mind. True love was supposed to work out forever, although I did notice that in the movies the film always ends before people get married.

I couldn't go beyond the idea that it wasn't supposed to be like this. Maybe she would change. Yet even though I kept in contact with her for several years, always hoping that things would work out, they never did. I had other girlfriends, but was always ready to return to her. It wasn't that she was beautiful, although she was. She wasn't that smart, but she was clever and quite amusing. But, bottom-line, what kept me hooked was that I couldn't have her, I couldn't control her, and that was the source of my passion—pure ego. And fortunately for me—in terms of the school of life truism—she stayed in my life on and off for seven or eight years, until I gradually realized that I couldn't control her, and that romantic preference, passion, is by its nature uncontrollable. I was chasing a rainbow. The closer I got to catching her, the faster she disappeared.

Anyway, at first I didn't understand all that and I just tried to make the world safe by finding a group of people who seemed dedicated to being nice and predictable. Plus, my mind was now focused on a beautiful cellist whom I had just met and was trying to get to know. She was a member of a notoriously cultish church in Boston called the Church of Christ. She was so gorgeous, she could have been a member of the Church of Satan and I would have happily joined.

Let's be clear. I knew it was a cult, but I was curious and willing to explore. I suppose I could have tried traveling, but this was much less expensive and just as exotic in its own way. The first thing I noticed was how enthusiastic and friendly everyone seemed. Of course, my cellist was there, but so were lots of other good-looking women. And they were all friendly. I was invited to Bible study groups. Being Catholic, I never had to read the Bible in any serious way, so I reasoned that this was not a waste of time. I asked lots of questions (to which there were stock replies), but I wasn't too interested in proving them wrong since I hoped they were correct. I enjoyed the conversations and was looking for a distraction from myself anyway.

The members of the Church all lived with one another and socialized exclusively with Church members or potential prospects. They all had confessors to whom they were supposed to "open their hearts." These confessors, who were in that position because they had been members longer, confessed the confessions to higher-up leaders who, therefore, were able to keep track of whatever sins Satan was pitching to the flock.

I remember one time in particular when Satan had been busy. We were summoned to a hastily called meeting of the quadrant of the church I belonged to, the "arts" sector. The room was filled with about 150 people waiting expectantly, not knowing what was going on that was so serious. Rumors flew around the room about a possible double sin, and then out onto a stage walked the lead minister of the church with two people, a girl and a guy. The minister began:

"We have a situation that requires Judy and Daniel to get their hearts right with us and God. They have shown their trust in Jesus by coming forward and voluntarily telling us about their transgression. We think they should explain it to you to protect you from falling into the same weakness that Satan is always waiting to exploit. Sister, will you begin, and tell everyone what happened?"

The woman, Judy, who was about twenty-five years old, stood up and began to speak:

"Daniel and I were baby-sitting, and fell into sin. We should have called someone. It was a dangerous situation because we were alone and the baby was asleep. We got carried away and we did it. We had sex. I'm so sorry and ashamed. Even though we're getting married in two months, that's no excuse. We could have kept this to ourselves, but our hearts were heavy and we knew we had to come forward."

Daniel, who must have been close to thirty, stood up and expressed his shame and desire to cleanse his heart and confess to us his fall from grace. It was all so embarrassing. But everyone started nodding in agreement, and then the minister made us all pray together. His directive was obeyed so readily and with such a oneness of mind that I thought I had been transported to Santa Mira, California to a town meeting of the Pod people. They had done the right thing. God and Jesus were very pleased.

In fact, openness was a highly valued gift of grace, we were told, and one that they all practiced on each other to keep everyone on the right path, at least the path that would build the church and keep everyone donating money, called tithing, to the leadership.

The leadership lived pretty well. They were always traveling around the country starting other churches, and living significantly better than the five thousand members. We even heard that they travelled by limousine in other cities. But they were leaders, after all, so God put them there and he was giving them the money, so what's the problem? I guess there must have been some problem, because soon tithing was no longer voluntary—members were required to submit their tax returns to the leaders, and ten percent was taken off the top.

I had never lived with any members. In fact, I lived alone, which always concerned them because it was easy to be weak with sin. And I must confess, I was awfully weak with sin, at least before I realized it was sin. It was a sin to read books on psychology because, after all, the Bible has all the knowledge you need and such extracurricular reading showed a lack of faith. For that reason, supplemental reading of any kind was greatly discouraged, as was having non-church-member friends. They would certainly lead you astray. I also had a non-church-member girlfriend. That really upset them.

The problem with the girls in the church, as I soon found out, was that a date was considered an entree to marriage, three dates was called going steady, and before you knew it, one or two more meetings and you were engaged, and this was announced to the whole church. It was like being in a department store full of all kinds of items to be examined and tried on for size, but anything you actually touched you pretty much had to buy—for life. So even though they all looked friendly and inviting, dating was constructed as a trap to ensnare you into lifetime membership. The babe girls were the bait. There were other social difficulties as well.

I remember a guy I thought seemed fairly interesting. He was from the Bahamas, an artist, with a sort of wild appearance, standing out quite dramatically from the clean-cut robot-like guys who were commonly seen in the church. The ultra-responsible, corporate, strong-but-religious types who all liked the same music, television shows, and of course, all sporting events. They were always high-fiving each other. I'm surprised they didn't pat each other on the ass.

Anyway, this guy seemed different so I figured I would get to know him.

We got together for lunch. We started talking about church stuff. That's all anyone talked about, aside from television shows and sports. Then he said, "I think you and I are pretty similar."

"Really? In what way?" I assumed he meant in our artistic interests.

"I've been struggling with the sin of homosexuality for years."

I must say that was quite a mood killer.

"Why bother?" I said.

Lunch was over in a few more minutes.

I mean why bother with the struggle just because someone says it's wrong? No one has to struggle with jumping off the top of a building, or putting their hand into an open flame, or taking a hot iron and putting it on your face. The thing is, if you know it's bad for you in your bones, you probably won't do it. But if it doesn't seem bad to you, then why control yourself just because a book written by a bunch of guys two thousand or more years ago says it's wrong? They didn't even know what the stars were. Why obey all these rules that someone else makes up?

Well, of course, because you'll go to hell if you don't.

The problem, though, is that you are obeying rules made up by dead people who claim to understand your life, and you comply because you are afraid you will be punished eternally. So instead of finding out for yourself what's true, you become dependent on other people's ideas of what you should be doing and what your life means. You become a robot with catch phrases and prefabricated answers for everything. Doubt is considered a lack of faith. You had better be lobotomized to really fit in.

And, in fact, some of them seemed that way; peaceful and dumb like a cow. But most of them seemed artificial and angry at the trap they had constructed for themselves. This lent a subtle edge to all interaction, even an air of malice if the covers were pulled too far back from the safety of the swaddling clothes they cloaked themselves in. The leaders of the church could never be questioned about their motives. That showed a lack of trust and often brought out their fangs.

After one particularly rousing sermon given by the main leader of the church, which whipped up the five thousand members into a religious frenzy of churchlove, I realized that his delivery of a poem he had read aloud, which by some odd chance I had recently come across, had given the impression that he had written it. Not explicitly, but through omission—by not naming the source. I went up to him and shook his hand in congratulations for the fine words he had spoken.

"There is only one thing, Brad. Maybe you should have mentioned where you got the poem from."

He approached me with a smile and reached out to put his arm around me. "Why, thank you for mentioning that, brother," and hit me so hard on the back that I nearly fell over.

All the women were referred to as "sisters." Our sister, Diana, our sister, Louise. Everyone also said they loved these sisters. This could get confusing. I remember one church leader named Bob. He had been a car mechanic before receiving the call to both lead and serve, and went from working under cars to working under God and over his flock. He was married with four kids, but definitely noticed a pretty sister when she would appear under his watchful gaze. In fact, he was always especially solicitous of the same sister I had joined the church to pursue. One day he noticed that I noticed that he noticed her and like one animal to another blurted out as if reading my mind, "I love my wife."

"That's great," I said.

He said it again, as if I didn't hear him.

"I really love my wife."

I nodded approvingly.

Finally he said emphatically, as if to stop an imaginary argument, "I'm in love with my wife!"

At least I was convinced.

Another time I was summoned for a heart-to-heart with another leader because I would not bring a Bible or notebook to church. This had been commented upon.

"We've noticed that you don't bring a Bible or notebook to church."

"I can't find where it's written in the Bible that I should," quite confident in the righteousness of my position.

The leader looked truly pained.

"It's a matter of your heart, Brother."

"I thought we're not supposed to be judging each others' heart."

"But you have to set an example."

And on and on. This leader was supposedly a scientist in his day job. He said he'd pray for me. I knew my days were numbered in this group. I was a truly bad seed, one that was not going to be bearing any fruit for them.

A useful exercise for religious deprogramming can be found in the Bible itself, *1 Corinthians 13*: "Love is patient, love is kind, it does not envy, it does not boast…it keeps no records of wrongs. It rejoices with the truth. It always protects, always trusts, always hopes, always perseveres." We are told elsewhere in the Bible that God is Love. If that is true, then the above statement is a description of God.

If we search the dictionary of antonyms we will find, reassuringly, that through inversion the text means that God could never be hostile or agitated, cruel, jealous or haughty. He keeps no record of wrongs, never attacks, never doubts, never damns, never gives up on anyone.

We throw around the name God very freely, but who even knows what it means?

It's like any word: if you say it enough it makes no sense. Take the word tree. A tree is a tree, we all know that. But the more you repeat the word the more arbitrary the word becomes. Besides, the French call it *arbre*.

Maybe everything is more mysterious than we can organize.

ACT IV

Power and Importance

CHAPTER 20

Instruments and Violin Dealers

Y̲ou cannot separate the success of the player from the quality of the instrument he plays. It was a common myth, and still is in musical circles, to authoritatively proclaim "such and such, or so and so, can play on anything. He's just that great." Of course, for some reason he never does; he, and all great players, have the fanciest equipment their money can buy. And for good reason. It makes a huge difference. The physical response of an instrument helps to create not only great sound, but promotes ease, or difficulty, in playing. But not all of us have millions of dollars to spend on a violin. And even if we did, are all expensive instruments great?

You have to know what you're looking for.

First, you have to know what a violin or cello, or any instrument is *"ideally"* capable of to know what qualities are possible to find in an instrument. To understand that, you must have experience playing great instruments. You have to know what you want, which depends on your understanding of technique and music. You have to know enough to determine if the "quality" that you're hearing—the sound, the "feel," the response—is all there is in the instrument (whether this is all that can be drawn from it), or if the instrument needs adjusting—the sound post, bridge height, fingerboard thickness—which is a whole field in itself, requiring the most subtle expertise.[1] The instrument's capabilities are not separate from your own; you are an equal, indivisible team. On top of this, when you are buying antique violins and cellos, which are the greatest, you are involved in a world market and with very few violin dealers who control it. How, then, to proceed? For the moment I will assume we are talking about finding a good violin for under $30,000.

First, the arching of the top must be flat, not too high. High-arched violins were the standard design in the seventeenth century, many with a beautiful,

---

1 Heifetz would only allow a luthier named Benny Koodlach to repair and setup his violin. Krachmalnick also went only to Koodlach for his violin's setup and, once it was done, would never tamper with it aside from normal maintenance.

refined sound. In those days concerts were held in churches and the rooms of palaces. But that design, generally, will not project the sound sufficiently to carry (be heard well) in our modern concert halls. Around 1700, Italian violin makers began experimenting with a violin design that had flatter arching on the top. This design projects the sound more efficiently than the older design and has been highly sought-after by performers ever since it was first introduced. The grain on the top must be fine, that is, close together. Otherwise the sound may be full, but will be broad and unfocused. Focus is important for projection and the possibility of nuance in the tone. The harmonics should be clear and easy to play. This shows the instrument has a fast response. This is important for clean playing—you don't want to fight to project the notes.

The response of the instrument is greatly affected by the setup. The height of the strings should be on the lower side for the technique of playing that we have been advocating. In this system, sound is released and coaxed, and we want smooth left-hand action. High strings encourage percussive finger action, overworking the left hand. They also force the right hand, the bow, to "dig in" to the strings to pull the sound. Some players favor this, but this setup results in wasted effort and a pinched sound. The strings should be low—not too low or there is no power; the bridge, standard height; the sound-post tight enough to provide resistance. If the violin is too easy to play there is nothing, in terms of sound, to release—no focus. Top-level violins have a sound that sizzles; it is alive with resonance, overtones. The sound should be strong, ringing, immediate, clear and rich, if possible. That is a lot to ask. All strings should have equal power within their different character.

Bows are also critical and it takes a lot of experience to understand what is good. They should be the standard, normal weight, not too heavy, which is about sixty grams. They should feel well-balanced and comfortable in the hand, not tilting one way or another when on the string, and they should not be too stiff. If they are stiff, the sound will be harsh. For smooth, connected playing you need the bow to be subtle—but not jumpy on long bows—and to have a fast response off the string. Round bows are usually better than octagonal.

My teacher, Krachmalnick, played many great bows. He thought, and I agree with him, that perfect examples of a maker, prize-winning bows (in other words, bows that have not been played much), are to be avoided. He said he always found there was a reason they have remained perfect specimens. They look perfect, but, for example, the sound may be harsh, or tricky bowings will feel awkward. Unknown, but latent problems often lie waiting, unveiled the moment you own it. These are bows for collectors, not players.

One may always bargain with violin dealers. They expect it. Usually you will get a break in the price. But *caveat emptor*. Be very careful with dealers. I have had some difficulties with them.

When I was twelve my father bought me a very great bow made in the nineteenth century by Dominique Peccatte which, at the time, the late 1960s, was around $2,000. Nowadays a bow by this maker would be over $100,000. I had owned it for three years, but the first time I had work done on it in another city—Philadelphia—I was told that it was cracked, which meant that they wouldn't work on it because it might break. Worse still, it wasn't worth anywhere near the money that had been paid for it.

So I had to send it back to my father, who got his money back from the dealer who sold it to him in San Francisco. The dealer, who was a friend of my father's, told him that he had been unaware of the break. Many years later, I saw the same bow in the private collection of a prominent businessman in San Francisco. This man owned many great violins and bows, which he fawned over like a spider attending to its web. He had bought this bow from the same dealer as a *perfect* specimen and brought it out to me with much pomp and circumstance.

In 1990 I bought a violin from Krachmalnick that he had acquired in New York many, many years before for $1,000. He said it was a Chanot, a maker who at the time, 1950, was not highly regarded because you could still buy a Strad for $25,000. But by the 1990s a Stradivarius could sell for close to $2 million dollars and a Chanot around $35,000. I bought it from Krachmalnick for $30,000. It had no papers of authenticity. I then took it to a prominent dealer in New York to be examined.

The proprietor was a Frenchman and quite a charmer. His family had been in the business for generations. He was well-known by everyone. He was always impeccably dressed, handsome like a movie star: tall, with black hair that had grayed perfectly at his temples as he aged, and of course, he was French. I had been going to his shop for years, buying strings and trying, but never buying, violins and bows. Jean-Louis was a smooth character. He never raised his voice. His manner was formal, but warm, with an elegant reserve. There was always a famous player there trying instruments—Isaac Stern, Pinchas Zukerman, Arnold Steinhart. Everyone went to Jean-Louis. His was the important New York shop once Wurlitzer's went out of business.

At Wurlitzers, in the 1960s, on any given day you could run into players like Milstein, Oistrakh or Szeryng. They needed new bows, other violins or repairs to their instruments, and they would play there in the middle of the shop for all to hear. You were expected to if you were good. There might be ten Strads in the vault in those days and they'd let you try them. I played two on my first New York visit when I was fifteen. Now this scene had moved to Jean-Louis.

I asked him what he thought about the violin I had brought, not letting him know that I owned it or anything about it, except that I had been told it was a Chanot.

He frowned. "Oh, no, I don't think so," he smoothly pronounced with a French purr. "No, no, no," he said again more gently.

"What do you think it is," I asked.

"German. Definitely German."

Poor Germany. It always seemed from stories I had heard from other players that the fall back position for a violin of dubious origin was that it was German, which was considered less desirable than French, or Italian, which was viewed as the highest level.

"What's it worth?"

"About $10,000."

I didn't flinch. I waited for his next move.

He saw the doubt in my eyes. "Let me call Laurent."

Typically, there is always someone in the back of the store who will settle the whole matter. Out came Laurent. Laurent was just as smooth, but of a different class, like the proprietor of a small restaurant and hotel in the countryside outside of Paris, happy to play on the confusion of a tourist between prix-fixe and à la carte. He knew his role. They exchanged a momentary glance. Laurent shook his head and with complete certainty gave the verdict.

"Definitely German."

"What's it worth?"

"Maybe $10,000."

"Are you selling it?" he asked with French nonchalance and a bit of ennui thrown in.

Another prominent violin luthier was in Philadelphia. The shop was owned and run by William Moennig III whose grandfather had started the business in the late 1800s. Bill was the third generation of violin makers and dealers in the family. Moennig's was one of the most reputable shops in the world. I had bought two great violins and a good bow from him. All the important violin shops had their own character. Moennig's was in the category of beyond rude. They always seemed annoyed that you had shown up at all. They were extremely formal and cold. It wasn't that they were tired of working there. It was like a formal restaurant where the waiters, who could never afford to eat there themselves, take the position that somehow you shouldn't be eating there either, even though you can afford it. For a while I thought maybe they were just singling me out as the one customer who should not be allowed in the store. My phone experiments seemed to confirm my suspicions. This was in the days when there was no way to know who was calling. The same woman always answered. For years.

"Hello, William Moennig and Son's," she said in a monotone.

I would ask to talk to an employee or sometimes Bill himself.

"He's not here."

They never were.

Silence.

"Could I leave a message?"

"If you want."

At this point I usually felt compelled to ask, "Will you write it down?"

"What's the message?"

As I said, I thought it might be me, but I once had an opportunity to hear and see her in action in the shop. I was relieved to realize she didn't discriminate.

The salespeople possessed an eerie Edgar Allan Poe-ish quality, as if I had entered a time-warp, or a dream from which Poe himself might draw inspiration, or where Dickens' Miss Havisham might be found still alive. There were only two assistants. One was an old, reserved man; very thin, with balding hair, who looked as if he had been selling violins there since the days of Stradivarius. His clothes must have been quite stylish in the 1940s, but if you wear them to work for that long they take on an otherworldly appearance, which made him look like the ghost of Christmas past.

The other salesperson, a much younger man named Jonathon, reminded me, to put it simply, of a Ken doll who smiled when you pulled on a string, having only a few programmed thoughts, as well as pale wan skin that made him look as if he had been stolen from a wax museum and programmed by Bill Moennig to obey his every order with mechanical dependency. He seemed to have very little muscle tone, yet somehow he could stand and move around. He looked young, but at the same time of an indeterminate age and manner that could have made him anywhere from twenty-five to fifty years old.

Bill Moennig, himself, had a bitter, patrician demeanor. He seemed as if he had grown up with privilege and possessed the nonchalance and rude manner common to that social set. He was always sarcastic and snide in his remarks. One day I was at the shop trying out some bows, all of which were between $20,000 and $30,000. For some reason he was more friendly than usual and sought me out to talk to. In an unusually candid moment, but still in keeping with his usual demeanor, he said to me, "You guys are always looking for something more, some better violin, a better bow. We depend on you guys being suckers. That's how we make our money." I didn't know what to say. I just smiled, shrugged, and left.

Two years after I had bought the Chanot from Krachmalnick I decided that I wanted to sell the violin and use the money to buy a great bow. I had another violin also. (I'll go into that story after this one.) So I went to another prominent violin shop in New York.

This, like Moennig's was one of maybe ten places in the world where you could buy and sell great violins. I showed the proprietor my violin. It still had no papers. I didn't tell him what it was. He said immediately, "It's a Chanot." I told him who had owned it. He was impressed. I also told him about Jean-Louis's opinion. He smiled knowingly. "I see."

We talked about price and decided to sell it for $45,000. We agreed that they could keep the violin for six months on consignment. When that matter was settled, the proprietor took out from his safe a Stradivarius that he had just purchased for $2 million dollars.

"Do you want to try it?"

It was a gorgeous orange-red color and had a thick, rich sound that played fast and easy. But on the D string, on B in the third position, there was a "wolf," which means the sound can suddenly choke. Usually this occurs, if at all, high up on the G string between B and C, which is a little more manageable. But on the D, I became worried for his financial future. How could he ever sell this to anyone who could play?

Well, the violin, my violin, as the months went by, was having trouble being sold they told me. They asked me to drop the price. I did. I needed the money for the bow. It still had trouble selling. Eventually, they called me to say they had finally found a buyer for $31,000. I agreed, but wanted my money immediately. They agreed. They sent me $15,000. They said the rest was around the corner. It must have been some corner of Cambodia because I waited six months for the remainder. I was glad to get it. I found out six months later that they had sold the violin for $65,000. The guy who handled the sale died a year and a half later of cancer. He was forty-five.

Anyway, I mentioned that I had another violin. I had bought this from Moennig's ten years before—a great violin, made in Cremona in 1739 by Lorenzo Guadagnini with every respected paper of authenticity imaginable. I paid $125,000 for it and by 1990 it had appreciated to $450,000. The violin's authenticity had been approved by every great violin expert on the face of the Earth, including Bill Moennig himself.

Then a bass player in the Philadelphia Orchestra wrote a book about the Guadagnini family and claimed that Lorenzo was a fake. He had existed, but he was a butcher, not a violin maker. Conveniently for this writer, only twelve violins that Lorenzo had made still existed in the world. Now no one knew what they were worth or who had made them, apparently. Except that they sound like a Stradivarius. They are great concert violins.

A well-known collector who made a fortune as a buyer of bankrupt companies, who, like me, owns a Lorenzo, along with a Strad, Guarneri, and case upon case of great bows, assures me that this whole thing is a scam. The dealers are trying to scare people into selling and these violins will be bought, and once they are in the right hands suddenly we will find that they are worth $3 million dollars apiece. He advised me not to sell. J.B. Guadagninis, which were considered comparable, are now worth $1.5 million. All I know is my violin is worth who knows what.

With the $31,000 from the sale of Krachmalnick's violin, I bought a bow, adding another $14,000—a $45,000 bow. Another Peccatte. I really liked this bow. I bought it from a famous dealer in a city I shall not name. It had all the great papers, including one from this dealer. A year later, while in San Francisco I showed the bow to a friend of mine who happened to be a bow expert. He looked at it and casually asked me if I had noticed the pin inserted into the stick near the frog. It was covered by color to hide it. But there was no mistaking it—the bow had been broken and repaired. It was worth maybe $5,000.

I was shocked, although by this time you would think that I would have expected it. I called the dealer and told him what I had discovered. He didn't believe me. I told him that it was a friend of his who had spotted the defect in less than a ten-second look and had added that it was an obvious repair to any expert with functioning eyes.

I demanded my money back. I sent him x-rays of the bow. He refused to give me back my money. He wanted the bow first. I told him that under the circumstances I thought that the burden of trust was on him. He wouldn't budge. I started getting calls from other dealers who somehow knew about the problem. "Why are you behaving like this?" they would ask. "These things happen. It's not a big deal." I'm talking about three separate dealers. I retained a lawyer and threatened to sue. I got the money back and sent him the bow.

I found out later that he was being sued for millions of dollars for allegedly undervaluing an old man's violin collection and reselling the instruments for a large margin. Several years later the dealer in New York who sold my Chanot was arrested in Europe and convicted on multiple charges of fraud.

Violin dealers are a tricky breed to do business with. The imbalance created by the buyer's lack of knowledge and the fact that the dealers control an unregulated market are uncomfortably similar to the dynamics at play between music teachers and students, which is a seed of mystification that grows into a web of confusion between musicians and conductors, soloists and music, and composers and their role.

CHAPTER 21

Mentors and the "Importance" of Importance

In my days, the 1970s, Curtis was in decline. Most of the students were high all day. No one seemed to care. The famous pianist, Rudolph Serkin, was the director of the school and could occasionally be seen walking around the building as if in a bubble. He looked like a hotel clerk in a German movie—wire-rimmed spectacles, a gaunt face—and he walked leaned over and moved fast, like Groucho Marx without any of the humor. He seemed a somber and stoic man—a good German. His main concern was practicing. He practiced seven hours a day and played concerts. That did not leave much time for directing a school. We knew he practiced that much because our English literature tutor, Liz, told us that he did. She was his daughter.

Serkin became incredibly nervous whenever he performed, even for the students. The first twenty minutes of his concerts could be a bit rocky. I suppose that's why he practiced so much. I remember hearing him play a recital at school. The first piece on the program was Bach's *Italian Concerto*. He was missing notes all over the place. Even I got nervous. But he gradually calmed down and played wonderfully. (Not that I knew enough then to know if he did. I just assumed he did.)

The school buildings were donated to Curtis by its founder, Mary Curtis Bok, who was the sole heir of the publishing magnate, Cyrus Curtis. His company published *The Ladies' Home Journal*, *The Saturday Evening Post* and the *Philadelphia Inquirer*. She must have been a very generous woman. The original idea of the school was to bring the greatest musicians of the world to Philadelphia and give students the finest European musical education that American money could buy. This was back in the Depression. The students went on holiday to Europe during the summer with their teachers, paid no tuition, and were given fine instruments to use—including great violins, cellos, and Steinway pianos. Josef Hoffman was the director, and Leopold Auer, the teacher of all the greatest violinists in the world, although well past his prime, was on the faculty. Leonard Bernstein was a student, as was Samuel Barber, who later taught composition there.

Mary Curtis Bok died in 1970. Whatever spirit of goodwill and care that may have imbued the years before me was not evident during my tenure there. There were no trips to Europe in the summer. If there was a collection of string instruments that could be used by students, I never had the benefit of it. I think most of the collection had been sold. Some members of the faculty were busy performing artists. They were almost never there. When they were, their minds were somewhere else, probably worrying about their upcoming concerts. So who was directing and monitoring your progress? You were truly on your own.

The Curtis Orchestra was conducted every Saturday morning by Eugene Ormandy, the world-famous conductor of the Philadelphia Orchestra. That didn't mean much to us. He was five feet tall, to us a midget, and had a nervous, hysterical disposition, which in addition to being bald and very short, made him hard to take seriously. He was, however, very serious about himself and lived next to Curtis in a fancy old hotel called the Barclay. It was a place stuck in a time long gone. The dining room had enormous chandeliers and waiters in tuxedos who seemed to have worked there for forty or fifty years. Meals in the restaurant were served with elaborate ornamentation and attention, everything brought on a silver tray, perhaps five waiters to a table because the place was nearly always empty. This is where Ormandy dwelled, alone with the staff, as if the days when Rachmaninoff had stayed there had never passed. He was out of step with the present day and the youth into whose midst he was thrown every Saturday morning.

Part of Ormandy's problem with us was that we hated playing in an orchestra and would never practice the parts. At least no one admitted to it. We had our honor to protect. We were sure we would be soloists. That's what we were told. No one stopped to think that the odds weren't too good. We just kept practicing concertos. Ormandy could sense our attitude about playing in an orchestra and often lectured us that most of us would end up there. But a little bald guy who has tantrums in front of the students is easy to dismiss. We wouldn't have known if he was a musical genius or not (he wasn't), but we could sense he was insecure and we took advantage of it. We thought he was probably the funniest person in the school and we were constantly laughing at him during rehearsals when he wasn't watching. But I think he knew. He tried to get us back with frequent tantrums, which, of course, encouraged our misbehavior. I remember one well.

We had to play a gala concert for Curtis in the Academy of Music[1] with Ormandy conducting the director of the school, Rudolph Serkin, in Beethoven's *Emperor Concerto*. In the final rehearsal before the concert Ormandy became exasperated with the student playing the timpani part. The student kept getting the rhythm wrong in one place. Ormandy had him try a few times. It still didn't work. Finally he exploded.

"Who is your teacher?" his face beet red.

"The principal timpani of the Philadelphia Orchestra," a meek and scared voice replied.

"I'm going to talk to him," he screamed. "You have no business being in Curtis."

We were in shock. Serkin just sat there. And then we just continued the rehearsal.

What happened to that student?

Who spoke up for him?

Thus, we see the spirit of the school embodied in two famous, important men. Fame can create importance, and importance can become a very serious affair. Of course, Ormandy and Serkin are not the only important people who take themselves very seriously.

IMPORTANT PEOPLE

There are people who become important by the contribution they make to human society. This type of importance is conferred, not sought after. For example, Albert Einstein became important, but I doubt very much whether that was his *raison d'être* and I would doubt that being important was very important to him. There are, however, very many people whose desire to be important creates the meaning of their lives. It is this type that we shall examine.

By what reasoning does one assume the *validity* of the crown of importance? Why is it so important to be important? The desperation with which people work, plot and grab for status gives the lie to the very thing they seek, for if they were truly important they would not need any outside confirmation to confer their validity or have to work so hard to get it. Because their quest is illusory, as we shall see, their actions are destructive to everyone around them—it is a hunger that cannot be sated and devours anything in its path. Interestingly, to be important, in the sense that we are examining, *requires* that others be *unimportant*. It is, therefore, essentially an assertion of separation. Yet if we investigate this claim, we can see that it is *not possible* to be important.

---

1 The Academy of Music is Philadelphia's equivalent to Carnegie Hall in New York.

Let's look at a stereotypically important person—the self-made man. If we could take hold of one and leave him alone, naked in the wilderness, we need not think very deeply to realize our important person could not survive for long. But we may go further with this thought experiment. If we also took away all trees, plants, animals, heat, water, light, air..., well I think we see the point—how separate is anyone from everything else?

Assuming our self-made man could make his way out of the wilderness, we must suppose that he did not self-make the language he speaks, the education he received, the clothes he wears, the transportation system he employs and all that he supposedly knows, including his name. We exist as an evolutionary system of constant unfolding interaction with everything at once. If we continue to peer beneath the facade of our societal assumptions, we will discover that there is no identifiable first cause for anything because what caused this was caused by that, which was caused by that. But there is also no separate entity to cause anything since the system of life works as a whole, simultaneously unfolding organism.

In reality, there is no such entity as a separate person. Therefore, if there is no possible way to be separate from everything else, there is no way to *validly and logically* assert such separation through the mantle of importance. *The assertion of self-importance represents an inversion, a distortion, of reality.*

Important people are always a let-down. This must be how Dorothy felt when she pulled back the curtain on the ominous Wizard of Oz and found only a nervous little bald-headed man. This man lurks everywhere that importance can be found. I have met my fair share of importances (actually, many of them), through musical events and the fact that classically trained musicians, even though they don't make a lot of money, often run in the same social circles as the socially elite, although not treated as a member of that social set. Through these interactions I have become adept at spotting behavioral traits that the species, importances, have in common. Additionally, for our study purposes, the species need not include people who have officially become important. "Want-to-be" importances are easily available for study everywhere one turns. In the following discussion we can easily meld importances and "want to be" importances into the same subject of study because no matter how important one becomes, there is no final point of arrival. Ultimately the members of the species are all "want-to-be" importances.

One can easily recognize unrecognized important people by the fact that they refuse to answer even the most innocent questions about themselves. They prefer to speak in broad generalities. They never speak about anyone or anything negatively, and if cornered into expressing an opinion that could possibly be construed as controversial, they will quickly find an escape, such as leaving to refill their drink, or saying that they see someone they know across the street and simply must talk to them this instant.

I have noticed that important people hate questions. I suppose they're not used to them. Or, the fact that they won't answer a question is a MacGuffin that makes them seem so removed from everyday manners that people start to get the idea that they know things that can't be explained. An important point here is that to pull this off one cannot seem at all concerned that a question has not been answered. That might make people believe you have no response. To answer a question must seem to be a waste of brain power or consideration and if one does this to enough people an aura of importance is thereby acquired and you are put in charge of something. That is why when one meets an important person who will answer a question, it is a shock.

I once had dinner with a very important person at a gala fundraiser for a musical cause of some sort. I was seated next to him among eight other important people. It was a fluke, but somehow I ended up at an important table. Not caring much about protocol, I began asking him questions. He told me about his family, his wife, his grandkids. He laughed openly and heartily and even talked about his investments. Up until this time the other important people at the table had listened with polite attention, but when he became candid about investments and money, even discussing his salary, the others at the table turned to each other in true horror, as if someone had just confessed to being a murderer or a Democrat. The gentleman seated next to me turned to me aghast and whispered, "I can't believe he's talking about THAT." I then asked him a question about himself. He excused himself from the table.

Invariably, important people always want to ask *you* questions if they don't know you. Once you start to answer, they know you're not important. The first question they will usually ask is "What part of the city do you live in?" Try not to be specific. They never are. If you live in Berkeley the correct response is "In the hills." It could be the foothills, it could be a slight rise in the street, but they won't have a follow-up. You're fine as long as you don't answer any more questions. If they ask you where you live and you say "Oakland," you should excuse yourself before they find an excuse to leave.

If you answer "San Francisco," you're alright. But they will try to follow it up with, "Where in the city?" Don't be trapped. Deflect them with "How about you?" That will confuse them long enough for you to gain the upper hand, as long as you express no opinions and ask no questions. The one permissible question might be "Where do your kids go to school?" You've got a good five to ten minute soliloquy ahead of you.

Strangely, I have noticed that important people, and of course "want to be" importances, are all quite afraid of each other, which leads them to be aware of social details that a normal person would overlook.[2] There are stock replies, coded queries not meant to be answered, sharp eyes watching for a wrong move, political understandings taken for granted, all of which must be carefully adhered to when in contact with the right set. They do a lot of standing around at social gatherings, staying within their circle, talking about other important people they know, sometimes with looks of grave concern about the information they are receiving about and from other importances. But that doesn't last long. Someone makes a joke and everyone is back to their good-natured banter.

To the watchful eye it becomes obvious that important people love meeting other important people. One can observe that as an important person approaches a group of importances a hero's welcome immediately materializes. It's not because they need the contacts or a new friend. It's because important people make important people feel even more important. Of course, there are levels of importance. They all like famous entertainers or artists and will do anything to meet them, but their interaction is usually somewhat upsetting because worlds of differing importance don't easily connect. A famous rock star and a real estate tycoon have little in common except importance.

The most important of the important are the "super wealthy who play political games." These people are untouchable, unreachable and potentially dangerous to other important people, who either want to be more important or are afraid of losing importance. My father once told me you can never have too much money. But I think at the bottom of it all is the fact that you can never be important enough. Their reason for life becomes this importance, and how they achieve that, or whether they merit it, is entirely unimportant. If they can get it, then they deserve it.

In my field encounters with those who seek importance they do not appear to be bothered by guilt, or feeling. They don't believe in the value of excellence because that introspective exercise might question the validity of their life paradigm. Their value is their bank account and their reputation. And that is quite enough. But is it? Are they really secure in this role they play?

---

2 Fear of another's opinion of oneself is a truth for everyone. The desire to be viewed by both oneself and others as "important" is an attempt to escape the judgement of others. Ironically, this strategy is dependent upon the judgement of others and, therefore, offers no hope for escape. Additionally, it is no answer for the satisfaction, the approval, of one's "self" by one's "self" since, as we discussed in Chapter 8 the "self" is really comprised of the "other."

There are unfortunate consequences for their lives (and anyone around them) by adopting this reason for existence. It means that they will do anything to achieve a position that will ensure their opportunity. They operate from a mental paradigm that is unfettered by fairness. They sell themselves. Because they become adept at that, they can be hard to spot, but they also surround themselves with like-minded importances, or "want-to-be" importances because that is what they value. They are, therefore, very threatened by everyone who makes up the world they have attracted.

They are, in fact, very sensitive. I was once standing around with some important importances: the president of a college, the head of a venture capital firm, and a mega-rich guy who had worked his way up to become the CEO of the multimillion dollar publishing company his grandfather had started. They were all having a good time gossiping about fellow importances. I made an innocuous remark such as "college tuitions are very high," and the next thing I knew I was being grilled about where I lived. I distracted the inquisition by saying with feeling, "Here!" I guess it sounded vaguely patriotic and I was let off the hook.

They, and all strivers for importance, are also very aware of how they are treated, hyperaware in fact. Whenever I am around importances I feel a tremendous pressure to make them feel alright. Did the joke they made fall flat? I feel compelled to save them from embarrassment and may laugh a little more than I need to. So does everyone else. I wouldn't want that kind of psychological carnage on my conscience. They are very delicate creatures, these importances. It is the supreme sensitivity of their sensitivity that expends so much energy that they can't be expected to have much energy for anything else. Being important is hard work. So I have found that they are incapable of noticing other people. I had a conversation recently with a person of importance. Well, more of a listening session.

I met him at an important party, again it was I fluke that I was allowed in the house. He was a short, fire-pluggy, shaved-headed, bulldog guy with a French Canadian accent. How do I know he had that particular accent? He told me. He told me lots of stuff and I enjoyed it. He said he lived in the Cayman Islands. I didn't think anyone really lived there, but apparently 35,000 other people do also, although according to him he is one of the richest. He said he was a movie producer and had made eighteen movies for Lifetime Channel.

He had recently lost his Rolls Royce in a tropical storm. That was not good, but it didn't bother him, he said. He still had his twenty-five-room house and his yacht, although apparently these brought him no joy. He had a girlfriend who was a dentist—the best, he said, in the Cayman Islands; good to know if I'm there and need some work done. Before settling down with his dentist, he had been a partyer. Everyone knew him on the islands, and in L.A., where he had also been a huge partyer. He knew a lot of people too, like Mel Gibson and Patrick Swayze, "What a shame," and he added, "and his wife was a real bitch." He talked to these famous types regularly. He had unwittingly snubbed the Prince of Monaco in L.A. saying, "Hey, dude," instead of addressing him as Monseigneur. But he was unconcerned. "Fuck him," he said.

He was taking all his friends on a Mediterranean cruise next week. He had had sex with hundreds of girls. There was only one problem, he said.

"I have everything anyone could ever want. I've made movies. I have a yacht, for God's sake. I have a great girlfriend. But I'm depressed."

"Everyone gets depressed," I said, trying to help.

"But I have everything. And I'm still depressed. I can't even go on board my yacht. It gives me no joy."

I was really starting to feel sorry for him.

"It's chemical. I'm on medication. I have no reason to be depressed. Other people do, not me."

"But what I'm trying to tell you is that everyone gets depressed. It's cyclical, like the weather. Lots of people get depressed. You don't need a reason to be depressed."

"You don't understand. I don't have a reason."

"That's precisely my point. That's normal."

"No. With me it's chemical. I have everything. I have no reason to be depressed."

He was getting frustrated with me.

I gave up. "I get your point. It's lucky you have the meds."

I said goodnight. This guy had just talked to me for an hour straight without asking me a single question about me or anything else. I couldn't explain to him that anybody with his mind would have plenty of reasons to be depressed. But that could not occur to such a brain. He could even ask his friends, if he had any. I'm sure they were depressed listening to him. Not only could he not have an interest in anyone else, he couldn't even have an interest in what anyone else thought of him. Is this really chemical?

He said he was also an investment banker.

Many people live their lives pretending to be something they are not to achieve status, respect and power. In their stampedic rush towards personal glorification, with no regard for whether they merit any distinction at all, they are often very destructive to everyone around them. Here is what the Russian philosopher George Gurdjieff had to say on the subject, as told by his pupil P. D. Ouspensky:

> False personality is based on pretense, especially imagining that you know something. The realization of our ignorance of even what we know can begin to undermine the tremendous power of the false personality. It is necessary for me to say that False personality always wishes rewards, medals, reputation, and all the rest of it. It is ambitious. It tries to keep going at all costs, and all this is pretense. And behind this pretense lies an enormous ignorance and helplessness which I call the dark side of a person, the side he will not admit and accept into consciousness.

> Personality whether false or real must be built up as strongly as possible. And that is why Gurdjieff said, "I can always talk to a man who knows something, such as a man who can make good coffee."[3]

Such a person understands something real.

EXPLOITATION

Pretense is a strategy used to acquire something, a ruse to gain an advantage. Perhaps it is donned merely for protection or to steal a slight edge over others. We all do this to varying levels. Charm can be a harmless provocateur if employed to procure an ice cream cone, or a dangerous beguiler if swindling you out of your life savings. Often, pretense leads to exploitation. The word "exploit" has several shades of meaning. At one end of the spectrum it can mean to cultivate, to utilize; and at the other end it can mean to take undue advantage of, to waste or use destructively. At this end of the scale, exploitation is parasitic. The use of pretense and the life paradigms it engenders breed ever more pretense. A small lie may create another to obfuscate an embellishment, until gradually, sometimes quickly, one's life becomes a rationalization of a small misstep taken but never admitted.

The need for outward approval to stifle some deep-rooted inadequacy has its comical elements. Take, for example, the idea of honorific titles. An honorific title is a prefix to one's name, adopted and coveted as a means of distinguishing oneself from everyone else. They are all comical by nature because of the discrepancy between the title's implications and the true nature of the person granted the honorific title. Let's look at the titles and expected protocol for religious luminaries who, if they understood their religion's deepest tenets,

---

3   P. D. Ouspensky, *In Search of the Miraculous: Fragments of an Unknown Teaching,* New York: Harcourt, Brace.

would no doubt understand the meaning of the word humility. Yet this does not appear to be the case: "His All Holiness" or "The Most Divine," "His Beatitude," "The Most Blessed," "All-Holiness," "His Eminence" or "The Most Reverend," "The Right Reverend Father," "The Reverend Father," "The Reverend Mother."

When in the presence of the Pope everyone follows elaborate rituals and procedures. He must be addressed as "His Holiness" or "Most Holy Father." Everyone else is referred to as his "most humble servant." At an audience with the Pope, His Eminence enters, carried on a throne by eight Swiss guards who transfer him to a fixed throne. Everyone is required to kneel until he blesses them. They may then rise. If allowed personal contact with the Holy Father, the ring on his finger must be kissed while kneeling before him. This is quite a contrast to the life and tribulations of the supposed founder of this religion who had no money, no home, and who was not in any social discomfort being around criminals and prostitutes.

I wanted to write a letter to the mayor of San Francisco and was surprised by the prescribed protocol. He must be addressed as "The Honorable such and such," which is interesting because I thought that he worked for me and I am not in the habit of addressing even my fellow workers, let alone a boss, with this level of deference. Apart from the upside-down reverence, the attachment of the title "Honorable" to any politician stretches irony to its breaking point.

Judges are called "Your Honor," other politicians are referred to as Senator This, or Congressman That, or Secretary This or That. I read that George Washington eschewed such verbal prostrations. Rabbis are referred to as such, doctors of anything may be referred to as Doctor. Generals are always referred to as generals, and those of other high military ranks are addressed by their position. We have Kings and Queens in some countries and they are called "Your Majesty" or "His Royal Highness," or "Your Grace" for a Duke, or "Prince" and "Princess" for whatever. One of the problems for the royal family in England has been that the media has exposed how utterly unspecial and unroyal they really are.

This demand for respect and subservience from others suggests that although religious leaders, government officials, and military men consistently and publicly profess a need to "serve" people, the reality is exactly the opposite, the *inversion*. They seek these positions so that people can *serve them*. The same need for the acquiescence of others can be noticed in teachers, parents, and anyone else demanding respect in the name of the service they supposedly do for people, including the supposed largess of the wealthy in the guise of benefactor. That is why they so are dangerous.

This state of pretense leads to, or is inexorably intertwined with, varying degrees of exploitation. They are mutually dependent. To protect a lie, you may need to exploit. The lie can be that you are important, that you are a self-made man, that you are a genius, that you are good-willed, that you are kind. What may have begun as a mechanism of protection can become a full-scale parasitic relationship to life. Sometimes it is simply a pure desire to exploit. You gradually forget where it all started. Maybe someone made fun of you as a child, taunted you saying that you were weak, or that your parents were losers, and you believed this because kids have no perspective. Maybe your whole life has been built to cover up some deep sense of shame, shame that is still there but that you longer notice. Or maybe you're just a bastard.

If you hunger for fame or money to become a worthy person in your own eyes or someone else's, you are in an impossible double-bind. If you believe that you are not important, you will find that no amount of importance will change that feeling. Money won't cure it either. The only way out is to see that the idea of importance is unimportant and *logically invalid*.

Perhaps your family has been rich for generations and you are spoiled and pampered and Daddy's little girl. At some point, perhaps at a very young age, you may notice that not everyone has the same privileges. That might cause a momentary disturbance and you might be prompted to ask Daddy why other people don't have their own airplanes.

"It's because we're very fortunate, Charlotte. Your grandfather was a great, important man, and because of that we have a special life." Except you wonder why you're so special because other people are prettier, better in school, more talented, and more popular. It's true that you are richer, but there is a nagging feeling that maybe you are not that special.

Examining this would destroy your entire life paradigm yet, if your mind can't go beyond that, it can't go beyond anything else. You will be stuck at that level of insight and creativity. Perhaps you want to paint or compose or be a scientist. That requires a free mind, but a free mind will let in thoughts that are unacceptable. The price that one must pay for creativity, genius, which is the ability to slip into new paradigms, is that one must be willing to shed the old skin.

If one is unwilling to do this yet still has the ambition to be "seen" as a genius or an artist, the adoption of the ruse of *eccentricity* can be utilized to con people into believing that one is a profound being, just as a kid will buy Michael Jordan's brand of toothpaste hoping to be able to improve their jump-shot. All of this is comedic on a certain level, but as the effects of pretense ripple out from simply blocking one's own creativity and start to affect other people, we are on the road to exploitation and parasitism. One's pretense may be that he is a man of action, a mover and shaker. This may have started innocently as a ruse for his father's attention because his father was an "important" person. Or he was a shameful nobody and you carry his shame with you. You've forgotten that. You are now a forty-five-year-old man with a wife and four children, a house in Tiburon, a prominent real estate developer, but with something to prove.

I met a guy who had bought over four hundred acres of pristine forest. He wanted to develop it, but was upset that California wouldn't let him. He complained to me, "I own that land! It's my property!"

"But what you do with it affects lots of other people." He walked away. That doesn't change the fact that his "ownership" of trees a few hundred years old and animals that have lived there for thousands of years seems to be an unimportant impediment to his ambition. He is, in essence, a punk.

Our system *creates* the possibility that these blowhards can be taken seriously, and *precludes* us from stopping such nonsense and destructiveness because most of us have been trained to seek such status for ourselves.

The basis of pretense is the desire to exploit at some level. No one drops this strategy without pressure. The pressure comes from others seeing through the act. Then the ruse is useless for advantage. This discussion quite naturally leads us where it must at this point in our investigation—the conductor, the epitome of an inverted relationship to reality.

CHAPTER 22

Conductors

I recently told a young conductor that I heard he had done well in a concert. "It's what I like to do," he confidently asserted. Yet the thought occurred to me (although not expressed), by what reasoning does he come to the conclusion that he has the right to direct a group of musicians at all? Why does he not doubt the very idea of "leading?" To conduct means to guide, to manage, to escort. What knowledge does our young conductor have that can successfully lead anyone anywhere?

If one reflects upon it, the ambition to be a conductor is similar to aspiring to be a politician. Socrates spoke with his usual insight on the subject of leadership:

> [Soc.] Of course you know that ambition and avarice are held to, as indeed they are, a disgrace?
>
> [Glaucon] Very true.
>
> [Soc.] And for this reason, I said, money and honor have no attraction for [good men]; good men do not wish to be openly demanding payment for governing and so to get the name of hirelings, nor by secretly helping themselves out of the public revenues to get the name of thieves. And not being ambitious they do not care about honor. Wherefore, necessity must be laid upon them, and they must be induced to serve from the fear of punishment. And this, as I imagine, *is the reason why forwardness to take office, instead of waiting to be compelled, has been deemed dishonorable.* Now the worst part of the punishment is that he who refuses to rule is liable to be ruled by one who is worse than himself. And the fear of this, as I conceive, induces the good to take office, not because they would, but because they cannot help it—not under the idea that they are going to have any benefit or enjoyment themselves, but as a necessity, and because they are not able to commit the task of ruling to anyone who is better than themselves, or indeed as good. For there is reason to think that if a city were composed of entirely good men, then to avoid office would be as much an object of contention as to obtain office is at present; then

we must have plain proof that *the true ruler is not meant by nature to regard his own interest, but that of his subjects; and everyone who knew this would choose rather to receive a benefit from another man than to have the trouble of conferring one.*[1] (italics mine)

To lead or guide responsibly requires, according to Socrates, regarding the needs of others above your own. To be able to understand and assist in fulfilling the needs of others requires knowledge, wisdom, and much kindliness—a rather unusual and highly developed human being, I would dare say. Yet interestingly, conductors nowadays start young. There are prodigy conductors who, one must assume, are apparently prodigy leaders. What exactly is the nature of their prodigious accomplishment? A conductor moves his arms about, yet he produces no musical sound himself. Is there any way to know that he knows anything at all? Is conducting difficult?

One of the most illuminating and amusing examples of the difficulty of conducting is often displayed in symphony fundraisers. A sought-after prize is the chance to conduct the orchestra for a brief moment. It makes no difference who wins; the orchestra doesn't miss a beat. By comparison we might imagine auctioning the chance for an audience member to play a Stradivarius or a Steinway nine-foot grand. How would that sound?

Conductors make a lot of money. James Levine's combined per season salaries from the Boston Symphony Orchestra and New York's Metropolitan Opera was about $3.5 million. A few examples will suffice: Keith Lockhart, conductor of the Boston "Pops" makes over $700,000 per season; Lorin Maazel was paid about $2.6 million per season from the New York Philharmonic; Daniel Barenboim made about $2 million from the Chicago Symphony in 2004. The San Francisco Symphony pays Michael Tilson-Thomas over $1.5 million per season. Many conductors are the music directors of several orchestras, thereby, collecting several salaries. This is not bad work if you can get it. But how necessary are conductors and how difficult is what they do? Or are they a tradition, begun as an expediency, that is "essential" because it has become an unquestioned "fact" of symphonic performance? Does the conductor's importance represent an *inversion* of reality made possible by the *confusion* of composers and performers?

Most conductors are not great instrumentalists. Some are middling good pianists, which is helpful in understanding scores, but not essential. I know many conductors who are percussionists. (I'm not sure that could be considered playing an instrument at all.) Such is the stuff from which the conductor springs. We might consider the following tale as a rather typical conductor's genesis.

---

1   Plato, *The Republic*, Book 1, "The Rewards for Ruling" (New York: Random House), 32.

It is a commonly known fact in musical circles that nearly all good violists (there are rare exceptions) were originally violinists who decided they would have more musical opportunity on the viola and switched instruments for reasons of expediency and inadequacy. Similarly, most conductors are average, or sometimes far below average, instrumentalists. Toscanini was a mediocre cellist. (Yet his lack of accomplishment in the actual playing of music did not stop him from attempting to push Vladimir Horowitz around. The poor guy even married his daughter.)

Let's for the moment imagine that our violist, often a "failed" violinist, has made the decision to learn how to conduct so that he can guide and escort other musicians through the complexities of performing. At first there is the confusion of learning something new. One notices a certain shyness and reserve in his manner and approach, a hesitation. He learns to read scores—something that any musician should know how to do. He learns to move his arms in the correct beat patterns. Thus far, there is still much awkwardness and humility in his demeanor. This is understandable because up to this point his experience in the world of music has been one of arduous work, yet still falling far short of being a great player. He has tried for years and couldn't do it.

The beat patterns of conducting, unlike the difficulties of playing an instrument, are mastered in a few weeks of work, perhaps two months, and the joy of it is that any normally coordinated person, even a four-year-old, can do it. Yet now comes the problem of leading. Our violist wants to look the part of a real conductor. He wants the orchestra to feel how much the music means to him; after all, that is why he is conducting—because the music means so much to him and the fact that he likes to do it.

The most obvious difficulty with asserting his musical expression is that as a conductor he makes no sound. It's like having sex with no genitals yourself and no physical contact with the other person. You want your partner to know how aroused you are; you want to excite her, but what can you do except grimace and make ecstatic faces? You can't have sex, or directly make music. Yet, paradoxically, it is at this point that our humble violist's ego starts to sprout wings, a metamorphosis whose dramatic character can only find its equal in nature—the change from a caterpillar to a butterfly.

Now our lowly violist is on a mission to make people understand and "feel" his soundless music. Miraculously, what he could not do on an instrument is now somehow legitimatized because *he can't be heard*. His mediocrity has been purged and his musical frustration pacified by this simple act of transformation. There are many conductors who fall into the category of wanting to express their inner selves. Yet they were never able to do this in a way that anyone would notice or take seriously as long as the playing of the music was done by *themselves*.

This is another sort of leading from what Socrates described as the good ruler. A leader of this ilk wants his subjects to be under his complete control so that he can express *himself*, not others. He wants to help *himself*, not those he "leads." And he does this because he *enjoys* it. A government of this type is called a tyranny and revolutions have been fought to end them. Yet here we have an instance of a person studying to become a tyrant, people taking this seriously, and other people volunteering to subjugate themselves. How can this be? Is there something strange in the training of musicians that makes them susceptible to accepting this dysfunctional relationship as normal. It could be that most musicians assume there is no other way to perform symphonic music. This is not true, as we shall conclusively show. But what a sad state of affairs it is for musicians that what no one would accept in their normal life—a tyranny—is legitimized, with nary a thought, as the reality of their careers. Once this strange arrangement is considered normal, other consequences must logically follow.

If one is granted total expressive control over a group of people, what else can this person be but important? What makes him, the conductor, so important? Why is the person who makes no sound and dances around on a podium paid so much more than everyone else on stage? How is it that his judgment is considered so much more acute and refined than any of the musicians he directs, *now that he can't be heard playing?* Before our conductor was a conductor, he was just a lowly violist, drummer, or average wind-player, or an accompanist to singers. Even if he was a fine player, why is he so well-respected and sometimes even revered now?

Do conductors really lead anyone or are they led by the *circumstance*? Clearer thinking suggests that they are dependent upon both the composer's composition and the quality of the players whose effort they seem to organize, although the true organization of effort is done by others—the composer's score has organized the players' interaction and the players' skill determines the quality of the interaction. Any conductor knows that an orchestra of good musicians can play without him. From Milstein's memoir:

> In the first years after the revolution Zeitlin played in the Lenin Quartet, whose cellist was our future buddy Gregor Piatigorsky. Later Zeitlin gathered the best musicians in Moscow and came up with this promising idea: Since we were living under new social conditions in the age of collectivism, there was no need for an orchestra to subordinate to a dictator conductor. Let's make

music collectively, decide everything by consensus, and in this way seek new paths to art.

Actually I think Zeitlin (who had been concertmaster for many years in Serge Koussevitsky's Moscow orchestra) realized that good musicians can easily manage without a conductor and decided that he himself would be the music director. And so it was. At rehearsals of Persimfans [the group's name] Zeitlin, who became concertmaster, gave instructions to the other members: he set tempos and showed them phrasing. But, in fact, there were also animated discussions and give and take that would have been impossible under a conductor.[2]

A person standing on a raised platform in front of people and directing them as they sit appears to be more important than whomever is seated. The focus on one person elevated in front of the seated members of an orchestra gives the public an erroneous impression of the dynamics at play. The orchestral players are at least as knowledgeable, and often times more experienced musicians, than the conductor.

An orchestra is comprised of an expanded string quartet, a woodwind ensemble, a brass ensemble and percussion. The strings play in small groups: first and second violins, violas, cellos, and bass support. A string quartet always plays without a conductor, as do woodwind and brass ensembles. In the symphonic repertoire, the winds and brass play solo parts in chamber music form. To coordinate an orchestra, the strings, as a block, have to mesh with the solo chamber groups of wind and brass. A conductor has to direct only two or three blocks (groups) of musicians at a time. He is not controlling a hundred people.

When Louis Spohr first stepped upon the podium in 1820, the orchestra was shocked. It had historically been the job of the concertmaster, the lead violinist, to direct the group *as he played*. This was often done somewhat crudely, by grimaces or the stamping of the concertmaster's foot to beat time. Spohr, who was a great violinist and well-known composer, created a sensation *by leading them all without playing*. This was done as an *expediency*. Spohr, *by conducting*, succeeded in *organizing* the players' efforts, all of whom played from individual parts and were, therefore, unable to see the *interaction* of their parts, which is written in the form of a score that displays all the parts at once, a format too cumbersome for the individual use of each player.

2 Nathan Milstein and Solomon Volkov, *From Russia to the West* (New York, Henry Holt and Co.,1990), 46-47.

Therefore, the use of a conductor can save rehearsal time and help organize a production in the same way as does a director in the theater. The position of conductor need not be so onerous to human dignity if the position became akin to a director of theater. But at this point, unlike a theater or movie director, the conductor never leaves the stage. This public position of authority that has thusly been bestowed upon him has elevated his importance beyond his actual function as an expediency. The medium is the message, as Marshall McLuhan has astutely posited; when one person stands on a podium in front of a group of a hundred people, the message transmitted is that he is essential to the proceedings. I would venture to say that if the principal oboist stood up in the middle of the orchestra whenever he played, he would inevitably increase his perceived importance also, and would soon demand more money.

Imagine a football coach shouting instructions while out on the field with the players during the game. I suspect he would interfere with the action of the people actually playing the game. A baseball or basketball coach may call the plays, but the athletes perform them on their own, which makes sense. Micromanaging during action inhibits the free flow of energy among the players and deprives them of the chance for inspiration, to catch fire. The coach does not need to yell instructions from the sidelines to the quarterback as he throws or as the receiver catches. That would interfere with their timing.

There are dark sides to the authoritarian control conductors have over the musicians in an orchestra. Here is an excerpt from Samuel Antek's, *This was Toscanini*:

> There is hardly a string player in a major symphony today…who did not turn to the orchestra as a last, grudging, desperate concession to economic necessity. To the string player a symphony orchestra offers little opportunity for personal expression or artistic creativity of his own. By and large, he resents the personal tyranny and artistic abuse of conductors. Like geisha girls who dance for whomever pays them orchestral musicians play to suit the taste and personal whim of whomever they play for, and their every musical instinct may be violated in doing this. They are in a sense self-expressive artists. Eventually they become only skillful automatons, giving no more, no less, than they are forced or cajoled into giving. As their original enthusiasms become dull and jaded, music making itself becomes a monotonous grind, and playing in a symphony orchestra but another way to make a living, one far removed from the dreams and desires that prompted the grueling work required to master

an instrument. Many musicians in large symphony orchestras actually grow to hate music and music making.[3]

It seems highly likely that wind and brass players are just as fatigued by this micromanagement. As I mentioned previously, an orchestra is comprised of *blocks* of players. Therefore, managing action onstage is not that complicated. Additionally, the standard repertory is so well-known by trained musicians that a major orchestra can play most symphonic works on their own. In practice, artistic decisions could be made by one person, a director, who is absent in performance. (Artistic decisions could also be discussed with players.) If properly rehearsed, a professional level orchestra should not need a conductor for a performance. Since a conductor is an expediency meant to *organize* a rehearsal and an interpretation, *ironically, his presence on the podium for a performance is a sign that the ensemble is not adequately prepared.*

Many conductors boast that they can memorize a score. Since the conductor does not play any notes this fact makes no difference. Perhaps Ingmar Bergman could memorize Ibsen's *A Doll's House*. This has little to do with putting on the play. Some conductors will say that to understand a score is difficult. Perhaps. But any well-trained musician should be able to do that. Must one be capable of analyzing every chord of a piece? Understanding the syntax of every sentence in *Death of a Salesman* does not mean you understand Willy Loman or his wife. Following the details of the score exactly, as many conductors will make a fetish of, means little, just as following the stage directions of a play literally is not enough. As we have discussed, the score must be *interpreted*, which requires insight, not simply compliance.

In theater the play comes alive through the interaction of the actors, yet the play is organized by the script. The director helps to coordinate the ensemble's effort in rehearsal and may succeed in helping to create an overall mood among the actors. But *he is not present* in a performance, although it might be instructive to imagine he was. To be comparable to a conductor, the director of a play would have to stand in the middle of the stage on a podium. As King Lear or other characters enter the stage, the actor must *wait* to speak until the director gestures that he may begin. The director continues to gesture for more sound, then less. As the action on stage heats up, the director might begin to dance around the podium in an ecstatic reverie. At the end of the performance, exhausted and sweating, the director takes a bow for everyone.

I suspect that such a scenario would interfere with the actors' ability to act and would most likely ruin an audience's ability to lose themselves in the drama.

---

3   Samuel Antek, *This Was Toscanini* (New York: Vanguard Press, 1963), 71-74.

(It might help in a comedy because whatever was being performed would seem laughable.) We have become accustomed to a conductor's dominating presence, but is the situation really so different? One may object to this depiction and state that orchestral scores are vastly complex, too intricate for musicians to negotiate without the help of time being depicted and cues given for various musical entrances. Yet even this is not as it appears.

I have a friend who has an unusual hobby. He goes to the San Francisco Public Library and borrows musical scores that no one has ever played or heard. Some modern compositions are incredibly complicated and, therefore, no one has taken the time to learn them. He is a violinist, not a pianist. But he is a computer expert. His hobby is entering these complex, unknown works into his computer. He punches in each note by hand. The computer plays the piece back in the voice of a piano or any other mixture of instruments the work calls for.

A student of mine was recently given the opportunity to perform in a master class Midori was giving on modern music. My student, only fifteen years old but an outstanding violinist, was given the score to a complex, twelve-tone, three movement sonata for violin and piano by Alexander Goehr. She had two weeks to learn it. This was an impossibility for her and her fifteen-year-old pianist. Even I could not have understood the score that quickly.

So I called Cohen and asked him to punch in the score. It took him six hours. He made a CD of the computer rendition. I listened to the piece, but was having a difficult time wrapping my mind around it. However, there is one feature of the computerized version that is truly amazing. I could slow the piece down at pitch. I could play it over and over at slow speed at the correct pitch and learn to hear it. The more I listened, the more the odd tonalities and rhythms began to seem as straightforward as Mozart to grasp. The slowness, at pitch, is what made the difference. The composer, after all, has all the time in the world to be able to hear it because he creates it slowly. However, once I understood it, I could help both students piece it together.

Cohen's CD had another helpful aspect. My student could rehearse on her own by playing along with the piano part at reduced speed at pitch, as could her pianist, playing with the recorded violin part. With this technology, and several rehearsals with each other, they were able to play the piece brilliantly in two weeks. Any complex score, or for that matter any score at all, can be realized by a computer in this way. To be done well, the score has to be entered by hand, a note at a time. It takes many hours, but once this is done, everyone in the world can have it. Stravinsky's *The Rite of Spring*, for example, could be studied at slow speed, at pitch, by every member of an orchestra. This technology also allows individual parts to be subdued at will, while others are amplified. Voices can be played against other voices or all the parts can be played at once. There is no pianist in the world who could do that.

And no conductor. This is, in reality, a new line of business: creating computer rendition study scores. Cohen's hobby has far-reaching implications. For example, a further use of this technology could be selling computerized versions of orchestral scores and chamber music scores to amateur musicians who could play along with them at slow speed for their own enjoyment. For all the expense of a conductor's salary, an organization could invest in creating a library of these types of study scores that would facilitate many more musicians being able to understand a score in depth.

There is another interesting aspect to Cohen's hobby. A musical score can finally be realized with perfect precision by a computer. As an experiment, Cohen entered a Beethoven piano sonata exactly as printed in the score. The computer played it back perfectly. It turns out, though, that perfection of this kind does not sound like music. What he realized is that for music to sound "human," each note has to be entered into the computer with a slightly different time span. Real performers, the people we like to listen to, play *unevenly*. This adds an interesting wrinkle into the intellectual debate about the sacrosanct nature of the score, and the oft-repeated platitude that everything you need to understand in a piece of music is already in the score. This is simply not so.

This experiment also puts to rest the notion that the ability to play metronomically is a musical virtue. (Yet, as we have mentioned, this is one of the main criteria for being a member of a major symphony orchestra.) A metronome is not rhythm. It is a machine. To play like a machine is anathema to every value our great composers had. Music is emotion. Its pulse is more subtle—making the beats obvious is to be avoided. Here is the great conductor Wilhelm Furtwängler on the subject of showing the beats:

> A strong downbeat has considerable disadvantages. It binds the movement of the piece to *specific points*, thereby restricting the natural flow of the music and reducing its expressiveness. A point remains a point...that is to say the purely rhythmic substance will be conveyed with the requisite precision, while the melodic substance, *everything that lies between the individual beats*...is left untouched. It is characteristic of such an interpretation, and a commonplace these days, that while the rhythm and the tempo receive due attention, the music itself does not.[4] (italics mine)

4   Wilhelm Furtwängler, *On Music: Essays and Addresses*, translated edited by Ronald Taylor (USA: Scolar Press, 1991), "The Tools of the Conductor's Trade," 19-20.

This is the most serious and *unsolvable* problem with the micromanagement of music by conductors—the beating of time accentuates the beat. The act of watching for a beat accents it, brings it into one's attention. It's like saying to someone "Don't think of a giraffe." *Therefore, a conductor's presence is itself a destroyer of musical values.* Playing together by watching a conductor's cues means the music cannot help but become mannered, not only because there must be a delay, an interference with the flow because of the distraction of waiting for permission to move, but more insidiously, a conductor's beat micromanages beats and bar lines, *which are killers of expression because they break the flow of the musical line.* Furtwängler was aware of this and tried to develop a technique for conducting that did not revolve around beats. Ironically, *a conductor's very presence as a beacon of musical direction that must be watched is unmusical.*

There is yet a further problem. As we have already mentioned, conductors stand on a podium over everyone else on stage, even in the case of accompanying a soloist. The audience's attention cannot help but be directed to his movements, not the music. The audience looks to the conductor's gestures with the dependency of a studio audience obeying cue cards. I am afraid that for audiences in our present day, the conductor has become a signpost for what is going on in the music. He gestures, he dances, he gets still. These are like silent captions to the music, but in essence a distraction to the orchestral performers' ability to create spontaneously genuine interaction and feeling with one another and therefore, robbing the audience of an "uninterpreted by sign language" musical experience. The excessive movements of a conductor are a sign of his disconnection with reality. Either he is afraid that no one will notice him or he is afraid that he is unnecessary and, therefore, draws attention to his leadership. Real control need not be broadcast. A minimalist conductor shows that by the mere raising of a finger he can make eighty people obey.[5] Yet this need for a display of power is an obfuscation of the fact that the conductor is fundamentally not essential to a performance. This is their greatest fear—that other people will start to understand what the conductor already knows.

Heifetz chose to do without a conductor for his last concert for television. When asked why, he replied, "We work together extremely well. They [the orchestra] understand that I would rather make contact than conduct."

For a successful musical event an audience needs to suspend belief. The belief in music to be suspended is that it is pre-written. In other words, it

---

5   If the reader could imagine the conductor yelling "Giddyup!" to the orchestra this would sum up the relationship between a conductor and the orchestra in a performance.

should sound improvised, free, made-up. A conductor's presence in front of the stage directing action suggests the opposite—that the music is planned and controlled. The focus of the concert becomes him, not Beethoven. It can be no other way as long as this practice continues. In addition, because the conductor is visible to the audience, his appearance can play into his popularity and is often an important factor in his selection. This distracts everyone from his true purpose—which is to *organize* the efforts of the orchestra. Does anyone care what the director of a play looks like? Does the director of the onstage action of an opera company remain in the midst of the singers during performance? Does the choreographer? Is it possible to safely do away with the presence of a conductor onstage during performance? Would performances fall apart? Would musical cohesiveness be lost? I think not.

Liszt agreed:

> ...the real task of the conductor, in my opinion, consists in making himself *ostensibly quasi*-useless.[6]

We can help make this a reality. A careful reading of this book will reveal that the opinions of this writer are not alone in objecting to the artistic compromise a conductor represents. A careful reading will also show that an answer has been supplied in our analysis of *bel canto* instrumental technique. Training musicians in the way described will eliminate the need for a leader depicting beats. We have seen that all ensembles can be held together—and the details of phrasing and nuance worked out—through the glue of the offbeat. In an ensemble, the interwoven and complimentary roles of the various instruments create a *self-binding* tapestry of relationship that propels a piece of music from start to finish. If phrased intelligently, the path of the music seems inevitable. Playing together is a matter of *phrasing* together, of *thinking* together. The interplay of offbeat to downbeat, which allows musicians to synchronize *themselves*, is where both the difficulty and solution lies.

This requires that the musicians of an orchestra play from music that shows the counterpoint, the interplay, between instruments. Unlike a play, where the script shows all the parts, traditionally the music used for orchestral ensembles shows only each individual part, not the whole. It is only the conductor who works from a complete score. This is only done out of practicality. If all the parts are shown, there are too many page turns to be negotiated and, additionally, the type is small because there are many parts per page. Yet computer technology can help in this regard and may have the democratizing effect that the printing

---

6   Eleanor Perényi, *Liszt—The Artist As Romantic Hero* (Boston: Little, Brown and Co., 1974), 292.

press and resultant availability of the Bible translated into local languages had in diminishing the power of the Catholic Church during the time of Martin Luther.

If music stands could be made with a computer screen (I believe such technology exists), individual music parts could be devised that would show whatever contrapuntal counterpart a player needed to play in relation to; through a touch of the screen, the entire score could appear if more detail was required. A music director could decide tempi at rehearsal, select particular ensemble difficulties, and display these passages—with an enhanced depiction of the score—on the computerized music stands. These areas could then be efficiently and thoroughly rehearsed. Sections of the music that remained problematic could continue to be shown on the screen with all counterparts necessary for reliable performance still visible. The computer screen could also be used for cues (a function a conductor often performs gratuitously), if necessary. Having a score, or even a partial score on the stand, makes cuing unnecessary because the music that leads into an entrance is visible.

Remember, as I said previously, a conductor only leads two or three choirs of instruments at a time. Individual string quartets play without conducting assistance, as do wind and brass ensembles. If players can view the part of the score vital to understanding the contrapuntal glue, there is little need for a human time-beater. If an organization does not wish to have a conductor at all, section leaders for each instrumental choir could rehearse and work out a musical approach before a general rehearsal. During a performance the section leaders could coordinate with each other both aurally and visually, leading the members of their respective sections.

This approach could even be used in opera performance. *Bel canto* instrumental technique and phrasing is naturally congruent with the subtleties of singing, as we have shown. A computerized score on the stand of section leaders, or even for all the orchestra members, would make following a singer quite simple, which brings us to an important point about ensemble playing. In reality it is the accompanying parts that control the solo lines, much to the chagrin and frustration of soloists. In an ideal musical world, an accompanying instrument is a true partner in the expression of the music, not a slave to the whim of a soloist. Therefore, an orchestra, should it wish to do so (as a pianist, in playing with a soloist), actually has complete control over a performance because they play the underlying harmonies, control the bass parts, and control most of the moving notes. Therefore, an orchestra can easily direct or better yet, cooperate with soloists or singers, without any need of a conductor. Pianists, in the role of accompanists, do this all the time.

In dance performances, dancers should be following the music, or in their own minds bringing it forth (not, as is often done, the music following the dance). Here again, there is no need for a conductor as long as the ensemble can play in a coherent and musical manner. Forward motion of the music, as I described in earlier chapters, is a result of proper phrasing, and should an ensemble play in this way—a great help for physical movement—dancers would have no need of a time-beater whose very presence and activity accentuates downward motion by the depiction of beats.

The myth of the necessity of a conductor is perpetuated by musical institutions. Students in elite music schools such as Curtis and Juilliard are *required* to play in an orchestra under the direction of a conductor. In fact, this necessity is the assumed position of music schools. Humiliatingly, students must even play with student conductors, allowing a fellow student to train himself to be their boss with their help and support. It would be far more educational to show students how to play major symphonic works *without* a conductor, which would begin to correct the inversion of musical reality that a conductor represents. Students would need to understand how to read scores, learn to listen and interact, how to make decisions about phrasing and the balance of sound between the various orchestral blocks of players—all skills that they should master anyway. Wilhelm Furtwangler urged that:

> We must discover guidelines for interpretation which take us beyond the sterile worship of the literal text on the one hand and the totally vague, all or nothing shibboleth of "creative interpretation" on the other.[7]

This book has discussed these guidelines and found that the movement of the offbeat to the downbeat and the interactive, expressive subtleties inherent in this understanding, can control an ensemble's cohesiveness and includes not only principles of phrasing, but phrasing of rhythm. The two are really inseparable since music unfolds through *time*.

The parameters of the music educational system *preclude* other more reasonable possibilities for a conductor's role to emerge. Our system *allows a* conductor to be in this unquestioned tyrannical position. Incredibly, as further proof of his dominance, he is referred to, without laughter, by his co-workers as Maestro. Maestro means "master" or "teacher" in Italian and is a title of extreme respect given to a master musician. Why does the conductor receive this title? Why does he not refer to his equally and sometimes more talented colleagues with this respectful title?

---

7   *Ibid.* 4, "Principles of Interpretation," p. 11.

A word comes to mind—arrogance—which means "exaggerating or disposed to exaggerate one's own worth or importance often by an overbearing manner."[8] Why would someone exaggerate his importance? Perhaps arrogance protects or covers something up. We have a clue from Nathan Milstein's memoir:

> Toscanini liked to sip champagne and converse in his mixed English-Italian. After dinner he usually went to his library. Horowitz and I would follow. Toscanini, gradually falling asleep, would mutter at us, "What you do is difficult! In order to play the violin or piano, you have to work, to think. For us conductors, others play. And I don't have to do anything!" As it applies to him and perhaps a dozen or so other conductors, Toscanini's words were, of course, a blatant exaggeration. But in principle I think he's right.[9]

Toscanini told the truth. Conducting makes it impossible to truly judge the conductor's musical sophistication—no one ever hears the conductor play. How many famous conductors of today can perform a major concerto on their instruments at a level equal to the musical expertise they claim? It might be interesting to contractually require that once a year the conductor of an orchestra give a solo recital on their main musical instrument. This would be quite revealing.[10]

Badly trained or amateur musicians may continue to need the help of a beat depicter, but musicians schooled in the manner we have described in this book will have little or no need for such direction. Eventually the conductor's onstage presence will become a silly and quaint anachronism, an expediency that was once turned into an industry benefitting a few wannabe emperors whose moment of relevance has passed. If I were the chairman of the board of a major orchestra or the director of a conservatory, I would give pause to these suggestions. To break the cult of the conductor, all that is necessary is to remove him from the stage. He is usually, at heart, an exploiter of other people's talent. There are exceptions, although salary differential is a good indicator of the relationship. The players will prefer it, the audience will enjoy a more spontaneous performance, students will learn to be better musicians, and the board can relax a little about raising money. *The cult of the conductor is an inversion of reality, a symptom of "institutionalized" professional amateurism, flourishing because there is a lack of real musical education.*

---

8 There are some conductors who are rare exceptions.

9 *Ibid.* 2, 164.

10 One could add that a qualification for ascertaining musical expertise would be an ability to compose, but what constitutes compositional skill has become so confused and, additionally, divorced from an ability to play an instrument, that the assertion of compositional expertise has become increasingly difficult to conflate with musical understanding and sophistication. We will examine this in Chapter 24.

CHAPTER 23

Agents and Soloism

They are inseparable.

A star is not born. She is made by businessmen, a marketing creation helpful to an agent's fee. Whatever will make an agent the most money is what they will promote. The larger the fees they can command for their roster of stars, the more money an agent makes. The easier a star is to sell, the more money an agent makes. The more scenarios that can be concocted to create a mass audience, the more money an agent makes. If this means Pavarotti will sing an aria with Sting, it also means an agent may be able to create a crossover market, which means more money. The stars are usually represented by the same agents. The star conductors engage the players that an agent wants. This is much better for the agent's business.

A small stable of soloists, a few conductors, and a few agents have what seems to be a monopoly on concert venues. What is wrong with this? Well, wrong is too judgmental. One might ask, "What does this situation create?" Stasis and an overvaluing of performers. This fact also contributes to a withering of artistic values because musical "style" and approach is set by a few people who are heard exclusively. And, judging by the fact that classical music is losing its audience base, it seems possible that attendance is habitual rather than compelled from true interest.

Here is what an agent, Ron Wilfred, a man who manages most of the prominent conductors' and soloists' careers, has to say about his own contribution to the art of music:

> My client is the artist—not the Philharmonic, not the Met, not anyone else, and I am absolutely ruthless if it comes to telling an orchestra to go to hell if I feel something is unfair to an artist of mine. I don't really care because if I have an artist they want, they will have to book him.[1]

---

1 Joseph Horowitz, *Classical Music in America* (New York: W. Norton & Co., 2005), 489.

In 1992 the American Symphony Orchestra League reported that orchestra costs had risen 800% since 1971, half the increase related to "artistic costs," fees paid to conductors and soloists, from which the agent takes a commission.[2] It is in an agent's interest and convenience to create monopolies and brand-name performers. An agent is not a promoter of art. He is a salesman and acts according to his nature.

Artistic costs for soloists and conductors are not paid for through ticket sales. The funds are raised through the charitable giving of a musical organization's constituency, usually with very few people bearing the bulk of the cost. This means that the funds to pay artists are raised by a different type of selling than an exchange of services. The selling that occurs must convince people to *give away* their money. A sale of this sort is complicated if the beneficiaries are not perceived to be in dire economic straits or compromised health. Therefore, the salespeople—the administration of the musical organization—must convince the donor that unless the money is raised he cannot have access to people whose ability cannot be replicated.

For this structure to exist, there must be agreement by both sides that this *scarcity* is a *reality*. Hence, it is in the interest of promoters and agents to fuel this paradigm. They, the agents, receive a percentage from the fees raised through donations. The supposed *scarcity* of the artists—which the agent would argue increases their worth and, not unimportantly, the agent's fee—is "sold" as a means to increase charitable donating. This approach is necessary in any situation where costs are not supported by an exchange of service. In Europe, musical organizations are often supported by the state, but the same ploy is likely used. It is a much easier sales pitch to claim scarcity, which also *requires* that the pool of players must be small. This means more money for everyone, as long as a few wealthy members of the public will buy into the pitch.

Yet to any reflective mind it must seem odd that in the field of music, unlike any other field, a handful of performers are deemed the only people who can sufficiently play or conduct music well enough to necessitate that they play nearly every major concert venue for two generations. But it can also be seen that this *contrived* situation benefits the people in that system enormously.

If charitable giving was not allowed for musical organizations, and fees and costs were collected through sales of exchange and not donations, I suspect that we would quickly find that these few soloists and conductors are not as in demand by the concert-going public as the situation seems to suggest.

2 *Ibid.*, 490.

Many of the performers who currently dominate the classical music world were promoted by Isaac Stern. Itzhak Perlman, Pinchas Zuckerman, Gil Shaham, Midori, Yo-Yo Ma, Sarah Chang, Schlomo Mintz and a few others are his protégés. Anne-Sophie Mutter is Karajan's creation. These performers are all very good. However, they are not in their positions because of an open process. Most of them never won major competitions, except for Perlman, who won the Leventritt, and Zuckerman, who did so, rumor has it, with the help of Stern talking his fellow jurors "into changing their minds so that nineteen-year-old Pinchas Zukerman…could share the [Levintritt] award with Kyung-Wha Chung."[3] Joshua Bell and Hillary Hahn have made careers without winning competitions. It's not that competitions are good, or even fair. It's just that all the effort young "hopefuls" put into winning them is often quite useless. The *business* of music is played by other rules. It is run by networked, close-knit relationships, as is the film industry or, in fact, any other business.[4]

Perhaps you may have noticed that year after year the same few performers appear everywhere you turn. They fly from concert to concert, able to play the same program over and over because they perform far away from where they played the previous night. The same people, year after year, play every major venue, every major concerto. They are paid a lot of money to do so, as are, consequently, their agents; money, as we mentioned, that is not supported in ticket sales. Some of them get $80,000 a night and more. This money has to be begged for by non-profits, that have an array of people on their payroll whose job it is to sell the public to give money not only to these performers, but to themselves as well, since their pay also comes from charity or public funding. Our current roster of soloists are expensive and their star qualities are hardly the level of a Milstein, Heifetz or Horowitz. In addition, their importance and achievements cannot be compared to the dead composers' "oevre" they live on. They have, in fact, been allowed to have an *inverted* relationship to music.

We see inverted values when we see ad lines such as:

HEIFETZ plays Beethoven

or

KARAJAN conducts Mahler

This may be good for ticket sales, but it is a sign that the art is in trouble.

---

3   *Ibid.*, 491.

4   Aaron Rosand claims that Isaac Stern interfered with his career. See "High Explosive: Aaron Rosand Accuses Isaac Stern of Sabotaging His Career," by Norman Lebrecht, Slipped Disc, July, 8, 2014, "My Life With Isaac Stern," by Aaron Rosand.

A few years ago I drove across the country. I was struck by the fact that everywhere I went the same chain stores, hotels and restaurants appeared. It was like being trapped in Bill Murray's endlessly recurring 24-hour cycle in the movie *Groundhog Day*, except that I kept changing cities. Likewise, as I mentioned, it is not uncommon for a soloist to dominate a world market for *forty or fifty* years, *which seems incredible and exceedingly strange* considering the fact that conservatories and colleges churn out *thousands* of performers *each* year. In men's tennis it is desperately difficult to dominate for one season, let alone two or three. The same is true in golf and every other sport. There is always a competitor at their heels. This is not true in music, which is odd no matter what way one looks at it.[5]

Of course, winners and losers are not so clear in music. Performers don't compete directly against each other—music is not a sport. There is another reason that helps explain this monopoly, aside from what might be discovered by an investigation into contractual agreements. In sports, video analysis of

---

5   Concert presenters within the same geographical area sometimes have an agreed upon protocol for sharing "top" performers from season to season. One season a concert presenter will book a "star," the next year another presenter in the same area can or cannot, by tacit arrangement between presenters, book the same artist.

    Additionally, presenters often organize and coordinate the timing of their bids for a particular performer. Several presenters, in agreement and coordinated action, will submit an identical bid in the same week for the same performer at an agreed upon, but discounted price.The agent and performer can, thereby, book several performances, albeit at a reduced fee, but accrue considerably more money than they would for a single performance at one venue for their usual fee. Yet equally important, or perhaps even more important, the performer and agent gain actual and perceived market share and dominance (demand). This industry practice means that many artists are shut out of the market. We begin to see, perhaps, why so many competition winners or other equally fine performers are rarely, if ever, heard in major venues by the public.

    This systemic situation offers little incentive for concert presenters to develop markets for less-known performers. It also reinforces the misguided perception of the general public and donors that there is a scarcity of "talent." This false, and perhaps calculated perception, fuels the rise in concert fees, the need for development personnel within musical organizations and the rise in ticket prices. This "arrangement" between presenters may give a false reading on the decline of interest in classical music—the lack of audience development may be due in large part to the monotony of the offerings.

    This systemic stasis is unlikely to occur in the arena of pop music because the "discovery" of new or unusual talent offers the presenter a chance for vast monetary gain. There is no similar benefit in classical music to presenters for "developing" new talents. Perhaps the hand-wringing over "developing" audiences should be, in fact, more about developing markets for new performers rather than "developing" audiences to be willing to see the same few performers for forty years, which is, quite understandably, a lost cause. This begs the question: is dwindling interest in classical music due to people's lack of education and changing taste or is it due to the fact that the offerings are monotonous?

players is common and has had the effect of greatly leveling the playing field. What one person may do to his advantage in the game is quickly discovered. Moreover, unlike music, the game is open to any qualified challenger.

We certainly can analyze how the greatest people play and learn from them, although we don't. As we learned from Nathan Milstein in a quotation previously mentioned in this book, he believed that it is possible and worthwhile to analyze the technique of great players. But, he added, most people are afraid to make the attempt. I would say they are *distracted* from making such inquiries because they believe that it is not possible to deconstruct "talent." Yet make the attempt we should because we can expect no help from the artists. If great players believe that their technique is their expression, their uniqueness, as Milstein stated about himself, we can never expect them to share their knowledge.

Therefore, the reason why Milstein would not teach in a serious way becomes obvious and logical. And it is likely that Horowitz, Heifetz, and other great players feel the same way. They do, in fact, have their secrets, yet they don't seem to see the irony of this position. They did not teach themselves how to play the violin or piano. They were taught by great masters. At best, they put a personal twist on something they were given.

I have a friend who is a very prominent musician, a fine player. One day over lunch I asked him if he could teach someone to play the way he does, to play on his level. "Yes, but I wouldn't," was his reply.

I have mentioned my ideas about analyzing the approaches of great masters to other well-known top performers. Their reply is always the same. "I don't think you can explain talent." To which I respond, "You may be able to explain ninety-eight percent of it." That ends the conversation.

From Charles Rosen's book, *Piano Notes*, we get a glimpse into the "generosity" of a famous performer towards his fellow musicians:

> Arthur Rubenstein, who had a great and humane wit, was once asked if he listened to other pianists, and replied, "If they play badly I feel terrible; if they play well I feel worse."[6]

Krachmalnick told me about an encounter that he had with the famous violinist, Henryk Szeryng. Szeryng was in San Francisco to play a solo with the orchestra. Krachmalnick was the concertmaster and, as I have mentioned, a great violinist. He owned a Guarneri del Gesù, a violin equal to a Stradavarius; his violin was considered to be one of the maker's finest examples. Szeryng also

---

6   Charles Rosen, *Piano Notes,* (New York: The Free Press, 2002), 109.

owned a del Gesù, and after the rehearsal asked Krachmalnick if he could take a look at it. Jake agreed. They met in Szeryng's dressing room. Krachmalnick took his violin from the case and presented it to Szeryng, whereupon Szeryng played it for about five minutes, finally stopping and proclaiming that he approved of its reputation. Krachmalnick then asked Szeryng if he could try his Guarneri. Szeryng took the fiddle from the case and held it in front of Krachmalnick's face: "You can look, but don't touch."

Another comment by Charles Rosen gives some idea of the arbitrariness and subjectivity of pianists judging other pianists in competitions:

> In any case as far as I can judge, concert pianists are often much less prejudiced than teachers about other pianists: they rarely want to hear an imitation of themselves, they prefer to think they own their performances and have a patent on the style. If I want to hear a piece played my way, I play it myself. From another pianist I would like something individual that has not occurred to me.[7]

Some stars refuse to ever leave the stage and contrive ways to remain in the spotlight. Often, once they are too tired or too old to play solos, many turn to conducting. This cements the same people into positions of power for generations.

One way to open opportunity and shake the system up would be to make esoteric knowledge *generally* available. If a school of music was created that scientifically analyzed virtuosos in the same manner that currently occurs in sports, and the results of these investigations were made available to the public, we would have an outpouring of excellence. We certainly can figure out how great players play. They are, after all, as human as anyone else.

Our current musical power structure will change greatly once this new paradigm is used in teaching and will lead to a democratization of the field. It may be true that we see the same players, as if watching constant reruns of old television shows, but it is not the fault of the concert agents, the players, or a conspiracy. It is a logical and inevitable outcome of the confusion at the foundation of music itself—education. Our unreflective system *precludes* the possibility of creating hundreds of outstanding players and makes scarcity of quality *seem* an *absolute* unchangeable fact.

Ironically, soloism is a *symptom* of the *ubiquity* of inferior teaching methods. It can only flourish where there is pervasive accidental and unscientific teaching. *It creates an incorrect, inverted relationship between the performer and the music he plays.*

---

7 *Ibid.*, 109.

The only way a performer can correct this is by becoming an excellent composer himself. Our current system of music education has not only created soloism—the *overvaluation* of the performer—it has unknowingly abetted this trend by neglecting the training of virtuoso performer/composers, who in the past were the source of nearly all musical composition. Where would soloists be without the two handfuls of composers who wrote the masterworks they play? Certainly not playing solo concerts. They have solo careers because of the great music written for their instruments.[8] Unfortunately, the art of composition is currently in a state of incoherence, as we shall see in our next chapter.

---

8   No one has composed a well-written concerto for the violin or piano for decades. Prokofiev's *Piano Concerto No. 3* was written in 1921. His *Violin Concerto No. 2* in 1935. Shostakovich's *Piano Concerto No. 2* was completed in 1957. Stravinsky wrote his violin concerto in 1931. Compare this with the world-wide *annual* output of material for actors.

CHAPTER 24

Composers

Sadly, the art of composition is suffering. Neglect, misdirection, and confusion are the causes. To start with, an unfortunate emphasis on the importance of originality *vis-a-vis* composing has created a black hole in music. This trap, a vortex which devours creative energy, is the belief that to be truly creative one must be original when, in fact, originality does not exist. If the evolution of all life is derivative, it follows that nothing can be original.

Additionally, most musicians are oriented by our current educational system to becoming "star" performers or orchestra players and rarely take even a course in composition or learn to improvise (we are not including jazz, which is a *style*, not a *method* for improvisation), which was a necessary skill for any musician in the Baroque era and was the wellspring of musical composition.

Nowadays those who do compose are a minuscule subset of musicians who have little interaction with performing musicians. Not only do music schools no longer train virtuoso player/composers, but often students who study composition *cannot play any instrument at all. Our educational system precludes the possibility that a composer of the level of Brahms, Beethoven or Prokofiev will be formed.* When composing music has become separated from the fact that it must be performed and the creator of the music cannot play what he wrote, or is not skilled enough to understand what might be unplayable, we have entered the realm of "theoretical" music.

Theoretical music has its place—somewhere on a shelf. Although there are many demands and pleas to support avant-garde music with grants, and societies formed to educate the public about its profundities, there is no need to support it, aside from making space for the scores in libraries. This is because the demands the composer makes on the performers, the audience and the instruments are antagonistic to the nature of all three groups. Therefore, after its first difficult performance, usually by a group of devoted friends, the score finds its way to a library shelf. There need not be any practicality to a composer's creation. Yet additionally, no one needs to play it, listen to it, or pay for it.

Our current educational policy of separating composing from learning to play an instrument has created this situation. On the one hand, performers do not learn what the written notes of a score represent to a creator: how much is impossible to convey, what immense variation there is in choices, subtlety, and complexity when bringing an idea or feeling from one's mind to a somewhat concrete realization on paper. They, therefore, tend to be too literal in their "recreation" of the music or, often, too insensitive to the nuance implied on the printed page. On the other hand, composers, if not outstanding players, cannot understand how to write well for performers: what is comfortable, what is difficult but worth the time to learn, what is technically challenging yet within the bounds of proper instrumental technique.

Instruments are based on the human voice. They are, in fact, different voices, and skilled composers treat them as such. A voice is used to impart information. In the case of music, that information is emotional. To liken this approach to that of a playwright, if an author writes a play that requires the actors to scream gibberish all night, it may be theoretically interesting, but who would want to act in it or watch it? Theater of the absurd goes only so far; we see the point in a couple of minutes. Additionally, playwrights do not write parts that are *inherently antagonistic* to the nature of the vocal cords. This is because writers are able to speak well; they are, in fact, experts of language. This is not true of composers who, as we have noted, often cannot play any instrument at all, let alone on an expertly fluent level. Their compositions for instruments are often comparable to the level of insight and language sophistication of a television soap opera or a children's show. Writers often work directly with actors to help transmit the spirit of their work. But what spirit can be conveyed to performers by composers who cannot play what they write or cannot understand the nature of the instruments they compose for?

Because instruments are voices, to ask them to be machines or simply noise makers is against the purpose of their creation. Additionally, music must have pattern for an auditor or player to derive any meaning from the sounds. Without understandable pattern, the music is not only horribly difficult to learn, it is also horribly difficult to listen to. This is perhaps easier to understand if we use the act of writing a play as a metaphor for composing music.

For example, let's explore the idea, "The dog went to the store," as a motif for a play. This can be made into many scenarios. How did the dog go to the store? What did he go through to get there? Whom did he encounter? Was it even open? Was it, in fact, closed, and is this not typical of his life, and now he feels sorry for himself, but there is a girl dog, or a nice human he meets, etc. This is a story. This has emotion.

What many modern music composers see in the idea, "The dog goes to the store," is quite different. For them it is not about a journey or situation, it is about the words themselves and how they can be cleverly manipulated. So this motif becomes "The store went the to dog," or "Store the to dog the," or "Erotsehtottnewgodeht," which is the phrase spelled backwards, which the composer can then throw into the air, watch where the individual letters land and see if they will make a sentence. Or a composer can arrange the letters into a pile and watch them. Maybe something will happen. Maybe meaning will appear.

This is very similar to the approach of many modern composers. Unfortunately, the play, the real story, which should be in the music composed, is not taking place. The only sense or message being conveyed is the absurd waste of everyone's time in playing and listening to intellectual gibberish that has little more meaning than a crossword puzzle. It may be enjoyable to push one's pen around some manuscript paper at home on a Sunday morning, but the use of ink will probably not result in the creation of anything one would pay to see performed.

> Individual caprice and intellectual anarchy, which tend to control the world in which we live, isolate the artist from his fellow-artists and condemn him to appear as a monster in the eyes of the public; a monster of originality, inventor of his own language…and the apparatus of his art. The use of already employed material and of established forms is forbidden him. So he comes to the point of speaking an idiom without relation to the world that listens to him. His art becomes truly unique, in the sense that it is incommunicable and shut off on every side. The erratic block is no longer a curiosity that is an exception; it is the sole model offered neophytes for emulation.[1]

Schoenberg was a great intellect and composer. But even Mahler, to Schoenberg's disappointment, had some difficulty comprehending a score of his, according to Schoenberg, saying, "I have conducted the most difficult scores of Wagner; I have written complicated music myself of up to thirty staves and more; yet here is a score (the first string quartet of Schoenberg) that I am unable to read."[2] Yet no one would, or should, dare to say that Schoenberg was

---

1 Igor Stravinsky, *Poetics of Music In The Form of Six Lessons,* translated by Arthur Knodel and Ingolf Dahl (Cambridge: Harvard University Press, 1970), 73-74.

2 Josiah Fisk, *Composers on Music* (Boston: Northeastern University Press, 1997), 193.

not a master of the art of composition. Rachmaninoff accurately describes our current situation:

> …I can respect the artistic aim of a composer if he arrives at the so-called modern idiom after an intense period of preparation. Stravinsky, after all, did not compose *The Rite of Spring* until he had had an extensive period of study with a master like Rimsky-Korsakov, and until he had composed a classical symphony and other works in the classical forms. Otherwise, *The Rite of Spring* for all its boldness would not have possessed such solid musical merits in the form of imaginative harmonies and energetic rhythms. Such composers know what they are doing when they break a law; they know what to react against because they have had experience in the classical forms and style. Having mastered the rules, they know which can be violated and which can be obeyed. But…I have found too often that young composers plunge into writing of experimental music with their school lessons only half learned. Too much radical music is sheer sham, for this very reason; it's composer sets about revolutionizing the laws of music before he has learned them himself…
>
> And yet there is this possibility; if you insist on becoming intimately acquainted with the old world before venturing upon a new, you may very well discover that there is room enough in the former, that there is no need for you to seek new paths…The only originality worth achieving is that which comes from substance.[3]

Most modern composition is a combination of poorly written parts for the instruments asked to perform the piece and a contrived attempt at originality—a product of intellectualism. Intellectualism is a refuge from feeling, a mask covering feelings of helplessness in viewing the confusion of life. If art does not make sense emotionally, if it is not from the heart or soul—unless its message is a nihilistic scream about the unknowable aspect of things—it is off the mark and self-importantly "deep."

The quest for "originality" is an illusion. Understanding the *craft* of composition and the instruments one writes for is what is essential. Audiences and performers will support new music if it is well-written for performers and the auditors like it. The art of composition is currently suffering from a *lack of skill* on two levels. Composers are not masters of an instrument in any way that would have been understood by the great composers and performers of the past. This circumstance is the result of a pervasive and nearly "institutionalized" lack of pedagogical seriousness regarding instrumental training, a foundational deficiency that

3   *Ibid.,* 235.

severely limits a would-be composer's ability to write intelligibly. This prevents composers from taking their rightful place within the musical world as the vanguard of musical value, tradition, and innovation based on the *mastery* of their medium.

ACT V

Teaching:
Values Create Culture
and Potentiality

CHAPTER 25

The Suzuki Violin Method

WHO'S WATCHING THE STORE?

Next we review the Suzuki Violin Method. Since its introduction to the music world in the late 1950s and early 1960s there has not yet been a serious review of its pedagogical approach. When a claim of expertise or knowledge is asserted, it is customary, indeed demanded by the professionalism of the field that such an assertion be verified by examination. The fact that Suzuki's method has never been seriously examined is, in itself, evidence of the lack of intellectual rigor in the field of music. Imagine, if you will, the published claim of any scientist that he has discovered a way to understand anything at all being unreviewed and accepted by the scientific community for fifty years without investigation. But in music...
It is time to start.

The Suzuki Method, initially used for teaching the violin but recently expanded to include other instruments as well, has become a brand name associated by the general public with music education in the United States.[1] Yet the assertion that one has a method, is not proof of its validity. Its coherence can only be demonstrated by scientific inquiry—an impartial look at the facts to determine what is beyond mere personal opinion and unsubstantiated belief. The Suzuki Method is now being applied to other instruments and promoted in several countries,[2] which makes its examination more urgent.

In a 2001 book, *Suzuki Twinkles*,[3] the author, Dr. Alfred Garson, an intimate friend of the founder of the method, Shinichi Suzuki, relates the following:

> After teaching several of his advanced students, I wondered if they would have made those same mistakes if they had been brought up with scales and etudes...I decided to ask Suzuki. He replied,

---

1 Margaret Mehl, "Cultural Translation in Two Directions: The Suzuki Method in Japan and Germany," (Research & Issues in Music Education, 7/1, 2009).

2 *Ibid.*, 1.

3 Dr. Alfred Garson, *Suzuki Twinkles* (USA, 2001), 37, 76.

> Scales and etudes are not necessary for learning the first eight books [of his method], but after that you may be right. That is why I always send my students on to study with a master teacher.

On another occasion a violinist told Suzuki:

> I still remember [the etudes of] Meerts, Seybold, Mazas, Sitt, Ševčík, Dont, Fiorillo, Dancla, Kreutzer, Gaviniès, and Wieniawski…They were not fun like the Suzuki Method.

> All the studies you have mentioned are unmusical and boring, [Suzuki replied.]

Born in Japan in 1898, little is known of Shinichi Suzuki aside from his primarily anecdotal writing and the hagiographic references about him made by music teachers employing his method. In 1868 the Japanese government began to introduce Western music into the country as part of a "Westernization" policy. Interest developed and grew. Suzuki's father taught himself how to make violins and by 1888 owned a violin factory that produced four hundred machine-made violins and four thousand bows per day. As a teenager Suzuki worked in the factory as part of the management. When he was *eighteen* years old he began to teach himself to play the violin by listening to a recording of Mischa Elman playing "Ave Maria." He tried to copy it by ear because he couldn't read music.[4]

He had to abandon his efforts because the long, smooth bows required proved to be too difficult. On the other side of the record was a minuet by Haydn. He decided to copy this, which he thought was easier, because as he put it, "Short, fast bows are easier to play than long, slow bows."[5] According to him, his "self-taught technique was more a scraping than anything else."[6]

He was invited on a world tour by his father's friend, the Marquis Tokogawa. His father gave Suzuki 150,000 yen to pay for the trip, agreeing that if enough money was left over he could study the violin in Europe. Suzuki was twenty-two years old, the year 1920, when he arrived in the capital of the Weimar Republic of Germany—Berlin. At a concert he heard the Klingler Quartet, whose first violinist, Karl Klingler, impressed him. Suzuki wrote to him and was accepted as a pupil. Suzuki recounted in his largely anecdotal book, *Nurtured By Love*, that the lessons were difficult for him. He was aware of his technical deficiencies and wrote that he "had no illusions about my performing ability."[7]

---

4   *Ibid.* 3, 11.

5   *Ibid.*, 81.

6   Shinichi Suzuki, *Nurtured By Love* (New York, 1983), 69.

7   *Ibid.* 6, 76.

Suzuki writes that he studied with Klinger for eight years, leaving Germany in 1928. He returned to Japan with his German wife, Waltraud Prange, and began teaching violin at the Imperial and Kunitachi Conservatories. According to Suzuki,[8] in 1931 the father of a four-year-old asked him to teach his son the violin. It was through this experience that he developed his method. He writes that during this period the thought suddenly struck him that all Japanese children possess the innate ability to learn their own language fluently. If the method that adults use to teach their children language was applied to other skills, children could learn them as naturally.

The astonishing ability of young children to learn and the educational opportunity it afforded from infancy was not a new idea. It was first developed into a practical approach based on a philosophy of pedagogy by the famed Swiss educator, Johann Pestalozzi (1746-1827) in the early nineteenth century.[9] His profound pedagogical insights, disseminated through his schools and enormous output of written material, influenced education throughout Europe.[10] Albert Einstein was greatly affected intellectually by a school he attended in Aarau, Switzerland, that was modeled on Pestalozzian principles of teaching.[11] We will discuss Pestalozzi's ideas in detail in Chapter 30.

Pestalozzi's concepts were continued by Maria Montessori (1870-1952) who, acknowledging his influence on her work, developed the Montessori Method. By the 1920s her schools were established throughout the world; her books published in several languages.[12] After spending eight years in Berlin, Suzuki claimed many of the same educational insights of Pestalozzi and Montessori in his pamphlet, *Talent Education and its Method*, published in 1949.[13] Suzuki asserted that he had discovered a unique method to teach young children the violin.[14] Is his method unique? Have young children never been successfully taught to play musical instruments?

The instruction of young children in the art of music has been a tradition in Europe for hundreds of years. European training produced all the composers

---

8 *Ibid.*, 1.

9 Johann Pestalozzi, *How Gertrude Teaches Her Children: An Attempt To Help Mothers Teach Their Own Children,* translated by Lucy Holland and Francis Turner (London, 1900), first published in 1803, reprinted Internet Archive, 2007.

10 Johann Pestalozzi, *Letters of Pestalozzi On the Education Of Infancy, Addressed To Mothers* (Boston,1830), Nabu Public Domain Reprints, 2012.

11 Walter Isaacson, *Einstein: His Life and Universe* (New York, 2007), 26.

12 Maria Montessori, *The Montessori Method,* translated by Anne Everett George (New York, 1912). Maria Montessori, *Education For A New World* (Kalakshetra, 1946).

13 Shinichi Suzuki, *Young Children's Talent Education & It's Method* (USA, 1949).

14 *Ibid.* 6, 2.

and performers who created what we call "classical" music. Bach, Mozart, Beethoven, Liszt, Paganini, and countless others were trained from an early age. Many toured throughout Europe as child prodigies. How were they taught? An excellent example of traditional European training for the violin is the *Graded Course of Violin Playing*,[15] published in 1926, written by Leopold Auer,[16] consisting of eight volumes of material sanctioned by another master teacher of the violin, Carl Flesch (1873-1944).

The Soviet Union—as did Russia, before the Revolution—made great contributions to musical pedagogy, systematizing the teaching of children into a science. The technical and musical excellence of the students trained by the Soviet/Russian system remains unrivaled. They produced four or five generations of the world's greatest musicians and still do so—Jascha Heifetz, Nathan Milstein, Leonid Kogan, David Oistrakh, Igor Oistrakh, Victoria Mullova, Vadim Repin, and many, many more. Among pianists—Sergei Rachmaniniff, Alexander Scriabin, Vladimir Horowitz, Emil Gilels, Sviatoslav Richter and countless others. How does Shinichi Suzuki's method of teaching, very popular in the U.S., differ from the traditions of Europe or the Soviet Union? Does he have unique insight or expert knowledge? Does his method achieve better results?

Suzuki derived his method of teaching the violin from his *self-teaching*, not his European lessons or available methods.[17] As he related to Dr. Garson:

> [Suzuki] Do you remember why I gave up on Schubert's, "Ave Maria?"
>
> [Garson] Was it because of the long, slow bows?
>
> [Suzuki] Exactly. When I chose "Twinkle, Twinkle, Little Star" as the foundation for my method, I realized that I could not start with that since it has to be played with long and slow bow strokes…
>
> The rhythm of the first variation…is the same rhythm that opens the Bach Double Violin Concerto. The other four variations are also typical Baroque rhythms…on the A and E string only, because that was easy for me…This was my own personal experience. I found this out *when teaching myself to play the violin*. That's why I planned *Book 1* the way it is…
>
> [Garson] In other words, the variations were put ahead of the theme for practical reasons based *on your own learning experience*?

---

15 Leopold Auer, *Graded Course Of Violin Playing*, Books 1-8 (New York, 1926).

16 Leopold Auer, *My Long Life In Music* (New York, 1923). Auer's musical background, experiences, and associations were remarkable.

17 *Ibid*. 3, 81.

> [Suzuki] Exactly. Short, fast bows are easier to play than long, slow bows. That
> is why I have all the variations played in the middle of the bow with short,
> fast bows.

It begs the question since, by his own admission, he had no illusions about his performing ability: Why would students want to follow *his* example? It also begs another. Why would he teach students the same foundation that had limited his own playing ability?

Shinichi Suzuki often stated, and is quoted in books published by the Suzuki Association, that the main purpose of his teaching is not to create performing artists, but to create better human beings.[18] We, therefore, have a violin method with a unique approach, one whose main purpose is *not* to make students masterful players.

The aforementioned Dr. Garson, himself a Suzuki method teacher, writes about the mother of one of his violin students who mentioned that another teacher had questioned the suitability of material in Suzuki's *Book 1*.[19] Garson replied,

> Madam, did he look at the book for maybe ten minutes, would you say?
>
> Yes, something like that.
>
> Madam, it took Suzuki more than ten years to write that book. Do you mean
> to tell me that after a ten minute scrutiny, your proper teacher is qualified to
> criticize Suzuki?

To an expert, a one-minute look is sufficient, yet we will examine each book and his method in detail, which will make for less interesting reading, but allows for a fair and thorough examination. Suzuki had his own approach to teaching the violin, based on his self-teaching, which was unlike traditional European/Russian methods of violin instruction, coupled with an observation about how young children learn.

Pedagogical methods for teaching very young children were well-known in educated European society at the time of Suzuki's Berlin visit and have been used to teach all manner of subjects, including music, since the nineteenth century.[20] One of the primary motivations and rationalizations for the early

---

18 John Kendall, *The Suzuki Method In American Music Education* (USA, 1966), 31.

19 *Ibid.* 3, 26.

20 Bernard Rainbow, "H.G. Nageli, Die Pestalozzische Gesangbildungslehre 1809," *Four Centuries of Music Teaching Manuals 1518-1932* (Great Britain, 2009).
   Lowell Mason, *Manual of the Boston Academy of Music, For Instruction in the Elements of Vocal Music On the System of Pestalozzi*, Intro. Ch. 1-4 (Boston, 1836), reprinted USA, 2012.
   Marjorie Lamberti, *The Politics of Education, Teachers and School Reform in Weimar Germany* (New York, 2002), 28-31.

childhood educational programs created by Pestalozzi and his disciple, Friedrich Froebel[21] (the "inventor" of kindergarten), in the beginning of the nineteenth century and continued by Montessori in the early twentieth century, is that a child's ability to learn without conscious effort is particularly keen before five or six years of age. Children readily absorb what they are exposed to without barrier, exemplified by their miraculous ability to unconsciously learn language. Therefore, it is supposed that this is a prime opportunity, which shall never come again, to teach them skills that will become a deeply embedded part of their very being, using an approach modeled on what seems to be the process of their unconscious language apprehension—reliance on sensory impression, repetition, and thoroughly learned incremental steps.

Therein lies the rub, for *what they learn is deeply embedded in their memory and shall not be forgotten.* Thus, as with all great opportunity, there is also considerable risk, the balancing of nature. *One may just as easily learn what is wrong.* The problem with the Suzuki Method is that the learning it inculcates at this tender age is indelibly recorded in muscle memory and is, regrettably, fundamentally incorrect. The step-by-step methodology he claimed to use[22] (a central pedagogical insight of Pestalozzi's[23]) is, in Suzuki's method, a *superficial* approach moving from a fundamentally incorrect start to error upon error. But to know what is incorrect one must first understand what is correct. This is the ground upon which all claims of pedagogical knowledge must rest, and without which no instruction can have validity.

HOW SUZUKI'S METHOD DIFFERS FROM A TRADITIONAL EUROPEAN METHOD

To learn to play an instrument requires that a student develop the skill to do so. From our analysis of violin technique in Chapter 18, we have seen that playing an instrument is a three-part system—the mind/body, the violin/bow, and the musical system, which must work in congruence as a mega-system without undermining any of the separate systems. The melding of these three components is called "technique." That which cannot satisfy the requirements of all three systems cannot be correct technique and is, therefore, destructive in developing the skill to play the violin. An analysis of Suzuki's method is its own best explanation of why it is *obstructive* to the development of ability. It will be

---

21 Friedrich Froebel, *The Education of Man*, translated by William Nicholas Hailmann (New York, 1898), originally published as *Die Menschenerziehung. die Erziehungs- Unterrichts- und Lehrkunst, angestrebt in der allgemeinen duetschen Erziehungsanstaldt zu Keilau,* (Keilau, 1826).

22 *Ibid.* 13, 32.

23 *Ibid.* 9, 78, 154.

shown that every component of the playing system is seriously compromised by his superficial method of learning the violin.[24]

A cornerstone, and one of several "key factors" of the Suzuki method,[25] is described in a pamphlet published by the Suzuki Association of America entitled *The Suzuki Violin Method in American Music Education*, written by John Kendall:

> Since this is a rote method, similar to the way a child develops language ability, regular listening to the music being studied is vital.

As defined by *Webster's Dictionary*, rote learning is "to learn by memory alone, without understanding or thought." This is not a complimentary "key factor." What scientific study has Suzuki or his followers conducted in how children acquire language and its alignment with the Suzuki method? He does claim to have researched how children acquire language skill in an unexplained statement in the Foreword to *Book 1* of his method: "From my research of the pedagogical methodology of mother-tongue acquisition, I have created an educational approach known as the Suzuki Method." Where is the proof of his research, or a description of this process? Even if we assume that language expertise is acquired through rote learning, this does not constitute a strong argument for its use as an educational approach, for it is, therefore, also true that *one's skill can never supersede what one is exposed to*. This observation was the basis of the play written by Bernard Shaw, *Pygmalion*,[26] more popularly known as the musical, *My Fair Lady*.

Shaw's premise was that even though at birth people have, for a moment, a somewhat equal start (although even this is not true), their future is unfairly circumscribed by the language skills they do or don't acquire in their immediate environment. If exposed to a limited and coarse environment, their language skills will be the same. If reared in an educated, cultured environment, the same child would be entirely different. Therefore, using Suzuki's theory of how children learn language, what he labeled the "mother-tongue" approach, a theory that was developed in Europe by Pestalozzi and Montessori many years before Suzuki discovered it (although they tried to *circumvent* the *serendipitous* nature of environmental influence by enhancing a child's learning through the

---

24 The views expressed in this chapter are the *author's opinion* based upon many years of research; ideas that, in his opinion, are easily verifiable by anyone willing to seriously investigate the findings, the theories, presented in this book.

25 *Ibid.*, 18, 14.

26 George Bernard Shaw, *Pygmalion* (New York, 2005).

intervention of their educational methods[27]), we can see the potential "Achilles' heel" of his method. As Suzuki himself stated, a student is a product of his environment and cannot be better than what he is exposed to.

Suzuki believed that his "despair" about his lack of performing ability "was brought about not because I had no talent but because I did not know how to develop it. I did not know that it was just a matter of repeating a piece hundreds of times in order to play it better … "[28] The use of rote repetition in learning a highly subtle skill is naively—and damagingly—simplistic. To wit, experience that prevents further good experience is not the sort of experience one needs. An experience may be "fun," but instill a careless attitude that prevents further growth. An experience may create incorrect physical and mental habits—muscle memory that is impossible to overcome. An experience may trivialize matters of great depth, thereby desensitizing the mind and encouraging superficiality.

The problems with his method begin with his decision to base his method of teaching the violin on how he taught *himself*, on his skill as a violinist, which by his own admission was not developed enough to be a performer. If he had achieved the skill of Jascha Heifetz, or understood his approach, he would have credibility, his method might have "traditions" to transfer. As we have seen throughout this book, potentiality is biased by underlying parameters that circumscribe development. These biases are the "values" and created "culture" of those values, which determine outcome and ultimate potentiality in learning to play instruments in a "classical music" tradition.

When Suzuki began to teach himself the violin he could not read music. His students follow the same path even though many children can read words at three or four years of age. Reading notes is not more difficult than reading words, and is, in fact, easily learned by children. (Ideally, children should read notes, play by memory and by ear.) Additionally, this "key factor" of his approach has an unfortunate side effect—it artificially limits the content that can be used in his method.[29] It makes the use of material outside his method books impossible, limiting the scope and, therefore, the depth of approach that can be used to teach fundamental skills. Perhaps Suzuki dismissed etudes as

---

27 *Ibid.* 9, Letter X, 149-157. Pestalozzi's observations about how and why to avoid the problems developed by unconscious language acquisition are remarkable.

Ibid. 12, "Defects of language due to education," *The Montessori Method,* 322: "… Such errors are acquired by the child who hears words imperfectly pronounced, or *hears bad speech.* The dialectic accent enters into this category; but there also enter vicious habits which make the *natural defects* of the articulate language of childhood persist in the child, or which provoke in him by imitation the defects of language peculiar to the persons who surrounded him in his childhood."

28 *Ibid.,* 6, 76.

29 *Ibid.* 18, 14.

boring and unnecessary because their inclusion would demand that a student be able to read music.

Another fundamental "key factor" of his method is Suzuki's insistence that mothers be involved in their child's learning process.[30] *This is not an insight.* Mothers have always been involved in their young children's education. Who else but a parent can help a four or five-year-old learn? But what is the point of instructing a mother in an approach that is fundamentally incorrect?

As we mentioned, according to Dr. Garson,[31] Shinichi Suzuki spent more than *ten* years writing *Book 1*[32] for the violin, which is *twenty-four pages of large-print music* and approximately one page, if spaced normally, of written material translated into several languages. It took Michelangelo *four* years to paint the ceiling of the Sistine Chapel. Perhaps Suzuki is more thorough. We have extensively discussed fundamental musical truths, examined in detail what constitutes proper technique, and how technique must align with musical values. With this knowledge as a template, we will examine Suzuki's method and see if it is congruent with a thorough, correct approach.

Book 1 starts with a variety of bowed rhythms on open strings and follows his own learning experience that short, fast bows are easier to play than long, slow bows. Unfortunately for his students, this is an incorrect foundation. Suzuki has mixed software for hardware, introducing content without meta-information. Short, fast bows are not a *basis* for anything. As previously mentioned, they are a *derivative* of correctly learned slow, connected bows. Unfortunately for students, the beginning of the method—the first experience with the instrument a student will have—teaches an exercise that will embed tension as a student's initial deep muscle memory *(ex. 25-1a and b).*

Suzuki spends only two pages on open strings, concentrating on the A and E strings (the D and A strings should be the core setting), again following his own unfortunate developmental process—he found the A and E strings easier

---

30 *Ibid.* 18, 14.

31 *Ibid.*, 3, 26.

32 Shinichi Suzuki, *Suzuki Violin School, Vol. 1 Revised Edition (USA, 2007).*

to play when he taught himself. There are no long, connected bows. In contrast, Leopold Auer wrote an *entire book* based on developing open string skill, which, to meet the requirements of the mind/body system, must be solidified before the introduction of the complexities of the left hand. Auer offered this advice in the preface to *Book 1* of his method:

> The underlying idea of providing a *whole book* of open string exercises is based upon the principle of separating and firmly establishing in the beginner's mind the radical difference in the functions of the left hand and those of the right, wrist and arm...It is all-important that the correct position of the body, and the holding of the violin and bow be first established, after which the pupil must become impressed with the importance of *tone production from the very start. Even on the open strings alone he must learn to produce a clear, round tone, capable of dynamic shading. Until this has been accomplished, the student's attention should not be diverted through the additional difficulties of learning how to set the fingers.*

This opinion is affirmed in the same preface by the great violin pedagogue, Carl Flesch:

> *The Leopold Auer Graded Course of Violin Playing* proceeds in conformity with what, in my opinion, constitutes an *entirely* correct basic principle, to the effect that, at the start, bowing and finger technique are entirely separated from each other: that the pupil continue on open strings until he has gained a certain amount of bowing ability...[33]

By way of contrast, Auer begins his *Book 1* with ex. 25-2.

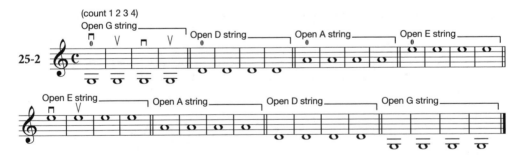

By the third page of *Book 1* Suzuki introduces the first three fingers of the left hand. On the next page he introduces the fourth finger. Not only have several months of preparatory work been skipped, but the student's physical sensation of playing will be completely confused. There has been no time spent learning how to bow on open strings, and *gradually* applying the fingers. Therefore, no

---

33 *Ibid.* 15, Book 1, Preface, A Word to Teachers (New York, 1926).

feeling for the separate function of the hands is possible, let alone spending the time to set each finger properly. A proper approach would be to spend considerable time playing open strings—perhaps two months—before adding the complexity of fingers.

Why is the addition of fingers a complicating factor? Each finger changes the feeling of the bow on the string because the length of the string is altered, which changes the tension on the string. To overwhelm a student at this beginning stage with such mind/body complication means that the student's deep learning is already tense—and trained even more deeply through repetition—because the foundation is based on an incorrect understanding of violin technique. His method is both incorrect and not systematic. We have reached only page four of *Book 1*.

As was mentioned previously, what is needed in the beginning is a foundation that is the *seed* from which complexity may *correctly* grow. Another way of looking at the process is that a template must be put in place to which content may be applied. In the Suzuki method, the mind/body system is already compromised at this point. Having no correct, relaxed feeling at the start, it is obvious that any intuitive process that may appear to the student's mind will be based on the wrong messages, unless his intuition is telling him that something is wrong.

We will examine several examples in each book of his method. The few little pieces (a few little tunes are essentially the substance of Books 1 through 3) that we shall skip are essentially more of the same—staccato bowings, awkward string crossings, and incomplete or nonexistent explanations of left and right-hand technique. The musical examples we present are excerpts from the Suzuki books. Our editorial comments are overlaid onto the excerpts and written in red. Piece No. 1 is "Twinkle, Twinkle, Little Star" with varied rhythms, ex. 25-3. The bows are short and fast, which is not a fundamental learning. Suzuki immediately adds several other difficulties.

He already uses four fingers. He introduces string crossings for the bow with no correct preparation (meaning no practice changing strings at slow tempo), but includes counterclockwise string crossings, which are awkward and difficult to execute properly (counterclockwise bowings are marked with red circles throughout this chapter).[34]

25-3

34 See Chapter 18 for a thorough explanation of bowing.

Piece No. 3, "Song of the Wind," ex. 25-4a, has staccato marks (short bows) over every note. This is an incorrect foundation for smooth bowing, an incorrect musical understanding—square thinking—and incongruent with the violin system, which requires smooth connection for proper acoustical release. Additionally, every string crossing is counterclockwise, which is bound to feel difficult for a beginner. Expert violinists would avoid these awkward string changes by using higher positions. A beginner cannot.

In measure 3 of the piece, Suzuki not only uses two counterclockwise bowings but adds a further complication—the third finger must play the interval of a fifth while the bow moves counterclockwise. He instructs the student to "Leave the first finger on the E string. Keeping the second finger in the air, place the third finger on the A string, then hop the third finger to the E string."

This is incorrect and another example of a lack of smooth connection. The third finger does not "hop" to the E string. The pressure is abated and the finger is then pulled laterally to the E string. Fifths across two strings can be played in three ways: one finger over two strings; the finger pulled laterally when moving from a lower to higher string; or the finger lifted and placed from a higher to a lower string. Fifths are an unnecessary complication at this point. Suzuki could, and should, have eliminated this problem by replacing the "D" in measures 3 and 5 with a second finger "G♯" on the E string.

In measure 7 of ex. 25-4a, if the first note is played with the fourth finger all the fingers must be used in support. If starting with an open string, fingers one, two and three must be placed on the A string before the bow plays the open E string. Either way, there is no explanation.

In measures 10–11 from the same piece, ex. 25-4b, there are two counter-clockwise bowings. The second finger of the left hand must be kept down while the open string is played, and in measure 11, the third finger must be placed on the A string before the open E is sounded. There is no explanation of this.

The retake of the bow (the two down-bows) in measure 11 is explained: "Here too, quickly retake the bow." Nothing should be "quick" at this stage. Everything must be smooth. Which direction is the circle the right arm makes to retake the bow? This is unexplained. (The circle should be counterclockwise for a down-bow retake and clockwise for an up-bow retake. The circles should be quite large and a relaxed motion for beginners. Otherwise they will develop a constrained and hurried movement—precisely what we do not want.)

A traditional approach would not have introduced the complexities of string changes at this point, with the additional complexities of using the fingers of the left hand, let alone complexities of this level. Suzuki's focus on the A and E strings is problematic for a beginner. The E string is the most difficult for a beginner to play for *both* hands. The middle two strings, A and D, are the core positions for both hands, the G and E are the outer extremities.

The same inappropriate difficulties can be found in the next piece, No. 4, "Go Tell Aunt Rhody," *(ex. 25-5).*

The first note, C♯, must be played with the first finger on B. In measure 3, the third finger, D, must be placed on the A string with the first and second fingers on B and C♯ before the bow leaves the open E string. If the fourth finger is used for the E in measure 3, the first, second and third fingers must be placed on B, C♯, and D in support of the fourth finger. This is not explained.

In No. 5, "O Come, Little Children," ex. 25-6a, there are counterclockwise bowings and, except for a few fingerings, no explanation for how the left hand should be played.

As was previously discussed, the number of fingers down should correspond to the number of the finger being played, especially in the case of beginners. If the first finger is to be played, it is down alone (although supported through a correct hand position); using the second requires the first finger in support on the same string on a note in the key, the third requires the first and second in support, and the fourth finger requires first, second, and third in support, as we have noted in red in ex. 25-6b.

If starting with the fourth finger E, four fingers must be down. In measure 1 the fourth finger, E, after the C♯, must be played with the third finger on D in silent support, meaning that all the fingers are down when playing the fourth finger E. This is the only way to train the frame of the hand.

In another look at this piece, ex. 25-6c, if beginning with an open E string, the second finger C♯, should be placed on the string, with first finger B in support. Both fingers remain down until measure 3, when the third finger, D, is added to this structure.

The abstract and complex nature of the violin makes such thoroughness essential. Unlike the piano, where each note is digitalized and can be seen, the violin requires a deep understanding of the relationship *between* notes, a knowledge of intervals, and how an interval on one string can by transformed by finger movement to form another interval covering two strings, yet maintain the same basic frame (form), as is the case of a perfect fourth on one string—formed between the first and fourth fingers—morphing to an octave when the same fingers cover two strings.

Preparation No. 1 on page 30 (actually page 10 of musical material, since the first nineteen pages of *Book 1* are filled with a brief introductory philosophy translated into four languages, a brief description of the parts of the violin, and some pictures of playing positions) has a one-octave scale in half-notes that, at first glance, might seem to be an example of teaching long, smooth bows *(ex. 25-7a)*.

However, the time signature is *"alla breve"* and the instruction accompanying the scale states that the exercise is to be practiced in *sixteenth notes* as a *preparation.* The exercises that follow—A, B, and C—do not explain the setting of the left hand. We will explain only one of them—A *(ex. 25-7b).*

In measure 1, C♯ must be played with two fingers; the first finger on B, the second on C♯. These stay down for the open string E, which is a counterclockwise string change. The third finger plays A on the E string while the first and second are held down on the A string for the open E in measure 3. The next C♯ has, therefore, been prepared and requires no change for the left hand. Examples B and C on the same page have equal levels of complexity that are *unexplained,* as well as counterclockwise string changes, also unexplained.

Piece No. 6, "May Song," ex. 25-8, has no in-depth explanation for the functioning of the left hand, and what explanation there is misses key elements.

In measure 1, as we show, the first C♯ must be played with the first and second fingers, which stay down through the counterclockwise string change to an open E. This allows the third finger, A, on the E string to be easily apprehended, at which point the first finger (which has been on B on the A string) is pulled laterally to F♯ on the E string. The third finger A, on the E string in measure 2, is played with the second finger on G♯. In measure 3, the third finger, D, must be prepared before the string crossing by having three fingers down—the first on B, the second on C♯, the third on D. The first finger stays through the C♯ in measure 3.

The first note of measure 5 must be played with four fingers down if taken with a fourth finger, or if taken as an open E, three fingers must be placed on the A string for the third finger D, which must be prepared before the string change from open E to the A string.

Piece No. 7, "Long, Long, Ago," suffers the same lack of explanation.

Piece No. 9, "Perpetual Motion," ex. 25-9a, has an ironic twist to its title, given the fact that the notes of the piece are all dotted—that is, staccato (separated). The instructions highlight the paradox by advising: "Use short strokes at the middle of the bow. Stop each note without pressing the bow into the string. Practice slowly at first and then gradually speed up the tempo." This is a prescription for tension, and will teach *that* as a *fundamental experience of playing.*

The exercise, ex. 25-9b, prescribed as an addendum to ex. 25-9a, is bound to build in *active* down-bow motion, precisely the wrong teaching for fundamental bowing skill, and yet another tension builder.

Finger exercise No. 1 on page 34, ex. 25-10a, has no explanation for the left hand action. Suzuki should have explained that the second note, G♯, is played with the first finger on F♯, the fourth note, A, is played with three fingers down, the fourth finger, B, is played with four fingers.

The "tonalization" exercise on the same page, ex. 25-10b, has counterclockwise string changes that could have been avoided by writing the first measure as an A, the second as a D. Counterclockwise string changes are more complex than clockwise and should be avoided, or *explained*, in the case of beginners.

Piece No. 10, "Allegretto," ex. 25-11, has dots on every note and accents on the downbeats. If the dotted notes are to be played off the string, this is much too advanced for a beginner. If the dotted notes are to be played on the string, the act of stopping the bow after each note will create tension and counteracts any notion of flow and smoothness (which should always be the essential teaching).

25-11

Accents on downbeats are an unnecessary accentuation of the beat and of down-bow motion, and *destroy the musical line.* As was previously discussed, the down-bow is passive, the up-bow active. The up-bow rises from the floor of the down-bow. Accenting down-bows is anathema to the development of the proper physical feeling for bowing, causing the "down" to be overemphasized. All athletic excellence is based on smooth connection of movements—flow. The same is true in music. Each note is bound to another, smoothly unfolding forward, in one exhalation of energy. Articulation is layered on top of smooth connection. It is based on it. Even rests do not break flow. Flow, connection, moves from start to finish.

Etude No. 12, ex. 25-12, which is four lines of music, is filled with counterclockwise string changes for almost every string crossing. These are very difficult to negotiate. There has been no preparation for them. These awkward string changes predominate nearly every string change in *Book 1.* This suggests that Suzuki does not understand the difficulty involved.

25-12

The directive *"sempre staccato"* (stopping the bow after each note) is a prescription for tension. A beginner should not be burdened with such unnecessary complications, which store tension as the muscle memory for bowing. Thus far, each page continually builds more tension as the basic muscle memory of playing.

Piece No. 13, "Minuet No. 1," shown in ex. 25-13a, is a transcription of a piece for clavier from the *Notebook for Anna Magdalena Bach* that J. S. Bach dedicated to his wife, Anna Magdalena. There is no explanation for the execution of the left hand except for a few fingerings.

25-13a

The first note, D, must be played with three fingers down, as must the G at the end of measure 2. However, in the latter instance, the first finger stays on B and the second finger plays F♯ in support of the third finger, G, on the D string.

In the excerpt, ex. 25-13b, suggesting: "Practice the following exercise to improve the accuracy of the second and fourth finger intonation," all will be for naught if the first finger is not held on "E" on the D string for the first example, and "B" on the A string for the second. These are also counterclockwise string changes.

25-13b

Piece No. 14, "Minuet No. 2," ex. 25-14a, from the same source as the previous piece (also a transcription from clavier), has minimal explanation for the execution of the left hand. Suzuki should have mentioned that before playing the first note of the piece, the first finger should be placed on B on the A string because *a finger must be placed on a string before the bow changes to the string*. This applies to the fourth note of the piece, G, on the E string, which must be placed simultaneously with the third finger, D, on the A string.

25-14a

There are numerous instances of fifths across two strings—the last note of bar 6, G to C of measure 7, and F♯ to B in measure 22, ex. 25-14b, with no explanation for the execution of the left hand as well as counterclockwise string changes (circled).

25-14b

There are three measures, 29-31, filled with difficult counterclockwise bowings, with no explanation about how to execute them smoothly *(ex. 25-14c)*.

Piece No. 15, "Minuet No. 3," ex. 25-15a, a transcription from the same source as pieces No. 13 and 14, has several instances of perfect fifth difficulties[35] in measures 1, 2, 9, 18, 25, 26, and 31, all of which may be played in various ways, none of which are explained. Expert violinists would avoid such problems by changes of position. A beginner cannot. In other words, this piece, as depicted, would be difficult for an expert to play well.

The piece is filled with counterclockwise bowing complexity, particularly measures 18-19 in ex. 25-15b, and 25-27 in ex. 25-15c. Starting up-bow at 17 in ex. 25-15b, and at bar 25 in ex. 25-15c, would eliminate the counterclockwise bowing. Also, the first note, B, in measure 17 of ex. 25-15b, should be played with four fingers down on the notes of the key—F♯, G, A, and B. In bar 18, the third finger, D, should be left down to measure 19. An advanced player may occasionally be less stringent in the grouping of fingers to make vibrating a little easier. Perhaps he might lift the third finger, D, in bar 18 to facilitate vibrating the G in bar 19.

---

35 The interval of a perfect fifth is not problematic for a pianist because it is the natural position of the hand as it lies on the keyboard, the interval played by the thumb and fifth finger. The perfect fifth, as we have mentioned, is problematic for the violin even though the strings are tuned to perfect fifths. The natural interval for the hand when playing the violin is the perfect fourth, when played between the first (index) and fourth (pinky) fingers. This is why when transcribing works written for the piano to the violin, there is not always a simple one-to-one match in the level of difficulty.

Piece No. 16, "The Happy Farmer," ex. 25-16a, introduces "hooked" bowing with no explanation for its proper execution. While the notation of a dot over the small note at the end of each bow is a traditional notation, the execution must *link, with smooth connection,* the smaller note—in this case an eighth note—to the larger note without stopping the bow.

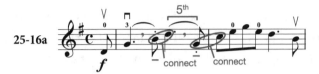

The dot is only on the dotted-quarter. This is not explained. There is an awkward "fifth" in measure 1 with no technical explanation. On the same page, Suzuki's application of this bowing to "Twinkle, Twinkle, Little Star" contains, in the first measure, a perfect fifth difficulty for the left hand in the last note of measure 1 to the first note of measure 2 of a different sort than the one mentioned above. How to negotiate this is unexplained *(ex. 25-16b).*

Piece No. 17, "Gavotte," ex. 25-17a, contains dots on nearly every note. Is measure 1 to be played off the string or staccato on the string? Either way, this is much too difficult for a beginner to execute properly. There are counterclockwise difficulties in measures 3–4 as well.

Measures 21–24 of the same piece, in ex. 25-17b, contain not only unnecessary short notes, but seven counterclockwise string changes in a row with dots over the slurs, which *disrupts flow* as a beginner's first learning. At a more advanced level, articulation may be added. Yet we have seen that *articulation is a less fundamental layer than connection* and must arise from a ground of smoothness.

Suzuki's method shows little or no understanding of the basics of violin technique. The book is filled with misinformation, unnecessary complications, inadequate preparation, skipped developmental steps, deeply incorrect fundamental development, and pieces that are far too complex to be educative for a beginner. Most of the pieces are set on the upper two strings, the most difficult for a beginner to play for both the left and right hands. There are no etudes, mainly naively complex pieces. The few exercises Suzuki includes are simplistic, as is his understanding of the purpose of etudes. Etudes are meant to *reinforce* technical and musical development *from many different perspectives*, creating deep structural learning. It's not children who find etudes boring, as Suzuki claims. How could they? He doesn't let them have the experience. Suzuki must have found them boring.

The violin is learned through sense perception. The sense perception offered in *Book 1* and inculcated through repetition can only lead to tension, and no "feeling" of correct technique. Rote learning, without a correct approach, is quite useless for the development of specialized skill. There is, however, a more insidious and deeply damaging lesson learned by this superficial rote approach. It instills in a student the belief that skills can be learned by *mindless* repetition. This way of learning affects all their future learning and creates the illusion that critical, analytical thinking is unnecessary, boring, and difficult—an unfortunate lesson that is bound to affect everything they do.

Suzuki observed that children learn through imitation. This is not a new insight, yet it is a superficial approach. He asks that students listen to, and play along with, recordings of great artists.[36] If it were true that one could learn by copying recordings, we would have thousands of great performers. Yet we don't. Imitation will not train a student. What one hears in a great performance is the result of principles that are hidden from view. These are only understood by those who can do them. It is true that students must listen to great performances. That is not a new concept. However, the knowledge that must be absorbed is not only aural. Learning is also based on physical feeling. This can only be transferred through hands-on teaching, and the hands that are laid on must be skilled enough to transfer the correct physical feelings. Learning is also based on mental paradigms that must be *understood* by the student. We can see in *Book 1* that Suzuki's method is incongruent with all three subsystems of playing the violin—the mind/body system, the instrument as a sound system, and the musical system, producing incoherence in the developing mega-system.

36 *Ibid.* 3, 36.

Book 2[37] is *twenty-two* pages of large print music. Suzuki advises students in the short half-page preface to *Book 2*: "Put your heart into your tone, your spirit into your tone, because our entire personalities are revealed in the tone we produce." A high-minded entreaty, but without proper instruction, whatever spirit is revealed in one's tone cannot be attributed to their heart.

The "tonalization" exercise, example 1a on page 9, has an incomplete explanation for the execution of the left hand. The second note, B, must be placed on the A string before the bow change *(ex. 25-18a)*.

25-18a

The first finger is held in place when playing the D of measure 2 and should stay down through the entire exercise. The second finger maintains its placement on G on the E string from the end of measure 2 to the end of measure 4, at which time it must move in support of the third and fourth fingers of measure 5 to C on the A string.

Examples 2a-4, similarly, have no detailed explanation for the execution of the left hand. What is indicated is insufficient. In the example below, ex. 25-18b, (ex. 4 in *Book 2*, p. 9) the third and fourth fingers must be supported by the first and second, as we illustrate.

25-18b

In Piece No. 1 nearly every string crossing is counterclockwise. His exercise at the bottom of the page does not explain the execution of the first finger. Does it stay down? Piece No. 2, "Mussete" is filled with counterclockwise string changes, particularly measures 12-15 *(ex. 25-19)*.

25-19

Piece No. 3, "Hunter's Chorus," is filled with staccato notes. His exercise on the bottom of p. 12, ex. 25-20, advises: "Place the third and first fingers simultaneously, and only then play the notes." It should be the first, second, and third fingers.

---

37 *Ibid.* 31, Vol. 2, Revised Edition (USA, 2007).

25-20

The variation of piece No. 4, "Long, Long, Ago," ex. 25-21, is filled with counterclockwise string changes. This is a destructive complication for a beginner that no one able to change positions would ever need to negotiate. And, yet again, we have staccato notes.

25-21

Every selection thus far has reinforced *small bows* as a *fundamental* element of technique. It should be the opposite—the inversion—long bows are the basis of short bows, not short bows the basis of long bows.

Piece No. 5, "Waltz" by Brahms, ex. 25–22, is also filled with awkward counterclockwise string changes that could easily be avoided by a non-beginner by playing in the third position. Note yet another stopped bow in measure 3.

25-22

Finger exercise No. 5a on page 15, ex. 25-23a, is a technically incorrect explanation of a crucial left-hand technique. Suzuki says to lift the first finger to lower it a half-step. The finger should be pulled back by abating the weight while remaining on the string.

25-23a

Example 8 on page 16, ex. 25-23b, contains no explanation for the left hand's organization when descending the scale, nor does example 9, shown here.

25-23b

This arpeggio, ex. 25-23b, requires an intricate left-hand explication that is too involved for this chapter. We have sufficiently made our point by the fact that the Suzuki "method" *offers no explanation at all.* Exercises 11 and 12, on page 19, contain no explanation for the execution of the left hand, aside from fingerings. In exercise 13, labeled "Perpetual Motion," nearly every string crossing is counterclockwise. If a teacher wanted a beginner to develop a feeling for playing separate bows at a faster tempo, why include any string crossings?

Piece No. 9, ex. 25-24, contains dots (staccato marks) over every note. The proper execution of this articulation is far too advanced for a beginner. He advises the student: "To be played lightly and separately." There has been no preparation that would allow a student to follow this suggestion. Short bows are a derivative of smooth, connected bows, not a fundamental learning.

25-24

On page 22, finger exercise 5b, Ex. 14, he advises the student to "practice lowering the first finger without changing the shape of the hand." He does not say how—lift the first finger or slide it back? Ex. 15 on the same page is a trill study with no explanation. The finger "trilling" should feel the "up" motion of the finger, not the down. That has to be trained.

On page 23, ex. 25-25, he teaches how to make accents on slurred notes, shown in the example below. The downward motion of the bow will surely add percussive action of the left hand on the strings, thereby destroying any possibility of legato in the left hand.

25-25

On the same page is a staccato exercise. His instruction says to use short bow strokes in the upper-half of the bow. How? What muscles? If one does not know what muscle controls the staccato stroke, the stroke is impossible to teach or learn. Additionally, this is a fancy label for an example that is not a true staccato.

On page 29, ex. 21a, line 2, shown here as ex. 25-26, there is no thorough explanation for the execution of the left hand. To play the fourth finger, D, in third position, the second and third fingers must support the fourth by being placed on B and C natural respectively. This is true for the same situations found in 21b, 21c, and 21d.

25-26

On page 31, "Waltz," by Brahms, ex. 25-27, line three, the shift in measure 2 from the third position to the first position is unexplained. The first finger must guide the hand to the second finger, C, by way of the first finger, B, in the first position.

25-27

This is a common oversight throughout his method books—there is little or no explanation for the execution of downward shifts. The same lack is found in measure 4 of "Gavotte" on the same page. This ends *Book 2*.

Even with the added information that we have supplied to *Book 1* and *Book 2* this method of teaching would still be devoid of any depth. The basic understanding of technique is incorrect for both hands—no frame is developed for the left hand and no connected flowing motion is developed for the right arm. Additionally, little pieces like this are not sufficient to provide any "in depth" experience of the fundamental techniques that need to be developed. The approach is shallow and *fundamentally* incorrect.

According to Dr. Garson, Suzuki could not teach vibrato,[38] yet there is a method in *Book 3*.[39] His explanation of the motion of the wrist used for vibrato is incorrect. The wrist motion, as used by a master like Heifetz or David Oistrakh, is more akin to the oscillation of a washing machine or screwing in a light bulb[40] than the motion described by Suzuki, which is back and forth. Although back and forth exclusively wrist motion is commonly used, it tends to create a vibrato that is overdone, nervous, and is not used by fine players.

The arm can be used with the wrist, although this is not mentioned by Suzuki. Moreover, the vibrato exercise he uses on page 9 will create down motion as the basic movement of vibrato *(ex. 25-28)*.

25-28

One should vibrate up to the note—the "up" motion is active. His exercise, as written, will make the "down" motion active. This is a subtle but important point. If the illustration was written so that it seemed the C♯ goes up to D, (as

---

38 *Ibid.* 3, 100.

39 *Ibid.* 31, Vol. 3, Revised Edition (USA, 2007).

40 Heifetz demonstrates this himself, unconsciously moving his left hand in a vibrato motion. This occurs in *Heifetz Master Classes, Volume Two,* DVD (Kultur, 2011) at 49:14, and is described in-depth in the Appendix of this book.

we have shown) not that D goes down to C♯, the vibrato would be developed
more correctly.

On page 8 of *Book 3* there is no thorough explanation for the execution
of the left hand. How to correctly play the descending scale in Example 2 is
unexplained, shown here in ex. 25-29a.

He should have mentioned that the descending scale in measure 5 of Example
2 (shown above) must have the first finger on B♭, the second finger on C, the
third finger on D, all in support of the fourth on E♭. Fingers two, three and four
must be placed on the D string before the bow arrives at the D string. Once
the "A" in measure 2 is played, with the second and third finger in support, the
first is placed on E♭. This process is repeated for the next string change. The
arpeggio, number 3 on p. 8, ex. 25-29b, is even more complex, an explanation
I will forego for the present.

Piece No. 1 in Book 3, "Gavotte," ex. 25-30, is filled with dots over notes and
accents on downbeats. This combination at this stage of a student's development
can only lead to tension. How could it be otherwise, with accents and constant
bow stoppings disrupting any possibility of smooth connection *between* notes
played by the left hand and the bow?

Piece No. 2, "Minuet," ex. 25-31a, carries on with more awkward string
crossings—fifths over two strings, and difficult fingerings because of the
limitations for a beginner of playing only in the first position. To play this
piece correctly (in other words, so that it would sound good), one would need
to be a far more advanced player.

Starting with an up-bow in example 25-31b, below, would eliminate the counterclockwise bowings. The explication of the left hand is complex and not explained by Suzuki.

25-31b

Piece No. 4 is "Humoresque" by Dvorak, ex. 25-32. Suzuki advises: "Use a very short bow stroke. Keep the bow on the string during the rest." It is not easy to understand how this matches the composer's marking of *leggiero*.

25-32

Piece No. 5, "Gavotte," ex. 25-33, is, yet again, filled with short bows, accents, built-in awkwardness, no explanation of the shifts, counterclockwise string changes if staying in the 1st position, and an amateurish musical conception.

25-33

His "String Changing Exercise No. 2," an addendum to the piece on page 19, is exclusively counterclockwise string changes *(ex. 25-34).*[41]

25-34

There is no explanation about the correct execution of such difficulties. Aside from the bowing complication, when changing strings, the finger of the left hand must be placed on the string before the bow changes strings. We will explain just the first two measures. After (or before) the open G, the first finger must be placed on B on the A string while the second finger, G, is placed on the E string. The B stays down while G of measure 2 is sounded, but, before the bow changes to play the third finger, D, the third finger must be placed on the string. The third finger, G, in bar 2 must be placed on the D string (before the bow changes to play the third finger, G); then follows an open D on a down-bow. The final note, B, must be placed on the G string before the bow plays it,

41 We have added the fingerings for clarity.

supported by the first finger, A. None of this is explained, and there has been no teaching in the method that would make this understanding evident.

Piece No. 6, "Gavotte," ex. 25-35, has dots over nearly every note. Starting down-bow would have eliminated the counterclockwise bowing, but not alter the continuing emphasis on short, unconnected bows, or the unexplained left-hand technique.

Piece No. 7, "Bourree," ex. 25-36, has counterclockwise bowings in measures 13-15 that could have been easily avoided by an up-bow start in measure 13, (with a few other bowing changes) that would have made the series of string crossings nearly all clockwise, which are easier to execute.

This, essentially, finishes *Book 3*, which has *eighteen* pages of large print music.

In the previously cited pamphlet, *The Suzuki Violin Method in American Music Education*, Kendall writes:

> Have any students emerged from the American Talent Education programs to become professional musicians or performing artists? Since the objective often emphasized by Mr. Suzuki is not to produce performing artists but to produce better human beings, the answer to such a question may not be relevant.[42]

Very few people learn to play the violin to become a better human being. By not trying to create performing artists as the goal of learning an instrument, Suzuki's approach has made an end before the start, and masks his method's superficiality and lack of knowledge as care for the development of the soul. Students want to learn to play well. That is the only valid goal. One must *strive* to do something excellently. Bad works hard enough on its own.

Book 4[43] is *twenty* pages of music available anywhere, with no pedagogical explanation or instruction. It contains a couple of standard student concertos, with a trill study that has no explanation. Suzuki has included several trill exercises throughout his books without ever mentioning the most important ingredient to developing a good trill—the lifting of the fingers, not the downward

---

42 *Ibid.* 18, 31.

43 *Ibid.* 31, Vol. 4 (USA, 1978).

drop. He includes a few exercises for shifting from the first to the third position with no explanation how to shift back to first. They are *identical* to those found on page 29 in *Book 2*.

On page 14 of *Book 4* he includes two unmarked pieces with the explanation: "fingerings, bowings, and phrasings have purposely been omitted in these Lullabies in order to give the instructor an opportunity to indicate his own ideas." As has been shown thus far, his omission of explanation has not been lacking.

Piece No. 4 is Vivaldi's *Concerto in A Minor*. He has added unnecessarily complicated bowings, a good example of which can be found on page 17, measures 60-68, shown here in ex. 25-37.

There is a reason for his complicated bowing. "Mixed" bowings are the only way to play the passage if one's bowing technique is mechanical and tense. *Book 4* ends with the second violin part to Bach's *Concerto for Two Violins* for which no adequate preparation has been made, at least if one expects a student to play it well. The first violin part will appear at the end of *Book 5*, which is odd. There is no difference between the technical level required for either part.

In *Book 5*[44] contains the slow movement of Vivaldi's *A Minor Concerto* and all three movements of Vivaldi's *G Minor Concerto*. There are *thirty* pages of standard pieces available anywhere and seven pages of large print exercises that could easily fit on three. The "tonalization" exercise on page 6 does not explain how to place the fingers of the left hand *(ex. 25-38)*.

He teaches the fifth position by shifting from the second; usually it is from the third.

"Etude for Changing Strings," ex. 25-39a, which is three lines of music on page 8, contains only short, unconnected, dotted bows. He suggests that the student change the bow direction—starting up-bow instead of down-bow—making the exercise unconnected, dotted bows in counterclockwise motion.

---

44 *Ibid.*, Vol. 5 Revised Edition (USA, 2009).

25-39a

He adds this additional dotted difficulty as shown in ex. 25-39b.

25-39b

Page 9 has a three-octave scale in G major (the only three-octave scale in his method) with no explanation for downward shifting. The arpeggio that follows also has no thorough explanation for the execution of the left hand. The same omissions occur on page 10.

Piece No. 4, "Country Dance," ex. 25-40, if played in the correct tempo, would be considered a virtuoso showpiece. There has been no preparation for the bowing difficulties, assuming the student is expected to play the correct tempo.

25-40

Book 6[45] contains *twenty-two* pages of music, eighteen of which are pieces with no pedagogical explanation. In this volume he includes exercises teaching the seventh position by shifting from the fourth. Most methods would shift from the fifth by way of the third. There is no thorough explanation for the organization of the left hand—how a student is to group the fingers.

Piece No. 1, "La Folia," ex. 25-41a, contains passages in double-stops from measure 161–196 for which his students have had no preparation.

25-41a

45 *Ibid.*, Vol. 6 (USA, 1978).

Double-stops are as foundational to left-hand technique as is the ability to play slow, connected bows for the right arm. Without this skill, left hand technique will never be solid. Double-stop practice also develops tone, the skill to differentiate the functioning of the two hands, and bow control. Suzuki virtually ignores double-stop technique. Here is another example from the same piece *(ex. 25-41b)*.

Book 7[46] is *nineteen* pages of standard pieces and no etudes. He includes four widely spaced, large-print exercises in preparation for the pieces, with superficial technical explanations such as "Play slowly with correct intonation and with quick preparation for the shifts," or "Draw a short stroke from the middle of the bow," or "Place the third finger close to the second" (an explanation of how to play a minor sixth). *Book 8*[47] is a continuation of *Book 7*. It has a few more Handel Sonatas, which, like all the other books in his method, contains only about twenty pages of music.

Books 9[48] and *10*[49] are Mozart Concertos No. 4 and No. 5, with cadenzas by Joachim, that are filled with double-stops that are much more difficult than the simple double-stops Suzuki introduced in *Book 6*. There has been no adequate preparation for such difficulties. These problems are compounded by unsophisticated fingerings and amateurish technical advice, such as is found on page 24 of *Book 10*: "If the pitch is found to be accurate in five successful trials, correct intonation can be expected." Correct intonation can never be expected, certainly if one never plays scales. Playing in tune is a daily effort, never overcome, reinforced by playing scales—the equivalent of daily bathing.

The instructions given the student in *Books 9* and *10* are unlikely to help a student overcome the difficulties of the concerti, due to the lack of correct methodology in the preceding eight books. A close examination of the inaccuracies and deficiencies of Susuki's explanations for the technical challenges in these two concerti would take another chapter to explain.

Upon close examination of the Suzuki method, there is little "method" at all, just the *assertion* of one. What Suzuki offers in his "mother-tongue" method is

46 *Ibid.*, Vol. 7 (USA, 1978).

47 *Ibid.*, Vol. 8 (USA, 1978).

48 *Ibid.*, Vol. 9 (USA, 1975).

49 *Ibid.*, Vol. 10 (USA, 1976).

an astonishingly *superficial* approach that has *serious foundational errors* and misconceptions that are ultimately *destructive* to the development of talent. The Suzuki Method has recently been applied to the cello, piano and other instruments. From this thorough examination of his approach to teaching the violin, there is no reason to believe that using the violin method as a template will be a harbinger of good results.

We will now turn our attention to Ivan Galamian's approach to learning the violin as described in his book, *Principles of Violin Playing & Teaching*. Since its publication in 1962, over fifty years ago, it has never been critically examined. Yet in any field where *reason* is valued, the assertion of a pedagogical method should be an invitation for a review.

CHAPTER 26

Galamian

Upon arriving in New York from Europe in 1937, Ivan Galamian was asked, "Now that you are here, what are you going to do?"

"I am going to become the greatest violin teacher in America."[1]

Ivan Galamian was born in 1903 in Tabriz, Iran, an ancient city dating from perhaps 1000 BC or earlier; some archeologists claim it was the site of the Garden of Eden. The area not only has a history of continual warfare—invasion and occupation by foreign armies—but cataclysmic earthquakes, both circumstances having conjoined to kill hundreds of thousands of its inhabitants throughout the centuries. Of more recent imprint and import, in 1826 the city was invaded and occupied by Russia during a two-year war with Iran. After a peace treaty was signed, the Russian troops were withdrawn. Yet Russian influence remained potent in the region. In World War I, Russia invaded the city again, retreating with the start of the Russian Revolution, whereupon Ottoman troops occupied the city, withdrawing after their defeat in World War I.

Little is known of Galamian's childhood or the start of his violin playing, but in 1916, at the age of thirteen, he was admitted to the Moscow Philharmonia School, a school for the training of orchestral musicians. His teacher was Konstantin Mostras, who had graduated in 1913 from the violin class of Boris Sibor.[2] Galamian graduated in 1919, three years after enrolling, and joined the Bolshoi Theater Orchestra.[3] The situation in Russia became increasingly dangerous beginning in 1917 with the start of the Russian Revolution. Galamian was arrested and imprisoned, released only by the intervention of the management of the Bolshoi Theater. His mother died during the Revolution, a topic he refused to discuss even among those closest to him.[4] In 1922, nineteen years old, he

---

1   Elizabeth A.H. Green, *Miraculous Teacher—Ivan Galamian and the Meadowmount Experience* (USA, 1993), 22.

2   Diana I. Seitz, *The System of Effective Violin Practice According to Konstantin Mostras* (dissertation, 3304217, 2008), 4.

3   *Ibid.* 1, 3.

4   *Ibid.,* 5.

escaped to Paris, forced to leave his father in Russia. Eventually he was able to bring him to Paris, but his father died shortly thereafter during surgery to treat his glaucoma.

Galamian studied for two years with Lucien Capet, eventually assisting him with several students. There was a substantial Russian émigré population in Paris in the 1920s that led to the founding of the *Conservatoire Russe de Paris* in 1924. Galamian taught there from 1925 to 1929.

In 1937, he emigrated to the U.S., where he established a studio in his New York City apartment on West 54th Street. He also taught violin at the Henry Street Settlement, a charitable institution that provided music lessons, neighborhood theatre, and medical assistance to the poor. In 1940, when visiting Gregor Piatigorsky, who was vacationing in Elizabethtown, New York, (Piatigorsky was a friend from his Russian school days and his sojourn in Paris) he met his wife-to-be, Judith, introduced to him by a mutual friend who also summered there. They were married in 1941. In 1944 he acquired property in the area, which served as a summer school for his students, known as Meadowmount. That same year, on the recommendation of Zino Francescatti to Efrem Zimbalist, who was the director of the Curtis Institute of Music, he joined the faculty of Curtis, and in 1947, the faculty of Juilliard.

Galamian taught at Juilliard and Curtis for thirty-five years. Through his own teaching and his assistants, he taught hundreds of students from around the world who attended both schools—the most prestigious music schools in the U.S. A few of his students became outstanding players, many excellent players. Because of this it has been assumed, *in this country,* that his approach is the highest level of violinistic understanding and teaching methodology. Yet to the connoisseur, the end-result of his teaching—the players that he developed—falls short of the players we have examined in this book. The results also fall short of what was *standardly* being produced by many teachers in Eastern Europe during the same period, who also fall short of the old Russian masters. What might account for this difference?

SCIENCE?

Galamian states in the book *Miraculous Teacher:* "The building of violin technique is no longer a matter of guesswork. It is now an EXACT SCIENCE."[5]

Science is the attempt to understand the world through observation and experiment. There is never a final point of absolute knowledge. Therefore, although one may attempt to be exact, there can be no final measurement, just as

---

5   *Ibid.,* 141.

one can never find the center of a point. Science is, more accurately, an attempt to find "something new that has a certain fundamental kind of significance; a hitherto unknown lawfulness in the order of nature, which exhibits *unity* in a *broad range* of phenomena."[6] Science searches for *fundamental explanatory principles*.

It therefore follows that a scientist would never say that his theory represented an "exact science." The best it can be is observant of what is, until a little more awareness comes along. Additionally, when a system uses "talent" as a fundamental explanatory principle for skill, which is common in all aspects of music education (not only in Galamian's approach), it is no different from saying that God controls everything and we need not probe his mysterious ways. In other words, this is an *assumption* that puts us in a double-bind. To teach or play we must *understand*, but if the common explanation is that talent is the *causative* factor in obtaining high levels of skill, we are left with nothing that can be studied, understood or improved—a poor educational model. We would have a far less evolved society if some people had not been interested in examining what most people take for granted.

It is instructive to remember Emanuel Feuermann's insight into how great players think:

> It is surprising how few rules and principles there are and still more surprising how completely they change the entire style of playing. Believe it or not, my dear friend, the really outstanding string players, whether Kreisler, Casals, or Heifetz, are similar to each other in the way they use their muscular systems and handle their instruments and bows. The main differences lie in their different personalities, talents, and ideas, and only to a very small extent in their techniques, for which, again, physical differences are accountable.

Feuerman implies that these great players follow rules, that they have a system. What are their fundamental precepts? This book has highlighted a few already. How does Galamian's approach align with these insights?

As we discussed in Chapter 18, technique is a three-part system. *Any* system will constrain—funnel—growth within certain parameters because what evolves does so from foundational settings, biases. Therefore, all future growth is *dependent upon the seed*. The seed structured by Galamian's approach and fundamental assumptions cannot flower into a musician on the level of a Heifetz or Milstein. This is because it is intrinsically antagonistic to each of

---

6   David Bohm, *On Creativity* (New York: Routledge, 2010), 3.

the three systems that constitute technique—the mind/body, the music system, and the instrumental sonic system.

We shall see that his description and understanding of left-hand technique *lacks* important fundamental parameters—information and approach—that affect future growth. We shall also show that his concept of bowing is the *inversion* of the technique of the great players we have studied, and likewise, has implicit shortcomings that curtail the development of virtuoso bowing technique. Additionally, it will become clear that his system has a *mechanical approach* to understanding music itself, which deleteriously affects *all* aspects of a student's development.

While his approach is far beyond the amateurism of Suzuki, it is nevertheless fundamentally flawed when compared to the technical/musical approach of the players we have been analyzing.[7] Yet we need not invoke their methodology as our only template of comparison. The use of reason will be a sufficient aid. We will examine Galamian's book on violin playing, *Principles of Violin Playing & Teaching*,[8] written by Elizabeth Green after several years of collaboration with him. I can testify that the book is an accurate description of his teaching philosophy and approach. We will follow the order of the book, which may not be the most satisfying journey literarily, but will be the most certain and clear path for our analysis. Short quotations from the book will be examined, as will a few representative musical illustrations. I will not comment on, for the most part, what is essentially aligned with what we have discovered about the technique of the masters we have studied. For clarity, we will use the subheadings found in the book itself.

Galamian writes in Chapter One:

> Technique has to combine with interpretation for successful performance, and the favorable issue of the performance depends upon the following factors:
>
> 1. The Physical Factor: consisting of (a) the anatomical make-up of the individual, and in particular the shape of his fingers, hands, and arms, plus the flexibility of his muscular apparatus: (b) the physiological functioning with regard to the playing movements and the muscular actions that bring them about;

---

7   The views expressed in this chapter are the *author's opinion* based on many years of research; ideas that, in his opinion, are easily verifiable by anyone willing to seriously investigate the findings, the theories, contained within this book.

8   Ivan Galamian and Elizabeth Green, *Principles of Violin Playing & Teaching* (New Jersey: Prentice Hall, 1962).

2. The Mental Factor: the ability of the mind to prepare, direct, and supervise the muscular activity;

3. The Aesthetic-Emotional Factor: the capacity to understand and feel the meaning of the music, plus the innate talent to project its expressive message to the listener.[9]

We have confusion at a subtle level. While it is correct that one student may have slightly differently shaped hands, different sized fingers, or different levels of innate tension, most of these factors have little to do with eventual outcome if the mental process regarding fluid motion and the physical training and setting of the hands are correct from an early age.

Careful attention to a correct start is of *primary* importance in the system of teaching in Eastern Europe. This requires *hands-on* attention, which means holding a student's arms and fingers in the correct position, putting their fingers on the string for them so they can experience the correct touch and balance of the finger, examining the thumb position of the left hand and its contact with the neck, which must also be done into the higher positions. This process of *hands-on* work from a teacher must continue for several years until the proper setting is instilled, habitual. The detail that is necessary in the teaching and playing of the violin could be likened to ballet training. Here is a comment from the great Soviet violinist and pedagogue, Igor Bezrodnyi:

> What is most characteristic of the Russian school? Firstly, the maximum naturalness of the handwork—I mean the violinist's motor process. I think the best Russian violin teachers were trying to instill in the violinist an exact realization of the fact that each hand had to be extremely productive—which part, which muscle or group of muscles to use. That's the way to achieve naturalness. I remember one of Abram Yampolsky's phrases: "Remember that the muscle which works when you play must be elastic."[10]

Correct early training mitigates most differences in hand formation because a child's hands are literally molded to the correct position, which means that a teacher must know the correct position, which again means that the *teacher must be a master player.* Additionally, one of the discoveries from our analysis of the great players we have studied shows that their left hand is biased to the outside, the "pinky" or fifth finger (fourth in violin terminology), by a slight turning at the base of the fingers to open the hand.

---

9 *Ibid.*, 3.

10 From an interview in *The Strad,* March 1998 issue, as part of a tribute to Igor Bezrodnyi.

In Galamian's system this fact is not known. (It is not known in Carl Flesch's system either.) If a player does this naturally, as did Michael Rabin[11] (perhaps his father, who was a professional violinist, taught him this), he will have an advantage that will be described as talent. Anyone who is trained with this setting may do the same and, thereby, acquire the same physical advantage. This is one the primary shortcomings of the Galamian system—*many important fundamental elements are not known and, therefore, unexplained.* The proper use of the muscles is virtually ignored. Yet while knowing which muscles to engage, or not, is necessary and important, the process of creating *flow* in movement is much more subtle.

One's mind—how one thinks—and mental state (biases, nervousness, beliefs) are indivisible from the proper functioning of the body. How one *thinks* about movement, consciously or not, determines the result. How one *understands* music, as we have seen, is a *primary factor* in *how muscles are utilized in playing.* Yet, how one thinks of movement—in terms of flow—and how one thinks about music, are also not part of the Galamian system.

Regarding the "aesthetic-emotional factor," the "capacity to understand and feel the meaning of the music" cannot be separated from the means, both physically and mentally, to actualize this feeling. Because music has no *specifiable* meaning, it requires *cultivation*—training—and emotional freedom to *understand* its contrived emotional world. Ham-feeling, common in musical circles because of the intense competition to stand out from others, is often mistaken for true expression and encouraged by ambitious teachers (and parents). It is not true musical feeling. The assertion that a student must have "the innate talent to project its [music's] expressive message" is an example of a destructive assumption in teaching. If one has the capacity to understand and project the "true" emotional meaning of music (not ham-acting)—which is inseparable from technique—one also has no need of being taught anything at all. Yet there has never been such a person born on this earth. As we shall see, the emotional message—the *aesthetic* dimension of music—is an *inherently absent* element in Galamian's system of playing.

Aesthetic sensibilities are implicit in musical values/culture. This affects one's concept of sound, of interpretation, of every aspect from which the technique to bring forth these musical values is born. *Without a sophisticated understanding of the music being played, the technique developed to express musical values can*

---

11 Watch Michael Rabin play the last movement of Tchaikovsky's *Violin Concerto, Great Violinists of the Bell Telephone Hour (1959-1964)*, DVD, Video Artists International, (2002). The outside bias of his left fingers is obvious.

only be mechanical. This is because the technique *is* an *outgrowth* of musical thought, as Horowitz correctly believed, whether one is conscious of this or not. Mechanical understanding of music = mechanical technique.

POSTURE

> *How to stand or sit should not be the object of exact prescriptions other than the player should feel at ease.*[12]

This is advice; it is not an explanation. Without correct posture a player cannot engage the muscles of the body correctly. Thus, it follows that there must be more, or less, ideal parameters in which the body can function most effectively. We must use the body to play. To stand with stability, the legs must be engaged in a subtle way by internally rotating the muscles of the thigh and externally rotating the muscles of the calves. This supports the upper body, which supports the raising of the arms while playing. The neck should not lean forward, which creates tension.

In other words, developing the proper posture for playing requires study and understanding and is as much a part of technique as playing in tune. A look at the performers we have studied will show that their posture while playing was astonishingly correct. Correct posture is fundamentally *indivisible* from technique, as we discussed throughout this book. The entire body must be in a state of relaxation *and* engagement, whereby the motion and the energy needed to play the instrument with expression flows from the center of the body, out. This means that the impetus of action is from *within* the muscles, not imposed by the skeletal frame to "force" action. This is much easier for people with a heavy build because, even if they do not engage their muscles completely correctly, the muscle mass allows more room for inexactness. For people of slight build, *more consciousness,* understanding, is required to engage the muscles properly.

Great players create sound from the *whole body working in unison,* coordination, to make a note—a tone—not, as many students assume, simply moving their arms or a finger. Playing is a sensual affair. In fact, the expression, the *emotion* of sound cannot be separated from the *sensual* aspect of producing it. To create different musical moods requires different touches and is a whole body engagement. Galamian's system falls short here. There is no explanation or mention of the physical engagement necessary to play with core sound and vitality. If one has this naturally, good for them. Yet this cannot be called a thorough approach.

---

12 *Ibid.* 8, 12.

HOLDING THE INSTRUMENT

> Some artists support the violin entirely with the shoulder and head and are
> obviously comfortable doing so.[13]

This is incorrect and can only lead to tension in the shoulders and neck and is
why so many "seriously practicing" violinists have marks on their necks that
look like an animal bit them. This common malady is a symptom of holding
the violin too tightly with the head and shoulder, and often leads to such skin
trauma that a student's neck will bleed. Galamian's book has no explanation
of how to hold the instrument other than, essentially, however you want.
(Carl Flesch's book, *The Art of Violin Playing, Book One,* also falls short here,
stating that the unavoidable irritation of the skin as a result of holding the
instrument is a professional "illness," and advising one to use ointment at
night or to shave carefully.[14])

Galamian states that the scroll should be high—how high?—to prevent the
bow from sliding towards the bridge.[15] However, he does not discuss other
benefits of not allowing the violin to be angled towards the floor.

One of the main reasons to hold the violin at least parallel to the ground
is that this setting helps keep the right arm lower than the wrist, which is
mentioned in his book, but not in this context. Additionally, holding the
scroll higher than parallel to the floor, at least when "setting" oneself to play
the instrument, engages the underside of the left arm—the triceps—slightly,
which helps the left arm feel weightless, which is correct.[16]

The violin is held by the left arm, subtly engaged from below so that the
arm is weightless, and the head and shoulders in the same position as when
standing, although the head turns slightly to the left. The main difficulty with
maintaining a relaxed hold of the violin with good posture is that the *motions*
of the right arm—the bow—and the left fingers influence the posture. An
active down-bow and active "down" motions with the left hand fingers *will
force the violin down.*

As we mentioned, Milstein, Oistrakh and Heifetz are very free and relaxed
throughout their shoulders and heads, so much so that they can raise their heads

---

13 *Ibid.*, 13.

14 Carl Flesch, *The Art of Violin Playing,* Book I, translated by F. Martens (New York: Carl Fischer, 1924), 16-17.

15 *Ibid.* 8, 13.

16 One can notice Heifetz and Milstein will always raise their left arm higher when *placing* the violin in its playing position. Is this merely a mannerism or is it done to engage the left arm muscles in the way we have described?

from the chin rest and continue to play, essentially undisturbed. This is because they do not have percussive downward motion with either the bow—the down-bow is passive—or the left hand. In other words, *to maintain good posture requires a high level of technique.* It also requires training. Standing in the correct violin posture (without the violin or bow) holding the arms engaged by the deltoids, relaxed, hanging, at both elbows and wrists, slightly more elevated than what is required for playing for several minutes at a time, will develop the proper muscular infrastructure to maintain correct posture. The upper body must be capable of supporting both arms while lifted, the arms hanging, relaxed, at the elbows, the arms *sinking* into the upper body infrastructure. *Without correct posture the proper angles for the bow and left-hand systems cannot be found.*

THE LEFT ARM

> Whatever its basic placement, it [the left arm] changes its position beneath
> the instrument as the fingers move across the strings.[17]

This is only somewhat true, and is, again, a matter of degree. The arm movement is almost imperceptible when crossing strings within a position, which is made possible by the fact that the left-hand fingers must subtly pull back from the base of the fingers as string changes are made from a lower string to a higher. The arm must move when shifting around the violin. This is properly explained.

This next example, 26-1a, from the first movement of Lalo's *Symphonie Espagnole*, is used as an illustration of elbow motion while shifting positions, and left-hand articulation, stating, "...the run requires a crisp, percussive articulation of the fingers...."[18]

Unfortunately, percussive articulation of the left hand jars the bow from its track—the groove necessary to make smooth, connected sound and flow. Anyone watching Heifetz or Milstein's left-hand action will observe that the motion is *never* percussive. Here, in ex. 26-1b, is another way to look at the same passage utilizing smooth, non-percussive finger action, and yet having the notes articulate, clear, smooth, flowing and properly phrased.

---

17 *Ibid.* 8, 14.
18 *Ibid.*, 14.

The passage is a repetition of a two-pair pattern—B♭/D is a separated double-stop, which we have previously named a "two-for-nothing" pair; E/G is a "set-shift." This pattern is repeated through three octaves and is a much easier way of playing the passage than what is suggested in Galamian's book.

The sections regarding the correct position of the left wrist, the left hand, and the left thumb are essentially aligned with what we observe in the technique of the players we have studied and agree with Carl Flesch's pedagogy, as described in his book.

THE MOVEMENTS OF THE LEFT HAND

> Reduced to their simplest types, the movements of the left hand are as follows:
> The vertical movements of the fingers: their dropping on and lifting off the strings. This is closely akin to the pianistic type of finger action...[19]

This is an unfortunate description of motion. The fingers do not drop onto the strings. Does one "drop" oneself onto a wooden chair? Not without injury. A more accurate description would be that fingers are insinuated, in the archaic use of the word, upon the string in a way that will not disturb the track—the groove—of the bow. The allusion to piano playing is misleading for both violinists and pianists. No fine pianist would "drop" their fingers on the keys. As we know, Rachmaninoff felt his fingers grew *out* of the keys. Why? To avoid percussive action, which is the enemy of flow.

Galamian's following descriptions of finger movement are correct. Galamian continues:

> Sometimes, however, a harder hitting will be in order where the music requires a certain percussiveness in passage work; or, a special accent on a single note may be called for, which can be, in a very characteristic fashion, produced by lifting the finger high and hitting it hard, resulting in what is called the "finger accent."[20]

Ex. 26-2a is used as an illustration of this technique—a proposed "finger accent" on the F♯ in measure 2, which is marked with a sforzando, (and which

---

19 *Ibid.*, 18.
20 *Ibid.*, 19.

is depicted with an asterisk) in this excerpt from Vieuxtemps' *Concerto No. 4,* measure 39 of the solo.

The "finger accent," "the lifting and hard hitting of a finger," is anathema to any conception of the violin as a singing instrument, and potentially damaging to the hand as well. It also, incorrectly, presupposes a break between the offbeat and the downbeat. There should be none in a vocal, *bel canto* approach—as is shown in ex. 26-2b—which is how this music is meant to be played.

The "finger accent" is an idea that is never used by the great violinists we have been analyzing. Eugene Ysaÿe, who studied with Vieuxtemps, relays that Vieuxtemps often said: "Pas de trait pour le trait—chantez, chantez! (Not runs for the sake of runs—sing, sing!)"[21] As we know, the old masters valued smooth connection, flow (which is a "cultured" understanding of music) from which articulation may arise, as a wave appears from the ocean.

INTONATION

Galamian uses this illustration, ex. 26-3a, as an exercise for improving intonation and as a way of understanding the octave frame within a scale.[22] However, if one plays this, it will become apparent that there is a considerable amount of wasted motion. Going up the scale, the fourth finger must continually come back from the setting of the octave frame on the higher string to play the lower string. Coming down the scale, the first finger must cross over two strings to preserve the octave frame.

21 Frederick Martens, *Violin Mastery,* Eugene Ysaÿe, The Tools Of Violin Mastery (New York: Frederick Stokes Co., 1919), 7.

22 *Ibid.* 8, 21.

Example 26-3b is far easier and shows that the primary formation of the left hand is the *perfect fourth*; intonation may be tested by fourth finger unisons with open strings. This is not just intellectual nit-picking. It is an important subtlety because within the formation of the perfect fourth, between the first and fourth fingers, lies the creation of all double-stops. A player must develop this awareness because advanced technique is based on the recursive possibilities implicit in simple fundamental settings. *This way of thinking is a key factor in seeing through the facade of complexity to its seed of simple and correctly formed primary elements.*

In his book, Galamian states that the first finger of the left hand reaches back from within a correct frame. Yet again, without the *open* bias of the hand, all physical sense of what pulling back a finger—or stretching a finger—feels like will be very differently understood. In the open hand feeling that I suggest Heifetz and Milstein employed (a subtle counterclockwise rotation, from the player's viewpoint, at the base of the fingers for all left-hand formations), the first finger will feel as if it is to the left side of the fourth finger, and not pulled back, at least not in the sense one would feel in the normally adopted closed position of the hand. The first finger will pull back when playing a scale upwards in one position. With this bias, the left hand is more relaxed, which also relaxes the right arm and, thereby, improves bow motion.[23]

Additionally, Galamian does not mention that the tip of the finger must pull back slightly, subtly, to form a cushion, as we have shown in Chapter 18, Fig. 18-g. This will round out the sound. The extra solidity of the finger contact with the string helps intonation and is a key factor in creating core sound and smooth connection from note to note—filling the space between notes with glue, with information. This raises a further issue. The setting of the fingers—the balance on the tip, the point of contact—is of crucial importance in shifting. *The finger tip must retain its relationship to the string*—the finger's shape—when shifting, albeit lifting the weight somewhat, in order to move.[24] This, yet again, brings up the issue of what is left out in explanation and must

---

23 This left-hand bias aligns—makes congruent—the movement of the left and right arms, helping not only bowing, but shifting as well, as was explained in Chapter 18.

24 Maintaining the finger tip's relationship to the string is essential for playing virtuoso passages in octaves, tenths, thirds, double-stop glissandos, etc.

be supplied by the student's intuition—or not—in the Galamian system. Yet this is a fundamental point of importance that is easily explained to anyone, an example where the *hands-on* intervention of a *master* player/teacher is necessary.

Galamian continues:

> The artist must be extremely sensitive and should have the ability to make instantaneous adjustments in his intonation. The best and easiest way to make such adjustments is by means of the vibrato.[25]

This is misleading. Intonation is secured by the *manner* in which the finger stops the string, not simply putting the finger in the correct location. Using vibrato to adjust intonation is like using water to put out an oil fire—it simply spreads the problem. The answer lies in the slightest shift of weight on the finger, which is enough to make the minor adjustment that may rarely be necessary by a fine violinist. This can only be done if the finger has the correct, full contact with the string, the "pad" we have talked about.

TIMING

> In the left hand the fingers often have to be prepared ahead of the time of the sounding.[26]

The fingers of the left hand are usually played in groups and formations. This is necessary for smooth connection, a *bel canto* approach. If the finger is already on the string before sounding, the string need not be disturbed by any "down" motion. Additionally, the left hand is *always* prepared before the bow moves—the left hand leads the bow.

DOUBLE STOPS

This section talks at length about the octave frame and its importance for reliable intonation.[27] However, the most important fact about the frame is that it is set from the outside-in—from the fourth finger (the pinky), the base of the fingers turning slightly, subtly, to the right from the player's point of view, which opens the hand. If the base of the fingers is slightly turned in the way I have described, which opens the hand, there is *almost no feeling of stretching* at all. The fingers move back in a very natural and relaxed way. The "stretching" is more between the web of the fingers and feels relaxed, not the strain of a stretch in the closed position of the hand.

---

25 *Ibid.* 8, 22.
26 *Ibid.*, 23.
27 *Ibid.*, 27.

SHIFTING

There is lengthy discussion about shifting that aligns with the opinion of Flesch.[28] However, several key ingredients are not mentioned, nor were they part of Galamian's teaching approach.

It is conceptually, and physically easier, to move around the fingerboard if one makes the central setting the fifth position. This means that the arm is set to play in the first position in relation to moving back from the fifth position. When playing in higher positions, the hand and arm move up from the fifth position. The fingerboard is divided into three areas—fifth position and back, fifth position and up, with the area around fifth neutral.

It is easier to shift from a high note, down, than from a low note, up. Therefore, the arm should be biased as if one were already "set" for the high note. Another way of understanding this: from the high note, one's arm moves back to "understand," to "feel" physically, the setting of the arm before the shift.[29] Additionally, all shifting is cleaner, and manifestly easier, if one thinks in pairs of "set-shifts"—the movement of shifting *is* the note—not as Galamian suggests, one shifts, and then finds the note, although a guiding note, as he correctly points out, is often necessary.

When shifting, *the journey is the note.* This includes all double-stop shifts and eliminates the technical difficulties he cites in ex. 26-4a.

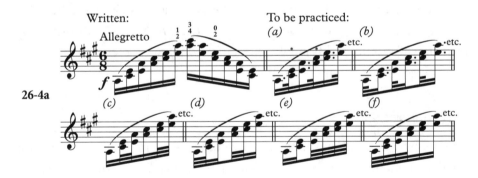

There is an easier way to solve the shifting difficulty he presents—playing in pairs of offbeats to downbeats. No matter what the rhythm, with this grouping the physical feeling to play the pairs is always the same *(ex. 26-4b).*

---

28 *Ibid.,* 23-27.

29 This is illustrated in the appendix section, ex. A-13.

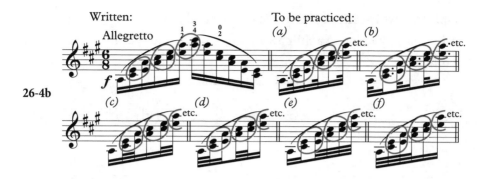

26-4b

Practicing as Galamian suggests, in rhythms, will build tension.[30] As we have discussed, the shift *is* the note. (This, of course, includes any guiding note.) This means that the shift is not different rhythmically from the value of the note as printed. The same is true for any note that is played as a "lift" or a "placed" finger. Speeding up the rhythm of the shift will create a "bump" in the overall motion and alters the true physical feeling of the passage, which is that the pairs of notes, offbeat to downbeat, *create* the rhythm of the phrase.

FINGERINGS

Galamian's fingerings[31] are based on square musical thinking, and are often unnecessarily difficult and theoretical, as in the following illustration of "creeping" fingering *(ex. 26-5a).*

26-5a

Galamian explains "creeping" fingering as a change of position by an extension of the fingers followed by a readjustment of the hand. The text explains the asterisk: "Extended finger. Hand adjusts to the new position on the following note." This technique is meant to eliminate shifts, or the sound of a shift. Yet correct phrasing often shows us another, much simpler solution, as I propose in ex. 26-5b. Correct phrasing puts the entire matter in a different

---

30 Practicing "difficult" passages in rhythms is a subtle form of desperation—forcing—and is pervasively used in teaching methods. The "problem" will always lie at a deeper explanatory level. The difficulty suggests a *lack of understanding,* a lack that is never addressed and is obfuscated, repressed, when one grasps at competency through willed assertion, which amounts to misguided effort.

31 *Ibid.* 8, 31.

perspective, which allows the frame of the hand to maintain its shape, while eliminating any sound of a shift because the correct musical grouping corrects the difficulty.

The same is true in the following *(ex. 26-6a)*.

The text explains the dagger: "Fourth finger is placed in tune by stretching. Hand adjusts to the new position while the fourth finger is sounding." The double dagger is explained: "First finger is placed on its note by stretching. As [the] first is sounding, the hand readjusts into the lower position."

Understanding the proper phrasing, as shown in ex. 26-6b, preserves the hand frame for both upward and downward shifts, while eliminating any sound of a shift. This is much easier than what Galamian suggests, which is not only musically naive, but technically less reliable.

The following excerpt in Galamian's book, from the first movement of the Beethoven *Violin Concerto*, measures 304–306, ex. 26-7a, is another example of intellectualism, not musical understanding. His fingering breaks the frame of the hand, which makes secure intonation more difficult.

The passage is really an ornamented melodic line, as is shown in ex. 26-7b and as such, one need not fear audible shifts as long as they align to the melodic contour of the music. In fact, *shifting often helps bring out the melodic line.*

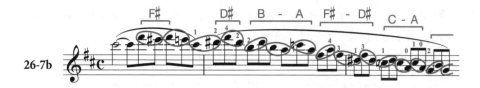

Fingering can never be separated from musical thought. It is a direct product of one's sophistication. Thinking in offbeat to downbeat pairs will require very different fingerings from those used in Galamian's editions of music and etudes. His fingering choices emphasize square, unmusical thinking, which, when used in partnership with his amusical practice methods, have a detrimental effect upon creating an artistic, expressive performance, *and* technical skill. They are also more difficult because they interrupt the natural flow of the music. *Fingering choices subtly develop the setting and muscular structure of the hand by encouraging a relaxed open position,* or a closed position, as we have mentioned, developing ease in shifting around the instrument, or not.

VIBRATO[32]

> "In general, the vibrato will have to be adapted to the dynamics of the bow, becoming more intense and wider in forte, more subdued, narrower and less fast in piano."

Is this how great singers sing? In fact, great singers use a variety of vibrato colorations, which they may even change from performance to performance. One cannot make such rules about expression. Vibrato is part of the "culture of sound," the knowledge of the "secrets of the traditions" of the great master players. If one does not "know" this "sound" (has never heard it), how can it be taught?

THE HAND VIBRATO

Galamian discusses what he calls a hand vibrato. If the vibrato emanates from the hand, the muscles of the hand will be overtaxed. The *muscular* source of the motion for this technique is not described by Galamian, (if, indeed, it is even valid as a vibrato method) another example of too much being left to chance if one is to assert a scientific approach. When discussing the training of the arm vibrato, he states: "At the beginning of the development of the arm vibrato, it is advisable to bend the wrist outward toward the scroll and to keep it locked in this position."

---

32 *Ibid.* 8. There is a discussion of vibrato from pages 37-43.

Try this and see how you feel. It puts tremendous strain on the hand, wrist and arm. Can this really be helpful?

Galamian writes:

> The vibrato motion does not normally occur exactly parallel to the length of the string, since this would deprive the vibrato of much of its ease as well as its range of motion. Rather, it directs itself across the string at an acute angle to the string's length.[33]

This cannot be correct. The motion of the arm or hand when vibrating moves parallel to the violin. If it did not, the hand would continually bang against the violin. The *fingers* are at an acute angle to the string, not the motion.

In his discussion about vibrato, and in his teaching, two key elements have been left out. Vibrato motion must be "up"—*to* the note. Just as the bow is a cycle of an active "up" to a passive "down," the vibrato is an active "up" to the note—the correct pitch. This is a crucial element for the focus of motion and, therefore, a focused vibrato. Also, vibrato is an *ornament* to core sound. Core sound places the instrument and player in a heightened state of focused energy and sound that allows for minimal movement in vibrato action, but maximum lushness of tone. As we have discussed, both core sound and vibrato are most easily accomplished on *up-bows*, which one may then transfer in physical feeling to the down-bow. One should maintain the "up-bow" sound and an "up" biased vibrating movement on down-bows.

Galamian's students lack a refined core sound with a rich, focused vibrato, which is a result of his technical approach. One may instructively compare his students to examples of Auer's students, such as Mischa Elman, Toscha Seidel, Nathan Milstein and Jascha Heifetz. In fact, this is an *elemental* difference between Auer's students and Galamian's and Delay's—the latter do not have focused, unpressed, core sound and vibrato. We may refer again to a comment from Igor Bezrodnyi:

> The second feature [of the Russian school of violin] is that a great deal of attention is paid to the violinist's feeling for acoustics and its possibilities. I mean the sound of the violin. Yampolsky and several other great Russian teachers made great demands on the sound, on its purity, richness and colourfulness.[34]

---

33 *Ibid.*, 42.

34 *Ibid.* 10. Yet none of the recently trained Soviet players have a sound like the old Russians, although far more refined than Galamian's students. They, also, do not have the bow arm ease of Oistrakh, the refined right arm movement, the subtlety of motion, or the understanding of phrasing that Milstein and Heifetz possessed.

While the element of beauty of sound may seem quite esoteric, when speaking of the highest level of playing, tone is an essential factor in the expressive power of playing. At this level it is not enough to just vibrate, nor is it enough in a scientific system to leave the matter unexplained, as has, historically, been the case. This is another example of something that many people can do if they are shown how, but is a "value" that must be understood.

THE RIGHT HAND

Galamian's description of the system of springs, the requirement of the pliability of fingers, wrist and arm in producing good tone, is essentially correct and aligns with the players we have studied.

HOLDING THE BOW

> The first finger is placed at a slight distance from the second finger and contacts the stick of the bow a little on the nail side of the middle joint. This placement of the first finger enables the bow to get a far better hold on the strings as the attack is made, to "catch" the string as it were, on the down-bow especially; and the hand acquires more directly the feel of the resistance between bow hair and string.[35]

This is a very subtle matter. For one thing, it is obvious from this description that Galamian bases bowing technique on an active down-bow motion, which is already a *fundamental* difference between his system and the playing of the great Russian masters. But, of more import and of a subtle nature, is the placement of the first finger (the index finger) away from the second and the feeling of the resistance of the bow hair when playing a down-bow. If the first finger moves in *opposition* to the motion of the hand and arm on the down-bow, the antagonistic movement will prevent the right arm's unimpeded movement. The finger must *move with the down-bow motion*, with the touch of the finger slightly feeling the "pull" on the hair. If the index finger is too "weighted," one will create *antagonistic* movement. This is a common, subtle, and pervasive source of bowing difficulties, even among professional players.

---

35 *Ibid.* 8, 46.

THE MOTIONS OF THE FOREARM

> The forearm can bend and straighten hinge fashion, in the elbow joint with the effect of closing and opening the arm. This is probably the most important of all bowing movements and it is used in almost every type of bowing stroke.[36]

The elbow joint is not a muscle. What muscle actually moves and controls this *most fundamental and important motion*? Galamian had no idea. Neither does almost anyone else, including Flesch. The great Russians did—the plug-in to the triceps, a small point the size of a fingertip (shown in Chapter 18, figures 18-a and 18-b) is the source of all bow motion, even staccato.

FOREARM ROTATION

> The forearm can rotate in the elbow joint around its own lengthwise axis so that it can turn the hand....[37]

This is a much more subtle issue than what is described and of key importance. Turning the arm from the elbow *joint* is a strain. The arm must be turned from the forearm, *very, very slightly and very subtly*, to allow for a transfer of arm weight to the index finger when the bow moves from the middle to the tip.

VERTICAL MOTION OF THE UPPER ARM

The upper arm should be described as the deltoid muscle, which acts as an elevator to move the right arm—as a whole unit—from one string plane to another.

---

36 *Ibid.*, 50.
37 *Ibid.*, 50.

DRAWING THE STRAIGHT BOW STROKE

> The straight bow stroke from frog to tip is the foundation of the entire bowing technique.[38]

This is misleading. More important is the fact that bowing is a *cycle*. While it is true that one must move the bow parallel to the bridge, this is not fundamental and is, in fact, the source of seriously incorrect teaching for beginners. It is the main reason that beginners in this country are taught to use short, stopped bows, in the hope that they can, thereby, control the motion. This statement also shows that Galamian viewed the *down-bow* (the frog to the tip) as the fundamental start of bowing, which is *fundamentally incorrect*.

The old Russian way to teach beginners is to start by playing long, connected bows, and is how Auer begins his series of books on violin instruction. This somewhat *amorphous* beginning is important because it teaches *flow* as a primary feeling, not separation. The students gradually learn to control direction, but with unimpeded flow as a basis for bow motion. We have very little information as to how Auer understood bowing, aside from the fact that in slow motion Heifetz's and Milstein's bowing is identical. But we will revisit an intriguing, and somewhat enigmatic, description made by Heifetz in an interview:

> The true art of bowing is one of the greatest things in Professor Auer's teachings. I know that when I first came to the Professor he showed me things in bowing that I had never learned in Vilna. It is hard to describe how I am able to hold my right arm so high with *unrestrained movements of the arm and wrist*, but ...bowing as Professor Auer teaches it is a very special thing. The movements of the bow become easier, much more graceful and less stiff.[39] (italics mine)

Galamian continues: "The chief problem in the straight bow stroke is to be found in the fact that action in the form of a straight line does not come naturally to the members of the human body."[40]

The actual difficulty lies in the fact that, as we have described, the *movement of the arm required for a bow motion parallel to the bridge is at a different angle from the angle of the bow across the strings*. This makes it difficult to map one's arm motion onto the direction that the bow must move. Yet, it is to the fluid movement of the arm *at the angle and direction of its motion when bowing* to

---

38 *Ibid.*, 51.

39 Dr. Herbert Axelrod, *Heifetz* (New Jersey: Paganiniana, 1976), 129.

40 *Ibid.* 8, 51.

which one must direct his attention, not exclusively to the motion of the bow across the strings. Attention to the motion of the bow, and not the movement of the arm, will impede and confuse one's arm motion. I suspect this is what Auer knew and why Heifetz felt he had unrestrained bow motion after Auer's intervention.[41]

These explanatory principles appear redundant and repetitive, which is unfortunate for the literary aspects of this chapter. Yet this cannot be helped and, in fact, as dull as this makes the reading, repetition does highlight the fact that this is to be expected if *all complexity is, in reality, a variation of simple fundamental ideas.* If one is unaware of the simple, underlying structure then everything appears to be a separate problem, a separate skill, a separate dilemma. As we proceed, we shall see how simple the solutions are to all of Galamian's assumed complexity.

TONE PRODUCTION

Galamian's use of the word "pressure" is an unfortunate description.[42] "Pressure" is from the top, from above, down. Pressure chokes sound. What should be used in playing is weight. The weight—the right arm—hangs from below the bow. Weight, combined with movement across the strings at the correct sounding point for core sound, creates spin on the string, which *releases* sound.

---

41 Most players and teachers believe that the right arm opens as a hinge from the elbow. As we know, the elbow is not a muscle. However, even if one knows that the motion of the arm is controlled by the plug-in to the triceps muscle, and even if we know that the up-bow is active, this is still not enough to explain Heifetz's and Milstein's bowing.

The common understanding of the right arm opening at the elbow for bowing arises because most people follow the track of the bow and do not concentrate on what would be the most *efficacious* movement for the right arm when bowing. Yet it is certain that Heifetz and Milstein have a more subtle arm motion than what is commonly understood. They pull their right wrist into their body on the up-bow, using the plug-in to the triceps muscle as the initiator of the motion.

This motion and the *very subtle* distinction between these two conceptions—the arm action as a hinge or the arm pulled into the body—is not easy to detect because the arm moves a short distance when bowing. Yet, awareness of this pulled inward arm motion makes bowing considerably more relaxed and allows for much more control of the down-bow *and* the up-bow. The difficulty in detecting this motion for the right arm is similar to the subtle awareness required to perceive the motion of the left arm when shifting, that, we mentioned, cannot be understood if the player aligns his attention to the left hand's movement up and down the strings. Both arms do move *parallel* to one another, but in shifting this is difficult to sense because the left arm, like the right arm, moves very short distances. Nevertheless, gaining an awareness for the *parallel* movement of both arms is a great technical advantage.

42 *Ibid.* 8, "The three fundamental factors for the right hand: (1) The speed of the bow stroke, (2) the pressure it exerts on the strings, (3) the point at which it contacts the string." 55.

THE SOUNDING POINT

There is a lengthy discussion about how to find the sounding point.[43] We can simplify this complex approach by realizing that the sounding point is between the bridge and the fingerboard. Auer writes: "It is within this compass that the tone is most full and sonorous."[44] This placement of the bow is easily discovered on *up-bows*—another fundamentally important factor that is easily taught—from which the sounding point should be maintained on down-bows. The sounding point is also affected by the cushion of the left fingertip and by the sonic *sophistication* of the player.

In other words, this is a matter of training and developed musical taste. If a student cannot hear a master "up close," live, he will have a difficult time understanding conceptions such as the sounding point, or core sound, which is a term Galamian never used.

Core sound and sounding point may seem to be synonymous. This is not so. The concept of core sound is more fundamental than where the bow must be to produce the sound, which could be called a sounding point. Core sound implies much more than where the bow is placed on the string. It is how the body must position itself, how the fingers must touch the string, how the notes must be glued to one another, and how the vibrato fuses with this basic sound. Core sound requires a certain state of the body, a state that develops the muscles in requirement with the needs of great technique. Core sound and great technique cannot be separated.

BOWING

Legato

> In the slurring of two or more notes on one bow stroke, which is called legato, we are faced with two main problems. One is concerned with the change of fingers in the left hand, the other with the change of strings. Considering the finger problem, we see that the basic need is that the bow must not be disturbed by what the left hand is doing.[45]

Any percussive action of the fingers on the string will disturb the track of the bow and physical flow. That is why Milstein, as we have seen, set his playing to the release of fingers, not the downward motion.

---

43 *Ibid.*, 58-61.

44 Leopold Auer, *Violin Playing as I teach It* (New York: Dover Publications, 1980), 21.

45 *Ibid.* 8, 64.

Ex. 26-8a is used as a practice approach for developing bowing not affected by left-hand action. Galamian writes: "On these slurs, the feeling in the bow arm should be the same as for the open string slurs."[46] Unfortunately, playing an open string will never feel the same as playing a string that is stopped because the addition of a finger changes the length of the string and, therefore, the tension.

26-8a

Ex. 26-8b is an easier way to have the bow not affected by the left hand. The correct phrasing, in pairs of notes played with one motion per pair, will mitigate any superfluous left-hand action that would disturb the bow's track.

26-8b

Galamian continues:

> Complete smoothness in changing strings will not always be desirable in legato (slurred) playing. Where a rather percussive finger-articulation is indicated (as, for example, in a loud scale or arpeggio run) a too smooth change of string on the part of the bow will disturb the unity of the passage, because the smoothness of the change of string will be out of character with the articulation of the rest of the notes by the left hand. It is important, therefore, to see to it that the legato string crossings *match in sound the percussion of the left-hand fingers.*[47]

26-9a

The example above, ex. 26-9a, is used as an illustration of such a situation. He writes that the asterisk explains: "Articulate the changes of string with the bow." The dagger explains: "Articulate by lifting the preceding finger, half pizzicato, in a sideways direction. The run, in general, is played with articulation in the fingers...."

---

46 *Ibid.*, 64.
47 *Ibid.*, 65.

Yet, as we have discussed, the great players we have studied never used percussive finger action. Percussive action is anathema to *bel canto* phrasing and flow, both musically and physically. The approach shown in ex. 26-9b will eliminate any technical difficulty with string crossing and left-hand movements, phrasing the music, and projecting the notes with great clarity and fullness. Notice the change in fingering required by the new conception of phrasing.

Detaché

Galamian discusses several variations of detaché (separate bows for each note).[48] These explanations of various bowing strokes are helpful to a point—they demarcate possible distinctions. But, at an artistic level, music is a far more subtle process because its *mettier* is emotion, which is ever-changing, channeled through an individual human who is, himself, in a state of flux.

Additionally, it is not possible to teach these bow strokes with *assured* success unless one knows the *muscle* that controls the motion of the right arm. This is yet another example of his system's lack of knowledge. If someone, by chance, did this correctly, he would have some success, although he would also need to use active up-bows and passive down-bows, which would also be "by chance" in this system. This double chance may have occasionally happened in, for example, Michael Rabin's case. Yet this is something that anyone can do if they are shown which muscle to use. Unfortunately, the more *active* the down-bow, the more impossible bowing becomes. So again, if by chance a student happened to play with less active down-bows, he might have escaped unscathed. Yet this is pure serendipity with his system.

Leonid Kogan came to visit Curtis when I was a student there, as I mentioned in Chapter 14, and was highly amused, in a disdainful way, when he heard us play. Many of these unknown and unexplained parameters and foundational settings were known in Eastern Europe. This is why nearly all Eastern European-trained violinists are better players than those who studied in the U.S. This is commonly acknowledged among professionals, at least in private conversation.

---

48 *Ibid.*, 67-69.

From the seed of slow, connected bows is born detaché, which is sped up legato pairs—slow, smooth bows—which give birth to all other bow strokes, except staccato. Detaché *is one of the most fundamental of all strokes.*

Galamian states:

> The detaché in particular will be helped by a good martelé…The martelé is decidedly a percussive stroke with a consonant type of sharp accent at the beginning of each note and always a rest between strokes.[49]

We again find the unfortunate word "percussive," which means to strike. How will this help detaché, which is a *smoothly connected* pair of *legato* (not accented) bows? In fact, if used as a basis for detaché, which it is in Galamian's approach, the ability to play detaché properly will be compromised and confused. The accent on the martelé note will create a *double motion* for the start of the detaché. (This is why one cannot play fast martelé strokes.) To use the martelé as a basis for detaché is a good way to teach a student how to "stutter," violinistically, that is, becoming tied into antagonistic muscle engagement.

His book then describes several theoretical uses of martelé, none of which should be done by a purely martelé stroke. Ex. 26-10a, below, from the first movement of the Brahms Violin Concerto, measures 3-4 of the solo part, is described as "quick martelé" using about one-half of the bow.

26-10a

Music must be *phrased properly* before we can even understand what the suggested articulation means, ex. 26-10b. How long is a note with a dot over it? *The printed music does not tell us this.*

26-10b

The music also does not explain the character of the stroke. In other words, Brahms does not say that the notes marked with dots in example 26-10a are to be performed with "a martelé bow stroke of a certain length and articulated character." This must come to the player by intuition and *sophisticated musical understanding.* Music is not comprised of bow strokes learned mechanically

---

49 *Ibid.,* 71.

and applied like the old "paint by number" children's toys. The printed page is an *incomplete* description of sounds organized by a composer that must be realized, made into music, through the mind and emotions of the performer. Additionally, articulation, which is the equivalent of consonants in singing, is hierarchically *less fundamental* than connected, flowing sound—vowels. *Bel canto* singers overlay consonants to the foundational connection of the vowels. Articulation must arise from underlying connection. This is a subtle but essential point.

Once a piece of music begins, *it is a single flow of sound*, psychological involvement, and expectation that does not cease its movement until the performance ends. From flow, *declamation arises*. Part of the confusion regarding articulation is that there is a misconception that connected notes cannot be clear. In fact, *properly connected notes are essential for clarity and power of expression*. Articulation is really added spice. This is an excellent example of the *impossibility* of separating technique from musical expression.

This next example shown above, ex. 26-11a, measures 29-30 from Saint-Saëns' *Violin Concerto in B Minor,* is explained as a "quick martelé" using the whole bow. This does not tell us much, although on another level it does—Galamian's approach is superficial. This selection is another illustration that, as Horowitz claims, technique is a product of musical thought. We have no way of knowing precisely what is meant by these accents. The composer does not tell us what bow stroke to use. What we can logically assume is that since Saint-Saëns was a friend of Liszt's he was probably equally obsessed with attempting to play the piano in imitation of the great singers of the time, in a *bel canto* style, as was Liszt's friend, Chopin. We must begin, therefore, with the *phrasing* and with underlying connection *(ex. 26-11b)*.

From there we may intuit what character these markings are meant to suggest. This will be no precisely definable stroke. Galamian's ideas are simplistic, mechanical.

This next illustration, ex. 26-12a, is an excerpt from the last movement of the Brahms *Violin Concerto,* measures 57-63. Galamian uses this passage as a description of "the sustained martelé," which he describes as "an expressive detaché stroke that has a martelé start...as soon as the attack is articulated, the short, rhythmic note of the fast martelé is replaced by a long sustained tone." This is marked in his book by the asterisk.

Yet what does this tell us about the music? It is from an understanding of the music that the articulation must arise. The phrasing of this excerpt, ex. 26-12b, shows us the proper left-hand technique and shows us Brahms' use of musical pattern, *which expresses itself through physical pattern.*

The octaves are all pairs of "set-shifts." From measure 1 to the beginning of measure 5, we have a scale, the little notes—the sixteenth notes—moving to the eighth notes. In measures 5–6 we have a pattern of two pairs of octave set-shifts—D/C♯, a half-step shift, then E/D, a whole-step shift. This pattern of movement and intervals is repeated—B/A♯, a half-step shift, then C♯/B, a whole-step shift. This passage must be practiced *legato,* from which the articulation will arise as a result of musical taste and emotional content. There can be no dot, no space, between the sixteenth note and the dotted eighth notes. Small notes lead to bigger notes, and there is simply no time to make a space. The connection between the two must be smooth, connected.

The analysis in pairs not only brings out the correct phrasing, but shows the repeated physical pattern inherent in the passage. This must be a first step in analysis before we can even decide what character the articulation must have. The music only gives us a clue. As mentioned before, the music does not tell us anything about the bow stroke to be used. This can only be understood by musical sophistication. In other words, it is a matter of taste, knowledge, intuition and feeling.

The violin part is part of an overall fabric. What is the orchestra playing during the solo part? How does the orchestra play similar phrases? These questions cannot be separated from decisions about articulation, bowings, the moods to be conveyed, and myriad factors that ultimately influence how a composition is to be performed.

He next describes a bowing called the "whipped bow:"

> ...derived from the accented detaché, but here the accent is produced by quickly (and barely) lifting the bow off the string and striking it down again with suddenness and energy. It is generally performed in the upper half of the bow, mostly starting up-bow, and should be practiced first in this manner. It must also be mastered, however, on the down-bow.

"Striking" the bow down with suddenness and energy on both up-bows and down-bows is simply *incredible*. No other word comes to mind.

Ex. 26-13a, from the last movement of the Beethoven *Violin Concerto*, is used in the book as a candidate for the application of this combative bowing technique. The notes to be whipped are marked by an asterisk.

26-13a

We can see, in ex. 26-13b, that this excerpt is actually a melodic line.

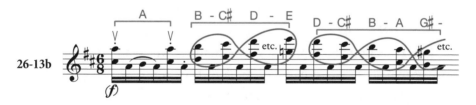

26-13b

Does it make sense to whip the individual notes of a melody? Not unless one is a sadist. The reason Galamian needs a "whipped" bow[50] to accentuate up-bows is because his system has no way to control the "up" stroke. Additionally, when, how, or why anyone would use a bow "strike" on a down-bow is impossible to guess, unless one views violin playing as a type of warfare.

In fact, the words attack, percussive, pressure, whip, command, are frequently used in his book when discussing technique, such as, "Gradually, the written rest should be shortened, the pinch replaced by a whip...."[51]

---

50 I am not sure which suffers more in this "whipping"—the bow, the note, the body of the player, or the ears of the auditor.

51 *Ibid.* 8, 87.

This refers to a bowing exercise. What entity, instrument, or body would enjoy being whipped, pressured, attacked, attacked from the air, simultaneously attacked, horizontally attacked, dropped vertically for a simultaneous attack, commanded, pinched, percussed, dropped, and slapped, all descriptors found with regularity in his book?

The "whipped" stroke is never used by the great Russians. Aside from the tension in the arm that it creates, it also produces a horribly harsh and ugly sound, which is against the *mettier* of the composers of Romantic music who were all obsessed with the desire to imitate *bel canto* singers, and the sonic requirements of the violin, which is designed to be stroked, not hit.

Staccato

His explanation of staccato is not helpful unless one knows the *muscle* that controls the stroke.[52] His discussion of ricochet bows is unnecessarily complicated,[53] *the illusion of difficulty*; if the down-bow has been trained to be passive after an active up-bow, a slight adjustment of the weight of the right arm will allow the bow to bounce from the string.

We have seen that every alternative solution I have given to Galamian's proposed difficulties, techniques, and solutions have been an *integration* of technique and thought, solving not only any physical problems, but musical, physical/mental, and instrumental problems at the same time. There is no separation between these elements in high-level playing.

PRACTICING

In this next section about practicing we shall see, yet again, that Galamian's entire system of practice is based on an *illusion* of difficulty. *The system has no fundamental explanatory principles.* It is, therefore, decidedly not scientific.[54]

Chapter Four of his book, *On Practicing*, is probably what Galamian is most famous for—infinite combinations of rhythms and unusual bowing combinations meant to train the mind and muscles to be prepared for any challenge or contingency. As he writes, problems encountered in playing:

---

52 *Ibid.*, 78-79.

53 *Ibid.*, 81.

54 Galamian's teacher, Lucien Capet, wrote a treatise on violin playing called *Superior Bowing Technique*, translated by Margaret Schmidt, edited by Steven B. Shipps (USA: Encore Music Publishers, 1993). Flesch, in his book, *The Memoirs of Carl Flesch* (New York: Macmillan Co., 1958), writes that Capet's "editions of classical works are so pedantically overloaded with complicated marks that it is impossible to see the wood for the trees," p 94. Capet's explication of technique is similarly pedantic, unnecessarily complex (technical examples that would never occur in well-written pieces), and mechanical in its orientation. Galamian's book does not fall far from the tree.

…should be handled by varying the practice devices, by changing the rhythms, bowing, accents, tempos…With this introduction to the method of solving problems of correlation and coordination, the reader should understand that the combinations given are by no means complete or exhaustive. *The number of possibilities is infinite and cannot be covered in a single lifetime.* The goal is not merely to play all of the possible combinations, but rather to master a few new ones each day so as to improve and to perfect gradually the coordination and correlation.[55] (italics mine)

Here is an example from his book *(ex. 26-14a).*

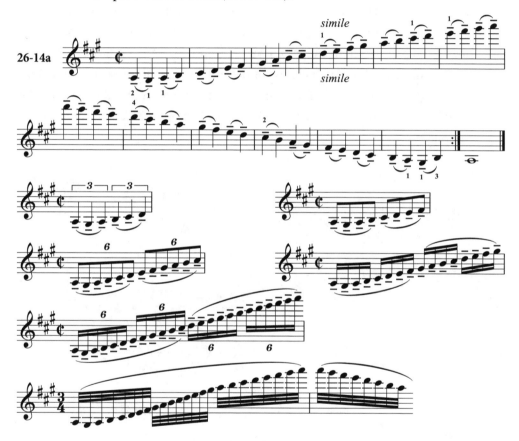

This approach complicates something quite simple. It reminds me of the joke about a man who complained to his rabbi that he was terribly cramped in his house.

The rabbi said, "Bring all the animals you own inside the house and then come see me."

The man did as he was told, complaining, "This is impossible. How can I live like this?"

---

55 *Ibid.* 8, 99.

The rabbi said, "Now invite your relatives to visit for a week."

The man came back, "Rabbi, I can't stand it. I'm going to kill myself if this goes on."

The rabbi said, "Now send your relatives back home and return your animals to the barn."

The man did as he was told and realized that he had always had ample living space.

The Galamian system advances the idea that to understand how to play a complicated passage one must complicate it further. This concept is *pervasive* in musical education and is widely applied and believed to be useful. Yet this approach will not make the musical passage easier. The original passage will merely seem easier than the mess one has imposed. This is a slavish, mimetic, and, ironically—despite all claims of developing the mind—a fundamentally unthoughtful approach. Is there an approach that will solve all the difficulties *simply*? In ex. 26-14b, we can see that beneath the assumed complexity lies simplicity.

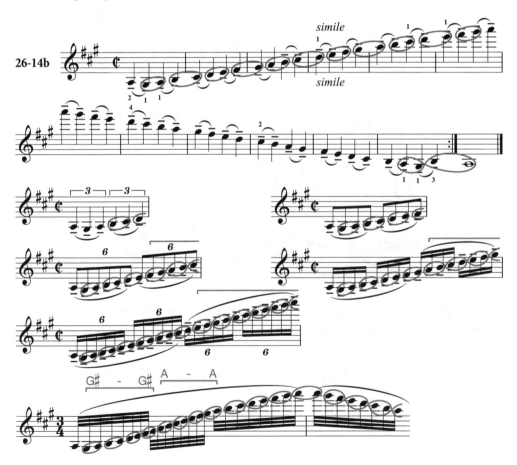

When these scales are properly phrased, no matter what the rhythmic pattern, the left-hand organization—the *pairs* of notes—*remains exactly the same*. Therefore the physical feeling and mental organization necessary to play the assumed complexities is a variation of simple elements and is not difficult.

I have chosen a few of the many depicted rhythmic groups in his book used for training the mind to illustrate another point. As shown in ex. 26-15a, one would not be able to see the underlying simplicity and unity of these examples.

26-15a

In reality, as we can see in ex. 26-15b, they are *exactly the same* if conceived as pairs of notes. This means that even if bowed as separate notes, or slurred, all the examples would feel *exactly* the same to play.

26-15b

This illustration from his book, ex. 26-16a, of assumed mental complexity is also suggested as a difficult technical challenge. The student is asked to group the examples as 2 + 6 + 4, and many variants.

26-16a

In ex. 26-16b, I have chosen at random one of the suggested patterns—1 + 8 + 3, yet this works for any of the patterns shown. As can be easily seen, when phrased as pairs of offbeats to downbeats, whatever pattern is imposed, the left-hand motion, the *pairs* of notes, will always be the same, as will the separate bowing pairs.

The differences in execution between the suggested patterns are negligible—essentially, nil.

26-16b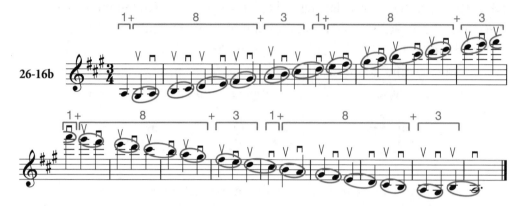

The "complexities" that Galamian presents in his method are illusions. They appear to be real because of wrong thinking and wrong technique.

The solution for all of the bowing problems that Galamian presents in his method books is the ability to play pairs of active up-bows and passive down-bows, and to think in groups of pairs. This makes all the bowing problems disappear and it becomes obvious that they are, just as was shown with his left-hand complexities and rhythmic puzzles, variations of very simple elements that repeat. Here is an example of assumed bowing complexity *(ex. 26-17a).*

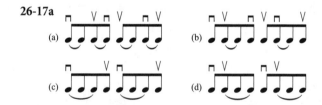

26-17a

In ex. 26-17b we can see that the first two examples, (a) and (b), *are identical* when understood as up-bow to down-bow pairs. Each pattern is three pairs of "up" to "down." One pair is separate and the other two are mirror images—two notes slurred, one note separate, and then one note separate and two notes slurred.

The next two examples of three notes slurred and one separate, (c) and (d), can be played with ease only if one has been trained to play with an active up-bow and a passive down-bow, otherwise the down-bow element will make it difficult to use enough up-bow to make the cycle smooth and connected.

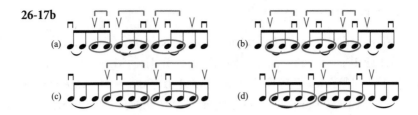

As I have said, to do that, one must know which muscle controls the "up" stroke. Why? Because to use the amount of "up" required to play detaché and mixed bowing groups smoothly will hurt the arm and elbow if a player does not know precisely where the "up" stroke begins. This is why so many contemporary players use little amounts of bow and stay in the middle of the bow. They cannot use more bow in fast playing because they do not know how to play an active up-bow. This "up-bow problem" is the source of much playing-related injury.

This is also why many performers cannot play clearly when playing separate bows at a fast speed. The inner beats, which are generally on up-bows, are not played with the same fullness that Milstein or Heifetz can achieve, hence most modern performers cannot approach the tempo freedom of these masters, and tend to play very square and rather slowly if they want clarity. As they approach faster speeds the offbeats are lost.

This next example of unusual accents, 26-18a, is again, much simpler than it first appears.

We can see in ex. 26-18b that the patterns of both examples are *identical*, just displaced. There is, again, no actual difficulty, just the *illusion* of one.

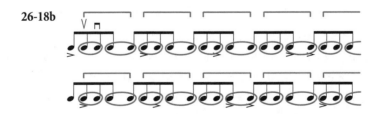

WHAT IS TECHNIQUE?

The word technique comes from the Greek "technikos," which means skill or art. What skill is there in *creating* difficulties? The skill, the art, is in *seeing through* the difficulties. Is there an underlying truth or system that is the substructure of what appears to be complex? Is there a simple system, which through variation, creates complexity? We know that there is. In the system of playing that I have proposed was used by Heifetz, and Milstein, instead of thousands of possible problems, we see simple solutions.

Additionally, the problems encountered in virtuoso pieces written by a great violinist will never be unviolinistic. They were written by performers—Paganini, Wieniawski, Sarasate, etc.—who made a living playing these pieces, which means that they wrote them for spectacular and unusual effects *that were doable*. These pieces were designed by their composer/performers to be played with a certain musical/technical approach in mind, a system. They were not written to be difficult "in theory." One can always find instrumental challenges that are nearly impossible. But who would write pieces for themselves that contained passages that were nearly impossible to play in public? The difficulties found in virtuoso violin pieces are always solvable using the method we have described.

A more insidious problem of the Galamian system of practicing, aside from the encouragement of an unthinking approach (while, ironically, claiming one), is that these exercises are devoid of any musical feeling, any expression, any understanding, or necessity for tonal color. Thus, the implicit assumption is that playing an instrument requires the practice of bowings and rhythms devoid of musical significance, which can then be overlaid to a musical composition. What actually happens is that the musical composition *becomes the Galamian scale system*, hence the mechanicalness of even the finest players that arises from such an approach is an *inherent* part of the system and of their playing.

This method favors the glib. The more expressive one attempts to be in a system aligned to downbeats, the more downward motion is accentuated, which breaks physical flow. Ironically, the more musically talented, the more impeded one is by this system, whereas an approach aligned to offbeats means that expression is highlighted by offbeats, which favors a release of sound and assists in fluid physical motion. The old Russians had this way of playing. Eastern European trained players were, and are, aligned to the downbeat, yet create sound by a release, and are better trained than Americans.[56] American trained players are, generally, either expressionless or, if attempting to play

---

56 This is also true of Eastern European pianists.

expressively, are more, or less, tied into physical knots. *This unmusical approach has defined our current music-making because of the system's ubiquitous presence.*

There is an intrinsic problem with a down-bow heavy approach, aside from the fact that it is inherently unmusical because it emphasizes downbeats. More insidiously, a heavy down-bow makes it difficult to use enough up-bow to get back to where the down started. As I mentioned, this becomes especially problematic in all detaché and mixed bowing—a combination of slurred notes and notes played one per bow in fast tempos. If the down is active at all, in fast mixed or separate bows there is not enough time or room to use enough "up" to make the bowing cycle sonically and physically smooth. This is what creates the need for contorted, unnatural solutions to use enough up-bow in these situations; hence the birth of the onerous and unnecessary "whipped bow."

Other solutions to the problem of not enough up-bow are to "dig" the down-bow into the string to slow it down, and then use a tiny "up" to get back. But this makes a very constrained, constipated sound and requires much slower tempos than what Milstein or Heifetz can play. Additionally, it is antagonistic muscle usage, which creates tension and a harsh, strained sound. This is what one generally hears among Galamian students.

Some avoid this intrinsic problem with more or less success. Itzhak Perlman, for example, flicks his wrist up, and thereby gets enough "up" motion to overcome any "down-bow" bias.[57] Most players are not that creative and have intrinsic, subtle problems with bowing that can be traced back to their confusion of the muscle controlling the "up" motion, and being trained to have an active down-bow.[58]

This down-bow emphasis, which is pervasive in string playing at this point, is the seed, the genesis, of what is called "orchestral" technique in string instrument playing. Because of the square conception of phrasing, which is static and metronomic, coupled with the physical constraint of an inability to play an active up-bow, this pervasive deficiency has been obfuscated and somewhat

---

57 Watch Itzhak Perlman play the Tchaikovsky *Violin Concerto,* the first or third movement, *Itzhak Perlman, The Philadelphia Orchestra, Eugene Ormandy,* DVD (EuroArts, 2006). He, also, clearly biases his left fingers to the outside.

58 Some players somewhat succeed in detaché bowing by playing in the middle of the bow and opening and closing the arm at the elbow using very little bow. This may "work," but greatly limits expressive possibilities because the potential sweep of the bow is constrained. Fast detaché is limited to the middle of the bow. At best, a player sounds "neat and clean." This approach is very different from the bowing technique of Heifetz and Milstein that we have described, which allows for more sweep of the bow, more control of the down-bow, more control in each part of the bow, and a much more *connected,* powerful sound with the potential for nuance when playing fast separate bows.

circumvented by using the wrist and fingers to flick the bow "up" and labeling this technique as officially "orchestral." *The alignment to the emphasized downbeat and the emphasized down-bow will always be limited in expressive possibility because it is contrary to the system of music and the system of the body.*

The argument made in its favor is that in order for sections of the orchestra to play in synchronicity, expressive technique is impossible. Therefore, it is demanded that all players align to the metronome, which aligns to downbeats and down-bows, as a sort of lowest common denominator of expression. Supposedly a conductor can mold this conformity into expression.

Yet this is impossible since the basis of the playing is machine-like precision emphasizing downbeats, with a built-in limitation for bowing technique. There is, of course, another way to achieve ensemble solidarity and expression— alignment to the offbeat, as we have discussed. *This requires an entirely different technique*, but would make conductors unnecessary for the performance of most music.

This shortcoming of technique is why all "orchestral technique" is essentially playing in the middle of the bow. When combined with square metronomic training this results in a manner of playing that is akin to typing out the notes that, while it may allow everyone to play in complete conformity, takes any sweep or flow out of the music, making it sound like everyone is typing in place. Nearly all string instrumentalists are trained to play in this manner. By comparison, if one were to watch old films of the NBC Orchestra with Toscanini or of the Berlin Philharmonic with Furtwängler (these are in the days of the Nazis—swastikas can be seen on the stage), the entire string section plays with much more bow motion. Or watch films of Casals. He bows like a great violinist, using a large amount of forearm motion. Most cellists simply move their wrist for most mixed-bowing combinations.

Because a majority of the players in an orchestra are string instrument players taught to play in this mechanical, typist manner, everyone else must conform. So the Darwinian process of orchestra auditions favors mechanical playing and those who do not notice the difference. This *mechanized* bias also selects the conductors, who must be approved by the orchestral, typist-players. If, as an experiment, one truly listened to current recordings of opera orchestras and symphony orchestras and imagined that it was one person playing, it would become apparent that the phrasing sounds like a mediocre student. This fact is obfuscated because of the enhanced sonority of so many instruments playing at once. But the sonority cannot eradicate the fundamentally mechanical approach to playing. This is why orchestral performances are so dreadfully boring.

We can see that Galamian's understanding of fundamental left and right hand technique is not consistent with what we have discovered was the approach of the great masters we have studied.

From *Miraculous Teacher, Ivan Galamian and the Meadowmount Experience*:

> It was as if he [Galamian] had three goals for the first lesson:
>
> 1. To clarify the beginning of the sound by isolating the attack itself and activating the fingers of the bow hand to accomplish this.
>
> 2. To increase the student's understanding of the gradual forward reach of the bow arm as the point of the bow was approached on the down bow and the necessary gradual retracting of that reach as the up bow got underway.
>
> 3. To introduce the "how to practice" methods through applying the routines of the A-major scale to the difficulties encountered in the etudes and the repertoire.[59]

Unfortunately, all of these primary goals are incorrect.

1. The beginning of the sound must come from where the motion of the bow starts—the base of the triceps muscle, a fact he knew nothing about—and the fingers of the right hand. The word "attack" should be used only in war games.

2. It is clear from his second goal that he viewed the down-bow as the start of bowing, which means that the down-bow is active. This is the start of his unfortunate and unnecessary complexity and misdirection.

3. It is this error that makes his practice routine necessary, and makes him believe that there are infinite possibilities with infinite solutions. There are infinite possibilities with very simple and few solutions. *It is also noteworthy that there is no mention of understanding music, itself, as a goal.*

Had Galamian taught in a school that had a scientific approach (which does not exist), his assertions of a scientific method, of having made violin playing an exact science, would have been subject to peer review, analysis and questioning from students and faculty. Interestingly, when searching for printed information about Galamian, there was a striking parallel with Suzuki—all that can be found are hagiographic descriptions of both him and his teaching, with very little information about his background and no analysis of his methods. The one critical comment I found came from the conductor,

---

59 *Ibid.* 1, 52-53.

George Szell, who regarded Galamian as "the worst thing that ever happened to music," which is left unexplained.[60]

IN SUMMARY

In reality, there is an underlying order in music, or level of explanation and perception, that lies behind the *apparent* order of the printed page. In the Galamian approach there appears to be thousands of notes, infinite combinations of bowings, and difficult to access musical meaning. We have seen beyond this superficial understanding—the technique of playing the violin is found to be a unity of flow. Diversity and seeming complexity arise from simple principles. Solutions and realizations are implicit in the essence of the music itself and a few key insights into the physical workings of the body and its alignment with the necessities of the music and the instrument.

Fundamental views, implicit and explicit, give form to implicate potentiality. These paradigms—views—determine the flow of psychic/physical energy. *How one thinks is what explains great technique—how the energy is channeled.* This is a different principle of explanation. Order is *enfolded* in the whole interaction—music, instrument, and mind/body. The simple order is pairs of notes, pairs of motion channeled through one's emotional, psychic structure.

In living structures the flow of energy and process is formed by *information*, DNA, which determines the parts from the *needs of the whole organism*. Different mechanical parts are not made separately and then sewn together. Therefore, *information* creates the substance and the structure of the organism as a continual process. This provides an apt comparison with playing a musical instrument. Are bowings (which create sound, tone) and left-hand technique—vibrato, finger movements, etc. *imposed* on the music or do they *emerge* from an understanding of the *musical necessity* organically? One approach is the imposition of discrete techniques onto written music. The other is a process oriented, "living" approach giving form to a *structure of technique* that *emerges by necessity* from a fundamental structure *implicit* in the music *beyond* the *printed page* (which is not really music, but only an abstraction of music). This *technique* is implicit in, and in conformation to, the mind/body system, which needs to be capable of subtle differences of expression that are inseparable from the requirements of the music (which are determined by the "values/culture" and "truths" of the nature and "laws" of music) and melded with the technique implicit in the ideal functioning of the tonal system of the instrument.

---

60 Roy Malan, *Efrem Zimbalist, A Life* (New Jersey: Amadeus Press, 2004), 262.

Therefore, what is essential in the acquisition of virtuoso technique is the mastery of the *correct fundamental skills,* which through their *recursive* properties potentiate virtuoso technique, and the ability to look at music in a way that sees through its superficial complexity. This way of understanding "technique" is a *different order of perception.* It is one whole movement of thought, which is inseparable from the physical act of playing, and which gives form to a *totality* of energy, *a psychic melding of performer and music,* in which analysis into separate but interacting parts is only partially relevant to outcome because the sum of the parts in interaction produces something far beyond mere linear addition.

CHAPTER 27

Responsibility

When I was a student at Curtis we had chamber music lessons with well-known performers on the faculty, many of whom were famous. One of the first chamber music coaches I met was Mischa Schneider, the cellist for the Budapest Quartet, who must have been in his late sixties when I first played for him. During lessons he sat in a big, overstuffed armchair and held a wooden cane by his side. He seemed very feeble and didn't speak much, at least I don't remember anything he said. I was sixteen and had no idea who he was.

Another chamber music coach was Jascha Brodsky, who had been on the Curtis faculty since 1932. Brodsky, who looked a little like Heifetz, was considered a second-tier teacher after Galamian, even though he was an excellent player, certainly far better than Galamian. It was rumored that he had played one of Prokofiev's concertos with the composer conducting. He also didn't say anything about how to play, explain anything, or demonstrate anything.

We used to go to the library and listen to recordings of Brodsky playing with the Curtis Quartet; he had the old style, the old sound. As I said, even that young one can recognize something, and it was obvious that he was different from the other player/teachers at Curtis. Yet he didn't discuss any general rules of playing chamber music with us and certainly never showed us how to play even two measures like the Curtis Quartet.

There *is* objective knowledge that can be taught about playing chamber music. Brodsky could have shown us how to rehearse, how to develop musical ideas, how to make a sound as a group. He could have discussed principles of phrasing, rules of balance, or invited us to watch him rehearse. Yet we received no applicable general knowledge. Chamber music lessons with him, and other teachers, generally traversed the same path as everything else—practice more. We would rehearse a couple of hours, go into the lesson and play. A few comments would be made. They were always the same.

"This is piano." That meant bow over the fingerboard and barely vibrate.

"This is forte." That meant press more with the bow or bang heavily on the piano.

"You missed a crescendo." That meant start quietly and then press more with your bow and left hand and move around a lot as you got louder.

"You must honor the score. Look at it carefully." No one knew what that meant.

"This composer is to be played with this character, and that character for another." This was an opportunity for piquant anecdotes about the composer or about the teacher's own personal experiences.

"You don't feel it; I don't sense your commitment." This meant move around more and make some grimaces or ecstatic faces.

Can this be what Kreisler's lessons with Massart, who was an ensemble partner of Liszt's, were like?

Is this how Vieuxtemps or Ysaÿe taught their pupils?

Are these the sort of musical insights one would have received in a master class with Liszt?

"Listen!" is one of the most overused admonitions in the verbal lexicon of the music world. It's obvious that what one does is aural. One can't help but hear something. The deception and mystification that accompanies telling someone to "listen more" is that it leaves out essential information—a student must know what to listen *for*.

"Listen, listen with your whole being!"

"Listen to your intonation, listen to your rhythm, listen to your dynamics."

"You have to feel music."

No explanation. Just feel it.

"Do something."

What?

Well, you could do this or that idiosyncratic thing, specific to this piece. Beethoven is this way. Dramatic. The score is your bible. Do everything in it and you are good. Except great players seem to be more than that.

How can a student simply "know" what good rhythm is, what good phrasing is, or what good sound is? In other words, *to listen well, one must know what he wants to hear.* This requires training. How can a student know what great sound is if he's never heard it? On a recording is one thing. Has he heard someone play like that next to him? How can a student "know" how to phrase, if he doesn't know how to phrase?

Unfortunately, most musicians' knowledge is personal, idiosyncratic. If you ask your teacher how to achieve better quality, the usual answer will be, "Listen more." This unexamined approach is ubiquitous in musical education at every level, from teaching beginners to teaching college-age players. Out of this confusion arises only one agreed upon answer—Practice. Practice. This is pervasive, not just a Curtis methodology. In fact, it is not just a geographical phenomenon. As far as I know, it is the way music is currently taught everywhere. If someone does something better, there is no explanation. They are just more talented. So one must practice more. This approach obfuscates a *pretense* of knowledge.

There were two great musicians who taught at Curtis who only pianists had access to—Rudolph Serkin and Mieczyslaw Horszowski. Serkin was always playing concerts, hence, rarely there. Horszowski had been a student of Leschetizky's (who had been a pupil of Czerny's who was a student of Beethoven's), a great player, and at the time old enough to have known Saint-Saëns. But neither I, nor anyone but a few pianists, ever met him or saw him teach. He was off-limits to us. Not purposely. No one thought of it.

This brings us to a fundamental question—is there a better way to teach? The great cellist, Emanuel Feuermann, wondered about this also:

> Why is it that in all other professions there is an effort made to raise the standard and the average, while in our profession, there is not even the slightest attempt to recognize existing lacks or more especially the need for correction?[1]

Nothing has changed since he made these remarks in 1940.

USELESS HELP AND HELPLESSNESS—TEACHING?

There is no need to apply for a license from the state to teach music; one may simply hang up a sign. If you are a certified Suzuki teacher students will come. To qualify for certification, essentially, a teacher must be capable of playing the Suzuki books, which is the equivalent in cooking school of being able to boil an egg at the same time as making toast.

Anyone can claim that he can teach music. Terrible players and terrible teachers often have droves of students. Parents, unless they have knowledge of the field, cannot know whether their child's ineptitude in music is the teacher's work or the child's inheritance. Additionally, there is the myth, conveniently circulated in music schools, that a teacher need not be a good player to be a good teacher. Unfortunately for everyone, there is only one chance to learn an instrument correctly. The fact is, good teachers are not good enough. Students need great teachers; and great teachers must be expert players.

---

1 Seymour W. Itzkiff, *Emanuel Feuermann, Virtuoso,* E. Feuermann, "Notes On Interpretation," (Alabama: University of Alabama 1979).

Astonishingly, as we mentioned previously, major conservatories often use the so-called method of Suzuki's to teach beginners. The fact that this approach has never been seriously examined, yet is seriously used and promoted by professionals, is both a symptom and proof of the illogical approach used in music education. It is commonly believed that great teaching is only needed for advanced students. Consequently, little attention is paid to the quality of teachers who teach beginners. In fact, the opposite is true—the end lies in the beginning.

Does anyone monitor what is being taught in private lessons at a conservatory or music school? Does anyone help the teachers improve? Does the school take responsibility for the correctness of what is being taught? Sadly, the answer is "no" to all of the above.

How can a parent or student be sure that what is taught is correct? They can't.

The unfortunate fact is that most teachers pass on to students the training they received from other mediocre player/teachers. Even if a teacher is an excellent player, I have never met a teacher of any instrument who had knowledge they could explain in clearly understandable detail that is *objectively* correct and deeply understood. They are the rarest of rarities, yet this need not be so. It is the educative isolation caused by the cliquish nature of the music world that creates the scarcity of people who possess real information. Players and teachers are fearful to protect what they have. Sharing knowledge, or admitting that one does not have it, is viewed as destructive to one's interest. Therefore, there is a pervasive lack of *assured* quality that is undermining the development of general public interest or, at least, more interest. This ubiquitous ignorance is a major problem in music education.

It is also *deeply* irresponsible.

Because of the lack of oversight and pedagogical seriousness by educational institutions, students and parents become "mystified" by the "faux" authoritative, and at the same time, passive stance of individual teachers. On the one hand, a teacher will *assert* his expertise based on his own personal experience, (which he must if he claims to teach); on the other hand, he will often rationalize or hide his lack of knowledge by *passively* claiming, without research, that talent is an explanation for skill that he cannot explain. *There is no way, as the educational system is currently configured, that a student can know with certainty that what he is being taught is the highest level of knowledge available.* My suspicion is that the supposed scarcity of major talent is not a reflection of the rarity of gifted students, but the inversion—the scarcity of teachers who have fundamentally accurate, deep knowledge of what they are teaching.

Equally irresponsible to students is that there is little openness (mainly coy, unexplained suggestions that one could do this or that) by teachers and musical institutions about the lack of opportunity in the field, should a student wish to become a professional. This is understandable. After all, without students believing that they can be professional musicians, serious music conservatories and colleges that offer undergraduate and graduate degrees in music would be out of business. So would their teachers.

This confusion, and resultant mystification, is perpetuated and rendered unfixable by a deeper problem: as a society we are enthralled by the idea of the *inexplicability* of talent. In the field of music, the word "talent" is uttered with nearly religious awe. This misbegotten reverence has affected not only instrumental playing, but composition as well.

For hundreds of years composition had been taught as a skill that could be learned through the direct *imitation* of masters:

> In one class with Krenek, the students asked him, What was it like studying composition in Vienna back in the early 20th century? Krenek answered that it was not like studying composition in the United States. Rather than individual lessons, they received group instruction, and a core element was a single large project which spanned the entire year. The first year, they were instructed to copy Bach's *Well-Tempered Clavier*. At this, the students gasped in disbelief. "Yes," Krenek said, "and for the second year, we copied the Beethoven piano sonatas." Horrified, the students asked why. Krenek responded, "Well, after a while, you stop having to look at the next note to know what comes next." What was the assignment for the third year, the students asked, with some trembling. He smiled: "There wasn't one; they figured, by that point, you knew what you were doing."[2]

This approach gradually changed when composers began to feel that the creative process was indescribable and not teachable, a matter of genius, divine inspiration, and originality:

> When asked about the amount of time that should be devoted to the study of harmony in the curriculum for young composers, Bruckner replied that

2 Joshua William Mills, *The Rhetorical Pedagogy of Music: Imitatio Techniques for Music Theory Instruction and Composition Training* (Dissertation, Master of Music, Peabody Conservatory of the Johns Hopkins University, Baltimore, 2010), 2. According to Mills, we *do* know how composers were trained in the past—modeling the great composers by direct copying of manuscripts, variation of copying, and many other interesting variations of this approach. This is how Bach learned, and how he taught his students, as did Mozart, Haydn and many other composers. This is a fascinating paper.

three years were absolutely necessary,... while for composition a few months would do, since composition was not really teachable anyway.[3]

Schoenberg agreed:

> The greatest difficulty for the students is to find out how they could compose without being inspired. The answer is: it is impossible. But as they have to do it, nevertheless, advice has to be given.[4]

Yet for hundreds of years students had been taught to compose, whether inspired or not, by literally imitating the great masters. This is how students were taught to paint in France—they copied the paintings in the Louvre. This is also the methodology we have used in this book to understand proper instrumental technique. Once what *is* known is understood, one may put their personal spin on it. This is what masters have *always* done, even though rarely remarked upon.

We know that Chopin and Liszt carefully studied the great *bel canto* singers. They also studied one another's playing and compositions, as well. We know that Horowitz seriously studied *bel canto* singers, and we can be sure that he observed Rachmaninoff quite closely, as Milstein must have been watching them both[5] and Heifetz, who I am sure watched others. Glenn Gould made his own analysis of Horowitz's playing:

> ...if I speak from a very personal standpoint, is the fact that there was one strange, quirky, utterly odd year in my life in which I imitated Horowitz like mad, and after that, I stopped doing it [laughs], as far as I know.[6]

Auer felt no embarrassment or futility in seeking out Wieniawski to learn from watching him play:

> Since Wieniawski was living in the same hotel in which I had registered...I took advantage of the opportunity presented, and every morning hunted [him]

---

3   Benjamin John Williams, *Music Composition Pedagogy: A History, Philosophy and Guide* (D.M.A. Document, Ohio State University, 2010), 54. Williams writes about the gradual shift that occurred among composers regarding the nature and source of their skill when they began to view themselves differently as a result of sociological shifts. This is a fascinating paper.

4   *Ibid.*, 49.

5   Milstein claims that, "Observing him [Horowitz] play, I learned how to imitate his sound on the piano." As we know, Horowitz mentioned in an interview in 1932 that he learned to shape passages as does a "good" violinist (Milstein). We quoted Milstein in Chapter 23: "We're afraid not only to criticize but even to analyze the work of the superstars, which is too bad." Nathan Milstein and Solomon Volkov, *From Russia to the West* (New York: Henry Holt and Co., 1990), 187. We must assume that he was not afraid to analyze master players.

6   Glenn Gould in a telephone interview with Glen Plaskin, September, 1979, researching Plaskin's book, *Horowitz.*

up...He would practice the violin for hours at a time, like a great artist—for his own pleasure—disclosing to me the hidden treasures of his genius.[7]

Bach, who we all agree was a genius, copied the manuscripts of master composers by hand, Vivaldi for one—not simply to procure the scores, but to study the methods of the composer. Haydn learned in this way and taught his students with this method—copying—as did Mozart, Schumann, Brahms, Liszt, and many other composers, using the masterworks of other composers as models for study and composing. All of these composers were geniuses, unique, individual, yet they learned by, literally, imitating and modeling other masters.

For the composers and instrumentalists mentioned above, studying masters, even modeling and imitating them, *did not destroy their individuality*, their voice.[8] They were exceptional themselves, yet had no *reluctance* in learning from other masters, not even hiding this fact. Incredibly, there is not a single music school that does the same as its policy. What is a reasonable and logical method of learning for masters, geniuses, is ignored by musical institutions.

This haphazard approach, biased by a confused understanding of the nature of individuality as an isolated, separate consciousness (a misapprehension that leads directly to our misguided reverence of "talent") and an illogical notion of originality (which does not exist), has created *educational incoherence*. We recall that Stravinsky lamented about the incomprehensibility of the work of young composers:

> "The use of already employed material and of established forms is forbidden him,...[which condemns] him to appear as a monster in the eyes of the public; a monster of originality....

There is a way to move towards rationality. As we mentioned, Rossini observed:

> Style is traditions, and the secrets of those traditions could be [surmised] by the young novice only among great singers, the perfect models consecrated by fame. [Traditions] elude scholastic instruction. Only the performing model, taken from life, can inculcate and transmit them. So that if those who possess the great, true traditions disappear without leaving disciples on their level, their art vanishes, dies.

---

7   Leopold Auer, *My Long Life In Music* (New York: Frederick A. Stokes Co., 1923), 92-93.

8   Writers have learned through direct imitation for centuries: "All great writing is in a sense imitation of great writing...For centuries, one of the standard...learning techniques has been imitation...even line-by-line imitation that enables the writer to learn 'from inside' the secrets of some great writer's style. John Gardner, *The Art of Fiction—Notes on Craft for Young Writers* (New York, Vintage Books, 1991), 11, 142.

Fortunately, because of printed music, recordings and film, the art cannot die *if one knows how to look*. This is the subject of this book—*how* to look. Are people really so different from one another *essentially*? If geniuses need to study geniuses to be geniuses, I would say not. Yet they are intelligent enough to realize: *What one person can do, another can figure out.*

If we remember the story in Chapter 16 of the pianist/composer who had access to Horowitz's piano, but was uninterested in exploring why Horowitz had set the piano up to play in that particular way, we can see a possible explanation of our collective reluctance to investigate master players' methods. He felt that this was just Horowitz's style, something personal. This is a common idea—it is believed that there is nothing to learn from studying other players because what they do is simply a personal style. However, some people's personal style allows them to play far better than others. Some people *are* objectively better than others. Clearly there is something deeper going on other than merely stylistic, idiosyncratic differences.

If we study only the superficial, we will stay confused. What this book has attempted to show is that if we can reach the fundamental level, the biases, we can begin to understand a great deal about why one person plays with more facility than another, or possibly how a composer writes more interestingly than another. If a school is not attempting to understand what it teaches in depth, what can they profess to be teaching?

People may say that even if a school made this information available to all students, each one would understand it differently. Some would benefit, some would not. This may be true. But this itself should be studied. After all, a school is devoted to learning. And learning about learning is a fascinating subject.

We have been diverted from a logical approach to educating ourselves by two distractions—the worship of talent and the idea of originality. They are really the same illusion. We want to believe in the unapproachable, incomprehensible specialness of certain people. This only benefits those deemed to be special and is a cul-de-sac of confusion and mystification that is preventing the continuance of the art. It is simply not true that skill cannot be studied and replicated.

If an educational system calibrates itself to the inscrutability of talent, the resultant system will deem the investigation and analysis of the causal factors of excellence as irrelevant. This assumption destroys the very purpose of a school, whose *raison d'être* must be that it is *possible* to learn and that phenomena become *understandable* through careful observation.

A system that precludes such a possibility, because its fundamental premise is that talent is unknowable, cannot claim to have anything of substance to teach.

This will bring a haphazard and desperate quality to the educational process, which makes it destructive of its very purpose. And, in fact, that is what we see in the field of music. We alienate, ruin, and discourage many more players and composers than we develop. The system, as it is, is self-defeating. It need not be.

ANOTHER WAY

What is scientific inquiry?

> [The search for] a hitherto unknown lawfulness in the order of nature which exhibits *unity in a broad range of phenomena...* [The scientist] wishes to find in the reality in which he lives a certain oneness and totality, or wholeness, constituting a kind of harmony that is felt to be beautiful.[9]

A school is a place where people go to learn and acquire skills. They are introduced to new ideas and thoughts. Hopefully, the knowledge imparted is coherently presented. Yet this is not good enough. A music school or a music teacher can be no better than their understanding of "the secrets of the tradition" that we have discussed throughout this book. This must be the *base* level. It is these "traditions" that a school ought to be transferring to new generations.

For many, many decades this has not been the case. As we have seen, the transference of knowledge has been disrupted by many factors. "Values" create "culture" and funnel potentiality, but we have seen that *we do not know* what those values are. This might not be a problem if we were on a higher artistic level than the past. But we are in a dead-end of non-creation, or confused creation compositionally, and a decay of quality in re-creative performance. This is leading the art into societal irrelevance.

If a school or a teacher does not transfer the actual tradition that *created* the great music and performers what are they teaching to students? They are teaching what they *guess* to be true, which inevitably results in a mechanical approach. We have defended our lack of knowledge by relativism. "I feel it must be this way, you feel another way." There is, therefore, at the center of education, no gravitas, no certainty about values. This confusion is eroding the entire edifice. Yet, we don't have to guess. We can seriously study the medium and the masters themselves.

A few reasonable questions for any music department or school to ask themselves would be: Is this a level of educative rigor and interaction that would satisfy Prokofiev, Beethoven, Bach and Tchaikoksky if they dropped by to observe composition classes?

---

9   David Bohm, *On Creativity* (New York: Routledge, 2010), 3.

Would Paganini, Wieniawski, Kreisler and Sarasate be satisfied with how the violin is being taught?

Would Liszt, Rachmaninoff and Chopin admire the piano department's pedagogical research?

Knowledge must be continually upgraded and refined. This is true in any field, yet this does not happen in music. It is quite a claim to say that you can teach someone. A school and its faculty are entrusted with a student's, and in the case of a child, a parent's hope. It is the responsibility, not only of an individual teacher, but the school as a whole to ensure that their claim of expertise can be supported with provable fact, not idiosyncratic opinion. Because we have "traditions" and power structures that need to be protected and may benefit from the system's current structure, any process that might be disturbing to the present way of doing things is considered anathema. This mental lethargy keeps us from developing a more logical approach.

Can we create a system? The danger of a system is that if there is no space for discovery it will eventually become dysfunctional. The system then becomes dogma, faith, belief—a dead concept. This is a natural and common occurrence in systems because by definition they are limited. *One will never find something truer than the system if the system precludes such a possibility.* Therefore, a system must include space for the search for what is true as part of its structure, its "values."[10]

Music is more unified than at first glance might be apparent. All musicians must use their bodies to play their instruments. There are rules about muscle movement that are true for everyone since, physically, everyone is essentially the same. How to use one's hands and fingers cannot be much different for an oboist, a violinist, a cellist or a pianist. As we have seen in previous chapters, music has underlying, fundamental "laws" and principles. Therefore, helpful insights about one instrument can be cross-utilized in others. Compositional insights apply to all musicians and will affect their technique.

However, we are currently divided not only into camps, but individual rooms. Pedagogical exploration should be brought under one roof and a

---

10 We are simply not used to looking at performers, composers, education, and music as an interconnected system. Some people may find this way of looking at art unaesthetic, unromantic, cold. I do not agree. A system implies *oneness, connectedness.* You cannot be much more romantic than that. Oneness (which *is* a system), when experienced, is more deeply mysterious, spiritual, and liberating than any organized religion can ever hope to promise. (This is obvious—they are all divided into separate "truths.") Additionally, a system does not have to lack creativity; it does not have to be mechanical. Does the universe, which is, itself, a system, lack creativity?

Nothing alive is mechanical—it is connected to the "source," which is the wellspring of intuition. Therefore, despite what scientists may believe about the possibilities of AI, nothing mechanical can ever be, or become, truly intelligent.

researched, holistic, non-idiosyncratic approach should be developed that uses the commonality of all branches of the musical world as a basis for a school's educational structure.

Because technique is a three-part system, as we have discussed, a school should research each aspect of the system:

- How to use the mind/body effectively;
- How to understand the music deeply, non-idiosyncratically;
- How an individual instrument's particular sonic system ideally functions.

This could serve as the structure for the creation of a template combining each facet into a comprehensive approach to learning that a school should *continually* develop. Additionally, a school should:

- Investigate and disseminate—publish, film—analyses of great players to both the students and teachers as part of its educational policy. (Great players, as we mentioned, have always done this, but no school.[11]) Using the approach provided in this book makes the process of analyzing *any* instrumentalist fairly straightforward. Ideally, a teacher should be able to explain how and what any player does—good, bad, or indifferent. Helping teachers do this, helping teachers and students gain knowledge, should be the main purpose of a school.[12]

- Teach students how to play the symphonic repertoire, *without a conductor,* from the beginning of their ensemble training. This would mean that students would learn to read scores. They would have to learn to play from the interaction of the offbeat to the downbeat, which we know is the "glue"

---

11 We can, perhaps, understand why schools do not study great performers. While this knowledge would be of *incalculable benefit* to the students, I suspect that it is not in the interest of the teacher/performers to give up whatever edge of knowledge and skill they may possess in a field that is *highly competitive* or, conversely, show that they do not have a provable edge in skill and knowledge over the students or other performers.

In athletics this sort of analysis is always used at the professional level. One factor that may explain why this is so, aside from the vast monetary differential between the fields, is that the athlete's career is over at thirty-five years old. Other performance fields are similar. An actor cannot play the same parts for fifty years. Neither can a dancer or a singer, whereas a performer/instrumentalist can perform in concerts until they are over eighty years old. Because of tenure in an orchestra, and through a false model of scarcity in solo playing, and because there are minimal employment opportunities generally, there is little *incentive and* little opportunity to help people "make their way."

12 We do expect, for example, that when we see a doctor they have sufficient knowledge to diagnose medical problems in a non-idiosyncratic, provable way, although this is also quite subtle. But even given the fact that there is an art to medicine, doctors are certainly helped in their role as "experts" by continually published new research in biology, medicine, neurology, psychology, etc. They are not diagnosing "on their own" entirely.

of expression and coordination in ensemble playing. They would have to understand musical "laws," which provide a non-idiosyncratic foundation to developing an overall musical conception for a composition.[13]

- Teach students to compose, at least to the level that regular schools require students be able to write an essay. We may utilize the methods used in the past—copying manuscripts, filling in figured-bass parts, and other pedagogical tools that were adequate for Bach, Mozart, Haydn and countless others to learn how to compose—that were relinquished after the first quarter of the twentieth century when composers decided that to be valid composers, students had to be geniuses and original and the old ways were of no use. If we gave up such self-aggrandizing "faux" lofty aspirations, we might find that many people can compose, at least competently. Must one be a genius to write a letter?

Could we develop programs to teach in incremental steps (from beginner to advanced levels), an integrated learning approach encompassing music history—including literary parallels—harmony, counterpoint, and composition (which, if taught correctly, is perhaps the best way to understand music) in a format that melds it with the technique of playing?

This proposed learning realignment for the field of music must occur in the *preparatory* departments of schools, not the colleges. If there are schools that can train people by the age of eighteen to be outstanding players who know at least the basics of composition (the equivalent of essay writing), this would allow serious music students to study other subjects in universities, perhaps with music as a double major. They would, therefore, not compromise their college years obtaining a degree in music, which currently teaches little but practicing an instrument for hours.

Some esoteric information may have been lost, yet we do have advantages over the past. We have technology that we can enlist to vastly improve our overall educational approach by integrating musical knowledge. The beginning steps in this effort may prove to be simplistic, but even a simplistic demonstration can be a springboard for further discovery. This will eventually help us teach students more thoroughly, more successfully. The task before us is to create a holistic approach. This has never been formally, in other words, seriously, attempted.

---

13 The usefulness of positing and utilizing musical "laws," which we have discussed extensively, if truly understood, allows for far *more* freedom in interpretation, more variety, than the constrained, mechanical, literally pedantic "method" of interpretation currently used.

The promise of taking the haphazard element out of musical education, the idea that there is real knowledge that can be transmitted and that all is not left to the mysterious process of talent, would be a powerful invitation for many more people to successfully participate in learning how to play music and vitalize the study of the art.

CHAPTER 28

On "Feeling" in Music and Life

As we have seen in the previous chapter, an oft heard entreaty from teachers of music to their students is the heartfelt directive to play with "feeling." Their plea is filled with hidden meaning. It is, at one level, an admonishment; at another, a challenge; at another, a mystery. What does it mean to play with "feeling?" If queried, a teacher will usually respond: "The music means something. You don't feel it."

Or, "This should be more intense."

"This should be quieter, more serene."

"This should have more grandeur."

"This is a Minor key, it should feel sad."

"This is a Major key, it is a surprise." Etc.

What is "feeling?" We normally associate the word with emotion, meaning an emotional response to the action and interaction of ourselves with the "stuff" of our lives—the world "outside" us. Our internal, psychic thermometer measures and labels our "feeling" about a situation, a gauge by which we determine who we are. Is this what is meant by "feeling" in an artistic sense? Are those "feelings" an aesthetic response to what surrounds us or a sentimental indulgence? What is the difference? Is it an important distinction? I believe so. Not only in living one's life, but also in understanding what constitutes artistic expression. We usually separate the two—by that I mean living from art. There really is no such divide, although in our society we have relegated the study of art to being an impractical waste of energy.

Art is the contemplation of beauty. The awareness and sensitivity required to do so is not only the source of all "feeling" in art, it is the only path to the subtlety—the "feeling"—necessary to have real relationships with people. It is only on this level of awareness that our embeddedness with all of life is obvious, and comforting—intimate. Only on this level can we live with one another and our surroundings and find meaning intrinsic to ourselves. A mind unaware of beauty is unintelligent, even dangerous, because there is no foundation of sensitivity.

Logic without "feeling" may be quite efficient, but with an effectiveness that destroys any human component and, ultimately, leads to stupidity:

> It was no less a scientist than Charles Darwin who demonstrated the consequences and human tragedy of a purely scientific, alienated intellect. He writes in his autobiography that until his thirtieth year he had intensely enjoyed music and poetry and pictures, but that for many years afterward he had lost all his taste for these interests: "My mind seems to have become a kind of machine for grinding general laws from large collections of fact… The loss of these tastes is a loss of happiness, and may possibly be injurious to the intellect, and more probably to the moral character by enfeebling the emotional part of our nature.[1]

Yet "feeling" without rationality is apt to be just as destructive. Emotions based on our "experience" are likely to have no more truth in them than the ravings of a lunatic, a mind unhinged from any objective reality.

An aesthetic interaction with the world is the essence of all art. The creation of art is our attempt to see what "is" from a whole mind, a mind that is perceptive and responsive, open to what unfolds under its scrutiny and free to be carried where it must. There is no separation of "feeling" and reason—rationality—at this level. By "feeling" I do not mean emotionalism. I mean emotion that is "clear." When we swim in a lake or walk through a forest or ski down a mountain, is there emotion? Is there feeling intrinsic to the act itself? You will notice that there is. Does one have too add a "touch of joy" or a "measure of excitement" to the experience to "feel" it? The act itself is the emotion, it is the "feeling." But to "see" in this sense one must free oneself from preconceptions.

I remember reading in Salvadore Dalí's book, *Fifty Secrets of Magic Craftmanship,* that to accurately "see" a subject to be drawn or painted, he advised students to view it through a device he concocted that, by the manipulation of mirrors, depicted the subject upside down, thereby making the artist's gaze free from preconception and enabling him to perceive the form without the filter of familiarity.

Everyone has feelings, emotional responses about everything we encounter. If you look carefully you will see that those feelings are made up of the happenstance of our conditioning, the "outside" world being the trigger that starts the engine of thought. Have you noticed the "feelings" we have about our name? If someone pronounces our name incorrectly, or purposely makes fun of it, it is likely

---

1   Erich Fromm, *To Have Or To Be* (London: Continuum, 1997), 122.

"feelings" will suddenly appear. Are we seeing the situation clearly enough to have a pure perception, or "feeling" of the moment? If not, if our reaction is based on preconditioned paradigms, we have entered the world of sentimentality.

Sentimentality is worked-up sensation through the spinning of the mind, a mental state which *produces "feelings." Sentimentality is a relationship with our conditioning, not with any objective reality.* Holidays are a good example. They carry the weight of the past, the burden of tradition, the comparison of time gone by, of aspirations unborn, of advertising and merchandising, of ideals. This puts the mind in a state of excitation and confusion, a whirlpool of conflicting realities between what is, what was, and what should be, leading to an emotional state of mind that may lead us to tears, numbness, or contrived, forced elation—a substructure that may not be visible to us. This is more akin to a dream state than a true "feeling" response. A person may genuinely have "feelings," but these feelings may have little or nothing to do with what is happening *aside from his imagination.* Therefore, sentimentality is a divorce, a separation, from accurate perception, usurping reality for effect, the effect of drawing attention to oneself—"ham-living." Similarly, in performance art, sentimentality is the source of all "ham-acting"—usurping the material of the play or the music to draw attention to the performer.

Our thoughts are words. Words create feelings. Words are also the thoughts that form the ego, which in turn creates self-imposed limitations because this "constructed" identity blocks—filters—clear perception, which is the source of intuition and creativity. In any "recreative" performance art, the transcriber's ego must be put aside, otherwise there can be no direct "feeling" or *communion with one's subject.* How does this work in practice?

In theater, the words of the script are, in essence, the psychological description of the character an actor plays. The words are the product of the character's thought process, and it is in the words that the truth of the character must be found. Are not words our thoughts? *Our thoughts are the content of our minds.* Thoughts create action. The actor, to be as "real" as we are, or he is as "himself," must become one with the words of the script. Those words must take over his body and mind.[2] The interference of his own words—his own thoughts—tangles the psyche of the character he portrays with his own "self"

---

2   There is an art, a skill, to this, of course. I suspect that Shakespearean actors, Lawrence Olivier, for example, are aware of the potential for shaping the rhythm of words in the same way as great musicians shape musical phrases; that they "play" with the "offbeat" (nonictic) of iambic pentameter by stretching the syllables and grouping the words that lead to "downbeats" (the ictus), conscious of the hazard of double-accenting the point of arrival. This gives the poetry a long line, with full syllabic detail and nuance, just as in music.

and creates a conflict that blocks true "feeling." Therefore, the actor's challenge is to make the words his own, as if he created them. To do that he has to be able to let the words take him over and flow so naturally from him that in answer to another character he can think of no response other than what is in the script. The "feeling" for the material is an inseparable byproduct from this process. How much room is there for his ego?

The actor has to train his mind and body to be a supple, subtle conduit for pure contact with the subject—the character he portrays. He must develop and train his voice to be a powerful yet malleable instrument of expression, train his body to respond in concord with his needs to interact with other characters with naturalness, and be aware of his movements on stage. This "whole" constitutes technique. To achieve contact with his subject—the part he plays—requires that there be no impediment to the actor's expression of the "feelings" of his character. To do this requires the focus of his entire being. The actor's "feeling" for the play and the part he portrays is inseparable from that attention. It is born from the melding of his psychic and physical forces in interaction with the script, the setting on stage, and other characters.

The same is true in music. The performer trains himself to become a perfect conduit of inspiration, coming directly from the music, and through him, to the audience. To do this requires that the artist have no physical or mental antagonism to the free flow of expression, expression that is one with the material, not added on by design. To "be" this requires technique. Without technique—skill that has become internalized—there can be no direct communion, hence, no true feeling. The "feeling" is the melding of the beauty of the sound, the subtlety, the nuance, the flow, the play of the rhythm, the organic understanding of the material, the physical presence and energy of the performer, the physical feeling of playing in itself, the touch of the string, the pull of the bow, the ability to create a "world" for an audience, the passion to work to that end, the pulling together of one's entire being for the purpose at hand. This is what constitutes feeling. It is not achieved by admonishment, or via sophisms such as play with grandeur, or in a piecemeal fashion. *It is a mind-set.*

The artist seeks to give to others a direct line to the essence of the subject being illuminated through himself. Since we all are in relationship with one another and everything else—because the world is one indivisible system—if an artist can create an atmosphere in an audience that begets self-forgetfulness, of suspended disbelief that the situation is contrived, the artist's mind can convey a direct experience with the music normally "outside" the capability of the auditors. To accomplish this transference, the artist's task is to "clean" himself psychically and physically from any impediment to expression, becoming one with the essence of what he performs. He must trust his intuition and inspiration. Two of the greatest impediments in artistic endeavor is a mind not free to run with intuition, and a public numbed to subtlety by the pursuit of distractions, the very purpose of which is to anesthetize the mind.

Art is study in the true sense of the word—looking with magnified attention at and into the subject and oneself. There is no end to discovery, and it is this journey into the depths of the subject that is the source of true "feeling." The main element necessary in art to convey true "feeling" is the possession of enough passion to get to the truth, the essence of the subject of study.

The source of a sentimentalist's actions are outside themselves. What they feel is regulated by their concocted persona, through which they *measure* their effectiveness. They sell. Since their persona is a collection of paradigms meant to please, their direct feelings, their intuitive process, is muffled or deadened completely. For a person at this level of psychic development, aesthetic feeling is not possible.

Freedom from inherited paradigms is not a loss of self. It is freedom from the limitation of one's conditioned thinking. When one speaks of the loss of ego as being a crucial component of art, the ego is the constraining, limiting factor. Loss of this ego allows one to harness insight and perception as a microscope peering into the complexities and subtleties of life, and to have the freedom to express "feelings"—emotion, which derives from care—in the highest sense of its meaning, a combination of reason and sensitivity, which is true intelligence.

So the dictum by teachers of art that a student play music with feeling, or act a part in a play with feeling, or paint or write with feeling, is not so easily met. If one does not live with genuine feeling and communion with the world, one has no chance of having anything but a sentimental, contrived, and ultimately frustrated response to that demand.

CHAPTER 29

Altered States

We have seen throughout this inquiry that what is deeply true is often the inversion of what, at first glance, seems to be true. This realization can occur in many realms. I recently discovered something interesting while hiking in the mountains overlooking Stinson Beach. The beach is an expanse of white sand about a mile long, bookended by the cliffs of California's coast. It is accessible by Highway 1, which follows the coastline north from San Francisco, or by way of Mount Tamalpais, beginning in the redwood groves of Mill Valley, over the hot, bare top of the mountain, winding through a redwood rainforest and ending on the beach. On the weekends it is quite crowded, traversed by trails and hikers, but during the week the trails are nearly empty.

It is the emptiness that allows one to imbibe the unusual air of the terrain while hiking through the forest. The dampness from the trees, because of the morning fog, heightens the aromatic properties of the ground and leaves, making the air perfumed. As one travels higher up the mountain, the heat penetrates through the sparse tree canopy and a fragrance of eucalyptus leaves, bay leaves, and dill—unique to Northern California—envelops the air. The forest smells like a Thanksgiving dinner.

For many years I had both calculated and hoped that while hiking I might be able to become "enlightened." Not that I know what that means, but I had read about it. Buddha, or some other mystic, would saunter through a forest and unexpectedly, overpoweringly "get it," understanding in a flash the whole of life, and in a state of ecstatic joy throw away his "self," his books, and his teachers, forever. I usually just breathed some fresh air, felt stronger, and became a little more calm.

Hoping for a new experience I often tried a few mental experiments. I would think, "Can I just be?" or "Can I really see that tree without calling it a tree?" "Can I stop my thoughts?"—(all the questions I had read that I should be asking). If I ran instead of walked, I was able to focus on the rhythm of my stride, or alternate leading with the right or left leg, or count my steps, for some reason never past four. Yet my mind always pulled me back to the same reverie in which I spied a beautiful, naked wood nymph peering at me from behind an upcoming tree, ran after her, caught her, and had sex with her on the forest floor. Clearly there were some benefits to exercising in the hinterland, but nothing that I would call profound.

One day I was walking from the beach up the mountain trail and something shifted. I was doing my same "non-stop-thinking-while-trying-to-see-something-deep" routine. The day was searingly hot, in the nineties. The air was saturated with fragrance, wafting through the forest by the ocean breeze. From a promontory I could nearly see the curve of the Earth on the ocean horizon. A thought appeared to me—my walking, my steps, were quite heavy, even aggressive. This was a new idea, one I had not read. I thought, "Let's see if I can think of raising my feet instead of putting them down." This did feel different. My walking was much lighter. I felt supported by the ground.

I continued; What if I stop looking "at" everything? What if I allow what's around me to come into me? So I tried it. I *let in* the trees, the aromas, the sun, the heat. The ground seemed to carry me along and something happened. My perception shifted. In a flash, my anxiety vanished. The world seemed to hold me, to wrap itself around me. There was no distance between me and "out there." My mind stopped chattering. I walked, but didn't seem go anywhere, going deeper into what was there without moving, as if I traveled *into* everything or through the lens of a microscope to a deeper view. And this happened automatically, like the shift your eyes make in viewing visual illusions that morph from two dimensions to 3D. The 3D is there all the time, appearing once one's perception aligns with it.

I've continued to allow this to happen and have discovered some interesting things. In this state, the world seems to move slowly. Without the noise from my thinking everything is quiet, deeply tranquil and devoid of anxiety. Seeing what's around me in this way is like watching a stoplight change in the middle of the night on a vacant street, or like the sound of the city after a huge snowstorm. All the noise is sucked out, except in this case the noise is my thinking. Colors are vivid and I notice odd shapes, the relationships of objects to one another are thrown into relief. I notice trees and birds, the sounds of animals, of my steps. People talk with one another, drive, shop, and stand around as if they had all the time in the world. Maybe we do.

This "disassociation" from identification with one's thoughts is the strangest aspect of the shift in perception that I have described. The most mentally disturbing and distressing factor in this experience is that to "unhook" from associating one's thought to one's identity, we must accept the idea that psychologically we are no one and nothing *in particular*. This seems insane compared to the way we normally think, but I must admit, as hard as it is to accept, it is most likely logically true, as least from the observation of my thinking. My thoughts are not really who I am. We have two biases, two realities—one filled with problems and stress, the other where these problems do not exist.

Subsequent interaction with people through my teaching and everyday experience has shown me that what I have noticed in myself is *generally* true. I think we are trained to be hyperaware of the opinions other people have of us. We learn this, in its primal form, as a survival *necessity* from our mother and the family unit. As noted in Chapter 8, we gradually and unconsciously form an identity that we call our "self." This "self" is, however, at its meta-level, the "other."

If we look carefully at our goals, our hopes, our dreams, we will see that they are framed within the possibilities and potentialities that exist in the *present* societal structure. It is the ideas, values, and paradigms of the present structure of the society into which we are born. These are *not* "eternal" never-changing values, yet they become our "selfs."

Children live, especially before the age of five, before the social conditioning of school, in a sort of dream state with the "other," a sort of extended maternal relationship with their surroundings and with adults who are part of the family network. This is easily noticed when teaching young children. Physically they are unafraid of close contact. They move and smile uninhibitedly with whomever is accepted into the family unit.

This seed of concern, born from maternal care, is gradually amplified in, and by, the child through interaction with the family system (colored by the parent's learned interaction with the greater societal system) into a *fear* of the judgement of *others*, which becomes a need to please the growing and evolving image of "self," and the recurring patterns of authority who eventually take on the parental and extended family role—teachers, peers, and everyone else one meets.

Personal interaction is continually tinged with the need to please or, conversely, the fear of disappointing. As we venture into the world, we encounter continual judgement from others and our "self," unconsciously and consciously, learning that to interact means, and hazards, fundamentally, the possibility of the rejection of one's "self" by judgement, which is "not-acceptance." This continual reinforcement conditions, teaches, the mind to assume the "truth" of this position—we learn that the meaning of life is to be found in the *pleasing of others and one's adopted "self,"* which is the "other" internalized.

Ironically, as one "theoretically" becomes more competent at functioning with one's own initiative and extends oneself into the greater world, *fear of the judgement of the other and the "self" grows*. It does not recede, as one might reasonably assume it would, with the growth of competence. This is because this psychological foundation is an inherently no-win situation, a double-bind, a paradox, within the depths of our psyche.

Pleasing can never lead to acceptance. Pleasing is born of judgement, and judgement is without end; *it is a state of mind*, and that state of mind can never be *finally* pleased. Our *meaning* in life can be summed up by our success in *pleasing* each other's "selfs" and the "other," or one another, which are the same. This means that our lives are based on the fear that we will not please, succeed, impress, gain approval, etc. We are essentially continually unworthy in the eyes of all these "selfs." Unfortunately, we can never be accepted, in a primal sense, if to be worthy we must *please*.

We all feel inadequate in some way or another. This is a result of conditioned thinking. *This conditioning* attenuates our ability to learn. Ability, even intelligence itself, is often blocked or brought forth, as we have discussed, by the most subtle shifts in awareness—intuitive shifts open to anyone. The fear of being judged as incapable often cripples intuition.

Since people's deepest desire is the acceptance of his or her "self," which is really the "other," all of our social interaction is subtly and essentially based on "fear of judgement," both externally and internally. Our "selfs" block any possibility of acceptance by either "side" because the "self" acts as a continual judge between both parties. Therefore, the possibility of being accepted without judgement, which is the primal state, the essential oneness, the connection with "mother" and all else, is impossible for everyone.

The underlying fear we have for each other is generated because we inherently *seek* oneness—we are *essentially the meaning and potentiality found in this acceptance* (in its true form), which is our *natural* state. This is not mystical. It is logical—the world is an evolutionary creation. This means that it is derived from a *single* source and is one interconnected organism. We sense this, maybe beyond conscious thought.

All people seek connection. They attempt to find it in the most creative and varied ways—religion, drugs, power, renunciation of power, and on and on. I think most people are not aware this (connection, oneness) is a *fundamental* need, and that most of what we desire in life is an attempt to fulfill *this* longing. Or, if vaguely aware, we are afraid we cannot have it, that this state is blocked for us. The way our lives unfold continues to teach us this.

The double-bind that makes this fear a reality is that we believe the "acceptance" we desire is the acceptance born of *pleasing* the other and our "self." This is the teaching of all the major Western religions—we must *please* God.[1] (Although no one knows what this is.) This yearning for acceptance is what makes religion so powerful and popular. It allows the small "self" to lose itself in a bigger idea of "self," a group of "selfs" all seeking the big "self"—God. This approach, this way of thinking, will never bring us real acceptance. *This* "acceptance" is based on judgement, which is essentially a form of fear, and therefore, not acceptance in the form we unconsciously hope for.

Judgement is inherently illusory. Within certain spheres of knowledge judgement, which is measurement, is useful. But, at a *fundamental* level, measurement and judgement are illusory because they are based on partial understanding, which is what all knowledge is. Measurement and judgement about a person's essence, our own or anyone else's, is therefore, in a deep sense, small-minded because it assumes *understanding*, which can only be possible with total knowledge, which is not, and never will be, within our grasp.

What we actually seek is "true" *acceptance*, which has nothing to do with *pleasing*. The interaction created by acceptance *of this sort* opens up entirely new possibilities of meaning. The acceptance that we seek, if one is observant of the workings of one's mind (*seeking* acceptance is the source of fundamental and ubiquitous fear) is commonly called love, and is probably the true state of existence, the primal state with mother. Why should it be so difficult to feel accepted and connected *without judgement* if this is the *actual* state of existence, which is again, logical, given that the world is one intertwined evolutionary system that doesn't care about our petty judgements at all?

Our common ambition for the *"fulfillment"* of the "self" is the *illusory* hope that eventually, when enough accomplishments and correctness have been achieved, the "self," (which surrounds us externally in the form of other "selfs" and internally in the form of our own little "self") will be satisfied and accept ourselves.

The source of evil, if one investigates one's mind, is the *rejection*, the attempt to *supersede* this need for acceptance, to escape the judgement of other "selfs," to be *beyond* pleasing the other. Yet, one cannot escape one's own "self" so easily.

What is evil and how does it arise?

---

1   The pleasing of God is remarkably similar to the sort of pleasing we all must do with one another. Christians, realizing that this pleasing is, logically, a hopeless quest, concocted the idea of "grace." Yet, can God really be so petty that He set up a world where everyone, including God, is filled with judgement about everything, where science has shown us that we barely know what is going on? That is, the more you know, the more you know you don't know.

It is a defensive strategy born of the pursuit of *power over others* to protect one's "self" from being "touched." It is, essentially, an attempt to become *"untouchable."*[2] To avoid being hurt, *one must be able to hurt others.* In other words, touch in its deepest sense is feared, and the *power to prevent being touched* is a protection from the disappointment of "no acceptance" from both the "self," which is the other, and the "other." It is the attempt to move beyond the need to please, but is born at the same level as this need, therefore, not really separate from this need and not a successful cure or strategy for escape. *The fear of judgement must be still there.*

Power over people is a common strategy because the world is filled with pleasers, which enables the "bully" to find victims anywhere. All forms of one-upmanship are indicators of this attempt at "self" protection. Because one's own "self" *cannot* be quelled with this strategy (which strengthens the "self"), the manifestation of power over others, the quest for "untouchability" may continue to grow to Stalinesque proportions if opportunity allows. Yet the "self" is a judge who never relents. There is no escape. Unless....

What is the inversion of all this?

The inversion is that one does not need acceptance from the "self," which is an illusion of completeness, or from other societally created illusory "selfs." All of these "selfs" are created by knowledge, ideas and concepts. But knowledge is limited, incomplete. There is, therefore, no solid knowable "self." Moreover this "self" is actually the "other," internalized. Acceptance, which is the absence of fear, which is love, is only found by the discarding of a "self." It is the "self" in us all that blocks people from what they truly seek—a primal state of oneness and acceptance with one another and life.

To discard the "self," one must see through the illusion—the desire to believe in a separate, permanent self—which is very difficult (and not an intellectual achievement). Without this step, one can never see clearly into anything. One will always become entangled in confused perception because an artificial observer, the "self," obscures accurate observation.

In reality, there is no permanence in anything; everything is continually changing, which is obvious from one's own observation or from the collective findings of science. In other words, there are no nouns, only verbs. Our language encourages the belief that separate, unchanging entities exist because language has evolved through time. Words are carriers of concepts tacitly implied from the world view of the era in which the word became commonly used. Usage has not kept pace with our developing understanding of reality. In an evolutionary

---

2   Yet, interestingly, still be "safely" connected to other people.

universe, everything is continually changing, yet our conventional use of words does not reflect this.

There is no unchanging, separate person that can be logically, scientifically, proven to exist. When one can dispense with the *intrusion* of a "self," there is breathing, heart-beating, walking, thinking. It is as if one is breathed, heart-beated, walked and *given* insight, empty of fear. One is carried, supported—expressed. We don't do; we are done.

There are no eternal, concrete thoughts or beliefs—there is believing, which is an *impediment* to understanding. Believing, which is *identifying* with thinking (as if our thoughts were total, all-encompassing, objective truth) *adds* an extra step—a "self"—the agent of action. The *illusion* that we are the agents of doing (even though we are actually being done, expressed) will, obviously, create confusion. If there is no separate self, no separation from everything else—but we act as if there is—we are in an antagonistic relationship to reality.

We all live in relationship to nature and to one another, reacting to situations. We are always being "done," and expressed (which is our reality, although in our usual state, our usual bias, we cannot notice this), but through the filter of our *identification* with the thoughts arising from these situations—both of which, the thoughts and situations, are always shifting themselves.[3] These continually generated thoughts (which arise because it may be the nature of reality to continually express temporary forms), are variations of our conditioned, inherited "display case" of ideas (interestingly, always synchronous with and derived from our current era), not insight. It *seems* as if we choose (free choice) among these thoughts and ideas. But these thoughts are derived from the illusion that there is a separate self who chooses, which means they are *ill-conceived thoughts.* We are not separate from these ideas, these confused "presented" thoughts, because it is from these ideas that we concoct, we piece together, our identity—our "self." This does not mean, however, that we are independent beings.

Belief in a separate controller, a watcher and coordinator of our thinking, is the equivalent of a double motion in playing. As in playing music, where we have shown that this extra step breaks musical and physical flow, connection, similarly, it is this extraneous, unnecessary step of creating a self as an "observer of action" that prevents, obscures, the realization, the noticing, that we are "being done," not doing. We, therefore, cannot perceive that we are, in essence,

---

3   The mind thinks that a "self" separate from all action, the overseer, can *control* reactions to thinking. The "self" bites and is hooked into reaction and the analysis of thoughts. This is an identification with thinking, which is a misperception.

"expressed" within a limitless, entangled *field* of continually, and similarly, expressed creating.

The thoughts, the feelings, the supposed intuitions and *reactions* born from our interacting (in actuality, complete enmeshment) with the world that arise from the psychological paradigm of belief in a continual "self" will be very different from the thoughts, feelings, intuitions and reactions that arise from our interacting with a bias with no controller, no thinker that is separate from thinking and doing. The bias of a "self" will create *continual conflict* with everything else because this bias is inherently incorrect—there is no separate self no matter how thoroughly one searches. As a matter of fact, the more thorough the search, the more a separate "self" consistently and loudly fails to appear.[4]

If one looks deeply, it is obvious that we *do* nothing. We are *done*; we are expressed. There is no thinker, no doer separate from entangled being and perceiving what is. There is only *this*.

---

4 Logic and unbiased examination will show that there is not only no "self;" in fact, there is no *separate* individual. This is implicitly understood, perhaps unconsciously, by the public relations industry. All effective advertising and propaganda is predicated on the premise that we *all* have stereotypical biases in thinking, which create irrational, muddled thought processes that can only see through the lens implanted by society, circumstance, education, advertising, and so on. Our way of "seeing" *presumes* a "self" *separate* and objectively removed from what is experienced (creating the *illusion* of an individual reality, an individuality interpreted and "birthed" through the *abstraction* of words and *socially* implanted ideas, which create feelings and experiences about our *societally constructed* reality—a reality that is, in fact, too intertwined, too mysterious, *to be parseable* by any abstraction). This is the essence of our *collective* mystification and confusion.

Because everyone is *actually* equally and inescapably enmeshed in the system of life *and the same habitual patterns of thought* there can be no logical, valid, claim of individual importance or achievement, which are outcomes of circumstance and situations *far beyond* the actions of any individual person (who does not exist, anyway). Any notion of *separate* achievement, importance or authority is a *small-minded* perspective. This *systemic view* is a paradigmatic shift that fundamentally alters one's ontological perspective, a shift which may be disturbing to the way we normally think, yet a fact that any serious investigation will prove accurate.

Thus, no person can logically—validly—claim authority over another, either in the name of "God," divine revelation or inherent right. All emotional appeals to the contrary, if examined rationally it will be found that claims of power are valid in only the most circumscribed, utilitarian cases. We may, by common consent, create organizational structures that operate through hierarchical "teams," but these are expediencies, they are not *intrinsic* truths, like the sun. They are cultural *artificialities*, not divine or Darwinian decrees of innate authority over others, since, unlike other animals, we can *learn* to see these distinctions, we can collectively "know better." We may create laws that make claims of power or ensconce people in situations that allow them to acquire power over others. In reality they remain "legitimate" only by the consent and *continual* review of society, not by the decree of authorities or the assertions of spokesman for "God." This confusion—

POST SCRIPTUM

An experiment with your self:

Write down every thought, unfiltered, no matter how strange, for two weeks (more or less). Then take these written thoughts and glue the pages together so they are strung out as a sort of paper collage. If you then tape this collage to a large mirror in such a way that this paper collage blocks your direct reflection, and then look into the mirror, you will "see" this written collage as your reflection.

This paper collage is "you." These written words and variations thereof are what form the content of one's consciousness, from which we form our identity. Our belief in this collage "taped to the mirror" is the *source* of psychological suffering, misperception of one's true nature, frustration, confusion, limited thought, etc., as is evident if one simply reads the content of the writing, the collage. This sort of collage, with slightly different particulars, is what forms everyone else's identity on the planet as well. These collages interact, thinking they are very different. But what they have in common is that they are self-referential. Can this be noticed?

The interaction of these self-referential collages and the stories created by their interaction is what forms society. Society is what forms these collages as well. Can this be noticed?

These collages gain a certain *seeming* particularity because each one's interaction with other collages and the surrounding societal collage forms a *story* seemingly particular to each seemingly independent collage. Can this be noticed?

Do these collages create reality—if one looks into what is actually happening at the moment of interaction between collages (not analyzing after the fact) in a deep sense—or are they made to *seem* real because the thinking *generated* by the *seemingly* individual collage and the interaction with other collages, which creates feedback (thoughts), suggests to us the *illusion* that this is bedrock reality?

If the collage of one's identity tries to analyze the contents of that same collage, is it possible to have any objectivity when looking at the collage? I would suggest not. This is why analysis of the contents of the collage by the

---

the mystification of most people about what is legitimate authority and what is simply a grab for power—"legitimizes" claims of importance and privilege in society no less absurd than what we observed from the conductor. A review of movies from the past such as D. W. Griffith's *The Birth of a Nation* or television shows from the 1950s and 1960s will show that society is continually becoming more aware of the arbitrariness of claims of power and that there has been a remarkable trend towards *explicitly* dismantling presumed and assumed acquiescence to traditional authority, power structures, and societal prejudices.

collage (the collage is what forms the identity, the "self," the "me") is a never-ending circle of confusion. One can never look from any viewpoint except the point of view formed by the collage one has taped to the mirror. Neither can another person's collage (a therapist, psychologist, for example), which is also similarly confused and limited—trapped in the same illusion—bring clarity to this *filter* to reality.

The next part of our experiment is: Can one understand experientially that there is no need to form the collage at all? This would mean that when one looked into the mirror one would see whatever is reflected without the collage. This would end psychological identification with the collage. Is this possible? It certainly is.

If one can really answer and *experience* the implications of these next questions, the *illusion* of a "self" separate from everything else will be understood experientially. Can anyone who thinks the way the "written collage taped on the mirror" demonstrates (which is essentially the content of one's consciousness, if one examines this carefully) truly be responsible, be in control, actually have the innate intelligence for the following?

Who is it that breathes when sleeping? Who is it that grows? Who is it that ages? Who is it that walks? Who coordinates all the muscles in the body and synapses in the brain to move? Who is it that beats the heart? Who is it that loses one's hair? Who is it that is doing, controlling, the dying? Surely if there was a separate self, one could control these circumstances.

If these questions can be *deeply* understood and *felt* "in being," the "self" will melt away. If you can really notice what is *actually happening,* you will apprehend that we are carried, we are breathed, we are grown, we are "expressed" by the whole fabric of what is. We are birthed from this fabric and we are evolved through time out of "what we are being," as well. We are, therefore, done, not doing. This is not mysticism or religion. This is simply seeing what is actually going on. If we substitute a God or something else as the *agent of action,* we will, as with using our own collage, set up another bump that prevents us from directly experiencing what is actually going on. If we look carefully, we can see that the *concept,* "God," is just another filter and creates the same confusion—a *filter* to direct experience of being.

It is this experiential seeing and directly being, with this insight, that shows us that we are not the collage at all. We can then see that we are "played" by the collage only if we identify with the collage. If we react to the collage, our life is as limited as the paper taped to the mirror. We will simply vary the order and contents of the collage.

As Einstein famously remarked, problems can never be solved at the same level of awareness that creates them. We have seen throughout this book that the great musicians we have been observing played with a fundamental bias that is *opposite* to what is pervasively taught. This bias allowed them to play without mind/body antagonism. Most musicians spend their lives immersed in attempting to solve problems that occur only because their fundamental musical bias *creates* those problems.

This applies to our lives as well. We spend our lives in "articulations," separations and distinctions that need not be, and are not, foundational to reality—artificial segmentations that have been created by countless generations of societal programming that has confused our perception. This *fundamental* misperception of reality *creates* our psychological problems and suffering.

This misperception is created and fueled by the *foundational bias* of our minds, which perceive reality through an outward, *assertive* focal point. This "setting" *creates* distinctions, solidifying separateness, because this focal point is, *in its essence*, an *assertion* that separates. Our ego, the sense we have of a separate "self," arises from this way of seeing and being, this focal point. The *outward focal point* is the *creator* of the conflict and fear that is integral to this way of interacting because this way of perceiving is "interacting with things that are outside of itself" (which is the essence of a separate self), obfuscating the truth of our actual *immersion* in totality. The focal point is, *in itself*, grasping, reaching out. The thoughts generated by this psychological setting, which is *inherently* separative, lonely and judgmental, are comprised of various forms of desire and fear (an effort by the psyche to alleviate this insecure, unpleasant state of being), constantly morphing, creating endless (unfixable in this perspective) and, therefore, *insoluble* phantasms of anxiety and desire (which are the same— they are co-dependent). These suggested "realities" are not unalterable truths of human existence. They are an inescapable, preordained result of a focal point that is, in fact, alterable. Our common perspective is *not* the *ground* of reality—it is a superficial, ultimately illogical and emotionally empty aperture,[5] making us easy prey for manipulation in endless guises. It is the root cause that *creates* our psychological suffering.

---

5   This aperture is the platform from which all debate, argument, and battle is initiated. All "sides" argue, in their opinion persuasively, from their point of view. Yet their beliefs emanate from a *common* way of seeing the world that *inherently* splinters it into various *arbitrary* segmentations. The segmentations, and their innately arbitrary nature, are *implicit* in the outward focal point. This is why all argument on this level of understanding, which is the level that creates the problems, is quite useless.

There is a level of seeing, accessible to anyone, that is beyond these distinctions [CONTINUED]

If we drop our identification with a controlling "self" by allowing the world to *enter* us, we can feel that we are breathed, not breathing, that we are walked, not walking, that we are expressed as is everything else, we will be freed from reacting to thoughts that arise *only* as a result of the feedback generated by our common *misperception* of reality. We will see our true nature with clarity, with no *filter* from the collage. The nature of the thought that arises will be, therefore, changed into something very different. What we are then *presented* with is insight into what is *actually* happening as we live. In truth the bird does not fly, he is flown; the tree does not grow, it is grown; the star does not shine, the dog does not move, the cat does not look, the fish does not swim. We do not express.

The deeply illogical psychological misperception of a separate self and the waste of energy caused by the confused feedback it generates, once released, would present to us a new dimension of existence and possibility. When we can see this, we understand that we live in a world of wonder, amazement and incredible beauty.

---

and punctuations. If the aperture is eliminated, by allowing perception to flow in, another level of "seeing" is accessible that is beyond common, but arbitrary distinctions. It is only by moving to this level of seeing that "problems" can be seen with clarity. As in music, their resolution lies at a deeper level of seeing. This view offers, if even for brief periods, the insight that our experience of "truth" may not be so true. This realm can be visited without the use of hallucinogenic drugs or religious ecstasy by anyone, at any time.

CHAPTER 30

The Development of Intelligence and Talent

ARE CHILDREN THE FUTURE OR OUR PAST?

We transfer our belief systems—our values/culture and inherent possibilities latent within this matrix—through the mechanism of becoming parents who, by design or inertia, often serve as blockers of creative potential, as do teachers. Through no fault of his own a child is enmeshed in a world created by the level of understanding of his parents, the interaction between the parents, and the relationship of child to parent; teachers are an integral part of this system. Parents need control over children to protect them—the world is complex and can be confusing, often dangerous. But how much control is necessary, particularly in the acquisition of knowledge?

One aspect of learning is acquiring knowledge and skill. Yet can this be done at a deep level without the accompaniment of understanding? Understanding is different from copying, memorizing, or doing what one is told. It implies direct knowledge of the deeper reasons for things: why we do what we do, the stories behind historical events, seen from an experiential level, without abstraction. Clear perception into the web of influences that make our circumstances the way they are results, perhaps at its highest level, in wisdom. It will coincidentally be observed that this process, this unfolding of learning, is endless, with no final answer, and must, therefore, be a way of perceiving that sees with an "unknowing" eye. Interestingly, children do this quite naturally—they often ask questions about commonly accepted "facts" that turn out to be impossible to answer.

Societal questions and answers—a catechism of a sort—are used to form our identity. Once this identity solidifies, the questions subside, asked only in the privacy of our thoughts at first and then relegated to the way things are. The ending of our questions is the ending of our creativity. Yet the child is an opportunity for us to remember ourselves before we were so sure that we knew anything at all. If we tried a simple shift in paradigm—or we could say perspective—I wonder how the process of educating a child would appear? Let's suggest this variation from our usual thinking: The child is our past and we are their future. We know what they will be, which is the sort of life we have. But they are what we were before everything was so set and known.

If this is so, how would we proceed? How would we change our life experience? How would we want to be taught? For example, in the more prestigious music schools, a teacher teaches and a student is generally expected to accept what is said. This is often quite severe—some teachers allow no questions. Unfortunately, as we have noted, because of the pervasive lack of knowledge (a result of our current educational paradigm) even if a teacher wanted to answer the questions a student asked there is often no real answer possible. This scenario encourages, perhaps unwittingly, a general passivity and insecurity among both teachers and students. Yet it is the accepted educational model of nearly all music schools and this common educational experience may explain the passivity of musicians in addressing and correcting the dysfunctional nature of the educative process in music. They have been *trained* to be unreflective.

If we look at a child and wish for them a better life experience than we had, what would we do about it? What did we have to face in life that no one prepared us for? What should we have understood better? To change the world we must change the past, not the future; we have it upside down. Are there fundamental concepts that can be experientially taught to young students that would apply to all knowledge, and assist their *process* of learning? Europeans—Montessori, Froebel, Rousseau and many others—have been investigating and experimenting with the potentially liberating power of education for several hundred years. It is now time to turn our attention to a man who was a champion of the kind of educational approach we are searching for. His name was Pestalozzi and his efforts radically changed our concept of education. Education, if it is at all serious, must investigate *how we think and learn.* This is what Pestalozzi began to do.

Johann Heinrich Pestalozzi (1746-1826) is considered by many people to be the "father" of modern pedagogy—the study of how we learn. Born in Zurich, his intellectual development was greatly influenced by Jean-Jacques Rousseau's book, *Emile,*[1] published in 1762, which advocates an education for children attuned to what Rousseau asserts is man's essentially free nature. A result of

---

1 Jean-Jacques Rousseau, *Emile—Or Treatise on Education,* translated by William H. Payne, (New York: Prometheus Books, 2005).

this approach, Rousseau speculated, would be that each man's powers of reason would enable him to create his own purpose in life rather than unconsciously serving the interests of the state. In his novel he demonstrates that such an education would show men the arbitrary power of the state and the Church and free them from their authority.

We must suppose that he proved his thesis quite decisively because the Swiss and French governments banned the book and declared Rousseau a danger to the state. His books were burned in Paris. Pestalozzi, age nineteen at the time, already an idealistic freethinker and investigative journalist, wrote several articles in his defense, finding himself in jail for his muck-racking bent. Rousseau's home was stoned by his fellow citizens and, facing immanent arrest, he was forced to flee to England. Several years later he was allowed to return to France upon the condition that he refrain from publishing any more books.

Pestalozzi's concern with the plight of mankind had been aroused not only from his acquaintance with Rousseau's novel, but also from his journeys with his grandfather who was a clergyman, to visit his parishioners in the Swiss countryside. The peasantry's extreme poverty made it imperative that their children work long hours in local factories. Their inability to improve this situation inspired Pestalozzi to find a way to empower them through education, as Rousseau's book *Emile* had suggested might be a possibility.

There is much similarity between Rousseau's and Pestalozzi's educational philosophies. It is beyond the scope of this chapter to enumerate what is particularly different or the same. One could make the general observation that Pestalozzi is less overtly politically oriented than Rousseau. His focus is on pedagogy itself—he investigates and attempts to articulate a description of how we learn, what we should learn, and what the process of learning might hope to create for human existence. He describes the unfoldment of his discoveries and understanding in a fascinating book, *How Gertrude Teaches Her Children: An Attempt to help Mothers Teach Their Own Children and an Account of the Method.*[2]

He reasoned that if he could devise a system of education that was based on the observation and understanding of what he termed the "invariable qualities in nature," uncomplicated by the abstraction of book knowledge as a first step to learning, he could teach people to see the world clearly, thereby giving them the means to discover how, through the manipulation of words, they were being entrapped into social systems that did not serve their interests.

---

2   Johann Pestalozzi, *How Gertrude Teaches Her Children: An Attempt To Help Mothers Teach Their Own Children and an Account of the Method,* translated by Lucy Holland and Francis Turner (London, 1900), first published in 1803, reprinted Internet Archive, 2007.

Traditional schools taught through a method known as catechism. The teacher, the sole authority, knows the question and the answer. This type of learning consists of the memorization of both the question and the answer, a process that gives the student the illusion that he is thinking on his own, of critical thinking. It is really indoctrination. This *usurpation* of one's own direct perception of reality to the predetermined truths of others is thought control—propaganda—rendering so-called education, which should be an unfolding of one's powers of reason, to the level of brainwashing. The student is considered to be an empty vessel into which knowledge is poured. (Have we made much progress since then ourselves?)

Pestalozzi's goal was to educate students to see the world by their own *direct* perception of nature, what he called sense-impression, which requires the *disciplined* use of words to describe with precision what is deeply true, the "invariable qualities of objects." He hoped that this clarity would free people from their susceptibility to manipulation. The blind obedience and mental confusion inherent in the acceptance of the *abstract* nature of words as a *fundamental* reality[3] creates a state of mind easily malleable to the promotion of the agenda of the state at the expense of individual freedom.

He believed that words should be used only as a *result* of feeling and seeing what is *beyond* words. Usually what is claimed as knowledge is simply learning the name of something, often something we've never experienced, seen or touched. We are, therefore, taught to live in *abstraction* and led to believe that what is educative is this type of knowledge—knowing a plethora of "facts"—and, more important, that a word is *primary* to the sensation the word abstractly attempts to describe. He believed that clear observation is a "feeling," which only through an inward process, can be formed into a word. Therefore, words cannot be foundational to knowledge since they are an *abstraction* of reality. Unfortunately, we are trained to believe they are the *ground* of reality.

Learning to use language properly is foundational to all learning. He writes:

> It is well known that Nature, in the first stages of the development of language...ignores the complicated and artificial combinations of complete grammar...only gradually by continuous practice in simple combinations does [one] gain the power of understanding the complicated.[4] Therefore, my exercises in language...inquire into the [fundamental] elements of language

---

3   Interestingly similar to how we are taught to understand music.

4   Again, how similar to music.

and give the child the advantage of forming speech in *exactly the same gradual way* in which Nature gave it to the human race.[5]

Therefore, one must be taught to use language properly from infancy or the abstraction of words becomes our reality. He believed that people are taught to use language in an artificially complex way, which leads to intellectualism and inaccurate observation of what is. Intellectualism, and one's immersion in the thought produced by this confused state, leads perception astray. What appears to be complex is based on simple elements; when one is perfectly clear about these, the most complex matter will become simple—a scientific approach to gaining understanding. *Teaching properly is based on the clear perception of the simple elements that are foundational to what is.*

He tried to discover the most effective ways of teaching any subject. Based on his observations of how children acquired language, he modeled his educational method on that process. He organized teaching and learning into small elemental steps, each of which must be thoroughly understood before the next stage can be attempted. He assumed that perfecting the beginning steps is essential to the correct development of each succeeding stage. One must pass from the foundation of a perfectly understood first step to the foundation of a perfectly understood second, to the third and fourth.

Conscious repetition reinforces learning. He noticed that with this method children develop an inner power and, quite naturally, teach other children. This led to his observation that "all true educative instruction must be drawn out of the children themselves; and be born within them."[6] He wrote, "... new life is nothing but the just awakened readiness to receive impressions... the awakening of the perfect physical buds that now aspire with all their power towards the development of their individuality."[7]

A teacher's task is to design a learning experience that promotes the continuous growth of that life force. Essential to this unfoldment is that if learning is to be deep and lasting there must be congruence between the impressions received by the child and the level of his current intellectual powers—the child must be developmentally ready to understand what is being taught. Before more complex subjects can be introduced, a proper foundation must be developed, which is, again, a step-by-step approach.

He believed that a teacher must continually expand a child's sense-impressions, reinforcing these sense-impressions, while giving them enough linguistic skill

---

5   *Ibid.* 2, 154.

6   *Ibid.*, 17.

7   *Ibid.*, 25.

to express what has been brought into their consciousness. Through this process, "indelibly impressed, *a general foundation for all kinds of learning are laid,* by which children and teacher together, as well as separately, may rise gradually, but with safe steps, to clear ideas in all branches of knowledge."[8]

A critical role in the educative process of Pestalozzi is played by the mother. An infant's primary relationship is with his mother and it is through her interaction with the child that deep fundamental learning begins. Through the mother's love, which is instinctual, a child forms the basis for his emotional response to life. It is through this relationship that the seed of love in a child is born. The mother shelters him—the seed of trust is born. The mother satisfies his needs—the seed of gratitude is born. According to Pestalozzi:

> Every step of … development must be completed before it can be subordinated to a higher purpose. The subordination of that which is completed, requires above all, pure holding fast to the beginning points of all knowledge and the most exact continuity in gradual progress from these beginning points to the final completion. The primary law of continuity is this: the first instruction of the child must never be the business of the head or of the reason: it should always be the business of the senses, of the heart, of the mother.
>
> The second law that follows it is this: human education goes on slowly from exercise of the senses to exercise of judgement. It is for a long time the business of the heart, before it is the business of the reason. It is a long time the business of the woman before it is the business of the man.[9]

The relationship of the mother to her child must be enlarged through the experience of education to be the seed that makes man have the same relationship of love for all beings of the natural world. As is the mother to her child, so is the developed man to all of life. This is the hope of Pestalozzi's educational process. Pestalozzi's insights influenced Maria Montessori, John Dewey, even Albert Einstein, and continue to impact educational processes in Europe to this day. According to a biography of Einstein by Walter Isaacson:

> It [Aarau] was a perfect school for Einstein. The teaching was based on the philosophy of a Swiss educational reformer of the early nineteenth century, Johann Heinrich Pestalozzi, who believed in encouraging students to visualize images…. The visual understanding of concepts, as stressed by Pestalozzi and his followers in Aarau, became a significant aspect of Einstein's genius.[10]

---

8   *Ibid.,* 51.

9   *Ibid.,* 189.

10 Walter Isaacson, *Einstein: His Life and Universe* (New York: Simon & Schuster, 2007), 26.

We rarely teach students experientially. Even after hundreds of years "catechismic" teaching, rote teaching, is standard. In keeping with the Pestalozzian spirit for the educative necessity of the "experiential" understanding of "invariable qualities" we could substitute the educational necessity for the "experiential" understanding of deep scientific principles.

To be of value and utility, what is learned experientially by students must have an application to other areas of study, what Alfred North Whitehead called "interrelated truths." Since the world is an organic whole developed through an evolutionary process, "as is this, so is that," relatedness must be a fundamental property of this wholeness. This suggests that the linking of like to like on ever-deeper levels inevitably presents to a student a world of metaphor and analogy that can be used to explicate the "pattern that connects" all life, a concept brilliantly elucidated in Gregory Bateson's book, *Mind and Nature—A Necessary Unity*. He wrote, "Break the pattern which connects the items of learning and you necessarily destroy all quality."[11] The "pattern of connection" between all life means that to know one subject profoundly, teaches us something about everything else and suggests that superficial exposure to diverse subjects is a confusing waste of a student's time. The ideas shown to *underly and connect* the diversity of information in school should be pithy and few, yet essential in demonstrating the interrelationship between the seemingly disconnected, disparate matters being studied. In other words, we need to form a "ground" of deep concepts applicable in explaining many seemingly varied situations and show the connection of the experientially "felt" concepts being taught to the entire range of subjects being studied. Can this be done in music lessons?

There have been many experiments using music as an educational, developmental tool. We shall not describe such methods, which tend to be superficial in both the experience and the depth of the musical training. We will propose another possibility—music, at any level of complexity, can be explained by deep scientific principles that can be understood "experientially" by a student. This creates a sophisticated vocabulary between a teacher and student that may be used to lucidly *discuss* advanced ideas with even very young people.[12] The following are but a few possible examples.

---

11 Gregory Bateson, *Mind And Nature—A Necessary Unity* (USA: Bantam, 1979), 7.

12 If one observes carefully, it can often be noticed that, frequently, "discussions" between children and older people consist of a child being talked about, talked at, or talked down to. It is exceedingly rare that adults, especially teachers, can create a field of interaction with young people that is free of fear, condescension, fake, or inappropriate, camaraderie.

Structure

The body is a structure. The body forms a structure to hold the violin, into which the violin (itself a structure, but now forming a new one with the body) is placed. A finger of the left hand is positioned on the string, the bow arm and bow made ready to play. Is the finger on the string an isolated structure or does structure imply an entire edifice of interaction—the alignment of the feet, the slight turning of the head, the relaxing of the neck and shoulders, the relaxing of the right arm, the left elbow under the violin, the angle of the finger on the string, how firmly the finger is placed on the string, etc.? The body will not stay still; it cannot really. We have not even moved the bow to play the note. This is a structure that moves, that must flow. Therefore, structure need not be static.

Does the structure of the finger on the violin include the person teaching this to them and the music they play, as well as the person who made the violin and the person who sold it to them? How deep does structure go? Is a system implicit in structure?

This is a lesson a seven-year-old can understand through the *physical* experience of putting a finger on the violin and relating that experience to a deep concept. I have used this method often with young students. The "experiential" understanding of structure by a student provides a vocabulary of interaction that allows a teacher, student, and parents to, together, explore many other phenomena that will eventually be seen to be a "pattern that connects."

Cycles

Bowing is a cycle from up-bow to down-bow that a student can physically experience and link as a fundamental explanatory principle to many other phenomena. What else is a cycle, in that there is no separation from one aspect to another? As we have up-bows to down-bows, we have sunrise to sunset, day to night, winter to summer....

Pattern

Music is based on pattern, as are the instruments used to play it. For example, the piano has the same pattern of black and white keys throughout the keyboard. Pattern is ubiquitous in all music, most obviously through the repetition of notes, sequences, rhythm repetition, and on and on. Pattern can be linked to anything that repeats a form—trees, birds, people, houses, etc.

The body and mind are one

Ask a student to make an ugly sound by pressing hard on the strings with the bow when playing the notes of a melody. Then have them sing the tune and imitate what they sang using their violin. Next, the teacher may sing the same melody differently and have the student imitate that. If this experience is framed properly by a teacher, it is a powerful lesson—how you *think* about something affects the result. This begins to open a student's mind to see the power of *visualization*, although it need not be called visualization for a five-year-old.

The state of the body affects the mind

Have a student tighten all their muscles as much as they can and then ask them if their head is tense and if it is easy to think about anything. Then have them relax their muscles and compare both mental/physical states.

Body awareness; subtle motion

How a student places their fingers on the string changes the sound. Move the finger slightly this way or that—the sound changes as does the intonation. How one touches the keys of the piano affects the sound. Exploring the concept of subtle touch may be directed to questions such as: What is a relaxed wrist? How do you walk? How tightly do you hold the pen when you write? These questions are provocative for any age student because very few people have subtle body awareness. This is the start of a conversation that can be applied to every aspect of a student's life, yet not in theory, because the inquiry has been connected to the *physical* experience of playing an instrument and the demonstration to the student that awareness of the subtleties of movement makes a difference in outcome.

The written note is not music

Play an open string—A, E, or G. Play middle "C" on the piano. Is the written note the actual note? What is the difference between the played note and the written note? This is a major problem in teaching music. Students assume that the printed music *is music*. Reproducing symbols is mechanical and affects a student's incipient "values" of what music *is*. What needs to be demonstrated is how to see through the abstraction of the printed notes to a direct experience of the *music* they represent.

Students must learn to read music, but, at the same time, to see through the abstraction of the printed note. This can be accomplished in several ways. Using what we have learned in our analysis of how great players interpreted the page we can begin to show in simple steps how the printed page can be looked at in a way that makes playing "re-creative."

The experiential demonstration of the reality behind the symbols of music can be used to bring awareness to the symbolic nature of language. What is the difference between the spoken word, "dog," the written word, "dog," and the dog itself? This can get as deep as any sutra, but on a level that an eight-year-old can relate to *experientially*. Interestingly, by the time we are thirty, the significance of this understanding can barely penetrate the intellectual edifice, the interface, that has been created as "identity."

We are a process of learning and change; everything is a process, therefore nothing stays the same

Today is not the same as yesterday. It may be just as sunny, but is it the same temperature? Aren't the days gradually getting shorter or longer? Are you, the student, the same? Are you growing? Is your violin the same or has it gone out of tune since yesterday? Do you play your violin the same today as yesterday? Is the water in a river ever the same? Does anything alive stay the same? Do the clouds in the sky, does the wind, does the temperature stay the same? This is called process. Everything is a process, never stopping, never the same. Everything we see is changing *all at once*, always.

Nothing is separate in a system

If the thumb of the left hand grips the neck of the violin, the thumb of the right hand grips the bow. If the fingers of the right hand hold the bow tightly, the fingers of the left hand will be tense. If a student can relax either hand, the other hand will be affected in the same way.

If the bow has no rosin you can make no sound. If the piano bench is too high or too low, it will affect the way you play. If the instrument is bad quality it will affect the way you play. All of this is easily demonstrated, experientially, to the student and has broad general application. What constitutes a system is a question that can then be introduced to a student's awareness.

Complexity is created from simple elements

Play a "C," then an "E" above it, and then a "G" above the "E" on the piano. These are three separate notes. Now play them together. A chord is formed from the three separate notes. Play a "C." Now play all the white keys one after another until you arrive at the next "C." That is a scale, but really made up of individual white keys going up in a row.

Therefore, complexity can be looked at with simplicity and shown to be created from simple elements. The teacher can ask a student to look at the alphabet. There are twenty-six individual letters that appear to be very different from one another. What elements are used to write the twenty-six letters? To write them requires only a line and a half-circle. Even musical notes can demonstrate simplicity within complexity.

There seem to be many notes written on the page and they all look different. But to write them we only need a line and a circle. What else is like that? What is the structure, since we can now use that word, of a tree? It looks complicated, but isn't it composed of ever-smaller trees? The close observation of a tree, the alphabet, a musical note or a chord not only demonstrates that complex structures are composed of simple elements, it also deepens the concept of variation.

Symmetry

The violin is symmetrical and so are you. What else is? Is a bridge? Is a cat?

Rhythm is in the body

The connection between musical rhythm and speech is essential for understanding musical rhythm, as is the variation of gait, heartbeat, and breathing to motion and emotion, and its parallel with the *non-mechanical* nature of rhythm in living systems and music, which is a creation of a living system. The non-mechanical disposition of natural rhythm stands, therefore, in stark contrast to the metronome, as evidence that the common metaphor that the body is a machine or that the universe is a mechanical, meaningless happenstance is an impossibility.

Memory is pictorial, kinetic, and aural; intuition is the inverse of this process

To memorize written music, a student needs to use four approaches: pictorial, (what the page looks like), intellectual, (what are the musical patterns), kinetic (what does it feel like to play physically), and aural (what does it sound like), a process which engenders quite a development for their brain. Memorizing is making what is *there* remain in the mind. Interestingly, this combination of visualizations proves to be a powerful tool in *bringing forth* intuition from the deep ground of the mind. Intuition is the inverse of the process of memorization; it is allowing something *that is not there* to appear.

Intuition starts as a wordless feeling, a wisp of something that seems important, gradually coalescing to a visualization/picture, a sense of coming into the body, finally forming, through words, into the abstraction of the "feeling"—to thought. Once put into thought-form, the intuition can be unfolded back into the depths, the source, of the original nameless intuition. Thus, an intuitive enfolded "feeling," once put into words (such as, matter and energy are the same), can unfold into a lifetime of discovery once it has reached consciousness as a word-thought, allowing one to move from the *word* back into the depths of the intuition. The word, the idea, that comes from the ground of intuition proves to be a point without center, but infinite depth.

Power is coaxed from an instrument or the body rather than forced; speed comes from relaxation

These ideas are counterintuitive and introduce experientially the idea that what is at first apparent may not be so. It seems obvious that to play loudly one must use force, yet this not only makes an ugly sound, it also injures the student. It seems unremarkable that to play fast one must force the motion, yet this will not result in the fastest speed. Speed is a result of fluidity, which is coordination.

This is a chance to introduce the idea of *inversion*—that quite often what seems true is the inversion of what is actually true. Obviously, this entire line of "experiential" teaching has vast possibilities for application in life: forcing compared to understanding, an inquiry into what is power, what appears to be obvious may not be so, the use of inversion in perception (that Dalí used, as we have already noted), the power of water to erode even the highest mountain (a metaphor common in Taoism), and the concept of paradox.

Power comes from coordination of the whole

A note, as we have already mentioned, is produced by a structure—body/mind, and instrument. A student must be shown that his *entire* body produces sound through a complete and integrated engagement; this is an obvious difference between a typist pianist or violinist and a great player. But this concept has wider application.

The power of coordinated effort is true in any type of business. Unless the organization is coordinated into a whole interactive structure, each part functioning optimally, the business will suffer. The same is true of one's health or in relationship to other people. *Coordinating with others must be done by minds that can coordinate*, otherwise a system fights against itself and tears apart.

Pairs

Pairing is ubiquitous in nature and is a fascinating concept to examine. It is experientially demonstrable to students as the pairing of off-beats to downbeats. Playing in this way not only sounds different, but feels different physically, which provides a good example of *thought* affecting motion. Pairs are found all around us and pairing as a concept is an obvious link to male and female, on and off, light and dark, dry and wet, etc. Older students will realize that DNA is pairs and that computers generate all of their complexity with on-off bits of 0s and 1s.

Pairing applies to speech as well. All words are composed of the mixture of two poles—vowels and consonants—a pair. Words, made of syllables, flow forward in time through the exhalation of the breath. An inhalation of breath segments the sound, although since breathing in and out is a cycle—another pair—the motion of speech is truly an unbroken flow. Words create duality (pairs); they are the source of the separation of "this" from "that." Insight into pairing is essential in understanding the concept of symmetry and waves (crest and trough). All of these examples suggest that pairing it is an *elemental* process, a *basic* factor in life.

Feeling is in the act itself, not applied

When a student plays music everyone hopes, and sometimes expects, that he "feels" something. We associate "feeling" with emotion, but as we discussed in the chapter on "feeling," in music this is not so easily explained or experienced. A simple way to begin this discussion with a music student is to encourage them to notice that *the act of playing*—the touching of the string, of bowing, the depressing of a piano key, or the physical act of singing—are *in themselves* a feeling. "Feeling" in music is the act itself, and for the person playing it may be as direct as the feeling of the sun on one's skin. This is an important lesson. To "add on" feeling is emotionalism.

Additionally, at first the abstract meaning or feeling of music may not be so easily understood, yet anyone can "feel" the touch of the piano keys without any intellectualization or concern that they may have no "feeling" for music. This is, interestingly, an essential aspect of our life experience. What do we feel when we walk or sit? What do we feel when we breathe or run?

I would suggest that we do feel something and that this is true emotion, which counteracts a common assumption that the world is devoid of feeling. The essence of emotion is that living, being alive, itself is a "feeling" and is, intrinsically, a *good* feeling. With this as an experiential foundation, we may begin to understand what are "true" emotions as opposed to melodrama and sentimentality. This lesson can be understood intuitively by an eight-year-old, but, as we have noted, it is a terribly convoluted affair to grasp at forty.

One can be no better than their thinking

This is made quite clear through the playing of an instrument. Ability, technique, is improved by the evolution of one's understanding, not very much by physical practice. We noted that Nathan Milstein had this insight, as did Einstein, who mentioned that a problem can never be fixed on the same level of thinking that created it. Is this applicable to a student's every day life? Can his essay writing be better than the level of his ideas or vocabulary? Can his effort in sports be better than his understanding of the essentials of the game? Eventually one sees that nothing can be better than the quality of their perception, and that is why wisdom is the highest level of mind.

Learning takes place on many levels

This is easily experienced by any student of music. One may understand the notes, the fingerings, the basic phrasing, but that does not mean that a student can play the piece. The body must also understand, and the body's understanding, which comes from practicing the piece, will change what the mind thought it, at first, understood. The deeper one goes with this process, the more one will realize that there is no final level of knowing and that one can never completely understand.

This is not intellectual; this is entirely experiential to anyone involved in a serious study of music. This is why it is nearly impossible to teach an adult to play. Most adults assume that they understand something if they can understand what is said verbally or if they feel that they can grasp its significance intellectually. But this has nothing to do with understanding music, or I would venture to say, much of anything else. A music student eventually learns this as a primary experience that, if applied to his interaction with the world, will give him serious pause before he ever assumes that he understands anything at all. Can anyone understand how we grow, or what keeps everything developing and changing?

Nothing living is mechanical

This is, again, quite obvious to demonstrate to a music student through his own experience. What is alive is a *process* that evolves: understanding evolves, learning a piece evolves, the student evolves through interaction with learning, which changes the mind of the student and, therefore, changes the *whole* of the student *intrinsically*. A machine cannot do this and will never be able to do this. A machine may degrade through use, which is change, but a machine cannot develop *intrinsically*. A machine has no access, and will never have access, to intuition from the "source," whatever *that* is.

Analogy, recursion is seen everywhere you look

Within a form lies latent possibilities intrinsic to the form. This is demonstrable by many aspects of violin technique: within a proper left-hand position lie all double-stops, within correct up-bow to down-bow lie all other bowings, within a chord lies an arpeggio, within a motive lies an entire piece. Even to a beginner, a young student, the concept of recursion can be made experientially clear: within a series of even beats, any time signature may be used to segment the flow of beats, within a one-octave scale lies the possibility of continuing the scale to other octaves or altering the rhythm of each note to create a melody. A triad has within it the possibility to be major, minor, augmented, or diminished. A single note is really every other note—a rearrangement of the overtone series. The structure of different notes is the same; they all come from the possibility within the form of a note itself. This sort of linkage to greater principles is an essential element of teaching, which is really showing students how to use their own minds to understand the world.

One factor in a system is not more important than another

In a system one aspect is not more important than another, because everything is interdependent. This is easily demonstrated to any student of music by experience. One hand cannot be intrinsically more important than another if two hands are required by the system to be able to play. Likewise, in the violin—where would the left hand be without the right? Unheard. Where would the student be without the instrument to play?

This provides an insight into the entire structure of what is meant by *importance*. In an interdependent system *everything* is important. This concept was used successfully in application to business by the famous systems analyst, William Deming, to great acclaim in Japan, but can be made obvious to a six-year-old experientially in a music lesson. In achieving quality, every component of the system is equally important. Interestingly, if one aspect appears insoluble at the moment, attention to the improvement of what is most accessible will begin to alter the problem that seemed insurmountable in the system.

The efficacy of the sum of the parts is beyond their addition because their interrelationship changes the potentiality of the system

The improvement of one aspect of a system improves other aspects. If a student uses his bow more correctly, the violin will sound better and his left-hand motion will be easier. The bow can even affect intonation. The effect of this change in skill will bring forth new possibilities to the mind. This is experienced directly by the student if the teacher brings this underlying principle into the student's consciousness.

Understanding requires feedback, which "appears" as intuition

A teacher can only *present* experiences to a student with which a student interacts. The student must be open to the subtle voice of intuition, which is how the student will begin to grasp the significance of the teacher's directions. *There is no explanation that is complete, and no knowledge gained thereby that is a final point of accomplishment.* This becomes obvious to a serious student of music, much to their frustration, especially because one must always reproduce a performance anew. Even a composition can be endlessly revised.

Measurement is useful, but an abstraction

This is a deep truth, but only helpful if a student can feel this viscerally. How does one measure, which means to assess? Where does one begin? Does the problem begin in the hand, the mind, the home of the student, or is it the fault of the teacher's teaching? And where did that fault begin? Thus, measurement is a useful theoretical parameter of investigation, but ultimately proves illusory when looking at the actual cause of anything at all.

One may kick a dog and say the animal was set into motion from the kick, but what made you kick the dog to begin with may ultimately go back to the common mother of everyone, "Lucy," and beyond that devolves into the slime we all evolved from. It is but a small step from the analysis of a student's problems into the futility of finding initial cause in anything. This again shows the indivisibility of the overall system. Therefore, in the big picture (and all smaller pictures are arbitrary measurements), *there is no first or single cause.*

The gathering of people in a performance amplifies an individual mind

Performance, although many times stressful, yields improvement in skill that can be noticed afterwards, even if the performance was not as good as was hoped for. This is a very strange phenomenon. My guess is that it is a result of an amplification of concentration during the performance, not only in the mind of the performer—the extra minds watching seem to enhance the performer's power of mind.

Students aware of this byproduct of performance can use the anticipation of this positive effect to mitigate the terrible pre-concert nerves that are part of any stage experience. This "enhanced consciousness effect" seems to imply the possibility that our minds are more connected than we are aware of, but I have no way to prove the veracity of this intuition other than it seems logical—to me.

Interaction must be constantly appraised; everything unfolds psychologically from parent, teacher and student and must be watched as it appears

As new learning occurs, new questions arise. This is a demonstration of the constantly unfolding process of life and that nothing stays the same. This means that the relationship between student, teacher, and parent is also unfolding and unearthing hidden assumptions and prejudices among all the participants in this learning situation.

What may have worked previously may no longer be effective and all participants in the teaching relationship must address these shifts by inquiring into each other's fundamental assumptions. Otherwise, a small difficulty may develop into something more problematic, which, at that point, may be much harder to fix.

In summary, these are but a few ways that the serious study of music ought to be linked to fundamental truths connective to all other subjects of study, including the most important of all, which is studying the way we think. I suspect that any subject could be approached in this way. Not many subjects offer the possibility of such *experiential* knowing because most subjects studied in school are overwhelmingly cerebral. Music is an integration of highly abstract mental processes, feeling, and evolved, trained physical coordination. This totality of essential factors is a combination far beyond that needed for sports or normal school activities. It may be that if music was studied in this manner, far from being an outlier of an educational approach, it could become an underpinning to a comprehensive educational paradigm.

DEVELOPING TALENT

There are realities in developing talent that are inescapable and often not well understood by parents. No one can learn music without hearing it consistently. Additionally, one must work hard to develop ability, and this work must be monitored. I think most people don't realize that there has never been an acknowledged "great talent" who was not helped every day by a parent or teacher and who did not practice for several hours per day, despite what is claimed to the outside world. The examples are ubiquitous. Heifetz's father practiced with him every day until he was twenty and for at least five or more hours per day. The pianist Evgeny Kissin's teacher lived with his family. With a Russian piano teacher living in his home, his practice regime must have been similar to Heifetz's. Rachmaninoff lived with his teacher. Horowitz's mother was his first teacher. Nathan Milstein's mother left her family, including her husband, to move to St. Petersburg when he was nine so that he could study with Leopold Auer. She watched him practice four to five hours every day. If this is what it takes to make a "genius," thirty minutes to an hour a day for a regular child does not seem like too much work. But, of course, this is not enough practice time to produce a great player.

When one teaches a child how to play a musical instrument, one comes face to face with a student's mental paradigms and one's own. If a student's outlook is more scientific, or in other words, if he tries to understand what he is being taught and will make adjustments within himself to support learning and developing, he will have success. If a student will not try with an open mind to understand the unfamiliar, he will struggle. Is the teacher capable of seeing what needs to be done to help a student change?

If one seriously attempts to understand how to play and posits that there is much more plasticity of the mind than is traditionally assumed, it will become obvious that people are usually much more capable than anyone would have thought. A simple ability such as singing in tune is normally thought to exist *a priori* to any encounter with music and to be unachievable if not "naturally" present. This turns out to not be so. In every situation I have observed, if no shame has been attached to an inability to sing in tune, within a year or two and occasional monitoring of a student's singing, anyone can learn to sing in tune.

We are very concerned that children should display and develop talent and intelligence. Yet should or can anyone judge a child's innate ability or potential? Therefore, anyone seriously interested in educating a child should be studying himself and the child to see if he or she is all tied up mentally (which may manifest itself physically in tension or illness) and seeing if they can free their child's innate ability. For many parents and teachers, this careful attention, this studying of a child or pupil is not easy. The child, an extension of the parents' image or sometimes a behavioral challenge to a teacher, represents a replication of their successes, fears and hidden desires. The child is a second try at life, but often with the same unexamined belief systems.

Perhaps the most helpful educative gift parents could bequeath their children would be to tell them the truth about what any self-reflective adult must feel—angst over how arbitrary our lives seem to be. The fear that life is a meaningless and useless endeavor is common to everyone. None of us knows the answers to the big questions. No one, not even a scientific genius, understands anything at that level of inquiry. If we could admit our ignorance in understanding life, we would give our collective children, and ourselves, the gift of doubt. And with doubt comes new possibilities.

THE INFLUENCE OF A NON-AUTHORITARIAN OR AN AUTHORITARIAN TEACHER ON A STUDENT'S EXPERIENCE

The quality of the interaction between teacher and student can be foundational to their perception of human interaction. An authoritarian teacher presumes that a student cannot or does not want to find out about or discover the world for themselves. A teacher of this sort assumes that there is a fixed point to knowledge and that the teacher can judge accurately from an omniscient gaze what is known, what needs to be known, and who is *intrinsically* capable or not. There is a difference between the authoritarian teacher and a true teacher. A true teacher tries to discover, to uncover what is not easily seen. A teacher is a studier. He learns about the student and about how and what he teaches.

An authoritarian "teacher" can suffer no question, cannot deviate from his armor or edifice of knowledge. Questions are derided, turned around and spun back as a mockery of the query. The authoritarian wants honor; the teacher wants people to learn, including himself. The authoritarian teacher wants to be admired, which requires that others look up from below; the teacher wants results, which requires that we look together. The *quality of the learning process* is fundamental in shaping a student's world view. In an authoritarian approach, what is most important is to eventually become important. This is a diversion from true learning. What is important in learning is to *understand matters in-depth*, which is essential in living one's life if it is to have any meaning at all and not be destructive to oneself and everyone else.

Authoritarian teaching tools are blame/shame. Blame and shame are one, simply different perspectives of the same accusation—inferiority. When one is blamed, shame appears. Initially, the blame can occur from an outside source, but when internalized by the student will function just as effectively. Blame can also be a teacher's cover-up of *their own* lack of understanding. Blame can be used by parents against a teacher.

If someone is upset with a result, unless one tries to *understand* what is happening, he is apt to fall into blame, which is really a sign of lazy thinking. Underlying this dynamic is the use of fear as a motivating force in learning. Where there is fear there can be no proper teaching or learning. Yet there must be seriousness, not camaraderie with no expectations, which is another common teaching model.

Both the authoritarian and the "comrade" teacher cover up something the teacher does not want the student to be aware of. The teacher may lack knowledge and skill himself and hides this fact by severity or camaraderie. Or, if the teacher is a well-known performer, he may hide his feelings of competition with either ruse. In a market model, which assumes and promotes the idea of the scarcity of quality performers, what incentive can a performer/teacher have in creating students who may equal or surpass his skill? If someone can be engaged who plays as well or better than the teacher, why should anyone pay his (the teacher/performer's) fee for a performance? In this situation the teacher will leave out essential information, or subtly sabotage the student's efforts, appearing to be helpful, but with no result that would compromise the teacher's position. This is well-known in the music world.[13]

It is common in authoritarian teaching, both the severe or the disingenuously friendly, that extraordinary results from a student are expected with little or no help from the teacher. This expectation produces not only a shame/blame psychology, but additionally, a more insidious effect—mystification. Mystification, which is chronic confusion, destroys the ability of the student to have any confidence in his own innate power of apprehension and intuition and, instead, focuses his confidence on the judgements of the authoritarian teacher, who careful observation will show, often knows little more than the student about how to realize great expectations, or may be deeply competitive and threatened by a student's ability, obfuscating these facts by a strategy of authoritarianism. In adult life we would call such a person a tyrant or a charlatan, yet in music we have little choice but to accept this mode of instruction because the system is functionally incoherent at the educational level—it creates this paradigm. The ubiquitous lack of serious pedagogical research for teaching instrumentalists, singers and composers creates a cloud of mystification that perpetuates the dysfunction and decay that needlessly pervades the *entire field* of classical music. With but rare exceptions, students are not given *solid* information about the *art* of music. Mystification destroys the *capacity* for intelligence in both the mystifier and the mystified and is perhaps the root cause of the suffering we have inflicted upon one another for centuries.

---

13 How would performer/teachers who are competitive with their students fare in a school that studied great player's methods as their policy? We can see, perhaps, why this is never done.

CHAPTER 31

Return to Curtis

I visited Curtis in 2008. I hadn't been there in thirty years. Even though I consider my experience there inane, and that the school was awash in useless teaching methods, I had no angst upon my return. Its values no longer had any meaning for me.

The building is beautiful—an amalgam of two mansions. A stone facade with marble steps and huge wooden doors lead to a vestibule. From there, two large wrought-iron framed glass doors open into the main entrance hall. As one enters the mansion, directly ahead lies a large fireplace, big enough to stand in, which is never used. To the left there is a security desk, and beyond that, the recital hall, which only seats about one hundred seventy-five people. This is where we played our orchestra concerts, even operas. It sufficed. Even though the orchestra was nearly the entire school, there was enough room for an audience of a hundred because the seats were movable.

I walked through the main hall, through the far doors—which are ten or eleven feet high and made of thick, heavy wood—to the entrance of the concert hall. A cello student was playing the *Rococo Variations*. I peeked inside. A master class was going on. There were probably fifteen people in the hall. I noticed Carter Brey, the principal cellist of the New York Philharmonic. The student finished her performance, and Carter stood up and made some comments. I thought they were pretty interesting, although a little superficial, but he seemed to be very considerate of her feelings. I looked around and noticed an old schoolmate of mine, Peter Wiley, a cellist. I had known he was teaching at Curtis, yet I could barely recognize him. I guess thirty years makes quite a difference. He seemed like an old man, even though we are the same age. He lifted himself out of his chair. He had gained a noteworthy amount of weight. He also made some comments. I guessed she was his student. He grunted a couple of remarks that I couldn't understand. The next student began to play.

I remembered that there was a back way out and I quietly escaped, unnoticed. A narrow passageway led me through the basement, which was like something from the time of Dickens—where cramped attics or subterranean hovels were the living quarters of orphaned children—past the old practice rooms, which were probably six by six feet. As I walked, I looked for the downstairs library where Portnoy and I used to listen to records of past Curtis students. These are private records made from the concerts they played as students. There was one of Krachmalnick playing the Tchaikovsky *Violin Concerto* with a piano accompaniment—amazing playing.

There were others that we would listen to—great players no one had ever heard of. Arnold Eidus was one. What did he ever do, we wondered? Fred Vogelgesang was another unheard of Curtis great. He had recorded himself playing all three parts of the Brahms *Horn Trio*—piano, violin, and horn—as well as many virtuoso showpieces, playing both the violin and piano part. I met Fred when I lived in New York. He was a buddy of Krachmalnick's. He played in the City Opera, somewhere in the violin section. I hung out with him a couple of times. He was very soft-spoken and self-deprecating, not in any way that was depressive, just not that impressed by himself. He had a bizarre recording of Heifetz, released under the name of Joe Hoyle, playing Saint-Saëns' *Rondo Capriccioso* like a joke. You could tell the guy could play well, but it was distorted and rushed and weird. This recording was an urban legend. I had heard only rumors of its existence. But here it was. There was also, supposedly, a recording of Heifetz playing scales. Fred didn't have it.

I couldn't help thinking, why was someone as talented as Fred sitting in the section of an opera orchestra? He lived alone in a tiny apartment in the middle of Manhattan, with shelves crammed with records and books, a piano, and recording equipment. I started thinking that it's too bad someone never interviewed or wrote about these undiscovered and forgotten greats like Vogelgesang and Eidus. Anyway, I'm rambling, but that's what walking through Curtis on that day did to me. I remembered all kinds of stuff.

The back passage led upstairs to the rear of the building where the classes were taught, and still are. At the top of the stairs was Louis Martin's solfège class. I remember he was droll, sarcastic, and flamboyantly gay. In those days of course I knew that there were gay people, that guys could be into guys. I don't think I really understood much of what that meant, except that I should avoid them. In solfège class we did a lot of singing by sight, and singing in different clefs, and took musical dictation—all of which I was pretty good at. At least that is my memory of it. So I never minded that class, although I had no idea what the larger point of it was. I just kept practicing.

I have always kept practicing, until I broke a finger on my left hand a few months ago. It healed fine, luckily. Until I broke my finger, I practiced violin every day for forty years. I was always busy with it and had no time for anything else. Once I couldn't practice, I had gobs of free time. I practiced only about three to four hours a day. What the hell was I doing all day? I have no idea. Oddly, when it was diagnosed that my finger was broken, I was shocked, but not so sure I cared if I could ever play again. What a never-ending psychological trap it can be. Every time you play well, it's erased. You have to start over. It can be recorded, but you still have to play live. It's not like painting, or sculpture, or writing. You can't keep what you did. It just vanishes, and it takes even more work than painting or writing.

At the end of the second floor of Curtis was where we had our high school literature class. This was taught by Rudolph Serkin's daughter, Liz. I don't remember anything about it except that we studied Syliva Plath and Liz always sat on a table. In the next room we studied history, not of music, but of the world. Our teacher was a man named Lawrence Cheeves, who seemed like a very smart guy. In the real world, I think he was a banker. He had a very quiet manner, soft-spoken and patient. His daughter, Janet, was a classmate of mine, a cellist, who I think I was in love with for a while. I don't think she ever noticed me. She had dark brown hair that she pulled back and braided. Pulled-back dark hair on a girl always made me fall in love from the time I saw the *Sound of Music* and fell in love with Liesl, the oldest daughter of the Von Trapp family. She became my model of beauty when I was a teenager. Any variation of her made me crazy.

The pulled-back brown hair variation lasted until I met and fell in love with the younger sister of a girl classmate of mine who I also had a crush on. Then for fifteen years I had an instant crush on any girl with her name or hands or body type. Then there was the older woman crush. God, I lusted for Sarah Jennings, a classmate. I was seventeen and pimpled and she was twenty-one and going out with, rumor had it, Burt Bacharach, the famous songwriter and thirty or more years her senior. She kissed me once at a party. A real kiss. But again I ramble on. Back to my history teacher, Mr. Cheeves. I remember only one thing Mr. Cheeves said. He looked at me one day in class and said in front of everyone, "You're way too smart to be a musician." I had no idea what he meant by that, but for some reason I never forgot it.

My French teacher was a beauty, and actually French. I can't remember her name. She looked a little like a twenty-five-year-old Rosanna Arquette. She always wore scarves and had a beautiful, fearless smile. She was crippled, with braces on her legs. I had a chance to talk to her once, outside class. Each Wednesday at three o'clock the students were served tea. Our hostess was always Mrs. Serkin, but one time our French teacher assisted her. Now was my chance to speak to her. The line for tea moved along and finally I was in front of her, outside of class. I had to say something. So I said, "Do you have any children?"

"I can't," she said.

I think I turned scarlet red. I know I moved away as fast as I could. I would like to think I said, "I'm sorry," but I don't think that's what happened. From then on I was embarrassed whenever I saw her.

I continued up the stairs to the third floor. This is where I had taken harmony class with Robert Levin. He was a skinny little Jewish guy, like a character from a Woody Allen movie. I would not have thought that then because I had never seen a Woody Allen movie. Still, I could see he was Jewish—the nervousness, the facial characteristics. Everyone said he was a genius. How they could tell that was beyond me, and how these rumors were propagated, I have no idea. He talked constantly and fast. And he played constantly. He played Bach fugues relentlessly. I am sure he must have been good. I had no idea. I was eighteen and had other problems. I know that I had no idea what the study of harmony had to do with playing well.

Today in the same classroom there was a class on how to buy and sell instruments, given by Jonathon, a salesman for Moennig's. Whether he still was there, I wasn't sure, because Bill had died of cancer a few years before and the firm had been through some changes. But here was Jonathon, a teacher at Curtis. How things change, I thought. I first met Jonathon some thirty years before at Moennig's shop. He was a very serious, prim, formal person, which made him seem much older than he looked, although I don't think he was more than eight to ten years older than I was, but he was like those young Republican priggish types. I got the impression that he could be easily shocked and that his response would be a hearty, "Oh my!"

Jonathon was smooth, in an unctuous sort of way. My god, he was smooth. He gave the impression of being beyond reproach, and maybe he was, but he had the charm of a statue. How amusing, I thought to myself, Jonathon teaching a class on buying and selling instruments to a bunch of kids who would never have the money to buy one because the prices had gone up so much. I stayed and listened. He was talking about how to look for flaws in bows, showing some examples of this or that bowmaker. Of course, not only could these kids never afford these bows, but they were nearly unfindable as well because collectors and older players owned all the good stuff. He didn't mention that.

On this visit to Curtis, after having walked around the school for an hour and heard some of the kids playing, and seen them running around and going to their classes with three or four other students in attendance, I couldn't dispel the idea that they were enormously naive. Like cows being led to the slaughter, they were all asleep, oblivious to what awaited them beyond the doors once they graduated.

The dean of the school had been a student at Curtis thirty years before, although I didn't know him. He took himself very seriously, with a haughty air of importance and condescension. He had graduated as a clarinetist and was now the dean—so much for progress in the outside world. He was very impressed with what the school was currently doing. He admitted to me that the seventies had been a dark time, but now, he reported confidently, the school was really trying to look after the students. They were building dorms in the city so that they no longer had to find their own apartments. They were counseling them on their future options. They were raising lots of money to do this.

The new, recently built library was located next door in a separate building. I thought I might walk over and see if I could listen to some recordings of Krachmalnick from his student days. I asked the librarian.

"I'm sorry, but we don't know where they are. Things have been moved quite a bit."

"No problem," I said, "but let me ask you a question. I've been walking around for a couple of hours, listening to the students and watching some classes. The thought keeps coming into my head: What do these kids think they're going to do? I mean, there aren't any jobs, and the little there are, are drying up."

"They don't think," he said. "They just practice."

"Look," he continued, "I'm a bassoon player. All I did through high school and college was practice. When I was thirty I realized I'm just playing gigs for no money. Now I work here."

I did not learn to compose, or play the piano too well, but my training is the norm in every music school. The days are long gone, and occurred mainly in Europe, when at least some people learned to compose a bit, as a basic part of their musical education. Even if I had learned to compose, it wouldn't have helped me socially. I seem to lack the desire to join in. This separatist inclination may have come from both my parents, neither of whom are joiners, which is probably why they married outside their inherited religions and countries. And since I am "technically" not Jewish, but was raised Catholic and "tainted" with a Jewish first and last name, therefore not fitting with either sect, being an outsider is natural to me. I had been encouraged and supported in my iconoclastic positions by both of my parents. My father is deeply skeptical of all authorities, a bias I must have inherited. Unfortunately for him, it meant that I was skeptical of whatever he said also, but there is a dark side to everything, I guess.

Krachmalnick and my father said two things to me that I never forgot. I had just made a sandwich in the kitchen when I was a kid, and my father came home early and noticed that I had left a mess on the counter. Looking it over he said to me, "Clean that up. Why should anyone else clean up your mess?" The other came from Krachmalnick. I was playing some piece, and he said to me, "You better practice more carefully. The only one you're fooling is yourself." For some reason those two admonishments never leave my brain. I certainly got scores of others that seemed to fly right through my head.

These two admonitions remind me of something else that Rafael Druian, longtime concertmaster of the Cleveland Orchestra when George Szell was in charge, told me about orchestra auditions. He said if you understand quality, you can discern a musician's level of skill within a few seconds. There is no need to have them play twenty excerpts. But, he added, because people don't know much of anything anymore (this was in the eighties and I don't think things have changed) audition lists are monumental. The auditors only know how to listen for mistakes, and that is why an orchestra committee requires a vast array of audition material, according to Druian. Toscanini auditioned people by listening to an applicant play a concerto or even a sonata.

CHAPTER 32

Can We Change?

…I have discovered in my scientific work that in the long run it is less important to learn of a particular new way of conceiving structure abstractly, than it is to understand how the consideration of such new ideas can liberate one's thought from a vast network of preconceptions absorbed largely unconsciously with education and training and from the general background.[1]

– David Bohm

The principal clarinetist of the New York Philharmonic, Stanley Drucker, was a graduate of Curtis. His first job as a principal player was at the age of sixteen with a second-tier orchestra. How many people auditioned for that job in the 1940s? I am sure it is nowhere near the four hundred that would send in their resumés today. He learned on the job and within a couple of years, in 1948 at nineteen years old, attained a position with the New York Philharmonic. He was a member of the orchestra for sixty-one years and held the principal clarinet position for forty-nine of them, which means that for sixty-one years one of maybe three clarinet positions in the orchestra was taken.

These jobs never become available because of tenure. Why should musicians have tenure? Why should anyone be protected in a job forever? Why should the justices of the Supreme Court have tenure? The possibility of tenure may be somewhat understandable in academia—protecting faculty who are going against the grain, although a contract without a lifetime guarantee seems more reasonable. But why give tenure to musicians? Why not make employment in music contractual without the forever part? You either get to stay, or not.

It wasn't until the middle of the nineteenth century that the idea of a public *solo* recital was conceived by Liszt. In those days, Berlioz could scarcely find enough good players to give a bad performance of his music. Yet in a city such as Warsaw in the early nineteenth century, when Chopin was a boy, one in three households had a piano. A piano in the home meant they had risen to the level of the bourgeoisie. The major orchestras of the United States were formed only as recently as the late nineteenth and early part of the twentieth

---

1   David Bohm, *On Creativity* (New York: Routledge, 2010), 48.

century. Interest in classical music grew with the middle class, and music schools sprouted up throughout the U.S. By the 1930s, you could begin to hear a Beethoven symphony well-played in Europe or the United States. Music was taught in the public schools.

Perhaps the height of playing was during the 1950s. That decade heard the greatest performers, the best orchestras. There was great public interest. There were still genius composers such as Prokofiev and Shostakovich creating music. Richard Strauss lived until 1949. Kreisler died in 1962. The Juilliard Quartet was playing in the tradition of the Budapest Quartet (whose first violinist was a student of Pyotr Stolyarsky, Milstein's first teacher). You could hear the lineage. Most of these players were like my teacher, Krachmalnick. They played in the way that surrounded them, the way that the singers of the time sounded. As we have discussed, when you listen to the old recordings you can hear that their sound, their tone, was entirely different, superior, to today's players.

Performers were friends with Shostakovich, Strauss, Prokoviev, and Bartok. Even Brahms nearly lived into the twentieth century—he died in 1897. Dvorak died in 1904. As recently as the early twentieth century Berg, Webern and Schoenberg wrote music, albeit difficult, that could be played on instruments in a way consistent with old-style technique. They still wrote music that, even if it was not traditionally tonal, was based on old and familiar musical forms such as the waltz. Even in my student days, many of the teachers at Curtis and Julliard such as Mischa Schneider, Felix Galimir, and Rudolph Serkin were from the "old world" of Europe. They did not create new music, but understood that bygone world, building careers in the U.S. playing the standard repertoire, something that many had not been able to continue to do in Europe.

Classical music in this country is, at this point, several steps removed from its source. Today's paradigm is to train orchestra players. They even do that at Curtis for violinists, something that was inconceivable when I was a student. We were trained to play concertos, which wasn't too brilliant either. Unfortunately, we should have been trained to be complete musicians, which ought to be the *raison d'être* of a music school. We were not trained to play our instruments with deep knowledge. We were trained to practice hard, which kept us unaware, not only of the quality of the education we were receiving, but also of the lack of opportunities we had upon graduation. In earlier times there may have been a reason to be a musician—that is, a real musician. But we have forgotten what that means.

During my visit I had arranged to hear a coaching with Peter Wiley and some students. The students were playing the *"Dumky" Trio* by Dvorak. I had not seen Peter in thirty years. He did not seem to remember me. As I said, I would have barely recognized him. But he let me listen to him work with the students.

They played the piece pretty well—nicely—"funly" is probably more accurate; at least that's the impression I got from watching their smiling faces. They seemed more than pleased with their efforts, except when one occasionally played out of tune or came in wrong. Then they laughed.

Peter didn't seem to share in their merriment. He had a real scowl on his face. He turned to the pianist, a young Israeli. "I hear that you won't be playing this in class next week."

"No. I have to play a concert in New York."

"But you're here in school. You have responsibilities."

"I already told you about this. I can't get out of it."

Peter was upset. He turned to the cellist. "You played this note with a dash, not a dot. The score has a dot."

"Oh, yeah."

"Why do we look at the score carefully?" Peter asked in an irritated voice.

"Because Dvorak is a better musician than me?"

They had been through this song and dance before.

"Because Dvorak is a better musician than you'll ever be."

Not much you can say after that.

It's all very well to say to a nineteen-year-old student that he will never be a musician of Dvorak's level, yet one might easily ask: What is he being taught that makes it so certain that he won't be? Why are the students in Peter's lesson so shallow and flippant?

The answer to both questions is that their training is shallow and flippant and this is why it is certain, it is preordained, that these students will never be musicians of Dvorak's level. Our system *precludes* this possibility. In this field we are just accidental. We are circumstantial. We are, as Milan Kundera put it, "unbearably light."

Why is this so? It cannot be otherwise in the system as it exists. The *structure* of the system *creates incoherence*. As a further explanation of structure I offer these ideas from physicist David Bohm:

> Structure is a hierarchy of orders…This is a universal principle of structure…
> The regular array of breaks or changes in the symmetry of one order is the basis
> of another level of order and so on to higher levels. This universal validity of
> this principle implies, of course, not only unending growth of a hierarchy of
> harmonious orders leading to the evolution of ever more encompassing and

unified totalities. It can also lead to the possibility of conflict and clash between different orders that will produce, not harmonious and unified totalities, but rather a process of destruction and decay of the partial orders... *This is well-defined order that is functionally wrong.*[2] (italics mine)

Even well-defined order can produce *functional incoherence* within a system. What is functional incoherence? A system in which foundational settings, biases, create order—function—that ultimately destroys the system.

In music, as a field, underlying suppositions incoherent with reality bias the system towards chronic confusion and mystification. This destroys creative energy, vitality. Without vitality there is decay. The chronic confusion *embedded* in the educational structure of music seeps into every aspect of the field, sapping and misdirecting creative energy by *misleading* interested students, keeping teachers *competitive and confused*, forcing professionals to *obey* a conductor for a living, and *creating idols* out of ordinary people, "talents" whose accomplishments, if examined rationally, are far from superhuman. If there is no energy left for creation, how can the system produce Dvoraks?

CAN WE CHANGE?

In Chapter 8 we examined our societal concept of individuality. We are not isolated self-contained units of action. We are creations of the natural world, which, psychically, includes the thousands of generations of thought that have preceded us. Talent and genius are subtle shifts in perception from inherited "norms," paradigms, which open an individual to another level of interaction *with what is known* and, therefore, to a different level of feedback from the deep sources of life. From this perspective one may possibly discover something not known, yet this is always derived from what *is* known.

Therefore, talent or genius *rests on multigenerational knowledge*. It is not an individual achievement, as we discussed in Chapter 9. When the transmission of the "secret" subtle traditions of music was destroyed, as we explained in Chapter 10, the bedrock, the correct and most efficacious bias for the utilization of this cultural creation of classical music was not available as a foundational setting for those who followed. Since then we have been guessing, and guessing wrong.

This wrong guessing has persisted because of the highly competitive nature of the field—the scarcity of jobs, opportunities, etc.—which has created factions. It has also continued because we believe that talent cannot be explained, that talent itself is an *explanation* of quality. This, again, can be traced back to our

---

2 *Ibid.* 1, 12-13.

confused idea of individualism and that talent will somehow "out." Yet all "talents" have been trained, and incorrect training, no matter who the "talent," will destroy ability.

From this misconception of individuality arises the *supposed validity* of the idea of genius, of importance, as *isolated* achievement. This can only persist when people have been chronically confused, through a certain type of education, the type of education Pestalozzi and Rousseau fought against, as we discussed in Chapter 30, but a type of education that is still pervasive in music. This approach does not seek *foundational* knowledge, what Pestalozzi called the "invariable qualities of nature." We may call this seeking what is true, searching for deep *explanatory* principles. In contrast, music education processes seek results, not *understanding*. Without proper understanding of what is to be taught, one can never have solid results. Without *understanding* the system fosters confusion, which leads to mystification. It is this mystification, this confusion, that creates and preserves the power systems that emerge from this foundational incoherence.

Mystification has created soloism—the *supposed* scarcity of great performers. This can only exist in a system where knowledge is protected or unknown. This chronic confusion fosters cultish teaching methods. If teaching institutions *took responsibility* for what is taught for *all instruments*, methods such as Sukuki's, for example, would have been thoroughly examined many years ago, as we did in Chapter 25. Even Galamian's approach and Carl Flesch's pedagogy, which are ubiquitously accepted, have serious flaws that should be corrected. If institutions studied great performers, as we have in this book, and incorporated their research into a pedagogical approach, *soloism would end*.

The conductor could not exist in his position of influence if musicians were *properly* trained, as we have shown throughout this book. Whatever a conductor asserts that he supposedly knows, any well-schooled musician should, and does, also know. If professional musicians decided to organize and train themselves to play without a conductor, and music schools began to teach students how to play minus a conductor, the conductor's power would simply *vanish*.

Disempowering conductors and solo players would diminish the power of agents and concert promoters, who depend on a model of scarcity for their market advantage. Because it is believed by musical organizations that an agent controls a scarce resource, the agent gains influence. Supposed scarcity allows the artist and agent to inflate concert fees, from which the agent receives an increased commission. *Remove scarcity and their influence evaporates.* This would also affect the fund-raising efforts and, therefore, the salaries of the business personnel in performance organizations—symphonies, opera companies—who also depend on a model of scarcity to demand monetary support, both for their organization and themselves.

As we discussed in Chapter 12, every year thousands of students graduate with performance degrees from universities and conservatories. What are they going to do?

They can create an alternative system.

Rocks, trees, and animals must succumb to how things "just happen." But humans possess the gift of self-reflection, which means, unlike a rock or a lion, we do not have to accept what "just happens," particularly within our psychologically constructed social paradigms.

IS THERE A BENEFIT TO TEACHING IN ISOLATION WITHOUT OVERSIGHT, REVIEW, OR RESEARCH?

For one thing it means that even though we may ask the question, "Is one teacher better than another?" there is no way to answer it. There are only different ways to teach and play. You may like this way, I may like this, and another may want that. This lack of clarity protects individual turf. Teaching in isolation helps create gurus and followers. That can be good for business. It also keeps anyone from asking another important question. Is there a better way to teach? Is there an approach to playing that is *superior* to another? These questions don't arise. Therefore, professionals are rarely faced with the questions, "Could they do more?" or "Do they have a lack of knowledge?"

In our current educational paradigm the answer to these queries, should they arise, is conveniently simple. Some students work harder. Some are more talented. The teacher just does his thing. Some students become good, some are just bad. You better practice more. It is true that some work harder and some less. Some advance more easily, some don't. Interestingly, or upsettingly, whichever way one wants to look at this, to learn to play badly requires the same time as to learn to play well. I assume that the badly taught and the well taught practice a minimal amount. One learns how to play incorrectly, one correctly. Same time, same years, very different results. Often the cost is the same.

In a field that is consistently losing its audience, where jobs are disappearing, and where the art form is spiraling toward irrelevance and decadence, can we afford to have a system of musical education that promotes subjectivity, idiosyncratic opinion, unverifiable comments, and psychologically damaging teaching methods? Don't we need to do something that is true, something scientific? If at the heart of the musical world, the training is based on nonsense, how can we expect that any of the rest of it will make sense? The foundation, which is education, must be solid. Now there is no rhyme or reason. There is only accident. Accidental teachers and accidental performers, accidental composers and accidental audiences. That is a house of cards. And it's falling.

The students continued playing. Peter stopped them, searching for the right words. In frustration he started to play his cello, angrily.

"You see, this is how to do it."

They all nodded in agreement, obviously cowed by something; I don't think it was the beauty of his playing. He was intensely aggressive. The entire time they played, the violinist, a girl, kept smiling. It didn't matter if the music was sad, tragic, happy, fast, or quiet. She was always ready to show how much she enjoyed playing Dvorak's piece by smiling as she played.

I thought to myself, this is it. This attitude is the essence of what I see here and probably was when I was a student. It is decadence.

Decadence. Yes, I thought. There is no essence. There is no feeling or understanding. The school is a caricature of what they are professing to teach. Only imitation with no depth. Teaching kids to be orchestra musicians, not musicians. It's corporate music. They are trained to fit into an empty system, playing music written by dead people. Pretending that it is art—creation—they are being trained for positions that don't exist or that require only their conformity and obedience.

The paint on the walls of the room was peeling off. There was a piece of plywood covering something, probably a hole, in another corner of the wall. Not a real repair, just a patch job to get by for a while. The coaching ended. I said "thanks" to the kids and Peter, and left.

CHAPTER 33

Some Answers

This book is predicated on the assumption that fundamental beliefs determine and circumscribe outcome, from which it follows that to improve the current condition of classical music one must first identify the underlying concepts both in society as a whole, and the music business in particular, that have led to this state of affairs. Therefore, part of the solution lies in understanding what is incoherent within the system, which, because it is a living system, will begin to alter the structure of the whole. This book has attempted to do so.

It cannot be denied that in the U.S. the audience for classical music is dwindling. Many books have been written on the subject, as well as studies by the National Endowment for the Arts that support this conclusion.[1] It cannot be denied that the employment opportunity for classical musicians is simply abysmal, and that colleges and conservatories that encourage students to seriously pursue employment in the field are, to be kind, misleading them, or at worst, perpetrating a scam. One may take exception to this second statement by citing the fact that colleges also award degrees in sociology, English literature, and many other liberal arts that also offer abysmal employment opportunities. However, the study of these disciplines does not direct students into a cul-de-sac of skillsets that cannot be easily transferred into other avocations such as journalism, marketing, law degrees, and so on. Being able to play in tune or beautifully has no useful purpose whatsoever. It is simply good for the soul.

It cannot be argued with any success that the foundation of music, which is education, has a scientific model as its basis for the transference of knowledge. There is not a single school that studies—as its policy—the most effective ways of playing an instrument or teaching the art. There is no school whose staff seriously investigates such methodologies and publishes the results. I am

---

1   James M. Doering, *The Great Orchestrator—Arthur Judson & American Arts Management* (Chicago: University of Illinois Press, 2013), 227. The NEA's 2008 Survey of Public Participation in the Arts "paints a bleak picture."

reminded of a lecture given by Richard Dawkins, Darwin champion and avid debunker of religious dogma. When asked by a member of the audience why he refused to publicly debate creationists, he replied that intellectual discourse has to have some standard. Would a geologist be expected to debate a person who claimed the world was flat?

In the music world, the flat world advocate is completely accepted because there is little or no intellectual discipline in the field. His stature and promotion is explained with supposed truisms such as he has an equally valid idea, a different point of view. In music the flat world geologist is made the head of a school or the conductor of a major symphony orchestra. This is a result— blowback—of our love affair with the *idea* of talent, a word that can be attached to anyone who has been deemed to possess some psychic force. This force can be sheer nonsense, but in art once the label is applied, the flat worlder is allowed any transgression. Talent, once ordained, requires no explanation. This paradigm *precludes* investigation, learning. It is time to disenthrall ourselves from the notion that outstanding playing and composing cannot be seriously analyzed in a way that can help people learn the same skills. But one cannot understand what one decides cannot be understood.

To compose a symphony on the level of Prokofiev or play like Horowitz is an intellectual and scholarly feat requiring vast knowledge and skill far beyond the simplistic explanation of talent, which mystifies, and trivializes at the same time, a discipline that has the rigor of any branch of science or mathematics. It is an art that must be approached, like all recondite subjects, with more than a little inspiration thrown in, and demands extraordinary precision of mind—and proper training. Sadly, unlike becoming a geologist, where exposure to a flat worlder teacher at a young age can be corrected by access to scientific information, in music a bad start is usually the end of the whole game.

We are free to explore. We have nothing to lose at this point. Because there are almost no jobs and music is continually becoming less and less of a viable profession, the whole field is free to go back to basics—training people to be fine musicians. Currently, the educational directive is to teach students to play like a machine, enticing them with the hope that they may win a disappearing orchestral position (that most people eventually hate). The situation is almost comically dire. In an attempt to attract audiences, concert promoters and musical organizations try every manner of outreach. They make the concerts more personable, less formal, the performers dress differently, the audience dresses differently, an expert explains the music, symphonies introduce jazz programming, orchestras play along with movies and program pop tunes. The one fact they never realize is that the way musicians have been trained to play is boring to listen to.

It's very commendable that performances are neat and clean, but unfortunately that is not the point of music. The elephant in the room is that the performances are dull. Vladimir Horowitz never had an empty seat in a concert. Imagine if an orchestra or an opera company could perform at his level of virtuosity and with his understanding of phrasing. I suspect audiences would be back in droves. It's never been the music that is boring. It's the performances that keep people home.

Interestingly, audiences for classical music may be dwindling, but enrollment for music degrees continues to rise, although there is almost no hope for employment. This shows that young people *are* interested in music. It is the older professionals who are destroying classical music, not the young people we easily blame for being uninterested. Yet the way we think about the young and the old, about time itself, is a paradigm that can be shifted.

Normally we think of the young as the future, the old as the past. This has the effect of transferring the responsibility for change to the young. We assume they have the energy and creative power to make a better world, or are intelligent enough not to ruin the present one. At the other end of the time scale, many older people hope to escape society to the leisure of the beach. But age may have responsibilities. How can the young know what awaits them? Only we do. Therefore, is it reasonable that once we have the means to leave the play, we allow them down the same unknown road we were directed to by those who knew our future? Instead of saying to ourselves, "I'm glad I made it through that," and running for cover, we could turn around and clear the path.

Consider how long it takes someone to finally understand what is going on in society. For perhaps forty or fifty years we simply follow along until at some point, if we are honest with ourselves, we wonder, "what were we thinking?" The young cannot solve the problems we are intimately acquainted with. To hope or assume that they will do any better than we did is an illusion. By the time they understand the situations ahead, they will be trapped by them, just as we are. We could be the scouting party warning those following behind what lies ahead, and *actively eliminating* obstacles we know are there.

If we could shift our perception and see that the future, past, and present are an indivisible movement of time, humanity could be seen as one organism or pattern of energy. This pattern exists in *all* possible states *at once*. Together, every person, when viewed as part of an inseparable human consciousness, is playing out all possible circumstances of the human experience *concurrently.* Therefore, it could be posited that I am the *future* to my young students and they are my past—the youth that is past for me. My *current* state exists for them in the future. For example, for me, from my position in life, my father is my future and I am his past, *existing at the same time.* In this way everyone represents an aspect of everyone else. This is one of the reasons we enjoy interacting with younger people. They are a time machine to what was, just as we are showing them a possible future. What can the future tell the past? What would we change about our past if we could? By adopting this thinking, combined with action, *the future can change the past.*

Entire societal structures have changed when fundamental shifts in consciousness become pervasive. The shift that talent can be explained is an empowering paradigm, as is the idea that music and the performance of it are an indivisible system of thought. Therefore, the most obvious place to begin to change course is the foundation. Let us create a school that trains students in a scientific, non-idiosyncratic way. We have made a start. The methods herein described will produce remarkable results. Our analysis shows that a *bel canto* approach to music is fundamentally congruent with truths about music, our minds, and our bodies. To solve the problem of teaching students to play in a way that allows for continual growth, it seems that all we need to do is to teach them in this way or perhaps find a variant, through research, that may be more effective.

But who is going to teach them to play in ways that are more deeply correct if one cannot find master players who already do so? Very, very few, if any, musicians are trained to play in this way. Therefore, the problem in initiating this new approach, in fact, the largest hidden block to progress in teaching music, may be muscle memory. Muscle memory means that it is nearly impossible to change a fundamental approach once it is stored in the mind/body system. An adult player who has reached a certain level of expertise will find it very difficult to change or understand different underlying concepts without years of work. It may be for this reason that musicians have been unwilling to prescribe and implement the most obvious cure for the music business's woes, which is to examine what we teach. It seems threatening and, perhaps, impossible. Yet this may not be so.

The greatest impediment to learning and changing in the field of music is society's deep rooted, erroneous belief that talent, great skill, cannot be investigated and understood. This is simply not true, which is what this book has shown. Furthermore, what can be understood can be learned. Therefore, *anyone* can improve their playing, their insight, their "talent," *if* they can proceed *without fear* in a spirit of scientific inquiry and curiosity. This situation requires a new garment, not patching the old worn-out sock. We have to assume that as educators, as musicians, our quest, our responsibility, should be to continually deepen our understanding, to critically examine how and what we teach and to *openly* discuss and debate what we learn with the musical community. If we do that, many things will begin to change.

A shift in fundamental approach, in the "values" and "culture" of the tradition being transferred to students, will change the *potentiality* of the educational system. This will alter relationships within the field, changing their hierarchical structure. Since there will be many more outstanding performers than we currently have, there will be less need for conductors, whose very presence is anathema to spontaneous performance, an inversion of their importance, and who should in the best of all possible worlds, or even a somewhat close approximation thereof, remain off-stage. Additionally, the creation of many more outstanding performers means there will be more "stars," hence, no scarcity of "stars," which will lower concert fees and diffuse the influence of individual concert agents. Since expertise will be more common, composers who are virtuoso players may reappear. This will correct our overvaluation of both the conductor and performer, ending soloism, and restoring the performer/composer to their rightful place as the vanguards of musical style, tradition, and innovation. They may even write music that challenges players in ways that develops their skill within the correct technique of the instrument, music that players want to play and audiences want to hear. The likelihood of this circumstance grows in direct proportion to their ability to write music that has understandable pattern, which as we have shown, is necessary for virtuoso performance. Pattern is also necessary for audience comprehension and for the ability of a performer to play from memory, which in itself increases audience appeal. More expert players means more interest and passion for music. More new music means vitality. Vitality means creation. And creation has no limits.

Appendix

APPENDIX

More ideas

Let's expand upon several of the ideas discussed in the book.

As mentioned, a useful concept is playing triplets *as pairs*. This brings out every note, and I suspect it is more natural for our brains to think in pairs. For example, in Tchaikovsky's *Violin Concerto* this passage, ex. A-1a, is much easier if played in pairs with neighbor note reduction *as a base of thought*—three notes can be mentally reduced to one.

In the first measure E/C♯/E is E, F♯/C♯/F♯ is F♯, and the next group, D/B/D, is D. Therefore, the first three groups of triplets in the first measure can be thought of as E, F♯, D.

This way of thinking can be applied to the entire passage *(ex. A-1b)*.

In this next passage, ex. A-2a...

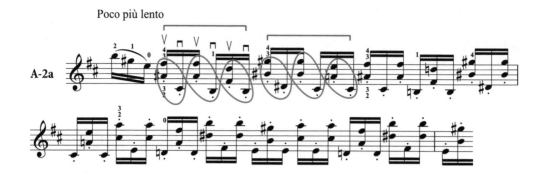

…the double-stopping can be thought of as triple stops *(ex. A-2b).*

The bowing pattern is *three* pairs of up to down clockwise cycles, which is easier than triplets because often, when playing triplets in groups of three the last note of each group of three will always be shortchanged; moreover, another difficulty is that each group will begin with alternate bows; one group of three notes with an up-bow, the next group of three with a down-bow. Breaking the triplets into pairs means a player uses only up-to-down bow motion. Additionally, if the bow angle is biased to the inside of the higher string and the inside of the lower string, the passage is much easier, albeit still difficult. (Auer thought that this passage was unplayable.)

Playing triplets or sixes in twos—pairs—is always easier. This is true of triplet playing in general, whether separate bows or slurred, as in this example from Glazunov's *Violin Concerto in A Minor* (bar 522), ex. A-3a, which is a combination of neighbor note simplification and triplet reorganization—the layering of thought.

This is a simplification of example A-3a, but can be done throughout this excerpt *(ex. A-3b)*.

Here is another example of this type of grouping, ex. A-3c, from the same piece, making the passage much easier to perform.

Ex. A-3d depicts a different grouping and longer phrase.

This type of passage, from Prokofiev's *Violin Concerto in G Minor*, ex. A-4a, is found throughout the first movement of the piece, which is filled with possible neighbor-note simplifications.

The example below, ex. A-4b, is a skeletalizing of the first measure…

…but as I have indicated, this can be done for the entire page and played as neighbor note reductions (that form pairs) or divided into pairs *(ex. A-4c).*

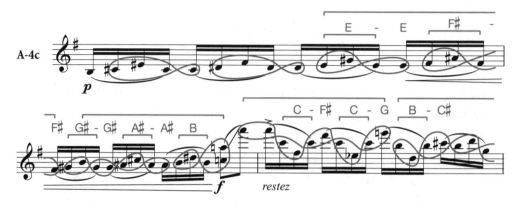

HELPFUL HINTS FOR BOWING

Jake Krachmalnick, a great violinist and, as I mentioned previously, one of my teachers, told me something interesting about his conception of bowing, unfortunately not until I was an adult. Yet it came in handy as I was trying to understand playing as a system of thought. I asked him, "How do you do this bowing?" He said, "There are no bowings. There is just up-bow and down-bow, and sometimes you use a little less, and sometimes a little more." So it would appear that he thought of "bowings" as variations of a basic cycle.[1] As we have seen, bowing, like the action of the left hand, is essentially legato—smooth connection. Any articulation (by that I mean accented strokes, bounced bows, etc.) comes out of the initial smoothness and connectedness. Articulations are *variations* created by bow angles, less weight of the arm, and other subtleties that are overlaid on perfect legato, just as the bow cycles themselves are overlays of a perfectly worked out legato of the left hand.

We also know that there are a couple of useful rules. The initiation of the movement of the up-bow starts with an impulse from the base, the plug-in, of the triceps muscle of the right arm. This moves the arm as a whole. As I mentioned, *the movement of the right arm is at a different angle from the angle formed by the bow across the strings.* If one puts their attention to the smooth functioning of the right arm motion, the motion of the arm when playing an up-bow will seem (in a way) as if one is pulling open a drawer, the arm and wrist moving towards the body. The down passively goes back to the position of the "closed" drawer as if drawn by a magnet.

---

1 Krachmalnick taught that the right wrist moving into the body led the bow, which is similar to how we have described Heifetz's and Milstein's bowing, although not as explicated nor or as deeply understood.

For a beginner, this may be too subtle an explanation. It may be easier to conceptualize the arm's motion when bowing by using a different metaphor. Put the right arm against the side of the body and raise the forearm, using the plug-in to the triceps muscle, as if having a drink of something. (The teacher can touch the triceps plug-in spot on the student's arm.) This motion raises the glass, and at the last bit, as you near the mouth, move the arm as a unit—upper arm and forearm. This would be for the last five inches of the bow near the frog. The difference between the actual arm movement of bowing and raising a glass to one's mouth is that bowing happens on a different plane. This exercise is *somewhat* similar to the motion of bowing, albeit at a different angle, and not as refined a method or explanation as "pulling open a drawer," which may be too subtle for a beginner to understand.

As previously mentioned, when playing the violin, or any string instrument, the deltoid muscle holds up the right arm, (it also holds up the left) with the support of the muscles of the back. The feeling is as if the right arm is a rope bridge, like the ones used to cross jungle rivers, with one end being the deltoid, and the other end the right hand. The arm sinks at the elbow, which is the middle point of the imagined "bridge."

A perfect look at the proper angle for the right arm can be found on a video of Heifetz playing Rachmaninoff's miniature, *Daisies.* At the end of the piece there is a shot of this angle when he is on the G string. This is the angle of the right arm that should be maintained for every string, and was the model for Fig. 18-e.

The deltoid raises and lowers the right arm, as a unit, from string to string, just like an elevator. The relationship of sinking elbow to wrist stays the same on each string. If the elbow is higher than the wrist one risks developing tendonitis. The bow hair must address the string at a 45° angle away from the bridge. Another crucial element to having an excellent bow arm is the negation of angles for string changes. *While on the same string,* the bow must maintain the *same angle* to the string or the sound will suffer. The shoulder must be down, but not "forced" down; the back's muscular infrastructure holds the right arm in place.

If all is done correctly, one should feel as if the bow hair is slightly "pulling" the string. The sound seems to be 'bubbling' up from the fingerboard through the left-hand fingers; the right arm is "hanging." (The bow "going through the middle of the string" is how Krachmalnick described the physical feeling of bowing.) Most players nowadays play "above" the string with their bow. To "pull" the sound, they press the bow into the string, attempting to scoop or push out the notes. This produces a harsh, or constrained, sound and does not connect notes.

The slight pull of the string needed to achieve sonic richness is aided by holding the violin nearly parallel to the floor when playing. This should not be exaggerated.[2] The relative flatness of the instrument in this position gives the right arm more relaxed weight, which assists the bow's engagement with the strings of the instrument.

COORDINATION BETWEEN HANDS

Krachmalnick had a clever way to practice the coordination between the hands—the left hand and the bow. He practiced using "hooked" bowings. The hooked bowings are the *actual* coordination of the right and left hands when slowed down. Ex. A-5 shows how he "hooked" bowings. The bowing is legato, connected.

The left finger is already down before the change of bow, which is the correct coordination between the bow and the left finger. The small note of the "hook" is gradually eliminated by becoming shorter, until all that is left are the main notes, smoothly connected. The "hooks" are too fast to be heard. One must make certain there is no accent when changing bow direction. This is not the same as practicing in different rhythms (which merely complicates passages of music) because this is the *actual coordination of playing the piece.*

THE BIAS OF THE BOW

Fig. A-a

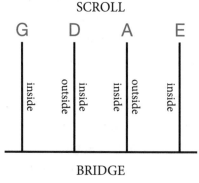

Figure A-a shows that on the E string, the bow is biased to the A. On the G, the bow is biased to the D. On the D and A strings, the bow is biased towards

---

2   The instrument is never parallel to the floor relative to the top or the back of the violin.

where it will be going. Let's analyze this small excerpt shown below, ex. A-6a, from the last movement of the Tchaikovsky *Violin Concerto* It is important to angle each up-bow correctly.[3]

It is easiest to think in *two* up to down pairs at a time (following the motion of the right arm, not the bow). In the first pair, C♯/E, (of the first two pairs), the up-bow, C♯, is biased to the inside of the G string; the down-bow plays E (this is a counterclockwise pair, the down-bow being half the energy of the up-bow). The next pair F♯/G has no string change (a same plane up to down-bow pair). The next first pair, of the two pair group, is E/A (another counterclockwise pair). The up-bow, E, is biased to the A string side of the D string; the down-bow plays the open A string. The next pair, B/C♯, has no string change. The next two pairs, A/B and C#/D, are both same plane pairs.

One of the trickiest bowing problems is found in Bach's *Prelude* from *Partita No. 3* for solo violin. This is called bariolage bowing. Here is an excerpt *(ex. A-6b)*.

It is important to angle each up-bow correctly. The pattern is *two* up-bow to down-bow pairs—clockwise, counterclockwise—that repeat. The open E of the first pair, E/G♯ (a clockwise up to down-bow pair), is biased to the inside of the E string; the down-bow, G♯, falls to the D string side of the A string. This completes the first pair. The up-bow, E, of the second pair, E/G♯ (a counterclockwise up to down-bow pair) is biased to the inside of the D string; the down-bow, G♯, falls to the E string side of the A string. This starts the cycle again.

You could say the down-bow comes down on alternate sides of the A string, and the up-bows stay on the inside of every E that occurs on the E and D strings, or that the bow is balanced on a plane on either side of the A string. To the player this feels as if he plays two pairs of up-bow to down-bow played on a single plane. This type of bowing difficulty is common. The first cadenza in Sibelius's *Violin Concerto in D Minor* is one example. Another is this passage in *Rondo Capriccioso* by Saint-Saëns *(ex. A-6c)*.

---

3 The start of the up-bow (which is understood as the right arm as a whole; the right hand as the tip of the bow) "sets" the angle for all bowing pairs. The arm's motion is initiated by the plug-in to the triceps. The player directs attention to the movement of the right arm, not the movement of the bow.

This pattern is *three* up-bow to down-bow pairs—counterclockwise, clockwise, clockwise. Each up-bow must be angled correctly. The up-bow, G♯, of the first pair, G♯/B (a counterclockwise pair), is biased to the A string side of the D string; the down-bow, B, falls to the E string side of the A string. The second pair, E/B (a clockwise pair), the up-bow, open E, is biased to inside of the E string; the down-bow, B, falls to the D string side of the A string. The third pair, G♯/E (a clockwise pair), the up-bow, G♯, is biased to the G string side of the D string; the down-bow, E, falls to the inside of the G string, and we start again.

The plane of the bow is in-between the A and D strings. Or you could think that, from the first pair, up-bow G♯ is inside, up-bow E is inside, and up-bow G♯ is outside. If done properly it should feel as if you do not cross strings—three pairs of up-bow to down-bow—counterclockwise, clockwise, clockwise—that, to the player must feel as if he plays three up to down-bow pairs on a single plane. One pair *plus* two pairs (three pairs) works well also.

Deeply understanding these passages makes all bowing much easier, because in addition to the concept of an active up-bow and passive down-bow, *the negation of angles is one of the most subtle and crucial elements of skill.*

As I said previously, the base, the fundamental level of playing for string instruments, is the organization of pairs of notes *in the left hand*. In detaché passages this is a simple overlay of the right on the left. Up-bow is the offbeat and down-bow the downbeat. Yet left-hand pairs and bowing pairs do not always align so straightforwardly *(ex. A-7a).*

Measures 1–3 of ex. A-7a break into bowing pairs that match the left-hand pairs. However, the bowing cycles of measures 4–6 break into three groups of up-to-down, slightly different from the left-hand pairing.

The passage, beginning in measure 4, can be thought of as descending thirds, another helpful simplification that can be seen in examples A-7b and A-7c.

Here is another useful simplification from the same movement, ex. A-8. The bowing cycle, starting in measure 4, is two pairs of up to down-bows. The neighbor note reduction shows the simplicity of the passage.

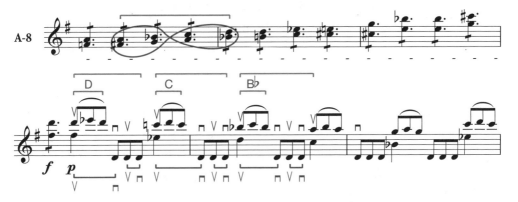

Here is a helpful way of negotiating this bowing from Bazzini's *The Round of the Goblins,* shown below in ex. A-9. The up-bow starts the cycle and is active; the down-bow passively drops, which allows the bow to bounce off the string. The left-hand pairs still have to be worked out as the underlying phrasing.

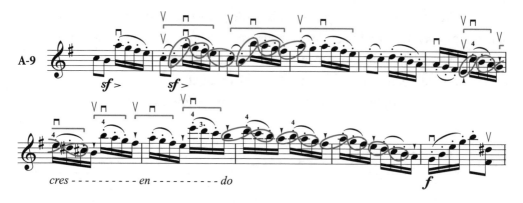

STACCATO

I cannot take credit for this information. It is the invention of my wife Audinga's violin teacher, Victor Radovich, who was a student of David Oistrakh's teacher, Pyotr Stolyarsky, and of Oistrakh. He taught this method to her. (It is exceedingly rare to find anyone who can teach staccato.)

The first staccato note sets up the rest that follow. To learn the stroke, one must practice it by learning how to play an enormously fast up-bow—the length of the bow from point to the frog—followed by a down-bow which "floats" passively back to the tip. The down motion, and any muscular engagement pertaining to the down-bow, *should be completely ended* before the up-bow is "set." If there is any residue of muscle involvement for the down-bow, the start of the staccato will be compromised by antagonistic muscle use. The up-bow is reset by concentrating on the base, the plug-in, of the triceps (which is where the muscle movement originates, but with only a subtle, yet concentrated engagement), and is released, moving to the frog again, as if it was shot from a cannon.

This subtle, concentrated muscle engagement is the energy needed to start the successive short "ups" that constitute the stroke. The stroke should feel as if it is one long slur, not individually enunciated notes. Once this initial impulse is mastered, the stroke will go by itself, although it is crucial that the down-bow that precedes the up-staccato ends *completely relaxed*. The weight of the arm and index finger of the right hand holds the bow to the string. *One must follow the motion of the right arm,* not the bow, when doing staccato. Additionally, the correct left-hand balance must be fastidiously worked out, which helps the track of the bow.

MORE IDEAS

All bowing is easier to practice as pairs of up to down bows if one holds the left hand to a relaxed open position—the actual abstraction we have talked about—while playing through the piece, or passage one is studying, by practicing with open strings. This means playing the actual strings and bowing pairs, minus the left fingers, but *imagining* the left fingers playing aligned in this way.

Here, in ex. A-10, is a commonly misunderstood rhythm and bowing, the most famous example found in Beethoven's *Symphony No. 7.* This rhythm will sound like triplets if one thinks that the rhythm starts with the dotted eighth. The figure is easily played if the start is the sixteenth note *before* the eighth. The sixteenth note "belongs" to the up-bow eighth note, not as is commonly heard, to the dotted eighth. The phrasing is eighth note to quarter note, which makes this usually troublesome rhythm quite simple and is a good example that *rhythm must be phrased.*

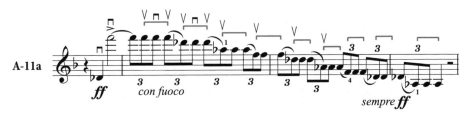

In this next example from Lalo's *Symphonie Espagnole,* ex. A-11a, it is easier to play and sounds much better if the notes are grouped as three Fs, three D flats, etc., each group starting with an up-bow.[4]

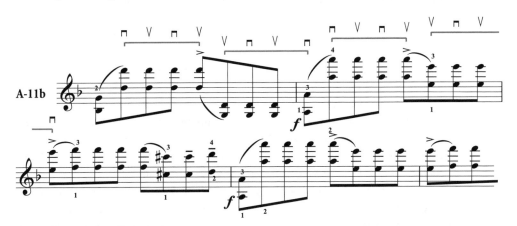

This passage from the first movement of the Sibelius *Violin Concerto,* ex. A-11b, is similar—four octave Ds (really a single, articulated, octave D), then three open strings, G/D, then four octave As, four octave Es, four octave Fs, etc.

One could also do this *(ex. A-11c).*

---

4 Listen to Nathan Milstein play this passage. This is certainly his approach.

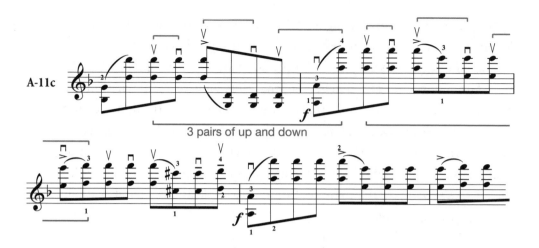

A-11c

3 pairs of up and down

FAST DETACHÉ, SLOW DETACHÉ AND EVERY SPEED BETWEEN

Detaché is the basic motion of the bow—up to down—with the "up" active and
the "down" passive. If the "up" half of the bowing cycle is not active enough
(by that I mean the motion, the amount of bow used), the "down" part of the
cycle has nowhere to fall. This is a crucial point. Most crunchy sounding bow
strokes are the result of too little up-bow or a too fast down-bow, and the
right arm not being relaxed. Fast separate bows should *feel* as if one played the
group, the phrase comprised of pairs, in one slurred up-bow (including the
final note, *slurred up*, which, as we know, is the first note of the next *printed*
group) eliminating all angles so the bow moves in one plane.[5] Separate bows
are the interruption of the up feeling of the bow by a slight down-bow. The
separate bows should feel extremely relaxed in the arm.

---

5   There is an interesting way to get a feeling for the relationship of up-bow to down-bow which,
    as we have discussed, is 2:1; the up-bow (the offbeat) approximately twice the fullness of the
    down-bow (the downbeat). If one were to play a group of detaché notes, let's say four pairs, for
    example, in one up-bow (cutting all angles; all motion emanating from the plug-in to the triceps;
    played at a tempo around 60 per pair), stopping the bow on each note, and giving the first note
    of each pair (the offbeat, which is each up-bow when played separately) twice the fullness of the
    second note of the pair (the downbeat)—if done correctly, in terms of the relationship of the
    offbeat fullness to downbeat passivity—this mimics the phrasing of both Heifetz and Milstein.
    This approach shows, if done correctly, the relationship of the up-bow to the down-bow which,
    once understood, is quite remarkable and extremely counterintuitive. Understanding this, the
    sound of it, the feel of it, the "play" in it, is a most subtle matter, an art.
        This experiment is useful only for advanced students. The understanding of flow must already
    be deeply inculcated before such demonstrations can be undertaken. Playing detaché (separate
    bow) passages in one up-bow, demonstrates many things: it is easy to understand how to play on
    a single bow plane, how to cut angles effectively, and shows the overall "up" feeling of all bowing.
    This experiment is just as informative using one unbroken up-bow (slurred), the last note of the
    phrase always being the first note of the next printed group.

Detaché at fast tempo is a faster cycle of up to down-bow, using, necessarily, less bow. To change detaché into a spiccato stroke, raise the right wrist slightly and turn the bow hair more on its side (the wood of the bow away from the bridge). The bow will seem to bounce off the string, but it should not really bounce. The actual interaction of the bow with the strings is more akin to skipping rocks across the water.

MOVING AROUND THE INSTRUMENT—SHIFTING

Heifetz and Milstein often replace one finger with another when the same note repeats in *cantabile* lines. Their transition from one finger to another is so fluid, so unusually smooth, that I began to think that their ability to do this suggested something deeper might be going on. The following exercise will lead one to the same realization.

A-12

This exercise, ex. A-12, develops the ability to shift while maintaining a constant "gluey" connection to the string with the left fingers, which creates a connected, legato sound. The base of the fingers is slightly turned out, as we know, so that the hand feels open *(Fig. A-b)*.

Fig. A-b

scroll

abstract open

frog of bow

arm

bow

tip of bow

player

Therefore, the balance of the hand is toward the fifth finger, the fourth on the violin, or as some may call it, the "pinky." This exercise should be played throughout the violin, on all four strings, using different notes. Playing this with careful attention will *present* to a player the imaginary, abstract line of shifting and left finger bias that makes one aware that both arms move parallel to one another, as was discussed in detail in Chapter 18.

All shifts must stay to this abstract, imaginary line. The illustration, Fig. A-c, reads, moves as a whole, from right to left, following the arrow. *But the numbers for the fingers (the fingerings), read left to right within each individual circle marked by an asterisk* because that is how the left-hand fingers line up when visualizing an outward bias to the left hand.

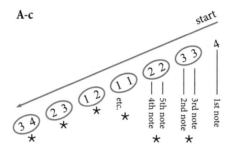

If this is done correctly one will realize that shifting down or up should feel, on the finger tip (to some extent), as if one is shifting up *to* the line. *In other words, shifting up or down feels basically the same* (another violin koan) because one actually shifts from one *point to another on the abstract line*, which does not feel "up" or "down" at this subtle level. Staying to this imagined line makes all shifting *much easier*—going "up," going "down," playing any double-stops, etc. The fingers also *play* on this imaginary line, which happens to parallel the line of the right arm, not the bow, which is moving across the strings at a different angle. The vibrato moves "up" *to* this abstract line.[6]

This also gives a player the feeling that the fingers are in constant, rather gluey, connection with the string, as if one were playing with only one finger that never loses contact with the string. This left finger "glueyness" is *critically important* for both the sound, the tone of the violin, and the "groove" of the bow. "Glueyness" should be maintained even when playing fingers consecutively, that is, when staying in the same position.

Conceptually and physically, it is easier to shift from a high note to a low note than from a low note to a high note. An excellent example of this can be

---

6   Whether or not someone has this visualization may not be the main issue. What is essential is the correct balance of the hand—that the base of the fingers turn out.

found in the last movement of the Sibelius *Violin Concerto,* ex. A-13, but this insight can be used throughout this concerto and the literature.

In measure 1, the D octave is a "set-shift" from the high D to the lower D. Then comes the octave scale in pairs—B/C♯, D/E, F♯/G—forming two chunks of three pairs, continuing to the high D in measure 4. Musically, this is an arrival, but in this case, technically, a "set-shift" *down* to the C♯/D pair of beat 3 of the fifth measure.

If the D octave in measure 6 is felt to be shifting *up* to the high E♭ at the end of measure 6, this is *actually* technically more difficult than if the high E♭ is the *starting point* of a *downward* "set-shift" to the lower E♭ of measure 7.

Measure 8 is the start of several "set-shifts:" a high F♯ down to a low F♯, then a high G to a low G, then a high G♯ to a low G♯, then a high A to a low A in measure 11, then a high B to a low A, from measure 11–12 and, finally, after the scale, we end with a high A to a low A. The whole passage is "set-shifts" from *high to low positions* on the instrument.

This thinking may apply to singing. It may also be easier *to sing* from a "set" high note to a low note. Big jumps "up" are more difficult than thinking of the note *before* the high note as a *finish point*, and "setting," or starting again from the high note. Once this is secure, the low note can be joined to the high, but only as a layering on of high to low notes.

Here is an example from the piano literature, the last movement of Tchaikovsky's *Piano Concerto No. 1,* ex. A-14. The hands "set" from the high notes, and the physical movement is down to the low note. There is no need to worry about how to get from the B♭ in the right hand of measure 2 up to the next note, F. (The same is true for the motion of the left hand.) The only motion one will be aware of is "setting" from the F and going down to the B♭. Getting back to the top F will take care of itself.

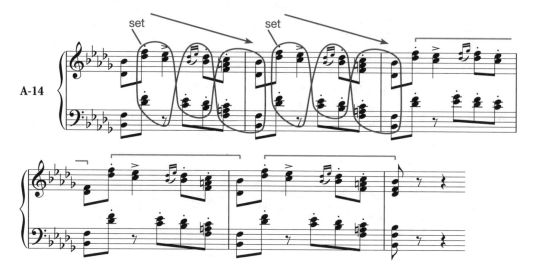

A-14

THE METRONOME

The metronome is a killer of musical expression. The mechanical rigidity imposed distorts the fluid and subtle forward motion of music. Yet if used in the way I shall describe, it can be a helpful tool for learning to play pairs of offbeats to downbeats.

If the beat of the metronome is aligned to the *offbeats,* the effect is entirely different from alignment with the main beats. This can only be done up to a certain speed, which is about 144 to the pair, beyond which the syncopated feeling is too hard to align with. This may be one way Heifetz and Milstein practiced. It effectually creates a syncopation, yet that is really too crude a description. It is, in essence, an undulation, a wave, a forward flow. The downbeat is scarcely there. The upbeat is like the skimming of a rock across a lake of the downbeat.

VIBRATO

Vibrato is an oscillation of a pitch from below the pitch and back *to* the pitch, never above the pitch as is commonly heard. The motion is also a cycle, whereby the up motion—the motion from flatter pitch back to the pitch—is active, and the motion to flatten the pitch, down, is passive. Additionally, the vibrato, like finger action, bow movement, and the basic phrasing itself, conforms to a figure-eight paradigm. (As I said previously, this does not describe the physical motion. The motion is back and forth. The figure-eight is a conceptual tool.)

Heifetz has an unusual motion to his vibrato that I would have never noticed except for an impromptu remark, and accompanying physical motion, that he made to a student on a videotape of one of his master classes. The student is performing the last movement of Brahm's *Sonata No. 3* and plucks the string with his left hand to make sure he has the correct note before making an entrance. Heifetz stops him and criticizes the gesture, encouraging the student to "take a chance." Heifetz demonstrates this himself with the violin.[7] Before he begins playing, he moves his left hand and arm, unconsciously showing his motion for vibrato in a way that is best described as the motion of the blade of a washing machine.

Most people use what is called an arm vibrato, and will move their arm back and forth to demonstrate the motion of their vibrato. Some might use their wrists, but in a way that *bends* the wrist, an approach that not only encourages tendonitis, but creates a vibrato that is too wide and often "bleaty," like the cry of a sheep. The motion of Heifetz's hand/arm is entirely different.

His vibrato emanates from the *touch* of the finger upon the string. In other words, the core sound cannot be compromised by the alteration of the pitch by the movement of the finger. This requires a very subtle feeling on the tip of the fingers, maintaining that "touch"[8] and relaxation as the vibrato expands from the touch of the finger on the string in tandem with the movement in the left wrist and arm. Any tension in the vibrato motion will degrade the sound and create tension in the right arm.

Vibrato is the icing on the cake of "core" sound. Nothing we have discussed is possible without core sound. The basic sound is the technical foundation

---

7   *Heifetz Master Classes Volume Two*, DVD (Kultur, 2011), at 49:14.

8   I am guessing that the touch feels as if the finger slightly pinches the string. Remember, the fingertip pulls back slightly to give more pad to the tip. The vibrato emanates from the intersection of the imaginary line for the left hand—the line created by the open hand position that we have previously described—and the direction of the vibrato, which is up *to* that line. The "pinch" is the finger "pinching" the angle created by the vibrato motion when the two lines meet. In other words, I suspect that Heifetz's vibrato is the *inversion* of what most players do, which is to move the wrist or arm to move the finger. The motion of vibrato, in Heifetz's case, seems to come from the *touch* of the finger on the string, out, in tandem with the motion of the wrist and arm. This is, yet again, *extremely subtle*, but quite different from the common understanding of how to vibrate a note.

Maintaining the "up" motion for vibrato is essential. This must be maintained on the down-bow, or the sound will suffer. This can be practiced effectively by playing each melodic phrase in one up-bow. This shows the overall "up" feeling for both the vibrato and the bow. Once this is understood, the passive down-bows may be added.

of everything else and follows its own laws for its production. In part, it is based on the sophistication of one's hearing, which means becoming attuned to, and trained in, the subtleties and nuances of sound production. In part, it is technical. But it is much more than that.

Producing a core sound is the basis of all instrumental and vocal technique. To achieve a beautiful sound, the body must work in harmony, guided by the mind's understanding of what that sound is. The sound is both the basis and the culmination of everything we have discussed. The sound, after all, is the vehicle by which the expression is conveyed. The greater the power, nuance, color and shading of the sound, the more skilled the control has to be over the mind/body system. All that we have talked about distills to this. Without *control through understanding* there can be no freedom to express oneself because the mind/body will work in opposition to your desires. Yet, one cannot conceive of those desires for expression unless the mind/body system is in a state to receive inspiration. Ultimately, it is all a matter of spirit, soul, or whatever word you care to use to define creative power.

Sources

Antek, Samuel, *This Was Toscanini* (New York: Vanguard Press, 1963), 1–74.

Applebaum, Dr. Samuel, *The Way They Play*, Book 1 (New Jersey: Paganiniana, 1972), 78.

Auer, Leopold, *Graded Course Of Violin Playing*, Books 1–8, Preface to Book 1 (New York, 1926).

———, *My Long Life In Music* (New York: Frederick A. Stokes Co., 1923), 92-93.

———, *Violin Playing As I teach It* (New York: Dover Publications, 1980) 7, 8, 21.

Axelrod , Herbert, *Heifetz* (New Jersey: Paganiniana, 1976), 124, 129, 131–132.

———, *Paganini* (New Jersey: Paganiniana, 1979), 16.

Bongard, M., *Pattern Recognition* (New York: Spartan Books, 1970).

Bateson, Gregory, *Mind and Nature, A Necessary Unity* (New York: Bantam Books, 1988).

———, *Steps To An Ecology Of Mind* (USA: University of Chicago Press 2000).

Bohm, David, *On Creativity* (New York: Routledge, 2010), 3, 16, 48, 59, 82.

———, *Wholeness and the Implicate Order* (New York: Routledge, 1980).

Capet, Lucien, *Superior Bowing Technique,* translated by Margaret Schmidt, edited by Steven B. Shipps (USA: Encore Music Publishers, 1993).

Chomsky, Noam and Halle, Morris, *The Sound Pattern of English* (MIT Press, 1991), 6.

Cooke, James Francis, *Great Pianists on Piano Playing*, Chapter 16, Rachmaninoff (New York: Dover Publications, 1999), 213, 215.

da Vinci, Leonardo, *Leonardo On Painting,* edited by Martin Kemp (New Haven: Yale University Press, 1989).

Dali, Salvador, *50 Secrets Of Magic Craftsmanship* (New York: Dover Publications, 1992), Chapter 1, 13.

Doering, James M., *The Great Orchestrator—Arthur Judson & American Arts Management* (Chicago: University of Illinois Press, 2013), 227.

Eigaldinger, Jean-Jacques, *Chopin: Pianist and Teacher* (Cambridge: Cambridge University Press, 1986).

Faulkner, Robert R., *Hollywood Studio Musicians* (Chicago: Aldine, Atherton, 1971).

Feinstein, Anthony, *Michael Rabin—America's Virtuoso Violinist* (Milwaukee: Amadeus Press, 2011).

Fisk, Josiah, *Composers on Music* (Boston: Northeastern University Press, 1997), 63, 64, 109, 157-158, 198, 211, 235, 257, 355.

Flesch, Carl, *The Art of Violin Playing*, Book I, translated by F. Martens (New York: Carl Fischer, 1924), 16-17.

_____, translated by Frederick H. Martens, *The Art of Violin Playing*, Book Two (New York: Carl Fischer, 1936), 79.

_____, *The Memoirs of Carl Flesch*, translated by Hans Keller (New York: Macmillan Co., 1958), 94.

Froebel, Friedrich, *The Education of Man*, translated by William Nicholas Hailmann (New York, 1898), originally published as *Die Menschenerziehung die Erziehungs- Unterrichts- und Lehrkunst, angestrebt in der allgemeinen duetschen Erziehungsanstaldt zu Keilau,* (Keilau,1826).

Fromm, Erich, *To Have Or To Be* (London: Continuum, 1997), 122.

Furtwängler, Wilhelm, *On Music: Essays and Addresses,* translated and edited by Ronald Taylor (USA: Scolar Press, 1991), 8, 11, 12, 13, 19-20, 21.

Galamian, Ivan and Green, Elizabeth, *Principles of Violin Playing & Teaching* (New Jersey: Prentice Hall, 1962).

Gardner, John, *The Art of Fiction—Notes on Craft for Young Writers* (New York: Vintage Books, 1991), 11, 142.

Garson, Dr. Alfred, *Suzuki Twinkles* (USA: Alfred Publishing Co., 2001), 11, 26, 36, 37, 76, 81, 100.

Green, Elizabeth A.H., *Miraculous Teacher—Ivan Galamian and the Meadowmount Experience,* (USA, 1993), 3, 5, 22, 52–53, 141.

Heifetz in Performance, DVD, (RCA, 2004).

Heifetz Master Classes, DVD, (Kultur, 2011).

Hoffman, Josef, *Piano Playing* (Toronto: Dover Publications, 1976).

Hofstadter, Douglass R., *Godel, Escher, Bach: An Eternal Golden Braid* (New York: Vintage Books, 1989).

Horowitz, Joseph, *Classical Music in America* (New York: W. Norton & Co., 2005), 490, 324, 342, 489, 490, 491.

Isaacson, Walter, *Einstein: His Life and Universe* (New York: Simon & Schuster, 2008), 26.

Itzkiff, Seymour W., *Emanuel Feuermann, Virtuoso* (Alabama: University of Alabama, 1979).

Kendall, John, *The Suzuki Method In American Music Education* (USA: Suzuki Method International, 1985), 14, 31.

Kirkpatrick, Ralph, *Interpreting Bach's Well-Tempered Clavier*, Chapter Four, The Rhythmic Approach (New Haven: Yale University Press, 1984), 68.

Laing, R.D., *The Divided Self* (England: Penguin Books, 1990)

_____, *The Politics of Experience* (New York: Pantheon Books, 1967).

Lamberti, Marjorie, *The Politics of Education, Teachers and School Reform in Weimar Germany*, (New York, 2002), 28-31.

Lee, Bruce, *Tao of Jeet Kune Do* (Ohara Publications), 43, 44.

Malan, Roy, *Efrem Zimbalist, A Life* (New Jersey: Amadeus Press, 2004), 262.

Martens, Frederick, *Violin Mastery—Talks with Master Violinists and Teachers* (New York: Frederick Stokes Company Publishers, 1919), 7.

Mason, Lowell, *Manual of the Boston Academy of Music, For Instruction in the Elements of Vocal Music On the System of Pestalozzi*, Intro. Ch. 1–4 (Boston, 1836), reprinted USA, 2012.

McLuhan, Marshall, *The Gutenberg Galaxy* (USA: University of Toronto Press, 1963).

Mehl, Margaret, "Cultural Translation in Two Directions: The Suzuki Method in Japan and Germany," (Research & Issues in Music Education, 7/1, 2009).

Mills, Joshua William, *The Rhetorical Pedagogy of Music: Imitatio Techniques for Music Theory Instruction and Composition Training* (Dissertation, Master of Music, Baltimore: Peabody Conservatory of the Johns Hopkins University, 2010), p.2.

Milstein, Nathan and Volkov, Solomon, *From Russia to the West* (New York: Henry Holt and Co., 1990), 18, 46, 47, 120, 130, 164, 191, 192.

Nathan Milstein—In Portrait, DVD, (Christopher Nupen, 2007).

Nathan Milstein, Mozart, Paganini, Falla, Novacek, etc., DVD (EMI Classics, 2008).

Mitchell, Mark and Evans, Allen, *Moriz Rosenthal in Word and Music* (Bloomington: Indiana University, 2006), 125: "Composers who are ambitious but lack in imagination prefer to express themselves with trumpets, trombones, and drum rolls. Platitudes are best delivered with a thundering voice."

Mohr, Franz, *My Life with the Great Pianists* (Grand Rapids: Ravens Ridge Books, 1992).

Montessori, Maria, *The Montessori Method*, translated by Anne Everett George (New York, 1912), 322.

———, *Education For A New World* (Kalakshetra, 1946).

Nicoll, Maurice, *Psychological Commentaries,* Volume 3 (Samuel Weiser, Inc.).

Ouspensky, P.D., *In Search of the Miraculous: Fragments of an Unknown Teaching* (New York: Harcourt, Brace), 20, 40, 949.

Perényi, Eleanor, *Liszt—The Artist As Romantic Hero* (Boston: Little, Brown and Co., 1974), 292.

Pestalozzi, Johann, *How Gertrude Teaches Her Children: An Attempt To Help Mothers Teach Their Own Children and an Account of the Method,* translated by Lucy Holland and Francis Turner (London, 1900), first published in 1803 (reprinted Internet Archive, 2007).

———, *Letters of Pestalozzi On the Education Of Infancy, Addressed To Mothers* (Boston, 1830), Nabu Public Domain Reprints, 2012.

Plaskin, Glenn, *Horowitz, A Biography of Vladimir Horowitz,* (New York: William Morrow and Co. 1983), 282.

Pinker, Stephen, *The Stuff of Thought* (New York: Viking, 2007).

Plato, *The Republic,* Book 1, The Rewards for Ruling (New York: Random House), 32.

Rainbow, Bernard, "H.G. Nageli, Die Pestalozzische Gesangbildungslehre 1809," *Four Centuries of Music Teaching Manuals 1518–1932* (Great Britain, 2009).

Rainbow, Charles, *Piano Notes* (New York: The Free Press, 2002), 97, 109.

Rousseau, Jean-Jacques, *Emile—Or Treatise on Education,* translated by William H. Payne (New York: Prometheus Books, 2005).

Schenker, Heinrich, *Harmony,* translated by Elisabeth Mann Borgese, (Chicago: The University of Chicago Press, 1980), 19.

———, *Counterpoint,* Book I, translated by John Rothgeb and Jurgen Thym, edited by John Rothgeb (Ann Arbor: Musicalia Press, 2001),19.

Schnabel, Artur, *My Life and Music* (New York: St. Martin's Press) 129, 138–139, 143.

Schoenberg, Arnold, *Style and Idea,* "Today's Manner Of Performing Classical Music" (US: University of California Press, 1984), 320, 321, 322.

Schonberg, Harold C., *The Lives Of The Great Composers,* Chapter 13, Virtuoso, Charlatan—and Prophet, Franz Liszt (New York: W. W. Norton & Co. 1981), 208.

Seitz, Diana I., *The System of Effective Violin Practice According to Konstantin Mostras* (dissertation, 3304217, 2008), 4.

Stravinsky, Igor, *Poetics of Music In The Form of Six Lessons,* translated by Arthur Knodel and Ingolf Dahl (Cambridge: Harvard University Press, 1970), 73–74.

Suzuki, Shinichi, *Nurtured By Love, translated by Waltraud Suzuki* (New York: Amereon House, 1983), 1, 2, 69, 76.

————, *Suzuki Violin School*, Vol. 1–10, Revised Edition (USA: Alfred Music Publishing Co., Inc., 2007).

————, *Young Children's Talent Education & It's Method* (USA, 1949), 32.

Taruskin, Richard, *Music in the Nineteenth Century* (Oxford University Press, 2010), 40.

Tulku, Tarthang, *Time, Space, and Knowledge*, (Berkeley, Dharma Press, 1977).

Watzlawick, Paul, and Hemlick Beavin. Janet, and Jackson, Don D., *Pragmatics of Human Communication* (New York: W. W. Norton & Company, 1967).

Wells, H.G., *The Outline Of History,* Volume II, "Twenty Years of Indecision and Its Outcome," Part 5 (New York: Garden City Books, 1949), 1131.

Whitehead, Alfred North, *Adventures of Ideas* (New York: The Free Press, 1967), 60.

Williams, Benjamin John, *Music Composition Pedagogy: A History, Philosophy and Guide* (D.M.A. Document, Ohio State University, 2010).

The Author

Violinist, performer, writer and lecturer, David Jacobson has appeared as soloist with the San Francisco Symphony, San Francisco Chamber Orchestra, and other orchestras throughout the United States and performed in recital in the major capitals of Europe. He is the founder and director of the San Francisco Institute of Music. Mr. Jacobson has spent many years analyzing the playing methodologies of great performers such as Jascha Heifetz, Nathan Milstein, Vladimir Horowitz, and Glenn Gould, attempting to understand how they achieved such unsurpassed levels of musical expression and technical skill, discovering their "secrets." Using this knowledge he created a unique system of teaching, employing what he terms the theory of "bel canto instrumental technique," now known as the SFIM (San Francisco Institute of Music) Method. He is a graduate of the Curtis Institute of Music, where he studied with Ivan Galamian, and has a Master of Music Performance degree from Boston University.